China in and
beyond the Headlines

China in and beyond the Headlines

Edited by Timothy B. Weston
and Lionel M. Jensen

ROWMAN & LITTLEFIELD PUBLISHERS, INC.
Lanham • Boulder • New York • Toronto • Plymouth, UK

Published by Rowman & Littlefield Publishers, Inc.
A wholly owned subsidary of The Rowman & Littlefield Publishing Group, Inc.
4501 Forbes Boulevard, Suite 200, Lanham, Maryland 20706
http://www.rowmanlittlefield.com

Estover Road, Plymouth PL6 7PY, United Kingdom

British Library Cataloguing in Publication Information Available

Library of Congress Cataloging-in-Publication Data
China in and beyond the headlines / edited by Timothy B. Weston and Lionel M.
Jensen.
    p. cm.
  Includes bibliographical references and index.
  ISBN 978-1-4422-0904-6 (cloth : alk. paper) — ISBN 978-1-4422-0905-3 (pbk. :
alk. paper) — ISBN 978-1-4422-0906-0 (electronic)
  1. China—Social conditions—2000- 2. China—Politics and government—2002-
3. China—Economic conditions—2000- 4. China—Relations—United States. 5.
United States—Relations—China. I. Weston, Timothy B., 1964- II. Jensen, Lionel
M.
  HN733.5.C4297 2012
  951.06--dc23

                                                                    2011030051

∞™ The paper used in this publication meets the minimum requirements of
American National Standard for Information Sciences—Permanence of Paper
for Printed Library Materials, ANSI/NISO Z39.48-1992.

Printed in the United States of America

For the next generation of Chinahands, may your footing be more sure, your vision be more clear, and may you benefit from the realization of how little we will always know this place and people with which we have fallen in love and for which we sometimes suffer.

L. M. J.

For all who are interested with an open mind and a sense of new possibilities in the China story, one of the most important and fascinating of our time.

T. B. W.

Contents

Chronology

1979	Joint Communiqué on the Establishment of Diplomatic Relations
1980	Gengshen Democratic Reforms; International Monetary Fund admits China as a member
1982	China National Off Shore Oil Corporation (CNOOC) is founded
1983–1984	Anti-Spiritual Pollution Campaign
1984	China is given membership in the International Atomic Energy Agency
1985	Hong Kong defeats China in a soccer match, provoking a violent riot; students rally in opposition to Japanese influence in China and in favor of open-door policy
1986	Anti-bourgeois liberalization campaign crackdown on cultural liberalism and influence from the West; widespread student demonstrations in support of democracy
1987	Fang Lizhi (1936–2012), Liu Binyan (1925–2005), and Su Shaozhi are expelled from the Chinese Communist Party (CCP)
1989	Student Democracy Protests Massacre, Beijing (a.k.a. Tiananmen Square Massacre)
1989	National campaign against pornography
1990	Promulgation of the Basic Law of the Hong Kong Special Administrative Region
1990	Asian Games are held in Beijing
1991	Massive floods in the east and southeast displace more than 206 million people
1992	Deng Xiaoping's Southern Tour, reaffirming the government commitment to capitalism
1995	Taiwan's President Lee Teng-hui visits the United States, jeopardizing Sino-U.S. relations
1995	Third summit meeting between the United States and China yields pledge for constructive partnership
1995	National People's Congress adopts the country's first banking law, the Law on the People's Bank of China
1996	China conducts an underground nuclear test
1997	Deng Xiaoping dies; Jiang Zemin becomes "president"
1997	Return of Hong Kong to Chinese sovereignty
1999	Portuguese entrepôt of Macao returned to Chinese sovereignty
1999	Falun Gong movement stages a meditation vigil involving 10,000 practitioners outside Zhongnanhai
1999	Government crackdown on Falun Gong

1999	Fiftieth anniversary of the founding of the People's Republic of China
1999	NATO forces destroy the Chinese embassy in Belgrade, killing three "journalists"
1999	U.S. congressional report reveals Chinese theft of U.S. nuclear secrets
2000	Original projected date for realization of the Four Modernizations (revised in 1994 to 2047)
2000	Democratic Progressive Party candidate Chen Shui-bian is elected president of Taiwan and signals ambivalence toward the One-China Policy
2001	Beijing selected by IOC as host city for the 2008 Summer Olympics
2001	U.S. reconnaissance aircraft down a Chinese fighter plane in the South China Sea; national anti-U.S. protests ensue; Chinese government conveys protesting students by bus to the U.S. embassy for demonstrations
2001	September 11 destruction of the World Trade Center in New York and attacks on the Pentagon
2001	United States launches Operation Enduring Freedom, an invasion of Afghanistan
2002	China is officially admitted into the World Trade Organization
2002	United States declares war on Afghanistan
2002	Promulgation of Jiang Zemin's Three Represents Theory: the party represents the advanced productive forces (business people), the advanced cultural forces (intellectuals), and the masses (workers and peasants)
2002	CCP announces that businesspeople may be admitted to membership in the party
2003	Sudden outbreak of severe acute respiratory syndrome (SARS); Chinese government intentionally misrepresents the extent of the problem, provoking international protest
2003	Onset of avian influenza (H5N1), or bird flu
2003	United States invades Iraq, beginning Operation Iraqi Freedom
2003	China's first successful manned space flight
2003	Hu Jintao becomes "president"
2004	Revelation of U.S. torture of prisoners at Abu Ghraib Prison
2005	Protests break out in Beijing, Shanghai, and Hong Kong following revelation that Japanese textbooks have misrepresented the Japanese invasion and occupation of China

2005	China hosts the opposition leaders of Taiwan
2005	China's second successful manned space flight
2005	Tennis Master Cup held in Shanghai's Qi Zhong Stadium
2006	Security forces repress violent antigovernment protests in Panlong, Guangdong
2007	China conducts a targeted antisatellite explosion in space, leaving a dangerous mass of debris
2007	Democratic elections of Hong Kong's Legislative Council
2008	Shanghai Anti-Maglev Protests
2008	Chinese Nationalist Party (KMT) candidate Ma Ying-jeou elected president of Taiwan
2008	First direct flight between China and Taiwan
2008	Sichuan (Wenchuan) earthquake
2008	China hosts the Summer Olympic Games in Beijing
2008	Government forces begin campaigns against resistance in Tibet and Xinjiang
2008	Propagation of Charter 08, a written appeal for democratic reform
2009	Government campaign against Xinjiang Uyghurs
2009	Liu Xiaobo is arrested for "inciting subversion of state power" and sentenced to 11 years' imprisonment
2010	China and Taiwan sign Economic Cooperation Framework Agreement (ECFA)
2010	China conducts an anti-ballistic-missile test
2010	China hosts the World Expo in Shanghai
2010	Sixteenth Asian Games held in Guangzhou
2010	Liu Xiaobo receives the Nobel Peace Prize
2011	Hu Jintao pays official state visit to the United States
2011	Popular protests in Tunisia bring down the government, igniting additional protests in the Arab world: Bahrain, Egypt, Jordan, Libya, Morocco, Syria, Yemen
2011	Popular revolution in Egypt leads to ouster of Hosni Mubarak and the first democratic election
2011	Chinese authorities block Internet access to Arab state protests
2011	Calls for a "Jasmine Revolution" are made in Beijing via new media
2011	Tōhoku Earthquake (9.0 magnitude) and subsequent tsunami in northeast Japan disables the Fukushima Daiichi Nuclear Power Plant, causing meltdowns of three reactors
2011	Chinese censors block Internet access to information about Japanese nuclear disaster

2011	Public Security Bureau initiates roundup of political targets, most prominently Ai Weiwei, acclaimed artist and human rights advocate
2011	Chinese National Museum reopens with the German exhibit *Die Kunst der Aufklärung* ("The Art of Enlightenment")
2011	Ai Weiwei suddenly released
2011	Chinese high-speed railway collision in Zhejiang kills 39; stalled investigation provokes public anger
2011	20,000 protest in Dalian against environmental threat of contamination from paraxylene chemical plant
2011	Wukan villagers seize government headquarters in uprising against corruption
2012	300 Foxconn industry workers threaten mass suicide in Wuhan over wage dispute
2012	Four Tibetans commit self-immolation in protest against Chinese rule
2012	A Chinese court sentences Zhu Yufu to seven years' imprisonment for his poem, "It's Time" which was posted on the Internet
2012	Vice-President Xi Jinping makes an official visit to the United States
2012	Politburo Member and Secretary of the Chongqing Committee of the Communist Party dismissed from leadership positions
2012	Twelve Nobel Laureates urge Hu Jintao to open dialogue with Dalai Lama
2012	China to complete construction on its national space station
2012	Dozens of self-immolations by Tibetans protesting Chinese policies in Tibet carried out in public between spring 2011 and spring 2012.
2012	Chen Guangcheng, an outspoken dissident, escapes house arrest and takes refuge in U.S. embassy.
2012	18th Party Congress and appointment of successor government and party leadership
2012	Planned first Chinese astronaut space walk
2012	Third Asian Beach Games held in Haiyang
2013	Sixth East Asian Games to be held in Tianjin
2014	China's proposed unmanned exploration of Mars
2020	China's proposed first manned lunar mission

Table of Equivalent Measures and Administrative Units

renminbi (RMB): lit. "people's money," national currency of China
6.29 Chinese Dollars (*Yuan*, ¥) = 1 U.S. Dollar
7.75 Hong Kong Dollars = 1 U.S. Dollar
TWN (Taiwan New Dollar): national currency of Taiwan; 29 TWN = 1 U.S. Dollar

centimeter	.39 inch
gigawatt (GW)	1 billion watts
gram	.035 ounce
kilogram	2.2 pounds
square kilometer	.38 square miles
megawatt	1 million watts
meter	3.28 feet
square meter	10.76 square feet
cubic meter	35.31 cubic feet
microgram	1/1,000,000 gram
milligram	1/1,000 gram; .015 grains
millimeter	1/1,000 meter; .1 cm
mu	.667 acre

ADMINISTRATIVE UNITS

There are three larger levels of administrative organization in China. Whereas the United States has states, China has provinces—eighteen of them in fact, as you can see on the national map on page xxvii. China also has municipalities such as Beijing, as well as ethnic autonomous regions (Tibet, Mongolia, Ningxia [Hui], Xinjiang [Uighur], Guangxi [Zhuang]). Under these are prefecture, county, county town or county seat, town, and village.

Figures and Tables

A Note on Romanization and Chinese Pronunciation

In a book that tries to make more familiar a China in the throes of an accelerated cultural, economic, political, and social transformation, it is surely unfair of the authors to begin with a tour of the unfamiliar, specifically a brief discussion of the alphabetic representation of the sounds of Chinese language. However, this is precisely what we must do, for the effort to know more about the contemporary phenomena of China requires that we draw closer to the texture of the place by becoming conversant with a number of its more significant expressions and terms.

In the technical parlance of the Modern Language Association, Chinese is one of a number of "less commonly taught languages." But with considerably more than a quarter of the world speaking Chinese, it is wise to give some thought to its status as one of the most widely used languages. And in China, it pays to remember that language is very complex, with a welter of "dialects" so distinct and different as to resemble individual languages. Indeed, Robert Ramsey, a linguist who has written on Chinese, claims that China has more than fifty languages!

Most readers of this book know that the written Chinese language consists of Sinographs, more popularly known as "characters," of which in the more complete lexicons there are more than fifty thousand. Literacy in Chinese, itself a contentious, because political, topic, requires a minimum active understanding of several thousand such graphs. To reproduce the terms Chinese people generally use for such things as "Internet," "economic growth," "political reform," "capitalism," and a host of others would be of little value for most of our readers because the written language is by itself unintelligible. Thus it is customary for authors of general-audience texts such as this one to provide the "romanized" or phonetic spellings of the

Sinographs. The objective in this instance is to offer access to the sounds of Chinese, but it is very important to recall in each of these cases that these are the Western-style letters that represent the sound of the "character," and that there are several systems by means of which these sounds have been represented, the first efforts having been made in 1605 by the Jesuit missionary Matteo Ricci in his work *Xizi qiji*, "The Wonder of Western Script." Such a phonetic imprint is better than nothing, but it is still not Chinese.

Students have long questioned this phonetic spelling because of the odd looking "words" it yields (i.e., *Xizi qiji*) and because there are other romanization systems that increase their confusion. The purpose of this note is to attempt to allay this customary confusion while explaining the reasoning behind current romanization and also trying to assist with pronunciation. Since 1980 the sounds of Chinese have been increasingly represented via the romanization system called *pinyin*, literally, "phonetic spelling." Owing to what we might consider a disregard for Western alphabet values, *pinyin* produces "words" like *zheng* that look very curious to the untrained eye and occasion the following reaction: How do you pronounce *zh* or *x*?

To account for the odd appearance of this popular phonetic spelling requires sensitivity to politics. One must know that *pinyin* grew from an earlier system of romanization called *Latinxua* (Latinization) that was produced in the 1930s in Soviet Asia and incorporated in China as Sin Wenz (New Writing). This system was subsequently adopted for use in the Communist base areas of Gansu, Ningxia, and Shanxi in the northwest in the 1940s. A few years after the Chinese Revolution, the government formed a committee to conduct scientific research aimed at standardizing the national language. From 1952 to 1958 this research was the foundation of a national policy of "language reform" that generated serious discussion about the abandonment of characters in favor of a purely alphabetized form of Chinese. In the end this did not occur, but a systematic simplification of the written language was realized and yielded an official promulgation of *pinyin* as the nation's romanization system and the northern dialect peculiar to Beijing, *putonghua*, as the standard spoken language. And because *putonghua* was the common parlance of the north and quite dissimilar from the speech of so many other regions, this decision complicated matters even further by giving the illusion of linguistic identity. For the purposes of drawing closer to the sounds of Chinese, we take advantage of this illusion throughout the book and provide the *pinyin* for critical terms. Lastly, the reader must be reminded that the greater ease of reading and writing *pinyin* is belied by its deficiency in representing the four tones of *putonghua*, which given the preponderant number of homophones in Chinese is a source of greater ambiguity.

Here are a few pronunciation tips, ones that you would do well to commit to memory so that the chances of your getting at an accurate expression are enhanced. We urge you to spend a few moments here at the start just trying out the sounds of these strange transliterated words since such effort will enrich your aptitude for the sounds of the street in China.

Distinctive Vowels

a is pronounced like a blend of the "a" in *father* and the "a" in *at*
ai is pronounced like the "ai" in *aisle*
ao is pronounced like the "ow" in *now*
e is pronounced like the "u" in *but*
eng is pronounced like the "ung" in *dung*
i is pronounced like the "ee" in *bee*, <u>except</u> when following *ch, sh,* and *zh,* when it sounds like the "r" of *sure*
ian is pronounced like *yen*
iu is pronounced like *yo*
ou is pronounced like *oh*
u is pronounced like the "oo" in *zoo*
ui is pronounced like the "ay" in *way*
ü is pronounced *yew*

Challenging Initial Consonants

c is pronounced like the "ts" in *nits,* so that *cao* sounds like "tsau"
j is pronounced much like *j* is in English, so that *jin* sounds like "gin"
q is pronounced like "ch" but with lots of air, so that *qi* sounds like "chee"
x is pronounced like "sh" but also like "sy," so that *xiang* sounds like "sheeang"
zh is pronounced like the "dg" in *judge,* so that *zheng* sounds like "jung," *zhou* like "joe"
z is pronounced like the "dz" in *adze,* so that *zeng* sounds like "dzung"

Preface and Acknowledgments

It has been nearly fifteen years since our inaugural conference, "China after Deng," from which was launched the *China beyond the Headlines* series. It has turned out to be a venture more successful than we could have imagined. For this opportunity we are grateful and excited to bring before students and the general public another guide to current Chinese affairs. Again under the incomparable aegis of Susan McEachern and the generous support of Rowman & Littlefield Publishers, we introduce the newest volume of our collaboration: *China in and beyond the Headlines*. With her exceptional knowledge of the culture and politics of modern China and an instinctual sense of how best to educate the public about its complexities, Susan deserves special recognition for our debt to her. *Wansui!*

As with the previous books, we asked a diverse group of individuals—academic specialists, activists, environmentalists, journalists, lawyers, and travelers—to help us compass the rapidly expanding terrain of information about, from, and on China. Our guidelines in selecting contributors have never varied: essays must be written in an engaging style free of jargon, they must be current, they must make comparisons to the contemporary United States where relevant, and they must engage with the moral issues raised by their topic. As editors we seek to provide comprehensible expert testimony on each topic and, by encouraging self-reflection, to open conversation across the chapters and with readers.

Above all, we wish to stimulate readers to think in new and open-minded ways about the role of China in the contemporary world and about the mutual entanglement of China and the United States as the two most important states of our historical moment. The number of essays in this volume is greater than in either of our previous two collections, a reflection of our interest in covering a wide array of views and in obtaining the greatest sample of China's current mixture of culture, economy, information, new media, politics, and society. Such coverage is complicated and enriched at the same time by the sophistication of the Chinese media, whose reporters cover real stories, and yet where the combination of self-censorship and forceful government oversight ensures that these stories are not as complete or as critical as they should be. Of course, the growth in sophistication and a modest increase in curiosity and willingness to investigate by the Chinese media are mirrored by more technically sophisticated mechanisms for constraining effective reporting and ensuring that the end result of such efforts does not reflect the full story. This is why investigative efforts by independent journalists and media experts in situ, such as Gady Epstein and David Bandurski, are so important. The benefits of this greater complexity and depth have, in our estimation, made this collection particularly valuable.

The adventure in U.S.-China studies made possible by our collaboration has proven very enriching for us both, expanding the orbits of our intellectual contacts with colleagues across the globe while also making more profound our intellectual and emotional ties to each other. This is the greatest gift of these years of work, and its preciousness cannot be measured.

In the course of this several-year effort we have accumulated a number of debts that require public acknowledgment. Institutions and centers were particularly supportive of the labors of this book's conception and completion. We are very grateful to the National Committee on United States–China Relations for financial support for the conference that brought most of the contributors to Boulder in April 2010. The National Committee's Public Intellectuals Program (PIP) and its inimitable director, Jan Berris, deserve particular and heartfelt thanks, as well as all the scholars in the PIP second phase. Many of the authors in this volume were, together with Tim Weston, fellows of that ongoing visionary program. We are very grateful for the Center for Asian Studies at the University of Colorado for its additional support of the April 2010 Boulder conference. The Institute for Scholarship in the Liberal Arts at Notre Dame and the Kellogg Institute for International Studies have again, as in the past, provided generous assistance in the production stages of the book, underwriting the creation of maps and figures as well as the reproduction of photographs for the cover and for most of the essays. The University of Notre Dame's Hesburgh Lecture and Teachers as Scholars Programs provided the ideal forum where some of the key ideas of the introduction were tried out.

Many thanks also to the participants in the yearlong China seminar sponsored by the Center for the Humanities and Arts at the University of Colorado at Boulder, and to Lynn Parisi and her wonderful Program for Teaching East Asia at the University of Colorado at Boulder.

At the Internationales Kolleg für Geisteswissenschaftliche Forschung (International Consortium for Research in the Humanities) of the University of Erlangen-Nürnberg, where most of the final editing took place, we must convey our appreciation for its generous provision of logistical and technical assistance. The auspices of the Kolleg made the final stages of manuscript production extremely enjoyable while accelerating the effectiveness of the entire process.

Individual contributions to the final form of *China in and beyond the Headlines* were numerous, but none as significant as that of Allison Wettstein, who read every page of the book manuscript, and wrote a critical review of each of the essays. The startling array of photographic imagery from today's China found on the cover and scattered throughout the book was very generously provided by Tong Lam, whose exceptional eye and feel for narrative distinguish his historical writing as well as his photography. We are also grateful to Christopher Dewolf for the remarkable photograph of the Shenzhen skyline that appears in Tim Weston's chapter and to Grace Baumgartner, Carrie Broadwell-Tkach and Alden Perkins for their industry in the final phases of the book's production. All but three of the maps were made by the cartographers at XNR Productions of Milwaukee. Yet, it was the inspired and very timely handiwork of Mr. Xu Yongli that resulted in the images of Sichuan, Chengdu, and Yongquan, Shaanxi. For this last-minute creative urge we (as well as our readers) are deeply appreciative.

In Erlangen, colleagues Chu Pingyi, Thomas Fröhlich, Patrick Henriet, Sophia Katz, Michael Lackner, and Richard Landes, who shared hours of inspired conversation and critique in discussions of enlightenment, freedom, human rights, and the intertwined fates of China, Europe, and the United States, were the greatest gift to the work. In addition, we must note the assistance of Philipp Hünnebeck, who read and commented upon the front matter and several of the essays. From the inception of the project, Lionel Jensen benefited from the unstinting support of Susan D. Blum, whose wide knowledge of China and keen eye for the golden glints enabled him to dispense with the dross of so much of the writing. For Jensen, the persistent and persuasive labors of, and discussions with, his research assistants, Matthew Lodwich, Allison Wettstein, and Deanna Kolberg (who, along with Dominic Romeo, prepared the index) made the work of writing and editing memorably enjoyable. For conversations and email exchanges that added meaningful dimension to the writing, we are grateful to Maura Elizabeth Cunningham, Bei Dao, Michael Davis, Michael Friedrich, Howard Goldblatt, Faye Kleeman, Terry Kleeman, Sylvia Lin, Jim McAdams, Scott Mainwaring, Victor Mair, Jonathan Noble, Steve Reifenberg, Holly Rivers, Sharon Schierling, Jeff Wasserstrom, and Xiao Qiang. Lastly, a note of appreciation is necessary for the students of East Asian Languages and Cultures 30104 at the University of Notre Dame for their intellectual commitment and spirited debate across the spectrum of the essays in this volume; their work has made it a better book.

Figure A. China and Its Political Borders.

Figure B.   China, Western Provinces.

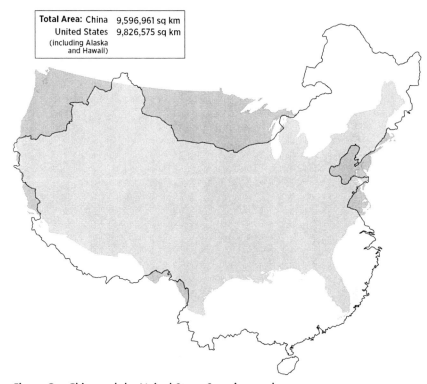

Total Area: China   9,596,961 sq km
         United States 9,826,575 sq km
         (including Alaska
              and Hawaii)

Figure C.   China and the United States Superimposed.

Introduction: China, the United States, and Convulsive Cooperation

Lionel M. Jensen and Timothy B. Weston

Nearly fifteen years ago this series on *China beyond the Headlines* emerged from a single afternoon of papers and discussion at the University of Colorado on several aspects of Chinese life as they were and were not represented to the U.S. public. China's former vice premier and head of the Central Military Commission, Deng Xiaoping, the chief architect of the country's economic and political reforms, had died a few months earlier. The focus of the conference was "China after Deng," but the interchange with panelists and the audiences circled around and above the paramount leader like rings from a smoldering fire. There were repeated questions about human rights, the freedom of the press, and the limits of journalistic and scholarly representation. In this case it was print and broadcast journalism: Why was coverage of China so predictable, and why did it break so little new ground in showing what life was like for Chinese? There were complaints about reliable information even on subjects that were obsessively covered such as economic reform. Would the reform policies initiated by Deng Xiaoping continue after his death? Was China still Communist? Is China a threat to the United States? What about the one-child policy and forced sterilizations and abortions? How could the Communist Party endure following the televised slaughter of countless innocent citizens upholding their constitutional right to protest? Should the United States confer Most Favored Nation and Permanent Normal Trading status on the "Butchers of Beijing"?

Our students[1] had prepared a survey of audience attitudes toward China. It was distributed at all of the conference panels and yielded startling results: a large number of respondents stated that China was a threat to itself and to world peace and that it was likely to face a military encounter with a foreign adversary in the future, while also experiencing the stresses of

1

rapid political reform. There was a genuine fear of the Chinese government along with a pressing sense of crisis. Still, a majority of attendees indicated a healthy appreciation for the Chinese people and their struggle to achieve greater individual freedom and control during an era of dizzying change in all dimensions of life—cultural, economic, political, social. Each panel was characterized by spirited exchange and even heated argument between panelists, who often were not in agreement, and the audience, some of whom denounced the boutique journalistic opinion on China provided by experts increasingly drawn to widening column space, live television interviews, and the prospect of policy engagement with U.S. government operatives.

There was a reactionary tone to some of the discussion, which had been a concern of Tim Weston's in organizing the conference to begin with. As trade with China was reengaged between 1993 and 1997, with local Denver companies like Samsonite getting back into the China market following the Tiananmen Massacre hiatus, many of the attendees expressed an anger that trade without sanctions was unacceptable. Such anger extended to the issue of Tibet and its violent occupation by the Chinese, as well as claims of a conscious political program to "thin out the gene pool," as one said, by moving great numbers of Han Chinese into Tibet to start businesses and lives among the people of Lhasa. Looking back at it now, it is apparent that the most we could wish for was to be partially right about what was happening in China, for all of us were talking about a place in rapid motion, trying to identify fixed shapes through blurred glass. For that reason, when we asked the conference participants to convert their talks into book chapters, we urged them to be self-reflective about how they "know" China and to adopt a stance of humility as they wrote about that most complex and fascinating of countries.

Our vision for the conference, as it has been for each of the books that have grown from it, was to reach outside the university, to practice public intellectualism by engaging the largest possible community of learners. This is why a critical dimension of its success was the encouragement of its participants to speak candidly, as citizens as much as experts, about their concerns in the current relations between China and the United States. One of the participants in the original conference in Boulder, Colorado, Richard Bernstein, a *New York Times* journalist, had just published a book, *The Coming Conflict with China*, in which he recognized forces of emergent reactive nationalism in China's rising with the passive acceptance by the United States of China's aggressive pursuit of expansion internationally. "China bashing" was the complaint most loudly spoken against Bernstein. But another popular book by Andrew Nathan and Robert Ross, *The Great Wall and the Empty Fortress*, argued something quite different, that the United States misperceived China's urge for security as an expansionist impulse when it was actually a reflection of the country's own reasonable fears. The air was thick with fear of imminent conflict, as well as a surprising degree of Cold War rhetoric concerning "Red China."

Nevertheless, most of the conference participants had traveled to China, some extensively, and saw beyond the hysteria of the great powers theory of rise and fall to focus collective thought on China's extraordinary economic progress and remarkable opening to the outside world, but also on corruption, tensions of ethnic diversity, labor unrest, rural poverty, environmental devastation, popular fiction and film, as well as human rights and China's "new authoritarianism." Given the quality of the discussion—a consistent, and welcome, feature of the conferences and book lectures we have conducted over the last decade—the papers delivered offered fresh insight into China, but more importantly into how it was analyzed by Western and Chinese observers.

If China was the story, the books that were produced from our running commentary were, in effect, on-the-spot reflections on how China's story was told at different points in time. While maintaining a consistent purpose with each collection, we early on concluded that the warp speed at which change in China takes place and the huge range of important subjects that make up the larger China story necessitated that each volume contain wholly new content and a range of new authorial voices. And looking back now, it seems that there was a lot to be learned from this metahistory. Our first book was made from this story as we and our contributors understood it then, and yet while the opening comments from our first volume may appear dated now, they are worth quoting here at the beginning of our third volume a decade into the second millennium:

> Demonizing each other may serve the immediate interests of China and the United States, but it is unlikely to lead to responsible decisions about the long term. Little is to be gained from one-dimensional understanding of the other, for this is mostly based in the very ignorance that . . . [we] seek earnestly to counter. It is our express conviction that a continued disinclination of the two nations to understand each other will prove perilous to the planet. We believe the information and range of perspectives contained in this collection will assist in . . . rethinking the meanings of "China," the "United States," and their increasingly intertwined relations so that the twenty-first century will be . . . notable for Sino-U.S. cooperation rather than conflict.[2]

The conviction is no less true for us today; still, it is difficult now in many ways to realize how little we knew then about the directions our studies of China would take us over the eleven years of editing these books. The fates of China and the United States are as intertwined now as we hoped they might be recognized to be in 1997. It is a reality today, and the amount of information it requires to assess this reality with evenhandedness and an open mind is daunting. But the techno-informational changes of the last few years *may* have rendered our prevailing conceit of "in and beyond the headlines" a metaphorical mistake.

THE END OF A METAPHOR?

Are there really any "headlines" anymore? Moreover, if so, it now must be recognized that China *is* the headlines, and not simply because of coverage—whether in their published or online editions—in the *Economist*, or the *New York Times*, or the *Washington Post*. China dominates the news everywhere because in the few years since we completed *China's Transformations*, the second volume in this series, this single nation's presence—culturally, diplomatically, economically, politically—has covered the earth. Today it is common to see stories declaring "the rise of China." This is a consequence of the confidence of the Chinese Communist Party's (CCP) development program, the limitless ambition for business expansion,[3] as well as China's investment in new media, which makes it very easy for people around the world to call up information and awe-inspiring statistics about that country with a few keystrokes.

In the United States one doesn't have to stay abreast of the latest mortality figures on Newspaper Death Watch (http://newspaperdeathwatch.com/) to understand that a declining number of U.S. citizens get, much less read, a daily newspaper. Most admit that what they know about the news they obtain from television or from the Internet. This is no less true for Chinese, although the number of them who use their smartphone or PDA device as the physical source of the information may be much larger. They still read newspapers, but about half a billion people have mobile telephones and 400 million are online, all of whom are a great deal more effective with these devices than most tech-savvy U.S. information buffs. And as readers will see from the essays in the volume, because information is *everywhere*, one has to determine reliable favorites. Increasingly these favorites also have forums for reader response and commentary, which is as true of the *Huffington Post* (www.huffingtonpost.com) and the *Wall Street Journal* (www.wsj.com) as it is of *China Daily* (http://bbs.chinadaily.com.cn/index .php). This is where one comes face-to-face with the less regulated thoughts and feelings of the online public. In China "BBS" (Bulletin Board System), "weibo" (microblogs), and "boke" (blogs), as Susan Blum demonstrates (see chapter 8), are informational conduits of considerable promise and peril. They provide windows on the daily experience and longings of "connected" Chinese. This is also where individual posts can be reconfigured as screeds by parties interested in posting apparently spontaneous rants when, in point of fact, many of them are skillfully manufactured statements of allowed dissent.

The obvious similarity of the information revolution in the United States and in China is one reason that the old journalistic metaphors of front page, back page, folds, headlines, and the rest *may* have outlived their usefulness. However, it is our opinion that it is the very transformation in the meaning of news and how it is transmitted and read and commented upon that gives the *in* and *beyond* the headlines a new, more urgent worthiness (see David Bandurski in chapter 1 and Gady Epstein in chapter 15). Determining which news is reliable and accurate is a tremendous task for the average reader, particularly when that reader is cycling through multiple windows of texts and images with the attentiveness of a blink. How in this context and with these reading habits can one understand the complexities of international news?

The Chinese government, in addition to monitoring and controlling popular access to the Internet through official portals, has an array of its own news sites with a sometimes bewildering display of advertisements, articles, headlines, images, videos, and shifting color palettes, all quite friendly and attractive. The *news* presented on the pages of the approved journalistic outlets, as when the winter 2011 revolts took place in Bahrain, Egypt, Libya, Morocco, Tunisia, and Yemen, was represented in a bold, multicolor banner headline announcing the unfortunate loss of Chinese tennis sensation Li Na at the hands of Kim Clijsters in the final of the Australian Open. Crowding the front-page space was also a dramatic piece on the eruption of Mount Aetna in Sicily, as well as the expected scattering of stories on CCP activities and lifestyle material on pop culture personalities. The epochal events in North Africa and the Middle East were simply not reported. The broadcast media were jammed. CNN was blacked out, Chinese censors conveying quite clearly the government's refusal to provide access to historical events for curious, connected citizens.

The reality of "open networks, closed regimes" makes the work of *China in and beyond the Headlines* even more important now.[4] With the book's scholarly commentary we believe the reader may obtain a deeper and more nuanced understanding of the more critical issues of the day: issues in and for China as well as the United States and China. And when one thinks of how much the very design of many websites and blogs owes to the headlines and bold type, folds and pages that make up the daily newspaper, the organizing metaphor of our book remains relevant and its reportage critical because its strengths come from the authors' candid accounts of what they observe and what they learn from interviews and from working on the ground. Engaged with agencies, citizens, local reporters, and officials, the contributors deliver a portrait of life that goes beyond the redundant wall of media representation: Olympics, World Expo, Internet censorship, urban growth, spectacular pollution, the stock market, trades, takeovers, investments, Communist Party proclamations (see chapters 5, 6, 9, 12, and 14 for examples of such engagement and reflection).

The book's core principles of engagement, honest reportage, self-reflection, and topicality have prevailed from the start, even with sensational changes in how information is obtained and the rise of the so-called 24/7 news cycle. The glut of news, nonnews, information, and infotainment must be *processed* more than reported. In 2012 there is unquestionably more information available about China than at any other time. It is one of the principal topics of world interest and discussion, but another reason for this popularity derives from a greater degree of meaningful Chinese cultural presence. A 2010 U.S. government survey reported that more than 1,600 public and private schools are teaching Chinese, where a decade ago there were but three hundred. The College Board, in concert with the Asia Society and its Partnership for Global Learning, is conducting a national campaign to accelerate this increase, calling for a goal of 10 percent of U.S. schools to teach Chinese. This effort at home in the United States has moved concurrently with the increasing global prominence of China, largely due, many commentators outside of China believe, to the success of the so-called Beijing Consensus.[5]

CHINA AND THE UNITED STATES: THE TENSE INTERTWINING

The Beijing Consensus was coined by *Western* policy analysts to describe the Chinese government's alternative model for development, one in which an authoritarian government may win friends and influence people by way of its example of integrated economy and strategic foreign investment. The term contrasts sharply with the "Washington Consensus," used for the last thirty years to refer to the specific economic policy prescriptions collaboratively applied by the U.S. Treasury Department, the International Monetary Fund, and the World Bank to "reform" or stabilize the failed economies of developing countries. Many people believe that the Chinese government has strategically followed a script of exporting advice, capital, plans, manpower, and cultural influence to beneficial effect on an astonished and admiring world.

Ironically, it is now the developing country, China, a member of the World Bank and the International Monetary Fund that possesses roughly $2 trillion of U.S. national debt and that is acting to stabilize the economy of the United States. This substantial investment is part of an explicit domestic and global strategy of *heping fazhan* or "peaceful development." Although China will continue to expend sizable sums on domestic and foreign defense ($91.5 billion in 2011) and even expand the ranks of its large military, the nation's leaders are carefully following a new policy imperative of *hexie*, or harmony.

In the language of the official Chinese press and in the eyes of almost every Chinese with whom we have spoken in the last twenty years, China's staggering economic achievements are the consequence of *gaige kaifang,* "[economic] reform and opening [to the west]" that was first announced by Deng Xiaoping in 1979. Although this vernacular term persists as the shorthand for the economic reforms, one may read Chinese press reports or think-tank analyses that refer to the *Zhongguo moshi,* "China Model." The successes of this model—"the realization of a prosperous and powerful, democratic, civilized and peaceful, socialist modernizing nation," to quote a Chinese source[6]—are the empirical result of more than thirty years of the policy of "reform and opening."

The overall effectiveness of this model in elevating the average standard of living and bringing China international respect is something about which the government and the people are immensely proud. In light of the country's succession of economic and social achievements, Chinese pride, even nationalist enthusiasm, is understandable. However, in a "developed world," still languishing in global financial stagnation, China's economic triumphalism provokes defensiveness and apprehension.

It is instructive in light of this anxiety to acknowledge some facts of Sino-U.S. relations—economically and politically the two nations are mutually dependent and have been growing ever more so for two decades. Since the mid-1990s China and the United States have enjoyed a "strategic partnership," reaffirmed in 2001 with a dedicated alliance in the "global war on terror" as well as China's admission into the World Trade Organization. China owns about eight percent of an ever-increasing U.S. national debt, while the United States is the single largest importer of Chinese-made goods. Trade in the other direction is also very substantial: China is now the second largest importer of U.S. goods after Canada.[7] Thus, for better or for worse, the two countries' current and future fates are necessarily intertwined. To the extent that they are aware of this fateful dependency (and most media-literate Chinese are, whereas U.S. residents have only more belatedly awakened to the reality), the people of both countries are not necessarily pleased. Today, Chinese and U.S. citizens know, or at least think they know, a great deal about one another, and what they know is held in a complex emotional mixture of admiration, competition, fear, judgment, and respect. On both shores their intertwined fates are understood as an unavoidable necessity of the current phase of their bilateral relations.

Even as one emphasizes their common bond, there are some critical differences that place China on much better financial footing than the United States. This fact is not lost on many U.S. citizens, 44 percent of whom in a 2009 Pew Research Center survey identified China as "the world's leading economic power." A February 2010 *Washington Post*/ABC News poll surveying global economic superiority found respondents equally bullish on China: 41 percent for the United States and 40 percent for China as the dominant economic power. With 20 percent of its exports sent to the

United States, China's heavily export-based economy also suffered from the U.S. and European financial collapses: countless Chinese businesses—large and small—were shuttered, enterprises went bankrupt, and hundreds of thousands of workers were laid off, as foreign demand even for cheap goods plummeted. And as the Bush administration was hurriedly enacting the $700 billion Emergency Economic Stabilization Act (creating the controversial Troubled Asset Relief Program) in October of 2008, the Chinese government put in place a substantial economic bailout plan valued at 3.9 trillion yuan ($589 billion U.S.). Whereas the bailout in the United States was highly controversial, in China, where the government has long played a leading role in the economy, most people eagerly supported its intervention. The Chinese bailout, which more closely resembled the New Deal program in the United States of the 1930s than anything the Obama administration was able to get through Congress, provided investment in public infrastructure (railways and roads), affordable housing, subsidies for social welfare, reconstruction of earthquake-devastated areas, urban renewal, advances in technology, and environmental projects in sustainable development. In the process the Chinese bailout created or saved countless jobs. In terms of the economic and social challenges they face, China and the United States are familiar, not strange, bedfellows.

In a number of very important respects, China and the United States are kindred nations. Their bilateral relationship, while marked by persistent tension, is fundamentally stable. Understanding the transcendent importance of this bilateral relationship, the governments of both countries have worked hard to achieve this outcome. "The relationship between the United States and China," President Barack Obama said soon after taking office, "will shape the 21st century, which makes it as important as any bilateral relationship in the world. That really must underpin our partnership. That is the responsibility that together we bear."[8]   When President Obama hosted soon-to-be-Chinese-President Xi Jinping at the White House in February 2012 amid an election cycle characterized by rising anti-China sentiment on the part of U.S. voters he acknowledged differences and tensions between the two countries, but went out of his way to emphasize that relations between the United States and China are vital and that cooperation between the two countries is good for the rest of the world. These two greatest powers are in turn respected and feared by other nations in Europe, Africa, the Middle East, and particularly Asia. Yet in East Asia—Taiwan, Hong Kong, Japan, and South Korea—the perspective on these two powers provides a view to their respective vulnerabilities, inherent weaknesses overshadowed by global reputation for financial and political might.

From the regional vantage, it is possible to recognize that China's global financial presence, its aggressive expansion into markets wielding substantial cash and demands for profitability, is belied by its inevitable, and very

Figure 0.1. "Obamao: Serve the People" T-shirt, Beijing. Photograph by Tong Lam.

frequent, domestic dramas. Although not overlooking the anxiety produced by China's escalation of defense (a particular provocation to Japan, which is now responding accordingly), it is China's domestic turmoil that is a concern to its neighbors. China is a newly industrializing economy; it is, by its own admission, a developing rather than a developed nation. No amount of speculating about the global reach of its capital investments and its purchase of U.S. national debt will change this or quickly wipe away China's multiple, complex domestic problems, such as its government's negligible legitimacy, storied corruption, and detachment from its people.

The GINI coefficient, a numerical measurement of any society's degree of economic inequality in which 1 represents complete inequality, is quite high for both China (.53) and the United States (.47) and distinguishes them as countries of marked inequality, and their inequality has grown markedly in the last ten years. Both countries' populations are sharply divided, consisting of small numbers of super rich who are becoming wealthier by the day, middle classes that are feeling squeezed, and expanding underclasses. Both nations are without a comprehensive system of health-care delivery for their citizens, and their governments sometimes act beyond the constraints of constitutional authority.

The global aspirations of the Communist Party are as ambitious as those of the U.S. government, as demonstrated in the former's spectacular hosting of the 2008 Summer Olympic Games and the 2010 Shanghai Expo, the largest such international exposition ever held. Spectacle of this nature has complemented the strategic spread of Chinese investment throughout the developing and developed world, where new relationships (and dependencies) have been formed. For example, China receives the bulk of its petroleum from sources in the Middle East, Eastern Africa, and Russia, while it is also the world's largest importer of soybeans. For perhaps as long as China and the United States have been engaged economically and politically (whether as friends or foes), each has regarded the other with a mixture of admiration, fear, and suspicion. Given our histories and our objectives, this emotional complex is likely to endure. However, with their above-mentioned strategic partnership and more than a decade of Permanent Normal Trade Relations (PNTR), as well as China's place in the World Trade Organization, fear and suspicion are less pronounced.

Still, with a significant portion of national debt in the hands of the Chinese, many people in the United States are concerned, and the impulse to fear or at least doubt is returning, as the 2012 U.S. election cycle makes clear. U.S. citizens' apprehension of China has risen together with the growing sense at home—and elsewhere in the world and perhaps in China in particular—that the United States is in decline. The perceived contrast between the two countries' trajectories has made China's "rise" that much more threatening to U.S. citizens. At the same time, the spread of popular discontent and rebellion among some Arab nations is believed by authorities in Beijing to be clandestinely choreographed by the United States.

Communism and the otherness of the Chinese resurface as threats to the U.S. way of life. Conservative impulses in U.S. political discourse call for a much tougher, confrontational relationship with Beijing, as evidenced in aggressive demands for the appreciation of the value of the yuan (the Chinese currency) on both sides of the aisle in the U.S. Congress. Yet it is the ability of the Chinese government to purchase large piles of U.S. debt that currently ensures the persistence of the unsustainable way of life that U.S.

citizens continue to enjoy. But even this investment must be placed in context. The total national debt as of this writing is in excess of $15.3 trillion (about $49,000 per citizen or $136,000 per taxpayer). Of that total, roughly 30 percent ($4.9 trillion) is owned by foreign entities, and among these China holds the greatest share, followed by Japan and the United Kingdom. Since the United States is currently not able to live within the limits of its budget, it must continue to borrow against itself in the hope that as the economy recovers and government coffers are replenished (with future as yet unannounced but inevitable increases in tax levies to individuals and businesses), it may pay back its debts and work its way back to solvency.

As the Chinese government and most U.S. citizens understand, tax reductions and tax incentives for large businesses, not to mention the financial assistance programs for General Motors, Chrysler, and AIG, Goldman Sachs, CITI, and others, can only be paid for by new borrowing or by the generation of new currency by the Federal Reserve. Thus, as the United States continues down the path of fiscal peril, the Chinese, among a considerable number of others, enable our deficit spending. Of course, this underwriting may have its limits, but as yet these have not been discovered, and concerns about such mutual financial dependency make many in China wonder what the future may hold for it and for the United States if the decade's pattern of indebtedness and indemnification remains unchecked.

THE PENDULUM OF PERCEPTIONS

This dramatic fluctuation between political extremes has characterized U.S. opinion toward China for well over a century, and one of the objectives of this book series has been to educate readers about the country's complexity. Greater familiarity, we believe, lessens the tendency to fear or dislike China as an adversary. In the recent past, say a decade ago, one of the reasons for that educational deficiency of U.S. citizens was the relative lack of access to reliable information on life in China in our schools and in the media. Another reason was the scarcity of Chinese language instruction and meaningful foreign travel. That was then; this is now. And now is indeed very different.

The emotional line that runs through the chapters that follow is the desire for intercultural communication, particularly as it is threatened by the enduring exceptionalist national ideologies of *both* the United States and China. Indeed one aspect of this exceptionalism, we believe, is a tendency in both China and the United States to understand their current bilateral relations in terms of a "rise and fall of great nations" theory according to which conflict between them is inevitable (see chapter 4). There is an undercurrent of unease with this prospect, considering that China and the

United States are engaged as never before in a wide expanse of multilateral economic and political engagements that intersect and crosscut national and regional identities in Asia, Africa, Europe, Southeast Asia, and Oceania. Bipolarity seems a very fragile foundation upon which to stand these complexities.

One of the objectives of this collection is to assist the reader in identifying the commonalities rather than the conflicts between these two powers so that the extreme oscillations of our perceptions may be stilled. We believe this is best accomplished by providing an access to dimensions of Chinese life largely unfamiliar to the U.S. reading public in clear, jargon-free prose. For this effort to be effective, candor and accuracy of reporting are essential, which is why we have asked all contributors to assess their own relationship to China as an object of study as they write candidly about China in order to bring it closer to the United States, so that it may be respected through greater understanding. Fear can be neutralized by reliable information and the willingness to think about what it means. Although not always unwarranted, fear often occurs for those among us who seek the threatening specter of foreign ideology or wish to make international politics fit the mold of an outmoded twentieth-century bipolarism. China certainly aspires to be a great global force, and these aspirations are in keeping with the objectives of its revolution but are also consistent with the achievements of its imperial past. This goal is, in certain very real aspects, within its reach, and yet there are other respects in which this greatness is undermined.

Indeed, moving away from Cold War–style polarity has proven to be halting and difficult. Following the Tiananmen Massacre of 1989, the most prominent area of public discord between China and the Western world was over China's human rights record and the related issue of the Chinese government's failure to uphold laws enshrined in its own constitution that guarantee the Chinese people's legal right to free speech and other civil liberties. The Western media gave full attention to China's human rights problem, as it did to intellectuals and activists who paid a high personal price for their brave attempts to take advantage of or expand their civil rights (see chapters 7 and 11). Today the Western media continues to cover violations of human rights in China, of course, but the relative weight of the issue in this reportage has declined dramatically.

This shift has occurred simultaneously with China's economic takeoff, as the United States and other policy makers were compelled to recognize that their countries' relationships with China touch on a wide variety of subjects and that overwhelming focus on human rights makes it extremely difficult to negotiate with Beijing on other critical areas of mutual interest. The Clinton administration's 1994 decision to delink the granting of most-favored-nation trading status to China with that country's human rights performance, followed by China's admission into the World Trade Organization in 2001, signaled that economics and trade had emerged as the most salient issue with regard to China's place in the world and that Western governments, much to the consternation of Western NGOs focused on human rights, had concluded that China is too strong and independent to be bent to Western standards on human rights in anything approaching a rapid fashion. Perhaps the clearest recent statement of this idea came in February 2009 from Secretary of State Hillary Clinton, who when asked by reporters before a visit to Beijing to comment on human rights in China, commented, "Successive administrations and Chinese governments have been poised back and forth on these issues, and we have to continue to press them. But our pressing on those issues can't interfere with the global economic crisis, the global climate change crisis, and the security crisis."[9]

THE BIND OF U.S.-CHINA MUTUAL DEPENDENCY

Disputes over human and political rights continue to bedevil relationships between Western governments and the Chinese government, a topic that will be taken up again below. However, the greatest controversy with China now is in the economic realm and focuses on China's ownership of United States debt and its manipulation of its currency. The common wisdom, at least as it is reported on CNBC, by the *Wall Street Journal*, and by Treasury secretaries in hearings before the U.S. Congress or at meetings of the G8, is that China's currency must be revalued. Its artificial pegging to the U.S. dollar undermines effective world trade and lessens the might of U.S. exports. But the common wisdom may be wrong, or at least has more unfortunate consequences for the United States than can be seen.

Many U.S. economists, policy makers, and politicians decry China's "currency manipulation." With the *renminbi* ("people's money") or yuan artificially devalued—so goes the story—Chinese exports remain cheap, U.S. goods too expensive, and the U.S. trade imbalance with China astronomically widening as unemployment escalates. Political ads in state and national races across the country always echo this imbalance regardless of the political year as they charge that someone has "shipped our jobs overseas to China." Pressure has mounted in Congress to counter with protectionism—proportional tariffs on unfairly subsidized imports. Even today when Democrats and Republicans are excessively polarized, the issue of China's undervalued currency, more than any other, dissolves their partisanship.

On September 29, 2010, the U.S. House of Representatives passed the Currency Reform for Fair Trade Act (HR 348-79), brandishing a punitive stick at China (and any nation manipulating its currency); the companion Senate legislation was to be taken up after the 2010 election but was delayed until October 2011 when the Senate passed the Currency Exchange

Rate Oversight and Reform Act, thereby increasing the likelihood of U.S. tariff retaliation. For more than two years President Obama and Treasury Secretary Geithner had directly registered their concerns on this issue in private meetings with President Hu Jintao and Premier Wen Jiabao, insisting that a modest appreciation of the *renminbi* would increase the flow of U.S. exports to China, thereby resulting in job growth at home.

The simple push and pull quality of this reasoning prevents U.S. policy makers from recognizing that the United States is in a bind that cannot be overcome by public declarations of unfair trade practices, high-level bilateral discussions, or even ominous protectionist legislation. The blameful fulmination of U.S. politicians is simply scapegoating rhetoric. In the same way, threats by the Chinese finance minister to shift his country's purchases to another currency like the euro is mere posturing. If U.S. rhetoric about the yuan is a genuine expression of belief that increasing U.S. exports to the Chinese will alleviate massive unemployment, then any policy based on it will come to grief. Neither the United States nor China would benefit from a trade war.

The debate about Chinese currency manipulation must not be miscast as a battle between China and the United States, and the latter must be honest in representing the complex causes of the country's economic struggles and the limited prospects for meaningful recovery. China, too, must level with its citizenry in explaining why an export-dominated economy with banks carrying massive volumes of bad paper will be unable to sustain the growth the nation must have to avert a financial and possibly domestic political crisis. Politics in such global trade situations always play a role in charging responsibility for the downturn of one or more nation's economies; yet the world is still recovering from the crisis of 2008, with Britain, Greece, Ireland, Portugal, and Spain in varying degrees of startling deficit. This seems at best an awkward time for the United States and China to engage their exceptionalist impulses.

U.S. officials must be candid with U.S. citizens that the real destructiveness of this currency manipulation is being played out globally, with nations like Brazil, Israel, Japan, and South Korea following China's lead and manipulating their national currencies. This was made spectacularly clear late in the fall of 2010 when ministers of the sixteen-nation European currency area meeting in Brussels recommended China undertake an "orderly, significant, and broad-based appreciation of its currency." One cannot help but wonder what the Chinese made of such pontification given the fact that some of those ministers had to be aware of their own imitation of China's protective model. Transparency in these matters is not simply China's problem.

The United States has much to lose if it causes China to lose face by officially condemning it for currency manipulation before the World Bank.

China is the world's largest purchaser of dollars. The last decade of U.S.-debt-led consumer growth was underwritten by the Chinese—something that government economists and most politicians, not to mention U.S. citizens, would probably like to see continue. Any substantive appreciation of the *renminbi*, or any attachment of specific duties on Chinese imports, will make goods more expensive. One wonders how Walmart, not to mention its millions of faithful shoppers, could cope with a sudden increase in price of the 80 percent of its goods that it imports from China.

But China is also in a bind. Its government, much like the U.S. government, is sensitive to domestic pressure from powerful interests. Chinese export industries that have benefitted maximally from a devalued *renminbi* lobby aggressively for their government to maintain the status quo and keep buying dollars at the rate of several billion a week so that they can preserve market advantage. At the same time, while China does not want to enrage the United States, it *does* want to ensure that it remains a good economic bet to pay back its colossal debt. Lately, that is in the first few months of 2011, there was evidence that China had become more anxious about this prospect, acting to reduce its investment in U.S. national debt by over $500 million.

China is a powerful engine of the global economy, but its leadership is struggling to determine the best path for its nation's development ("socialism with Chinese characteristics," "peaceful rise," "harmonious development"). Maintaining social and political stability is of the utmost concern to the Beijing government. Given this, recession, unemployment, and popular unrest are the principal focus of the Chinese leadership, as China faces staggering domestic problems—some of which also plague the United States—that threaten its stability each day.

While many observers accentuate the differences between the United States and China, it is important to remember something that we have stressed from the very first volume: that mutual concord between these two "favored" nations is critical to the unique codependence upon which international harmony rests. This is a bind worth acknowledging and, if necessary, submitting to. It is essential that both countries recognize their common interests, challenges, and high level of responsibility on the global stage and that their bilateral relationship be handled in an honest and pragmatic manner that avoids the idea that one nation's gain is necessarily the other's loss. In this moment of populism and resurgent nativism in both China and the United States, it may be politically expedient to portray China as solely responsible for increasing U.S. joblessness. At a time when both countries are passing through political transitions—certain in China, possible in the United States—aspiring leaders in both countries find it difficult to resist the temptation to adopt tough poses in relation to the other. However, this is not the Cold War, China is not an implacable U.S. enemy, and the loss to both from miscalculation would be immeasurably great. The two nations must be better at conducting global dialogue, even developing consensus, about currency and trade and a wide range of other thorny issues, with an awareness of this U.S.-China bind.

Even as we insist on the reasoned need to work more collaboratively to overcome mutual misunderstanding and demonization, there have been incidents since the fall of 2010 and continuing through the winter of 2012 that indicate just how difficult a Sino-U.S. cooperation in key issues will be. Human rights have again risen to the fore as a highly divisive issue. This disagreement is not likely to be easily managed.

THE LIU XIAOBO CASE AND THE LIMITS OF CHANGE

October 8, 2010, will forever be remembered as the day that the third Chinese national citizen received a Nobel Prize, this one to Liu Xiaobo, for peace. The other two of course were the Fourteenth Dalai Lama, for peace in 1989, and Gao Xingjian, for literature in 2000. It was a tremendous honor for Liu, one of the eight principal authors of the stirring democratic manifesto Charter 08,[10] but no less so for his native country. His fellow citizens were undoubtedly proud of this achievement, because it conferred a dimension of international recognition China has long desired—the Nobel Prize. However, in the words of the Chinese government, Liu is a "criminal who violated Chinese law." Yet according to his wife, Liu Xia, who was brought to see him on October 9, it was his jailers (Liu had been in jail since 2009) who first informed him that he was the peace prize recipient. It seems that national pride trumps political ideology.

The pull of nation over ideology was evident again on Tuesday, October 12, 2010, when twenty-three retired Communist Party luminaries submitted an open letter to the Standing Committee of the National People's Congress calling for the elimination of censorship and honoring China's constitutional guarantees of freedom of speech and the press. Still, the official media organs of the Chinese state were working overtime to cast aspersions on the Nobel Committee and all of its members, who were denounced as "clowns": an embarrassing display to say the least.

Since 1992 (as Jensen discusses in chapter 13), the Chinese government has schooled its population in "patriotic education and socialist spiritual civilization." Unfortunately, it was Liu's alternative, and broader, conception of Chinese civilization and its democratic emblems of national greatness that earned him eleven years' incarceration in 2009 for "openly slandering and inciting others to overthrow State power." It is difficult to imagine how the words of a single individual heralding the prospect of a greater Chinese future might be taken as "slander."

Because official media went dark, most Chinese initially were unaware of the Nobel announcement. Yet for those who did learn on October 9, there were impromptu celebrations. These were met with police crackdowns and arrest. In Beijing authorities apprehended some of those posting comments or congratulations via Twitter or on Sina Weibo. All such commentary was erased. But fireworks still went off at Beijing University, historically a bastion of democratic thought and activism.

CNN coverage of the live broadcast from Oslo, Norway, was preempted; instead viewers saw a black screen of six minutes' duration. China's principal online information sources featured the latest "news" from the Shanghai World Exposition and a host of other "current" topics. At first it was *almost* impossible for Chinese to learn of the honor of their countryman as the Sina, Sohu, and other Internet portals interdicted all searches for "Nobel" and "Liu Xiaobo." On mobile phones his name was blocked. Still, those who wished to post their feelings about Liu's receipt of the prize did so furtively (and successfully) by what the Sinologist Victor Mair has identified as numerous "circumlocutions" of the name Liu Xiaobo (some of these are discussed in chapter 8).

Owing to proxy server access and popular will, a great many Chinese netizens knew of this national honor that very day. As so often is the case in China, it was simply not possible for the news to be repressed. In fact, knowledge that information is being repressed in and of itself stimulates greater curiosity and determination to know on the part of many Chinese citizens. By the evening China's official *People's Daily* acknowledged that the "lawbreaker" Liu had received the Peace Prize. Three days later the Ministry of Foreign Affairs inveighed against the Nobel Committee for "meddling in China's internal affairs" and contributing to "the suspicion that there is a Western plot to contain a rising China."

With the house arrest of Liu Xia and China's sudden withdrawal from talks with Norway's fisheries minister, it was clear that the Chinese government was struggling mightily with what *it* can only understand as a challenge by foreign powers to its legitimacy. This is why it had threatened Norway in the first place, unwilling to acknowledge that the Nobel Committee is a fully independent entity.

Most observers could have predicted that the Beijing government would view the Nobel Peace Prize going to Liu Xiaobo as an affront, as an attack on its human rights record. The CCP insists that foreign countries and nongovernmental organizations have no right to meddle in Chinese "domestic" matters and that China's human rights record is improving steadily. In recent years China has gained some traction with this argument, especially in light of the grievous human rights violations committed by the United States at Guantanamo. To be sure, the choice to award the peace prize to Liu may be viewed as a provocation intended to get the Chinese government to open a more vibrant dialogue on the subject of human rights.

However, rather than see the Nobel Prize as a disparagement of China or the Chinese people, as the government in Beijing claimed, it is worth considering that Liu Xiaobo's honor may also be viewed as having been bestowed in a spirit of recognizing how far China has come, having delivered more than a quarter of a billion people from absolute poverty and opening itself to the world. Awarding the prize to Liu conveyed clearly that as it becomes a world power the expectations for China are high. Indeed, these are the very expectations China must meet if it is serious about global recognition of its greatness and if it intends to cast off the frequently conjured yoke of a "century of humiliation."

Recognizing an imprisoned figure of conscience in spite of threats, rather than a criticism intended to cause the government to lose face, could just as well be taken as the cost for China of being a great nation on the world stage. If this international honor is "criticism," then it is the kind that comes from respect and hope. This is what many Chinese see and are proud to embrace. In its official reaction, the Chinese government, unfortunately, revealed an intransigence that placed national honor and achievement beyond an implicit understanding (that China has entered the arena of the world's great nations) that its own citizens—and the very world they wish to join—already possess.

China's official reactions to the announcement were nothing short of astonishing, as were the many pointed threats it made to a great many of its world trading partners, harshly warning them of the consequences of attendance at the official ceremonies in Oslo. (In the end, only seventeen of the invited nations threatened by Beijing, including the Russian Federation, did not attend.) There were editorials and planted articles in Chinese papers and online publications identifying Oslo as part of a "world conspiracy" to deny the proper Chinese recipient or to maintain their hegemony over lesser nations. The language exceeded diplomatic protocol, as did the numerous real and implied threats (see John Kamm's afterword) to international relations and trade. As if this was not enough, the Chinese government quickly invented its own newly created peace prize, the Confucius Peace Prize (*Kongzi hepingjiang*), valued at 100,000 yuan ($15,288 U.S.), which it awarded to the former premier of Taiwan, Lien Chan, for representing the values of peace, harmony, and goodwill synonymous with the figure of the ancient sage.[11] Shortly after the announcement, reporters in Taipei asked Lien about his reaction, only to discover that, according to a spokesman from his office, "he knew nothing about the award and had not been contacted." His office added that Lien "had no plans to accept it." The 2010 award was not conferred and the Ministry of Culture announced its cancelation in September 2011, only to have the Confucius Peace Prize reappear two months later with the announcement of a winner, Russian Prime Minister Vladimir Putin.

ADVANCING THE GLOBAL CHINA
AND MANAGING ITS NEW IMAGE

Under the leadership of Hu Jintao and Wen Jiabao, the Chinese government has invested significant amounts of financial and political capital to enhance its global image. Public diplomacy is a prominent concern of the Hu regime, which has created a public relations juggernaut that extends from Beijing to the far corners of the globe. Since 2009 in particular when the government announced the investment of nearly seven billion U.S. dollars to launch its bold global media drive, China's greater presence in the world, literally and figuratively, has brought measurable change in popular perception. The media surge also includes the creation of new Internet and television programming offshoots of *Zhongyang dianshitai*, China Central Television (CCTV), to give the party multiple hip looks for the transformational era (see chapter 2 by Jonathan Noble). Party propaganda has gone twenty-first century so that only the Chinese themselves really know which programming is "free" of the hand of the "mother-in-law" (see chapter 3 by Jessica Teets). Before long, perhaps, we may expect the announcement of a CCP media "app store."

Many observers have taken note of China's new international profile, and the benefits of this strategic investment have been demonstrated in the global change in opinion about China. In a 2010 poll conducted by *Forbes* magazine, Hu Jintao was identified as the world's most influential and powerful leader; Barack Obama ranked second. Conducted annually, the Pew Trust global attitudes survey has most of the developing world respondents reporting a quite favorable view of China in world politics since 2005. The investment in good public relations combined with strategic global investment has enhanced, although not transformed, world opinion toward China and its government. For example, in the Gallup World Poll of 2007, 48 percent of all respondents reported a favorable attitude toward China; however, this same poll taken in 2009 in the wake of the Beijing Olympics revealed that China's favorability had fallen to 41 percent, where it remains today. In fact, if one were to take the data from the BBC World Service Poll from 2005 to 2009, measuring attitudes toward China's "influence in the world," one would have to conclude that the jury has returned on the early phases of public diplomacy and found China's world influence to be "mostly negative."

The Beijing government's reaction to the Liu Xiaobo Nobel Peace Prize certainly has not helped China's image in the past year, nor did the recent arrest of the internationally acclaimed artist Ai Weiwei, whose piece *Nian* (Missing) is a 240-minute-long MP3 reading by volunteers of the thousands of names of the children killed in the collapse of their schools in the 2008 Sichuan earthquake. Before the recorded reading Ai is quoted as saying, "It represents the memory of the lives that have been lost and the anger at the covering-up of the tofu-buildings. Respect life; refuse to forget."[12] More than seventy thousand were killed in the disaster. After the Public Security Bureau destroyed his new studio in Shanghai in January 2011, an event to which Ai had sent a public invitation via Twitter and received more than ninety thousand RSVPs, he was subjected to constant surveillance. Government authorities installed surveillance cameras around the perimeter of his studio in the contemporary arts village of Caochangdi outside Beijing. Stationary cameras were deemed insufficient to track his actions, so the Public Security Bureau had mobile surveillance units parked on the street outside his studio.[13]

For reasons that remain confusing and contradictory he suddenly disappeared on April 3 as he attempted to board a plane for Hong Kong en route to Taipei.[14] Thereafter authorities entered his studio and took possession of computers and hardware, CDs and DVDs, and his notebooks while also detaining his eight assistants. The police remained through the night interrogating Ai's staff through vague inquiries about projects, income, the studio, travel plans. As befitting these all too frequent occasions, officials threatened them with "inciting subversion of state power." More than forty days after Ai's disappearance, the Chinese government indirectly acknowledged his detention by allowing his wife, Lu Qing, a fifteen-minute visit with him on May 15, 2011. Until that moment his whereabouts were unknown. Moreover, it would appear that Ai was never told why he was disappeared. Lu Qing reported that in the course of their meeting, "He didn't say anything about his case. I don't even know if he knows the reasons he has been detained." Yet, suddenly, as swiftly as he disappeared, Ai reappeared on the evening of June 22, 2011. Xinhua, the official press agency of the government, reported that the Beijing police had released him "on bail" and his wife confirmed later that night that he was again in his studio.[15]

These repressive actions in the fall of 2010 and the spring of 2011 continued into the first months of 2012, when a series of self-immolations by monks protesting Beijing's harsh policy in Tibet drew widespread international concern. All of this dramatically displays the limits of China's much extolled policy of "peaceful development" and international harmony. It has also reminded its many trading partners of the importance of maintaining a healthy suspicion about the Chinese government's willingness to open the country to fresh political possibilities. But there have been many other examples of the limits of cooperation simply on the matter of annual human rights dialogues, which we learn from John Kamm's afterword have become willfully distorted in their intent and expectation by the wiles of the Chinese Foreign Ministry and the central government. The most glaring of these examples may be that of China's controversial execution of an EU citizen, Akmal Shaikh, in December 2009, even after repeated stringent protests and passionate appeals for clemency by the British government and a host of human rights organizations including Amnesty International and Reprieve.[16] The Chinese government, specifically the Ministry of Foreign Affairs, responded to the protests by complaining that the British requests had "hurt the feelings of the Chinese people." Thus they had no choice but to cancel the scheduled round of human rights dialogues to be convened in Britain in January 2010.

A quality of noblesse oblige extends beyond the diplomatic negotiations with foreign powers to academic and cultural events involving foreign dignitaries from universities. The newly opened National Museum in Beijing was the site of a noteworthy event in the early months of 2011. China was the host in this case, and yet as happens with all such events, the foreign guests had to pay for the right to exhibit materials that are part and parcel of the celebration of their newfound engagement with China in sciences and humanities. Every square foot of the portion of the museum that was to be used by German officials in the opening exhibit was paid for—and handsomely—by the German government along with the Stiftung Mercator Corporation. The hosts merely provided the space and the entertainment. It should be noted that Germany is one of the EU countries that has been holding human rights dialogues with the Chinese since 2003, but in this instance it was treated, according to Professor Michael Lackner, "like a vassal state."[17] In a curious reframing of the universal ideals of the Enlightenment, for twenty-first-century China it is not man but *money* that is the measure of all things.

This is not the way to win friends and influence people. Actions speak louder than money and resources, and it is in this calculus that China and the United States alike have a great deal to ponder in order to "reset" their relations against the background of a range of world involvements that are inconsistent with, if not invalidating of, the constitutional ideals by which their exceptionalisms are guided. It is incumbent upon the United States and China to interpret each other differently—not as enemies that are "other" but as nations whose economies, ideologies, and politics are different than, but not necessarily inimical to, one another. The burden of this responsibility is shared; both must overcome ingrained misrepresentation, yet it may be that greater weight will be borne by the United States, owing to more open networks of political communication and potential capacity to recognize the dramatic changes China has already made.

If anything, citizens of the United States must adjust the compass of their political navigation, perhaps even to acknowledge the emergence of a genuine alternative to the postwar dialectics of Western-based globalism. This they may well have to do in advance of their own political leaders, many of whom remain tethered to a rising-power ideology derived from the Cold War era and who are only able to see law as a means to an end: the endurance of U.S. dominion. A similar engagement with the facts on the ground

Figure 0.2. "Under Construction," Pavilion of the Future, Shanghai World Expo. Photograph by Tong Lam.

may be more difficult in China, but it is no less necessary for Chinese citizens, who must resist the reflex to deny the constructive role of the United States in collaborative engagement with China on issues such as national defense and international security (see Andrew Erickson in chapter 4), environmental and legal reform, along with human rights. It is our wish as editors that the honest accounting offered by the reflections in this volume make a small contribution to a reconstruction of the disturbing disinclination of both these "favored nations" to accept the mutual responsibility for the troubling dynamics of the present.

As well, we hope that our work here may assist U.S. and Chinese citizens and leaders to make the hard choices to take action of benefit to both nations and even greater benefit to the world that they will bequeath. With a presidential election ahead in the United States and a Party Congress in China that will lead to the election of a new president, 2012 will be an interval of prominent discussion of the countries' special bond. As we have argued in all of our work—in and beyond the headlines—the relationship of these great nations is of critical significance to the fate of our larger shared world. Our concluding hope is that China and the United States are aware that their relations must be cultivated with the care and concern that grow from the seeds of a deeper understanding planted in the spirit of mutual respect and one day harvested in the bright sun of their respective promises of democracy and human fulfillment.

NOTES

1. Elisa Holland and Erika Kuenne, two of the finest students of China and Chinese graduated by the University of Colorado, conceived of the questions and organized this survey, the value of which remains undiminished.

2. Timothy B. Weston and Lionel M. Jensen, "LEAD STORY—Favored Nations, Intertwined Fates," in *China beyond the Headlines*, ed. Timothy B. Weston and Lionel M. Jensen (Lanham, MD: Rowman & Littlefield, 2000), 8.

3. Chinese business people have canvassed the globe in creating opportunities, much of it self-exploratory and not driven by political calculation of influence, as Jensen learned in the summer of 2007, when he arrived in Addis Ababa, Ethiopia. Waiting in the customs line for foreign entry were two Cantonese speakers. In a brief conversation in Mandarin he learned from these businessmen that they had started a business in Addis and had made many trips to Ethiopia.

4. See Shanthi Kalathil and Taylor C. Boas, *Open Networks, Closed Regimes: the Impact of the Internet on Authoritarian Rule* (New York: Carnegie Endowment for International Peace, 2003).

5. "Beijing Consensus" was coined by Joshua Cooper Ramo in 2004 to describe a new paradigm for development in the wake of the collapse of the "Washington Consensus, the breakdown of the WTO talks . . . [and] the implosion of Argentina's economy." Joshua Ramo Cooper, The Beijing Consensus (London: Foreign Policy Centre, 2004), 60. Some Chinese commentators have started using this term very recently. See also Stefan Halper, *The Beijing Consensus: How China's Authoritarian Model Will Dominate the Twenty-first Century* (New York: Basic Books, 2010), and the insightful critique by Arif Dirlik, "Beijing Consensus: Beijing 'Gongshi.' Who Recognizes Whom and to What End?" *Globalization and Autonomy Online Compendium* (2006), http://www.globalautonomy.ca/global1/position.jsp?index=PP_Dirlik_ BeijingConsensus.xml.

6. "Zhengque renshi he pingjia Zhongguo moshi" (Correctly Recognizing and Evaluating the China Model), *Guangming ribao*, January 10, 2011, http://theory .gmw.cn/2011-01/10/content_1505420.htm.

7. This is according to the U.S. Census Bureau, http://www.census.gov/foreign -trade/statistics/highlights/toppartners.html.

8. "Remarks by the President at the U.S./China Strategic and Economic Dialogue," press release, July 27, 2009, http://www.whitehouse.gov/the-press-office/ remarks-president-uschina-strategic-and-economic-dialogue.

9. "Clinton: Chinese Human Rights Can't Interfere with Other Crises," CNN, February 21, 2009, http://articles.cnn.com/2009-02-21/politics/clinton.china.asia _1_human-rights-china-policy-chinese-president-hu-jintao?_s=PM:POLITICS. Secretary Clinton's candor proved prophetic because by January of 2012 IMF Managing Director, Christine Lagarde had invited China's assistance in an effort to solve Europe's worsening sovereign debt crisis.

10. Charter 08 was published on December 10, 2008, and was modeled on a similar manifesto, Charter 77, written by a group of Czech dissidents, including Václav Havel. Published on the one hundredth anniversary of the promulgation of the first Chinese constitution, Charter 08 called for the government to meet nineteen demands (many of which are already listed in the 1983 Chinese

Constitution), including democratic elections. The full text of the document (as translated by Perry Link) and the names of those who originally endorsed its prescriptions and vision for democratic reform may be accessed at http://www .nybooks.com/articles/archives/2009/jan/15/chinas-charter-08/.

11. Former premier Lien's selection was undoubtedly linked to his leadership of the Pan-Blue coalition of the Guomindang (National People's Party), which made a historic visit to the People's Republic in April of 2005. It was the first high-level exchange between the adversarial political parties since 1949. It must be noted, however, that the meeting's endorsement of the One-China Policy was not acknowledged by Taiwan's ruling government, at the time under the direction of the Democratic Progressive Party and President Chen Shui-bian.

12. "Tofu dregs" was the term used by Ai Weiwei and others to describe the abysmal shoddiness of the material used to construct the school buildings in Wenchuan. All the schools collapsed, killing more than five thousand children, while the official government buildings in the village withstood the damage.

13. These conditions of his daily life in the fall of 2010 and winter of 2011 are well documented in Alison Klayman's film *Ai Weiwei: Never Sorry*.

14. Evan Osnos, "Ai Weiwei, Disturbing the Peace," *New Yorker*, April 4, 2011; "Police Detain Artist Ai Weiwei, Question Staff," *Asia Pacific News*, April 3, 2011. See also Lionel M. Jensen, "Ai Weiwei and the 'Age of Madness,'" *History News Network*, April 11, 2011, http://www.hnn.us/articles/138386.html.

15. On May 20, 2011, several days after Lu's visit, the Xinhua News Agency reported that Beijing Fake Cultural Development Ltd., the firm responsible for production of the artist's designs, "was found to have evaded 'a huge amount' of tax" and also to have "intentionally destroyed accounting documents." However, Ai Weiwei is not the director of the firm and in all likelihood has no knowledge of its accounting practices, so the vague charge of economic crimes would appear irrelevant. Upon his sudden release, it was reported that Ai was "out on bail after admitting guilt over charges of tax evasion and agreeing to pay the amount he allegedly owes," demonstrating that the May 20 gambit was the key step in the government's extrication from their self-imposed diplomatic and human rights disaster. As Wen Jiabao was preparing for high-level visits to Germany and the UK, where the protests in support of Ai have been the most energetic and sustained, the release of Ai Weiwei would likely reduce the degree of his discomfort and embarrassment.

16. Mr. Shaikh was arrested in 2008 in Ürümqi with five kilos of heroin in his luggage. The circumstances of his arrest are unclear, but the Chinese authorities concluded that he was a drug smuggler and so should be sentenced to execution in accord with Chinese law. There was strong evidence that Shaikh was suffering from mental illness at the time of the crime and very likely was not even aware of his transport of the drugs. He had manifested multiple symptoms of mental distress in the years before the incident as well as after his arrest, but Chinese authorities refused to submit him for psychiatric evaluation though Chinese law explicitly states that persons determined to be mentally impaired during a crime are not to be subjected to corporal punishment. Authorities also refused to inform him of the date and time of his execution. It turns out that he learned from two relatives who paid him a visit in the final twenty-four hours of his life that he would die by lethal

injection. No one was permitted to attend his execution. Shaikh was the first EU national since 1951 to be executed in China.

17. Henrik Bork, "Nach der Festnahme von Ai Wiewei: Lasst uns über was anderes reden," *Süeddeutsche Zeitung*, April 10, 2011, http://www.sueddeutsche .de/kultur/china-nach-der-festnahme-von-ai-weiwei-lasst-uns-ueber-was-anderes -reden-1.1083525.

I

IN THE HEADLINES

Photograph by Tong Lam.

1

Jousting with Monsters: Journalists in a Rapidly Changing China

David Bandurski

Thomas Jefferson, a staunch defender of press freedom, once said that given a choice between "a government without newspapers, or newspapers without a government, I should not hesitate a moment to prefer the latter." In China, where the Chinese Communist Party (CCP) still regards the control of information as critical to preserving its one-party rule, leaders would certainly respond that neither of Jefferson's choices is acceptable. Clearly, they would say, the government must *control* and *direct* the newspapers. How else can it manipulate public opinion in its favor?

Press control is a fact of political life in China. The legacy hearkens back to the revolutionary leader and founder of the People's Republic of China, Mao Zedong, who said in 1959, after unwelcome criticism of his policies, that, "In doing news work, we must have politicians running the newspapers."[1] More recently, in 2001, as China charged ahead into the age of the Internet and new media, the party reiterated the concept of "party control of the media," or *dang guan meiti*, in an internal document circulated among top Chinese leaders.[2] Even today, as blogs (*boke*) and microblogs (*weibo*) reshape the ecology of information, CCP leaders garnish their speeches with buzzwords like "guidance of public opinion," the idea that press control is essential to maintaining social and political stability.

Press control is also real and immediate. At the level of the individual reporter or editor, control is applied through fear and uncertainty. Can I report this information? What will the consequences be if I do? The Central Propaganda Department in Beijing, and various regional propaganda offices under the command of local party leaders, send out regular directives banning, limiting, or directing news coverage. Report nothing about this corruption case, one directive might instruct; use only official press releases and do not send reporters to the scene, another might say. For those, such as bloggers, working outside the formal press system, there is a vast technical system (sometimes called the "Great Firewall") designed to block access to overseas websites and prevent the posting of sensitive material, and an even more formidable human system of eyes and ears designed to root out language regarded as a threat to the government. In August 2010 Wu Danhong, an assistant professor of law at China University of Political Science and Law in Beijing, had his microblog shut down by a private Internet website under government pressure. Wu, who writes not about politics but about the rule of law, was told by the website in question that he had posted "large amounts of language attacking the government."[3]

Stories about China's lamentable record on press freedom sometimes find their way into our own news headlines about China. We read about an editor removed for overbold coverage—as was the case in May 2010 with Bao Yueyang, an editor at a newspaper that dared to report on hundreds, and perhaps thousands, of Chinese children who were seriously injured by substandard vaccines. We read, though less frequently, about publications shut down or suspended for upsetting party leaders—as was the case in January 2006 with the journal *Bingdian* (*Freezing Point*), which had for more than a decade earned a reputation as one of China's most outspoken publications.

But while *control* may be a real and salient feature of China's media landscape, it cannot capture the full picture of what is happening in the country. If we understand contemporary China only through the prism of political control, we stumble quickly into the richness of this nation's contradictions, particularly where information is concerned. How can we possibly explain, for example, the existence of "super-blogger" Yang Hengjun? Yang, a former diplomat and entrepreneur, criticizes his country with merciless tact, arguing the virtues of democracy and freedom to a daily audience of more than 150,000 readers (a number that would rank him individually among America's top newspapers by circulation). How can we explain the way hundreds of Chinese journalists managed to ignore, with impunity, a May 2008 propaganda order instructing them against going to China's western Sichuan province to report on the devastating earthquake there?

Control is only half the picture of information in China today. And understanding the complex transformations that have taken place in China's media landscape over the past two decades is critical to understanding modern China—socially, culturally, and politically.

A vibrant tradition of investigative reporting is one of the most surprising things to appear on China's media landscape over the past decade. Given the tenacity of government press controls, it may surprise readers to learn that investigative reporters have existed at all in China, much less been relatively active since the late 1990s.

The story of China's investigative reporters provides us with a much fuller picture of how Chinese media have developed over the past twenty years and how the role of journalists, and of information, is changing in the country. The story also tells us, unfortunately, how press controls are themselves being modernized, transformed, and reasserted.

Before I take up the story of Chinese investigative reporting, it is important for readers to bear in mind the extreme complexity of China's media environment today. While this particular story highlights the more courageous examples of professionalism in Chinese journalism and shows how information is changing, we must not forget that press controls are themselves being transformed and reasserted. Nor can we forget that corruption is endemic in China's media and by some accounts has worsened considerably over the past decade, fueled by economic growth and epitomized by such practices as accepting cash payments, known euphemistically as "transportation fees," for covering corporate and other events and "gag fees" in exchange for not reporting sensitive news stories.

CONTROL, CHANGE, AND CHAOS: THE STAGE FOR WATCHDOG JOURNALISM IS SET

Up to the start of economic reforms in China in 1978, media were seen as "mouthpieces"—literally the "throat and tongue"—of the party leadership, and information was monopolized by the party through a limited number of state-run publications such as the *People's Daily*. During the Cultural Revolution, from 1966 to 1976, Mao Zedong was able to launch ideological assaults against his political enemies through the newspapers he controlled.

The death of Mao Zedong in September 1976, and the subsequent overthrow of the leftist political faction known as the Gang of Four, marked the end of the Cultural Revolution. In the years that followed, as China's new "paramount leader," Deng Xiaoping, encouraged a period of reflection on the extremes of past decades under Mao, journalists began their own process of self-reflection, exploring the role newspapers had played in the chaos of the Mao years. During this period, media were still effectively tools of the state, but there was a movement away from the "falsehood, excess, and emptiness" of the Cultural Revolution, and this came with a greater emphasis on news that served China's new development prerogative, Deng Xiaoping's policy of economic opening and reform.

By the late 1980s, economic reforms had brought new prosperity to China, but they had also hastened the development of new problems, such as corruption, that deepened resentment in Chinese society. Supporters of greater political liberalization, including then premier Zhao Ziyang, believed that one way of adding resilience to the system and tackling problems like corruption was to empower the press in a more active role, allowing them to reflect issues of popular concern. In 1987, at a full session of China's top party leaders during which the policies of the next five years were laid down, Zhao Ziyang spoke of the need to encourage "watchdog journalism," or what is called in Chinese "supervision by public opinion." Zhao's call, which essentially gave the press the green light to investigate and expose problems in Chinese society, was the first explicit sanction of press supervision by the CCP.

Zhao Ziyang's "liberal conception" of watchdog journalism was unfortunately short-lived.[4] Massive student demonstrations broke out in late April 1989, shortly after the death of a popular former party leader, Hu Yaobang, who had himself been a proponent of political and economic reforms. Demonstrations were still going strong in early May, and the party leadership was divided on how to resolve the situation. Premier Zhao Ziyang, who believed that the demonstrations would dissipate with time, was in favor of a light-handed response. In fact, during a May 6 meeting with top propaganda ministers, Zhao reportedly encouraged them to "open things up a bit."[5]

The rest of the story is all too familiar. Zhao Ziyang was forced aside by party hard-liners, who declared martial law on May 20, 1989, and eventually ordered the June 4 crackdown that brought the democracy movement of 1989 to a violent end.

June 4 marked the beginning of a new political era for China, and also a new era for press controls in the country. When Jiang Zemin stepped in a reclaim order, he criticized Zhao Ziyang for his light-handed approach to unrest that spring. In particular, Jiang criticized Zhao Ziyang's open-press policy, which he said had encouraged "support for the student movement" and "wrongly guided matters in the direction of chaos."[6] From this idea the policy of "guidance of public opinion," the conviction among hard-line leaders in the party that the failure to properly control, or "guide," the media had led to social and political chaos in the spring of 1989, was born. "Guidance of public opinion" underpins media controls in China to this day, although a number of changes have lately been introduced under Jiang Zemin's successor, President Hu Jintao.

The 1990s began, then, as a period of intensified media controls in China. Change soon crept into China's press landscape, however, as the country was propelled forward into a decade of unprecedented economic growth and reform that completely transformed Chinese society and, by extension, its relationship to information.

In the years immediately following the Tiananmen crackdown, hard-line elements within the Communist Party actively opposed the path of economic reform and opening on which Deng Xiaoping had set the country. But in the spring of 1992, Deng Xiaoping made his so-called southern tour, visiting the southern Chinese cities of Guangzhou, Zhuhai, and Shenzhen and urging China to accelerate economic reforms. This set China on a path of renewed economic development that would hit all sectors of China's economy, including media.

Given the political sensitivity of the media, economic change in the media took longer than in other sectors of China's economy. But by the mid-1990s, commercial development had seized the media as well. Before the mid-1990s, in fact, no one spoke of a "media industry" in China. No such industry existed, as media remained effective organs of the party-state, supported entirely with government subsidies.

Soon, however, so-called metro newspapers started to spring up in China's cities, responding to huge unmet demands for more quality and relevant news and enabled by a number of other factors addressed below. These newspapers were commercial spin-offs of the party-run newspapers at the city and provincial levels, but unlike their official counterparts these papers relied on advertising. They had to survive in an increasingly competitive media marketplace. And that meant also that they had to create content that was more relevant to their audiences. So while party newspapers continued to publish banal accounts of the doings of Communist Party leaders, China's new commercial papers offered more animated accounts of life in the city, sections on cars and other consumer products, and a whole range of consumer fare that appealed to China's increasingly wealthy and savvy urban population.

Why would China's government encourage or tolerate the commercialization of media to begin with? There were a number of reasons. As China's economic connectedness with the outside world grew and the country worked toward membership in the World Trade Organization, the prospect of competition from foreign media became more real. By pushing media out into the market, China could prepare its fledgling media sector for competition with the media giants of the West: the "coming of the wolves," as it was called. This was the generalized fear that as China opened its doors to the world, its domestic media, which had never operated by market principles, might find it impossible to compete with tried and tested international media. For China's party leaders this was a political concern more than an economic one; if foreign media were successful in getting an edge in China's domestic media market, this would inhibit the CCP's goal of controlling information.

Second, state-run media were increasingly a burden on government budgets. In the early 1990s most media were still supported by various party or government interests, and in some cases government agencies even pressured subordinate government offices to subscribe to their official publications as a way of generating revenue. This was a substantial drain on local governments and at the same time resulted in a glut of low-quality publications that lowered the effectiveness of core party publications such as *People's Daily* by crowding the airwaves, or so party leaders believed. By cutting off government funding to these publications, the central government could achieve two goals at once, relieving burden on local governments and enhancing the impact of core party mouthpieces.

Last, but certainly not least, a rapidly commercializing media sector would help contribute to China's economic growth, both by providing essential information and by driving a growth in advertising and consumption. Reductions in spending on state-run media came in tandem with broader reductions in social spending in China in the 1990s and less state involvement in the lives of ordinary Chinese.

It is important to emphasize that the media commercialization of the 1990s was not a process of media reform. There was never a move on the government's part to redefine the role of the media, and control, under the post-Tiananmen notion of "guidance," was still the first rule.

Despite the fact that media control was never, formally speaking, loosened at all, the changes of the 1990s created a new climate for Chinese media. One of the most important changes was the rise of the reader. Suddenly, Chinese were *media consumers* in a way that they never had been before. They could determine at the newsstand which newspapers they found valuable and which they did not. And this meant that commercial media, which relied on their readership base to generate advertising revenues, now effectively had two bosses—the party and the reader.

The emphasis on the media market and the growing orientation toward the reader also created a new environment for journalists with their own professional ideals. As media commercialization distanced newspapers financially from the party-state, and as public information demands rather than political considerations increasingly drove the editorial process, many journalists began to feel that they were working for a broader public interest rather than a narrow party interest. Even if media were still subject to party control and "guidance," Chinese society was growing ever more complex, and journalists could find ways to push the bounds of news coverage by deftly exploiting this complexity.

These changes may not seem dramatic on the surface, but the net effect of this rise of the reader, of journalistic professionalism, and of broader social change in China—including the rise of the Internet by the end of the 1990s—was electric in ways that did make a difference.

Journalistic professionalism is a complex issue, and even Chinese journalists disagree about its meaning and origins. But broadly speaking, the emergence of a professional journalism community in China can be glimpsed in several trends. First, while the party continues to define the "profession" in terms of its own interests—maintaining social stability and party rule through "guidance of public opinion"—a sense of social mission has risen among Chinese journalists, many of whom now envision themselves as serving the public interest rather than the interests of the Communist Party. Second, and of course related, there is growing emphasis on "truth" in the news, at least among a core of journalists whose self-identity lies outside the dominant party press culture. Third, there is much greater coherence, thanks in part to the Internet and social media, among journalists and media who believe they should serve an agenda-setting function (or social mission) beyond that defined by the party.

In 2010 there were two prominent examples of growing professional cohesion. In the first case, on March 1 fourteen newspapers in China signed a joint editorial calling for an end to China's highly unpopular *hukou*, or "household registration system," which effectively segregates China's population into urban and rural classes and denies certain rights to rural migrants working in China's cities. And on June 28, more than one hundred journalists signed an open letter pledging a professional boycott of the *Chongqing Morning Post*, a commercial spin-off of the official *Chongqing Daily*, after the newspaper spoke out against journalists trying to get to the bottom of the police questioning of several *Chongqing Morning Post* employees accused of "fake reports." Signers of the letter believed the newspaper was not doing enough to stand by its reporters and ensure their safety.

Qian Gang, a veteran Chinese journalist and media scholar, describes these shifting dynamics in China's media in the 1990s with a formula he calls the "three Cs": control, change, and chaos. The idea is that while *control* (in the form of propaganda directives, for example) has persisted in China's media, larger forces of economic growth and social *change* have created an environment of *chaos*, in which journalists have been able, though often in limited ways, to push back against control.[7]

Another factor that proved useful to professional journalists was the party's mandate for "supervision by public opinion," a legacy of the 1980s reform era. In fact, President Jiang Zemin included this party buzzword in each of his political reports to senior CCP leaders, although his view of the practice differed significantly from that of his predecessor. For Jiang, press control remained paramount, but "supervision by public opinion" could serve an important role as a top-down monitoring mechanism, by which central party media such as China Central Television (CCTV) could expose corruption at the local level. Supervision of this kind had the advantage of being both immensely popular, tapping into and diffusing public anger over rising corruption and deepening social tensions, and largely innocuous, not touching on more sensitive high-level cases that might undermine the legitimacy of the central party. In the 1990s newcomers on the media scene like CCTV's *Focus* investigative news program helped to build an audience for investigative news content. But these party watchdogs were also criticized by some for pursuing only cases involving small-time businesspeople and lower-level cadres. They swatted at flies, as Chinese journalists often said, and let the tigers run free.

By the end of the 1990s, however, conditions were ripe for a whole new brand of investigative reporting in China. Journalists now had savvier audiences, hungry for information, and newspapers had both a professional and a commercial incentive to go after exclusive news stories readers would find interesting and relevant. And despite the ubiquity of press controls, the party mandate for "supervision by public opinion" to some extent legitimized media supervision of power. At no point in the 1990s did the CCP relax its formal restrictions on the press, but the changes China's leaders set into motion created new challenges for their goal of controlling information.

ENTER THE ARMIES OF DON QUIXOTE

In the new environment of the 1990s, professional Chinese journalists developed a number of metaphors to describe how they could manage to circumvent *control* and promote *change* in the midst of this *chaos*. Journalists in China routinely talk, for example, about "hitting line balls," or *da cabianqiu*, a sports metaphor referring to news reports that push the bounds without flagrantly violating propaganda rules.

Examples of "line ball" stories happen all the time in China's media today, but one good example occurred after the devastating Sichuan earthquake in 2008, even as party leaders were trying to rein in coverage of the quake's aftermath. Just over a week after the quake struck, the Central Propaganda Department issued a ban on coverage of shoddily-built school buildings that had collapsed unnecessarily, killing thousands of schoolchildren. This story was highly sensitive, touching on the issue of local government responsibility in failing to ensure the safety of school buildings. Media were told to keep their stories positive and avoid coverage of school collapses. A reporter at the state-run Xinhua News Agency responded by writing a positive story about a poor local schoolteacher who had scraped together his own money in the months before the earthquake to single-handedly shore up his schoolhouse. Not one of his students died in the quake. It was not exactly a direct and hard-hitting indictment of government negligence, but the deeper substory was clear enough—one poor schoolteacher had managed to accomplish what local governments in Sichuan could not.[8]

One of the most interesting, if somewhat revolting, metaphors came from Shen Changwen, the longtime editor-in-chief of *Read* magazine. Shen described the way journalists could seize the opportunity afforded by the misfortunes of other publications. If, for example, one newspaper was facing serious disciplinary measures from government authorities as a result of coverage that crossed the line, other media could seize this moment to push a bit further with their own coverage. Propaganda authorities, after all, could not be everywhere at once: particularly as disciplinary action itself proved increasingly unpopular and could draw international criticism. Shen Changwen drew his metaphor from the Qing Dynasty classic *The Dream of the Red Mansions*, in which the servant of an aristocratic household, Jiao Senior, has his mouth crammed full of excrement after an act of insubordination. Journalists, said Shen, could not always be Jiao Senior, stepping out on their own and incurring a high price. But they could be more strategic, striving to be "Jiao Juniors" who break the rules on the sly while the master is dealing with the unhappy Jiao Senior.

For China's professional journalists, one of the most enduring and relevant metaphors comes from the comic Spanish literary classic *Don Quixote*, in which a bedraggled Spanish noble, Don Quixote, rides off on a series of ridiculous adventures, fancying himself an errant knight of the sort he has read about in romance novels.[9] In one chapter of the novel, Don Quixote and his squire, Sancho Panza, come upon a plain where there is a group of large windmills. Believing the windmills are giants, the foolish Don Quixote rides after them with his lance, which breaks upon impact, and he is hurled aside with his horse. It is from this passage that we get the phrase "tilting at windmills," which means to fight futile battles or attack imaginary enemies.

In the context of Chinese investigative or in-depth reporting, the enemies are only too real. The windmills *are* monsters, and they are the sum total of the social and political ills from which China suffers and the myriad challenges facing the journalists themselves—entrenched local power, corruption, state propaganda controls, greedy corporations, and the list goes on. But professional Chinese journalists understand and share the sense of futility that Quixote jousting with the windmills seems to represent. In many ways, they are fighting an impossible battle, but they are driven on by the sense of professional mission described earlier in this chapter. In a society where corruption seems to be everywhere, and where journalists themselves routinely accept "red envelopes" of cash in exchange for favorable news coverage, these investigative reporters make it their business to serve a greater public interest, like romantic fools on a hopeless errand.

Investigative reporter Lu Yuegang once said before going off on a dangerous reporting assignment, "Often, the opponent we face is like an army, or like a monster with countless arms. If one person, or a few people, face off against something as vast as this, something webbed with self-interest, we are like Don Quixote, or at best like a band of Don Quixotes."

The image of Quixote and the windmills can also help us to understand the complicated nature of China's media environment, and how a mess of social and political factors in contemporary China can both obstruct journalists and offer them new opportunities. Recapping our discussion of changes in China since the 1990s, we can associate a number of visual characteristics in the Harker image of Don Quixote (see note 9) with aspects of the Chinese media environment and the professional journalist as I have described them.

Quixote's Shield

We can see the shield in the hapless knight's hands as the CCP's mandate for media to conduct "supervision by public opinion," or the monitoring of power by the media. Despite the persistence of press controls, party leaders have to varying degrees stressed the importance of "supervision by public opinion" ever since Zhao Ziyang first used the term openly in a party document in 1987. This remains a weak mandate, but it has nevertheless been an important tool for professionally minded journalists in China, and particularly for investigative reporters. While party leaders may tend to understand "supervision by public opinion" as a top-down process of monitoring by powerful state media of small-scale local corruption ("swatting at flies"), professional Chinese journalists envision it differently, as a Chinese cognate of the kind of press monitoring that has in the West been called "watchdog journalism." In China, in fact, the term *freedom of speech* remains politically sensitive and is only rarely used. Journalists and others who support greater freedom for China's media often couch their arguments in terms of "supervision by public opinion."

Quixote's Steed

We can understand the horse that carries Quixote off to do battle with the windmills as representative of broad and rapid changes in Chinese society. Many of these changes, as I said before, have come about as a result of economic reforms, of which the two-decade-long process of media commercialization (and the emergence of the media consumer) has been an important part. We can also include in this category the rise and growing ubiquity of new technologies, most notably the Internet and new media.

Quixote's Lance

All of these economic and social forces can help drive journalists toward their targets. But journalists must first have a sense of professional duty and mission, a belief that resisting and exposing power are worthwhile exploits. This is where Quixote's lance comes in. Quixote's lance is journalistic professionalism, and the sense that journalists must work for the public interest over narrow political interests. The professional spirit is of primary importance here, but professionalism is also served by the skills and norms of journalism (protection of sources, confirmation of facts, etc.), as well as the strategic use of political opportunities to ensure that risk to the journalist and to the publication are minimized.

Windmills

The image of Quixote on the plain gives us a rather full picture of professional Chinese journalists, and particularly investigative reporters, in their present social and political context, with all the tools and advantages that serve their professional objectives. But what about China's windmills? What about China's giants and monsters?

Since the late 1990s, Chinese investigative reporters have pursued a range of issues, including threats to public health, corruption and abuse of power, and even corruption by journalists themselves. Examples include Zhao Shilong, a reporter for Guangzhou's *Yangcheng Evening News* who in March 2002 went undercover to expose a government-run hospital that was selling female drug rehabilitation patients into prostitution; Zhai Minglei, a reporter for *Southern Weekly* who in 2002 blew the whistle on the official embezzlement of funds from a state-run charity, Project Hope, which was meant to support impoverished rural schoolchildren; and Zhang Jicheng, who in January 2000 exposed the mass infection of poor Chinese with HIV-AIDS through a blood donation racket backed by top government officials in Henan Province.

The best way to gain a clearer picture of China's media environment and how Chinese journalists work is to look at the specific stories they have pursued and the obstacles they met along the way. The following is the inside story of one case reported in 2003 by Li Yaling, a journalist working for *Chengdu Commercial Daily*, a major market-oriented newspaper in the western Chinese city of Chengdu, in Sichuan province. Li Yaling's case in fact involves little real investigation, unlike the reporting work of Wang Keqin, for example, who routinely works grueling weeks and months to dig deeper into his stories on subjects such as a fraudulent securities company in Gansu province fleecing ordinary people of millions, or government-backed corruption in Beijing's taxi industry. But Li Yaling's case, which has never been fully told, is a good illustration in miniature of the types of pressures journalists face in reporting tough stories.

CASE: THE GIRL WHO DIED OF STARVATION

On June 21, 2003, Li Yaling, who had been working as a professional news reporter for eight years, was preparing to head home at the end of her shift at *Chengdu Commercial Daily* when the head of the paper's news desk, Cai

Jun, called her over and said they had received a lead on a story. In Qing-baijiang, an outlying district of the sprawling Chengdu, a three-year-old girl had died of starvation. According to the source, who had called the newspaper's telephone hotline, the girl had relied entirely on her mother for support. Her mother had been missing for more than a week. "You're a new mother yourself, so you might have some feeling for this story," said Cai Jun.[10]

Li Yaling took one of the newspaper's cars and drove the eighteen miles out to Qingbaijiang. When she arrived on the scene, the child's body had already been removed, but the smell of death lingered in the apartment. Trying her best to keep her cool, Li interviewed eyewitnesses, neighbors, police investigators, and local community officials. One police officer was gruff and closemouthed about the case but said Li Yaling was welcome to tell the story. As he saw it, this was a tragedy, plain and simple. The girl's mother was a drug addict, and she was still actively using, so this clearly was not an accident. The case could serve as a lesson to the public about the evils of drug addiction, he said.

Li quickly learned that the child's name was Li Siyi, and that she was three and a half years old. The child's mother, Li Guifang, was indeed a chronic drug user, and according to neighbors often went out and left Li Siyi locked in the apartment by herself. They all said Li Guifang had adored the child but had found it difficult to provide for her. The child, they said, had seemed accustomed to this way of life. She never cried, and she would often poke her head out of the window and say hello to passersby while her mother was out. The last time Li Guifang went out, she had left the girl locked in an inner bedroom. If she had pleaded for help, no one would have been able to hear her.

Li Yaling was choked with emotion as she hurried back to the newspaper to file her story. Nothing at all seemed to matter in the face of the brutal fact that a three-year-old girl had been left to die in this flourishing city. She filed her story at around 1 a.m. and made sure the proofs went through. It was a story tinged with shock and anger. After running through the essential facts she had from sources at the scene, Li Yaling wrote, "Where is Li Siyi's father? Where is Li Siyi's mother? How could a mother be so heartless as to lock her daughter inside and not come back? We hope anyone who knows about this case will call our hotline with more information."

Li Yaling had no idea, as the morning paper went off the presses, that the full story behind Li Siyi's death was far more sinister.

The next day, Li Yaling sat down with her editor to talk through a follow-up story on the Li Siyi case. At this point they were still quite sure the girl's death was an accident. They decided initially that they would pursue the drug addiction angle, exploring the vagaries of drug use. Perhaps they could get police familiar with the mother's drug history to speak about the case.

Based on the newspaper's experience with the police, they expected their request for cooperation to be accepted on the spot. Much to their surprise, the police refused to cooperate, and Li Yaling could sense from the tone coming out of the Public Security Bureau that they had hit some sort of snag in handling this particular case.

Very quickly, an answer presented itself. Having seen the Li Siyi story in *Chengdu Commercial Daily*, a reader called the newspaper's hotline later that morning. The caller refused to identify himself, but said in a hushed voice that the girl's mother, Li Guifang, was not missing at all. Nor was she dead. She had been arrested for theft and dragged off to the police station, the source said. When police found out she was a drug user, they committed her for mandatory drug rehabilitation. The caller claimed to have seen Li Guifang with his own eyes as she knelt on the ground before police and pleaded with them, saying she had left her three-year-old daughter alone at home. She had asked to go home and see to her daughter first before reporting back for treatment. The police refused to listen, the source said. He was even able to tell them where Li Guifang was being held.

Li Yaling phoned the drug rehab center immediately, identifying herself as a relative of Li Guifang's. Sure enough, they could confirm that Li was being held at the facility. They told her, however, that the patient was not allowed to speak with relatives or receive visits. When Li Yaling checked up on laws and regulations governing drug rehabilitation centers, she had a good hypothesis as to why the police were so reluctant to cooperate. The law obliged them to notify the relatives, work units, or residential committees of drug rehab patients within twenty-four hours of committing them for mandatory treatment. In Li Guifang's case they had failed in this critical step, a fatal act of negligence.

Recalling this key juncture in the story years later, Li Yaling wrote, "My tears stopped, and my sense of despair hardened into grief and indignation. I quickly put on my best professional face and began investigating the case. I learned the truth quickly."

By noon on June 4, 2003, Li Guifang had found herself utterly penniless. A friend of Li Guifang's treated her and Li Siyi to a simple lunch. Afterward, Li Guifang locked her daughter in the bedroom at home and went with her friend to Jintang County, another district of Chengdu about six miles from Qingbaijiang. There the two women planned to shoplift at the Red Flag Department Store. Li Guifang tried to steal two bottles of shampoo and was caught by security. At the Jintang Police Station, Li was given a drug test that came back positive. The police decided to send her for mandatory drug rehabilitation. Li cried and knelt before the officers, saying she had locked her three-year-old in her apartment. At first they didn't believe her. Finally, before sending Li Guifang away, they promised they would call the police in Qingbaijiang to have them check up on her story. It was seventeen days before the unmistakable smell of death alerted neighbors to the fact that something was wrong.

Just before 8 p.m. on June 22, as Li Yaling was busying herself to finish her follow-up report on the death of young Li Siyi, a call came from top officials at the newspaper saying that Li was to put a stop to all reporting on the case. Having worked in the news business in China for eight years, she was no stranger to prohibitions on news reporting. But on no occasion before, Li Yaling later said in her case study on the story, had she been so outraged by restrictions on the reporting of a story. At the time she was the only journalist who knew the full facts. Despite the difficulty of her situation, she felt her silence on the story would make her complicit: "If I chose to be silent, even if it was not me who was killing the story, was there really any difference? I am a journalist, and reporting the facts and the truth are my duty and obligation."

Li Yaling weighed her options for about ten minutes before finally deciding that she would post her story on the Internet. She went to Journalist's Home, a well-known professional online forum for journalists hosted at the website Xici.net. The title of her online post conveyed the full thrust of the story and her own professional and human motivations for telling it: "A journalist driven by a mother's anger: police arrest and take away a mother without notifying her relatives, and her three-year-old daughter dies of starvation at home."

After giving a full and professional version of the story, Li Yaling explained her gut response to the attempt by the police and local officials to bury it. "I've been a journalist for eight years," she wrote. "I've witnessed so many dark things, and rarely do I ever cry anymore. But the blackness of this order [against reporting] infuriated me. I am not only a journalist, but even more I am a mother, and how I have cried for this child! I cry to see such a mother, such police, such a society, such a world!" Li made a point of using her real name on the post to demonstrate that her story was not baseless rumor. She even included her mobile phone number so that other journalists could reach her about the story.

The post quickly drew attention from Chinese Internet users, who posted hundreds of comments within minutes. Before long, calls came in from editors at other newspapers such as *Beijing Youth Daily* and *Southern Weekend*. Within an hour, however, police in Chengdu had been alerted to the post and contacted the paper to demand it be deleted. Someone in the newspaper's external affairs office quickly learned about the post too and severely reproached Li Yaling, saying she had heaped trouble on the whole paper by her actions. Li Yaling was obliged to place a phone call herself to Xici.net, asking that the post be removed from the site. Before she placed the call, however, she made another quick post to the site urging Internet users to copy the original post. Ten minutes later, the post vanished.

The next day, journalists from around China arrived in Chengdu to follow up on the story of Li Siyi. By day three, Li Yaling was receiving calls from Western journalists, some of whom were also en route to Chengdu. Li Yaling, who now had to fear for her safety and well-being as political pressures closed in around her, met with none of them.

On the morning of June 23, the day after she posted the Li Siyi story at Journalist's Home, two officials from the propaganda office of the Chengdu police met with Li Yaling's boss at *Chengdu Commercial Daily*. They demanded to see Li, but her boss refused, saying it was inappropriate for the police to deal with her directly. Once the police officials had left, he sat down with Li Yaling and told her about the visit. Still furious about the whole matter, she was in no mood to talk. "I don't regret my decision for a minute," she said animatedly. "If I could go back, I'd do exactly the same thing. Even if you held a knife to my throat I would make that post!" Her boss told her to go back to her desk and cool down.

But the story would not cool down. It kept getting bigger and bigger, as reporters from around the country crowded outside the offices of the Chengdu police and city government. Top city leaders held a meeting three days later, and Li Yaling learned from her own sources that a senior leader had spoken out against her, saying journalists like Li Yaling had to be weeded out of the local press corps. She was certain her career as a news reporter was finished.

Knowing the ax would fall at any moment, Li Yaling decided to take the rest of the day off. She tried to relax by going to her regular salon for a facial. It was impossible. Her colleagues kept calling with the latest whispers of information about her situation. The word was that she would definitely be disciplined for her act of defiance. They told her to ready herself. She shut her eyes, listening to the voices at the other end of the line, tears coursing down her cheeks. Her stylist, finding the facial impossible, came around and held her tightly as she wept uncontrollably.

Later that day, Li Yaling received a call from someone in the Chengdu Party Committee saying a senior official wanted to meet with her. She met with the official and insisted that if they were going to fire her, now was a poor choice of timing. Foreign journalists were already on the story, and firing her would further politicize it. That would be bad for everyone involved, Li Yaling said. She even agreed to speak with foreign journalists in an attempt to set the facts straight and defuse tensions, being careful about what she said. The official tentatively agreed. That night, however, a telephone call was arranged with another senior city leader, and she was told to report to the Party Committee the next morning, June 27, at 8 a.m.

When she arrived at the offices of the Party Committee the next morning, there were several senior officials there, who told her resolutely that she was to post a letter on the Internet "clarifying the facts and cleaning up the whole mess." They were asking, essentially, that she retract her story. She insisted that this was a bad idea. Changing her story would only fuel speculation that she had broken under official pressure, giving media another handle to grab on to. The officials present were divided in their views. One camp wanted Li Yaling to retract her report publicly. Another camp said such an action would "only make the situation stink worse." They should let the story take its own course and settle down naturally, they said. Ultimately, the first camp prevailed.

Li Yaling refused to write a retracting statement herself. She suggested they write a statement for her, which she would then post. Her thought was that if she posted the statement just as she received it, the document would speak for itself, making it clear to everyone that she had been pressured. In that sense, the statement itself would be a historical document of sorts, a dark footnote in China's press history. Chengdu leaders ultimately decided that the propaganda office of the Public Security Bureau would write Li Yaling's retraction. She would then edit it to suit her style, and she would post her version on the Internet only after it had been approved.

It was 2 a.m. before the retraction finally came. Reading it through, she left every word just as it was. After she delivered it, she phoned the head of the news office at the Chengdu propaganda department and once again urged against posting the retraction on the Internet. The next day, she received a call from the Party Committee. They had changed their minds, deciding not to post the retraction. Instead, they wanted to create the impression for foreign media that Li Yaling was under no pressure at all. They ordered her newspaper to ensure that her byline appeared in the newspaper every day.

For a time, everything seemed to return to normal. Still, Li Yaling knew the ax would fall as soon as all sympathetic watching eyes were gone.

In early October, Li received a dinner invitation from a self-described "Internet user" who said he was traveling to Chengdu and wanted to give her a recording of a song someone in Beijing had written in memory of Li Siyi. Feeling obliged as he had gone through so much trouble, Li Yaling agreed, and she arrived at the restaurant to find that a number of her fellow journalists had shown up as well. She had no idea this innocent dinner engagement would become the pretext for her removal as a news reporter.

On October 8, two days after the dinner, top officials at *Chengdu Commercial Daily* approached Li Yaling and asked her whom she had met with on October 6. She had nothing to hide and told them exactly what had happened. They insisted that the "Internet user" she had dined with was in fact a former leader of the 1989 democracy movement and that her colleagues at the dinner had also been involved in the democracy protests. She had stepped into an invisible maelstrom, and nothing could save her journalism career.

Her bosses insisted the matter was beyond their control. She would be removed from her position as a news reporter and shifted over to another department at the newspaper, where she would be responsible for commissioning freelance articles and selecting news from the wires. If she wished to keep her pay, she would meet with no one and speak to no one.

In March 2004, unable to withstand the monotony of her exile from news reporting, Li Yaling asked to be transferred to a department where she could return to writing. Reporting news was out of the question. But short fiction had long been one of her passions, and the newspaper finally agreed. Li Yaling would be allowed to write serialized fiction.

In the Li Siyi case, Li Yaling had faced what she later described as "a journey into hell." Her career as a news reporter, which she had thought would be her lifelong profession, was now officially over. An erstwhile Quixote jousting with the monsters of Chengdu, she now turned to a less perilous calling, writing stories of modern-day romance.

NEW CHALLENGES FOR PROFESSIONAL JOURNALISTS

There have been many changes in the media environment in China since Li Yaling broke through the silence on the Li Siyi case more than eight years ago. The picture is a mixed one, and again we see the pattern of *control*, *change*, and *chaos* at work, at once inhibiting the work of journalists and offering them limited opportunities.

One of the most recent developments on China's media landscape has been a high-level change in approach to news and propaganda policy. In a major media policy speech in June 2008, President Hu Jintao talked about the need for the party to more effectively "channel public opinion" by putting its own messages out more aggressively. Essentially, this was the idea that controlling information, or shutting it off, was no longer sufficient in the age of the Internet and twenty-four-hour news coverage, and that the party had to become more adept at spinning stories to its advantage. One major impetus for this policy shift was the feeling that China had committed a major blunder in March 2008 by issuing a blanket ban on coverage of unrest in Tibet without effectively communicating its own version of the "facts." By closing Tibet off, China's leaders had created an information vacuum. This had not succeeded in controlling information, but instead had allowed foreign media to dominate the information space. In the aftermath of Tibet, many CCP leaders came to believe that China had lost control of the agenda on Tibet, essentially yielding it to international media.[11]

What Hu Jintao advocated in June 2008 was a more strategic use of both information control and information release. "Channeling" meant pushing aggressively with selected coverage of breaking news stories—with authoritative official information, as leaders liked to call it—and resorting to more traditional information controls where necessary to keep coverage within bounds. Since 2008, largely as a reflection of this policy, we have seen more coverage in China of natural disasters and so-called sudden-breaking incidents, including strikes or work-related tragedies. In a limited sense, the change is a positive turn, signaling that Chinese leaders recognize it is no longer feasible to bury information.

But Hu Jintao's policy is a change in strategy, not a change of heart. Media control remains a critical priority, and the question is not whether or not to control information, but how. What we tend to see in the case of natural disasters and other breaking stories is blanket reporting of surface details. News coverage focuses on the who, what, when, and where. When did the earthquake occur? How powerful was it? How many people have died? What is the government doing to deal with it? The question of *why*, however, remains highly sensitive.

Heightened restrictions on in-depth reporting stemming from this new policy have been a step backward for investigative reporting in China. Government restrictions on investigative reporting, however, go back even further to a 2005 CCP document prohibiting the practice of what is called "cross-regional reporting," or *yidi jiandu*, in which media from one government jurisdiction investigate government or corporate misconduct in another local or regional jurisdiction. Since media began investigating stories more actively in the 1990s, cross-regional reporting has been one of their most important tactics, enabling them to some extent to circumvent local press restrictions and make more full use of the party mandate for watchdog journalism, or "supervision by public opinion." In 2005 provincial leaders in China pressured top propaganda officials in Beijing to curb the practice of cross-regional reporting, which they said was putting them under intense pressure and making it hard to focus on priorities like economic development.[12]

The CCP decree has not been enforced to the letter, but it has strengthened the hand of local officials working actively against press scrutiny. And this brings us to one of the latest developments working against investigative journalists in China: the noxious combination of authoritarian political power and commercial self-interest. This new monster, what some have termed Market-Leninism, or "the combination of relatively free-market economics and authoritarian one-party rule,"[13] is arguably the single most important obstacle journalists face in China today.

While in the past, directives from propaganda authorities have been concerned with "the party line" or the broader goal of maintaining social stability, many actions against the press today stem directly from vested commercial interests that have backing from connected party or government officials.

In the midst of fierce competition, a number of leading financial publications have actively investigated Chinese listed companies in the past few years. These media navigate through the *chaos* of China's political environment to push professional coverage in a direction relevant to their audiences. But the companies they investigate respond increasingly, and with growing effectiveness, with their own pressure campaigns. They employ special "intermediary structures" that operate like public relations firms with powerful government ties, able to suppress coverage or pay for the removal of undesirable content. They seek protection from government officials and agencies. And they use the state media control apparatus to intimidate journalists and media.[14]

There were numerous cases in 2010 of reporters being sought for arrest or physically attacked after writing critical reports on listed companies. In one case, Fang Xuanchang, a science editor at *Caijing* magazine, was attacked by hired thugs. In another, Qiu Ziming, a reporter for the *Economic Observer*, was placed on a national "most wanted" list after he wrote a series of reports on alleged insider trading by Kan Specialty Materials, a manufacturing company.

These developments tell us that state media controls and other pressures on Chinese journalists are undergoing constant change. It is fair to say that in the last few years Chinese journalists, and investigative reporters in particular, have suffered many setbacks, owing to both political and commercial pressures. Li Datong, the former editor of *Freezing Point*, said in 2009 that "investigative journalism has been in a clear cycle of weakening over the last two years."[15]

But journalists are changing and developing too. Despite immense pressures, Chinese journalists are finding ways to push back against the pressure. Following a toxic spill in July 2010 at a facility in Fujian operated by Zijin Mining Group, two commercial publications, *New Century* magazine and *Time Weekly*, reported aggressively on the incident, exposing close collusion between the local government and the company, which had many officials on its payroll. In a follow-up report, the newspaper *China Youth Daily* revealed that Zijin Mining Group had tried to pay off news reporters to cover up the toxic spill.[16]

The dynamic jousting match between *change* and *control* in China's media is one of the most exciting stories unfolding in China today. The outcome will depend in large part on the professional efforts of journalists themselves and the extent to which they are able to push open new areas of coverage. Ultimately, however, protecting and empowering journalists in their role as monitors of power will require deeper political change.

SUGGESTIONS FOR FURTHER READING

Books

Bandurski, David, and Martin Hala, ed. *Investigative Journalism in China: Eight Cases in Chinese Watchdog Journalism.* Hong Kong: University of Hong Kong Press, 2010.

Polumbaum, Judy. *China Ink: The Changing Face of Chinese Journalism*. Lanham, MD: Rowman & Littlefield, 2008.

Shirk, Susan L., ed. *Changing Media, Changing China*. New York: Oxford University Press, 2010.

Zhao Yuezhi. *Media, Market, and Democracy in China: Between the Party Line and the Bottom Line*. Urbana: University of Illinois Press, 1998.

Websites

China Media Project, http://cmp.hku.hk

China Digital Times, http://chinadigitaltimes.net/

NOTES

1. Zhao Zhongxie and Yong Li, "A Modern Reading of 'Politicians Must Run the Newspapers'" (Zhengzhijia banbao de dangdai jie du), *China Journalist*, March 2006, http://www.cqvip.com/QK/96951X/2006003/21283215.html.

2. Chan Yuen-ying, "A Scholar's View: The State Media Have an Iron Grip and Grand Plans," *Global Asia* 5, no. 2 (Summer 2010): 62–65.

3. Wu Danhong, "Why Was Wu Fatian Completely Killed on Sina Microblog?" (Wu Fatian wei he zao dao xinlang weibo quan mianfeng sha?), *Wufayan Biao*, http://laws.fyfz.cn/art/717324.htm.

4. Li Fung-cho, "The Emergence of China's Watchdog Reporting," in *Investigative Journalism in China: Eight Cases in Chinese Watchdog Journalism*, ed. David Bandurski and Martin Hala (Hong Kong: University of Hong Kong Press, 2010), 167.

5. Qian Gang, "Guidance/Supervision/Reform/Freedom: Plotting the Direction of Chinese Media through an Analysis of the All-Important Buzzwords," *Twenty-First-Century Bi-Monthly*, June 2006.

6. Qian Gang, "Guidance/Supervision/Reform/Freedom."

7. Qian Gang, "Guidance/Supervision/Reform/Freedom."

8. Zhu Yu, Wan Yi, and Liu Hongcan, "The Risk Prevention Consciousness of a Rural School Principle in the Disaster Zone" (Yige zaiqu nongcun xiaozhang de bixian yishi), *Xinhua News Agency*, May 23, 2008.

9. For readers' reference, the subsequent discussion of Don Quixote is keyed to the celebrated pen and ink drawing by G. A. Harker, which may be accessed at the following site: http://www.brudvik.org/2011/02/statkraft-mener-vindkraft-er-feil/.

10. Li Yaling, "A Full Account of Reporting on the Li Siyi Case" (Li Siyi anbao dao qianhou), case study on file with the China Media Project, Journalism & Media Studies Center, University of Hong Kong, submitted May 28, 2005. All details from this story and quotes from Li Yaling in the following pages are from this source.

11. Du Yongming, "Renewing the Theory of Party Control of the Media" (Dangguan meiti de lilun chuangxin), *Hongqi Wengao* (published by *Seeking Truth*), June 13, 2010, http://news.xinhuanet.com/theory/2010-06/13/c_12217842.htm.

12. David Bandurski, "Jousting with China's Monsters," *Far Eastern Economic Review* 172, no. 2 (March 2009): 46–50.

13. Ian Buruma, "In the Land of Market-Leninism," *New York Times*, September 18, 1994.

14. Bandurski, "Jousting with China's Monsters," 46–50.

15. Chan Yuen-ying, "Politics and Pressure: How Will Freedom of Speech Come to Mainland China?" (Zhengjing shi yanei di chuanmei ziyou he lai?), *Hong Kong Economic Times*, September 13, 2010.

16. Bandurski, "Jousting with China's Monsters," 46–50.

2

Youth Culture in China: Idols, Sex, and the Internet

Jonathan S. Noble

The larger landscape of contemporary China is marked by breathtaking change along a number of faults: culture, economy, society—all have undergone seismic shifts. And China's youth (those fourteen to twenty-eight years of age) have been especially affected by these changes. In the history of twentieth-century China, the registry of change in the lives of youth is prominent. Indeed, the establishment of modern China a century ago was inseparable from the empowerment of "youth" (*qingnian*) as a new political classification that challenged the hierarchy of patriarchal elders and laid the popular groundwork for a "New China."

A New China was called for by youthful reformers to replace the imperial dynastic reign whose declining rule jeopardized China's sovereignty in the face of threats from Japan and from Western powers inclined toward occupation of its territories. The New China required youthful vigor and fresh ideas, many of which were brought back to China by Chinese students who had studied abroad in Japan, Europe, or the United States. They called for "enlightenment," for gender equality, for the widespread use of *baihua* "plain speech," for the sovereign rights of the individual, all in the spirit of modern, Western, scientific, and technological advocacy. If the premodern concept of youth in China focused on obeying the elders in most of life's activities, especially in the "most important event in one's life" (*zhongshen dashi*)—marriage—then the New China developed the concept of a "new youth" (*xin qingnian*), which was to be divorced from, and in some ways antithetical to, arranged marriage and the social precepts maintained by the traditional patriarchal hierarchy.

The founding of the People's Republic of China was built upon this new youth, of which almost all of the early Chinese Communist Party luminaries (including Mao Zedong and Deng Xiaoping) were self-conscious members. These youths devoted themselves to the fight against imperialist aggression, especially by Japan in the so-called War of Resistance, and to the adaptation of Marxist ideology that sought to liberate all Chinese from the shackles of the old feudal China. Yet today the political power of China's youth, despite this legacy of activism, is grossly overshadowed by older government officials. There is an ironic reversal of roles, wherein the party of the "new youth" seems, in practice, to value obeisance and political didacticism over independence and intellectual autonomy.

When defining youth, we are subject to specific cultural values and contexts; however, new technologies, such as the Internet, have enabled youth from around the world to connect with one another and contribute to the possible creation of a global youth culture. Throughout this essay, the definition of youth is not entirely defined by age, though as a reference members of the Communist Youth League of China (*Zhongguo gongchan-zhuyi qingniantuan*) (CYLC) are always between fourteen and twenty-eight. The concept of adolescence and certain phases of adolescence, such as the preteen and the teenage years, are less pronounced in China than they are in the United States. However, it is common today in China to differentiate generations as post-'70s (now in their thirties), post-'80s (now in their twenties), and post-'90s (now in their teens). According to Baidu.com's Baike (Baidu is China's Google; Baike is China's Wikipedia), the post-'90s generation has the following characteristics: (1) a high aptitude to adapt to change; (2) self-absorption but lack of self-confidence; (3) an interest in promoting one's individuality; (4) tendency to pursue hobbies that are not understood by adults; (5) "growing up" early; and (6) inhabiting a world expanded by the Internet yet one that is somewhat empty. Like the post-'80s generation, the post-'90s generation is characterized by an increasingly wealthy, and materialistic, society, the pervasive influence of new technologies, and a social structure in which most families only have a single child because of the national family-planning policy.

Given that the development of the category of "youth" in modern China has been distinctly political, it follows that today "youth" continues to be a status "protected" by the government. This is seen most directly in state institutions, such as the CYLC, which was founded in 1920 in conjunction with the New Youth Movement (*Xin qingnian yundong*). CYLC's importance to and connection with the Chinese political leadership is clear. The first secretary of the Youth League is also a member of the Communist Party's Central Committee, and China's current president, Hu Jintao, served as first secretary of the organization from 1984 to 1985. CYLC is essentially a Communist Party institution that functions to organize the nation's youth into local groups, usually affiliated with schools that support the state's ideological dominance and the Communist Party's supremacy. Entry into the Youth League is often seen as a prerequisite to academic and professional success, and so it is not surprising that the CYLC Central Committee reported around 73.5 million league members at the end of 2006.[1] In April 2011 the CYLC announced a new program that will send ten thousand college graduates to serve in China's western ethnic regions (mainly Xinjiang and Tibet) to assist with improving basic education, health care, and agricultural technology.

In addition to the Communist Party's formal organization of China's youth, the Chinese state regularly launches campaigns to protect the nation's youth from "spiritual pollution," which includes criminal activities, such as drug use, prostitution, and pornography, as well as cultural activities that are deemed deleterious, such as addiction to online gaming and engagement with vulgar online content and television shows, such as the production of satirical videos (*egao*). The blocking of certain Internet sites and monitoring of online content by the Chinese government help to prevent youth from accessing, creating, and circulating content that is deemed harmful to them, society, and the state.[2] Green Dam Youth Escort (*lübei huaji huhang*), a sophisticated content-control software, which was originally mandated by the Ministry of Industry and Information Technology (MIIT) to be installed on all new personal computers sold in mainland China starting in July 2009, aimed to prevent access to prohibited sites. The mandate represented the Chinese government's effort to control and monitor use of the Internet, especially targeting China's youth, but this particular effort seems to have failed as government funding was stopped.[3] It should also be noted that the proclaimed goal of "protecting China's youth" is often manipulated by the Chinese government as a justification for a broader censorship that is extended to the entire public. Yet given the complex interweaving of the lives of today's youth with the desires for wealth and recognition and involvement in illicit activities, the party-state's concern about censorship is not simply a matter of political repression.

YOUTHFUL AMBITIONS AND SEXUAL AGENCY

In tandem with China's explosive economic growth, Chinese youth today are keenly focused on the desire to advance their social standing and financial well-being. Opportunities to do so vary significantly, but access to secondary and tertiary education has grown dramatically for youth in China. For example, the number of young people attending college has increased from 120,000 students in 1949 to 27 million students in 2008. The number of Chinese attending college outside of China has also increased significantly. In 2009–2010 for example, 18.5 percent of the total number of international students studying at U.S. universities were from China

(127,628), more than double from a decade earlier.[4] Whereas a resident in a wealthy suburb of Shanghai may aim to attend a top-ranked university in the United States, the vast majority of China's young people is not college bound (at home or abroad) and typically join the ranks of the migrant population as they move from rural to urban China.[5] This is quickly verified by a visit to most rural villages in China, where one will overwhelmingly find older generations. According to an estimate by an official of China's national population and family-planning commission at a forum on World Population Day in 2010, nearly 40 percent of China's floating population—estimated at 211 million—was born after 1980.[6]

Although exact numbers are difficult to verify, the population of Dongguan, one of China's largest migrant cities, is around 8 million. Dongguan is located in the Pearl River Delta close to Hong Kong, and its estimated 6 million migrant factory workers are female, predominantly under the age of 25, and have migrated from small rural villages.[7] The iPhone photo of the very young female factory worker that became viral on the Internet around the world, as well as the string of Foxconn suicides, represent the inhumane alienation experienced by many young factory workers in Dongguan and beyond.[8]

The socio-economic divide between college-bound and non-college-bound youth is significant, and it plays an important role in defining their future lives. However, a college education is financially more accessible in China than in the United States, because the college entrance system, in most cases, ensures that the students with the top scores will attend the top universities, often with full scholarships. Nevertheless, a college education in China is no guarantee of favorable employment. In fact, China's economy is struggling to absorb its escalating number of college graduates. Mounting social and financial pressures at college have also resulted in serious problems. Growing numbers of college students are committing suicide, and there is an epidemic of college-age prostitution. Suicide and prostitution are real social problems faced by China's youth in factories as well.

Dating and sexual behavior are often viewed as defining characteristics of youth. In China the preponderance of opportunities to trade sex for money—massage parlors, escort and mistress networks, online sex dating, KTV (big screen television karaoke palaces), and discos—has led to an inordinate percentage of female youth either directly participating in the sex trade or in some fashion having informal links to it. Some young women and some young men as well regard the economic opportunity of the sex trade as a short-cut to acquire funds for designer clothing, the latest gadget, or even a car or a condo. It is also seen as a quasi-legitimate way to raise start-up capital to return to one's hometown and invest in a family business, such as a hair salon, restaurant, or clothing store. Other youth may justify prostitution on the grounds of filial piety and dedication to one's family—such as helping to provide parents with medical care or assisting a sibling, often male, who needs money for school or marriage.

Therefore, whereas in Europe and the United States young people are characterized by recreational or leisure activities such as athletics or music and a focus on individual personality and autonomy, in China the relatively commonplace monetization of sex blurs the boundaries for many between recreation and livelihood and between competing perceptions of morality. At the same time, despite the relatively widespread phenomenon of the commercialization of sexual activity throughout Chinese society, China's rigorous national entrance exam system for primary, secondary, and tertiary education places a very high demand on youth to study intensively. Entrance into the most competitive primary and secondary schools is seen as a prerequisite for admission into China's elite universities or for studying overseas.

The elite high schools, especially those located in China's largest and wealthiest cities, are minimally affected by the monetization of sex. This is because the financial motivation for such activity is lower for youth from middle-class and wealthier urban families and their prospective gains, both intellectually and financially, from attending competitive universities either in China or abroad discourages such youth from engaging in the practice of monetized sexual activities. In a speech on the occasion of Tsinghua University's centennial on April 23, 2011, President Hu emphasized the need to infuse China's higher education system with moral integrity. This is recognition from China's highest political level that the country's education system must address more effectively those issues relating to the moral values of China's youth, even as students demonstrate extraordinary academic performance. Indeed, there was quite a stir caused in both Chinese and U.S. media when fifteen-year-old Shanghai students had the highest scores in math, reading, and science on the Program for International Student Assessment (PISA). On the math assessment, the Shanghai students finished first, scoring 600, and those from the United States finished thirty-first with a score of 487.[9]

THE REVOLUTION OF POP IDOLS

During the Maoist era, government directives and political campaigns dictated cultural practices. The most familiar idol was Chairman Mao himself; he dominated the popular imagination and could not be usurped by any competing icons. During the Cultural Revolution, he was worshiped by the millions of youth who joined the Red Guards, and he exploited youth rebellion and transgression to maintain his political supremacy until his death in 1976. Other popular figures during the Maoist era were political icons that were popularized in order to enforce Chairman Mao's hegemony. For example, the "white-haired girl," (*baimao nü*) popularized through the model revolutionary opera (*yangbanxi*) of the same name represented Chairman Mao's directive to renew class struggle and weed out class enemies. The martyr Lei Feng represented the Communist Party's ideological dictate to sacrifice oneself for the nation. Other icons popularized through the state's cultural-production apparatus also followed such ideological models, and their circulation was largely controlled by the state.

In the post-Mao era, the production and consumption of youth culture, as a commercial practice, developed in tandem with China's market reforms first introduced in the late 1970s and early 1980s. As a critical component of the market reforms, the "open-door policy" resulted in the increased flow of capital, people, goods, and ideas from outside China, especially from Hong Kong. The popularity of Taiwan's Canto-pop star Teresa Teng (1953–1995) in early 1980s Mainland China is an important example of how China's open-door policy and market reforms helped to shape China's new emerging popular cultures. Celebrity stardom in China today is big business, with the top mainland Chinese actors—Zhao Benshan and Zhang Ziyi—earning 95.6 million ($14.7 million U.S.) and 69 million yuan ($10.6 million U.S.), respectively, according to *Forbes*.[10]

The impact on Chinese society of the array of economic reforms cannot be overstated, although it is clear today that the market economy has not overcome the rule and authority of the one-party state. Rather, market reforms over the last thirty years have in many ways bolstered the legitimacy of an evolving Communist Party and Chinese state. Therefore, in the United States the rise and fall of celebrities is rarely a result of political (dis)approval; but in China the state can have a much larger influence on the fate of celebrities and the landscape of popular culture. This is largely due to the fact that the Chinese state, for the most part, controls the means of celebrity production, namely the media (Internet, television and film, newspapers, etc.) and the modes for distribution and consumption of pop icons. However, the state is less in the business of producing pop icons than involved with regulating the cultural industry, including popular and youth cultures.

One case in point is the reality TV program known as *Super Girl* (*Chaonü*), first broadcast by Hunan TV in 2004 as *Happy China Super Female Voice* (*Kuaile Zhongguo chaoji nüsheng*).[11] The program maintains the record for the highest viewership of any television program broadcast in China other than China Central Television's (CCTV) annual Spring Festival galas.[12] Modeled after *American Idol*, the televised singing competition *Super Girl* produced a number of China's popular youth icons (such as Li Yuchun, Zhang Liangying, and Shang Wenjie). On one level, the program simply represented the youthful desire to achieve overnight stardom as a shortcut to wealth and success. Of course, such a path to fortune is anathema in a meritocracy based on a system of rigorous education organized by the Communist Party. In fact, throughout China's history the civil service exam system, conceived as a meritocracy, rewarded literacy, scholarship, and especially knowledge about the canon of Confucian classics. This system generated a class of scholar-officials and a merit-based evaluation of a particular type of learning.

When the civil service examination was dismantled in 1905, foreign educators and missionaries established new universities in China. These universities imported educational values from Europe and the United States that emphasized the role of arts and sciences in understanding the human and natural worlds. Then during the Communist revolution and the Maoist years (1949–1976) that followed, China's educational system imported elements from the Soviet curriculum and focused more on utilitarian subjects, such as engineering, and ideological ones, such as Marxist-Leninist Thought. The meritocratic system was supplanted by a new one, which emphasized "technical ability" (*zhuan*) and "redness" (*hong*), meaning zealous commitment to the Communist Party. Market reforms initiated in the post-Mao era created new paths to achieve wealth, success, and status while at the same time promoting a rigorous national entrance exam system for primary, secondary, and tertiary education. Within this historical context, *Super Girl* represents a glorified path to success that circumvents the rigors of the entrance exam system and rewards winners for talent, character, and performance ability rather than book learning. Instant stardom (and its consumption) supported an ideology of eternal youth that shirked a more official and pragmatic path to adulthood. After all, the program's motto was *Xiang chang jiu chang! Yi chang wei ben!* ("Just go ahead and sing! Singing is your life!").

In 2006, due in part to the unprecedented popularity of the program, CCTV and the China Bureau of Broadcasting and Television (*guangdian zongju*) instituted some new policies, including implementing a minimum age of eighteen for contestants, increasing the authority of the judges, and limiting national coverage only to the finals. In addition to popularizing youth icons and associated trends, the program also exemplified the role of various technologies in the production and consumption of youth culture, such as the blogosphere (including blogs, bulletin boards, instant messaging, etc.) and cell phones. For example, there were an estimated 2.4 million postings on Sina.com in connection with the *Super Girl* finals in 2006. *Super Girl* also introduced the cell phone as a tool for representing one's views—namely, by voting for one's favorite contestants via text messaging.[13] In the finals, the top three finalists were chosen not by the judges but by the audience's text message votes. One cell phone user could vote fifteen times at a cost of five *mao* (about eight cents U.S.) per vote. Owners of China Mobile cell phones could vote thirty times.

The competition was made more dramatic by introducing the concept of "PK match-off." PK means "player killer" and originates from MUD, multiuser dungeon interactive computer video games. In the PK, those contestants who had already been eliminated could be invited to rechallenge finalists. The great success of *Super Girl* sparked the adoption of the program model by other networks, and the PK format has become extremely popular—possibly a fusion of the familiar competitive nature of China's education system with the popularity of multiplayer video games. Some view this *Super Girl* voting as an important development in terms of political consciousness (see below).

The popularity of the reality TV program was closely connected to blogosphere discussions. Different topics were discussed online, including singing techniques, gender identity, and behind-the-scenes manipulation. One question discussed on the message boards and in online forums in China, as well as in the international news media, was whether or not *Super Girl* and its voting mechanism could generate some type of political impact, that is, promote political reform in China. Some interpreted the program as representing an opportunity for Chinese society to embrace democracy. Jim Yardley of the *International Herald Tribune* viewed *Super Girl* as one of the largest "democratic" voting exercises in mainland China.[14] One of China's official newspapers, *People's Daily* (*Renmin ribao*), quoted Zhu Dake, an authoritative cultural critic, who opined that the show "blazed a trail for cultural democracy. . . . It's like a gigantic game that has swept so many people into a euphoria of voting and selecting, which is testament of a society opening up."[15] One blogger with a distinctly political sensitivity viewed the program as representing the development of civil society in China:

> The existence of Super Girls shows two things. The people's happiness does not have to depend on the government, for the people can create their own source of happiness. When society no longer depends totally on the government, when society has gone ahead to form its own self-perfected, self-reliant, self-operated and self-maintained system (and this was formed during the practical experience of Super Girls by the television station, the program participants, the viewers and the advertisers) and when the system can continue without needing the government to do anything, then it won't be too long before a civil society emerges. Thus, the Super Girls is a glimpse of the future Chinese civil society.[16]

However, others were skeptical of the efficacy of voting: "How come an imitation of a democratic system ends up selecting the singer who has the least ability to carry a tune?" (referring in this instance to Li Yuchun, who won but was regarded by many as insufficiently talented).[17] Such skepticism was also expressed in the *South China Morning Post*: "Democracy is not about the sending of a text messages or reaching for the remote control to change channels—it is about people having the right to rule themselves and determine their own government. Television shows do not provide that."[18]

One infamous blogger at the time whose alias is "Anti" wrote, "I don't think that I will ever get to vote [for] a president in this lifetime, so I'll choose a girl that I like. Super Girls is obviously not the same as democracy, but it is the fantasy for the 1.3 billion Chinese people who do not have democracy. When I think about this, I feel sad for China."[19] Liu Xiaobo, the well-known intellectual and winner of the 2010 Nobel Peace Prize, stated:

> In real life, the people of China had very few opportunities to make their choices based upon voting. Therefore, the Super Girls game rules offer the citizens [a chance] to see the possibility of practicing these common values, and a participatory democracy may evolve out of how the Super Girls are selected. . . . The greater likelihood is that the many dissatisfactions inside the people can only be allowed to be expressed in a virtual entertainment world but not in any critical fashion within the system of dictatorship. In that case, the Super Girls is only a River of Forgetting that lets people release their dissatisfactions through the joy of entertainment.[20]

In an online forum Xu Jilin, another intellectual and critic also expressed his skepticism: He remarked that the show created an "entertainment democracy." "Behind the Super Girls there is an invisible hand—it is the hand of money, it is the hand of power and it is the joint conspiracy of power and money. . . . When the results are revealed as expected and people are cheering for the 'victory of the common people,' the really happy one is that invisible hand behind the curtain—the hand that stole, toyed, and manipulated public opinion to realize quick commercial profits."[21]

In an article in the *Asia Times* on Aug. 29, 2005, a reporter commented:

> As for certain overseas persons thinking that the SMS [Short Message Service] voting on Super Girl is an alternate rehearsal for Chinese democracy, that kind of talk is like saying that underground lottery betting or Hong Kong racehorse gambling is useful for opening up the country for development. Other than amazing people with the fervid imagination, those comments have no value beyond bringing unnecessary political terror onto Super Girl.[22]

This reporter's comments proved prophetic. Due to the great popularity of the show, as well as the fact that a bunch of spin-offs, such as one for male singers (sponsored by Sprite), were also becoming popular, the State Administration of Radio, Film, and Television (SARFT) issued new rules in April 2006 governing such shows. The new regulations state that the shows should contribute to "constructing a harmonious socialist society. . . .

[They] must not make a hubbub about things as they please and must avoid creating stars." They must also "avoid vulgar or gross styles" and protect the morals of the youth of China. It seems as if obeisance to the self-proclaimed moral authority, therefore, remains a primary part of defining the qualities of youth in China; however, youth are not simply passive but actively pursuing their interests, passions, and futures, facilitated by new technologies and an ever-accelerating global network of communication and access.

Li Yuchun, the winner of *Super Girl* 2005, entered the pantheon of Baidu's ten mythical creatures in 2009 as the popularity of the online meme with a cross-dressing theme exploded. The motto "Brother Chun Is All Man, a Real Iron-Man" is accompanied by manipulated images that feature her head atop the body of Bruce Lee and depict her in religious scenes—as a Buddhist deity and as the messiah.[23] Baidu's ten mythical creatures, originally hoaxes to satirize Baidu's censorship of keyword searches, represented a form of creative resistance against China's censorship.[24] Whereas different types of censorship typically can be found in most countries, the institution of censorship in China is focused largely on the idea that national security cannot be guaranteed unless the state controls the flow of information—including different types of media—print, visual, and new (Internet).[25] In this way, each individual in China, including non-Chinese visitors to China (like me while I am writing this essay), are subject to the laws of the PRC that limit access and circulation of certain types of information that are deemed harmful to national security. It has also been in China's commercial interest to block or ban major Internet portals and sites such as Google, YouTube, Twitter, and Facebook since then China's own companies, respectively Baidu, Youku, Sina Weibo, and Renren, can monopolize these vast markets in China and possibly beyond.

YOUTH CULTURE, TECHNOLOGY, AND NEW MEDIA

During the last several decades, China has experienced a veritable explosion of technological products and technologically driven media. According to MIIT, there were an estimated 900 million cell phone users in China in May 2011.[26] China had about 420 million Internet users in 2010, including 277 million mobile users who access the Internet over their phones and 142 million users who shop online, according to the China Internet Network Information Centre (CNNIC).[27] Near the close of 2010 there were an estimated 230 million blog users in China, according to Wang Cheng, minister of the State Council Information Office.[28] China's largest micro-blogging provider, Sina Weibo, reported in October 2010 that it reached over 20 million registered users since its launch in August 2009.[29] Although the new technologies are used by different age groups, youth in China have higher rates of utilization and more quickly affect the ways in which the new technologies are adopted and utilized.

The Chinese blogosphere has developed into a dynamic mode of communication and expression for the nation's youth.[30] The increased popularity of blogging is directly linked to one of the key narratives of youth culture—namely, sexual exploration and expression. Blogging took off in China at the end of 2002 when Li Li (pseudonym of Mu Zimei) put an explicit log of her sex life online at blogcn.com. She wrote, "I have a job that keeps me busy, and in my spare time I have a very humanistic hobby—making love." Its enormous popularity caused servers to crash all over China. A year later Sina.com claimed that Mu Zimei's site received 10 million visitors a day. Accused of harming public order, Mu Zimei lost her job as a reporter for a magazine in Guangzhou as the Central Propaganda Department ordered her blog deleted and recalled a collection of her best diary items from bookstores just days after it was published. The Mu Zimei phenomenon represents how the use of technology—Internet and blogging—was adopted by the youth to participate in the exploration—and voyeurism—of sex, which had previously been a relatively inaccessible, nonpublic, and a somewhat taboo subject.

Blogging (and now microblogging) also provides a semipublic forum to display and discuss issues that may be subject to censorship through traditional print media and websites that are more easily monitored.[31] When bulletin boards or online forums get axed, blogs are serving more and more as the repository of the evidence. For example, after the Peking University–based online forum Yitahutu was terminated, discussions about it were immediately preserved in the blogosphere. Several bloggers were particularly noted for pushing the envelope, such as "Sai Sange Biao" on his *Massage Cream* blog, who often criticized the state of journalism in China due to extensive censorship and widespread corruption, and "Anti" (Michael Anti), who discussed questions regarding democracy.

Vlogs, or video logs, and recut trailers became another online phenomenon in China popular among the youth. The *egao* or satirical videos mentioned above are mainly video and flash spoofs that use digital editing techniques and voiceovers with lampooning as their primary goal. Revolutionary martyrs, such as Lei Feng, have been lampooned, but one of the most prominent spoofs was of Chen Kaige's high-budget fantasy epic *The Promise*. The film is parodied in a twenty-minute online spoof called "Murder Over a Steamed Bun."[32] The spoof brought instant fame to Hu Ge, its creator. SARFT issued new regulations that block Internet broadcasts of short films that satirize officially approved cultural products, including films, celebrities, and Communist Party icons.

Under regulations issued by China's censors as part of Beijing's race to keep control of Chinese cyberspace, anyone who wants to post short videos on the Internet will need approval from the managers of those sites (such as China's popular video hosting sites Toodou.com, 56.com, and Yoqoo .com). Internet users are banned from posting content that humiliates or libels, or infringes the legal rights of others or the regulations of the state. Liu Jianhui, a censorship official at SARFT, said, "SARFT has established a quite advanced Internet audio-visual monitoring center and plans to set up monitoring centers in Beijing, Shanghai and Guangdong. Connected with each province, a timely, effective monitoring system will be formed."[33] Hu Ge, China's most famous spoofer, remarked, "Individuals will still be able to make a 'flash.' It will just be more difficult to share it with others. But there are so many Chinese 'YouTubes' at the moment that I guess the authorities will find it difficult to manage."[34]

Addiction to the Internet (commonly referred to in the media as "Internet Heroin") by some youth in China is recognized by the Chinese government as a major public-health and even national security risk. Beijing's Military General Hospital created the country's first center to cure Internet addiction in 2004, years before the first Internet treatment center, reStart, opened in the United States. The Qihang Salvation Training Camp opened in Nanning in May 2009—now one of about four hundred camps—to cure youth of their addiction to the Internet.[35] The Chinese government claims that the Internet is linked to the majority of high school and college dropouts and most juvenile crimes. According to a 2010 study by the Chinese Academy of Social Sciences, almost 14 percent of the 236 million netizens in China who are under twenty-nine years old are addicted to the Internet, which means they spend more than ninety minutes a day online outside of work or school.

A recent announcement by the government indicates that there is much more than online content and addiction that it is currently trying to manage. On March 31, 2011, the State Administration of Radio, Film, and Television issued new guidelines for television programming in which it discouraged the airing or the production of shows featuring "fantasy, time-travel, random compilations of mythical stories, bizarre plots, absurd techniques, even propagating feudal superstitions, fatalism and reincarnation, ambiguous moral lessons, and a lack of positive thinking." This discouragement of the imaginary was a strongly worded, nationalist advisory that "TV dramas should not have characters that travel back in time and rewrite history" because it is contrary to China's cultural heritage.[36] A month later SARFT conveyed growing concern that Chinese citizens were watching too much entertainment programming. According to their findings, more than 10 percent of the population was devoted to such viewing, such as the spectacularly successful Jiangsu Satellite TV dating program *If You Are the One*, which has now spawned a number of matchmaking imitations (all very cheap to produce and very popular) on other channels.[37]

On January 1, 2012, following the Communist Party's Central Committee meeting in October 2011, government regulators issued a new policy to limit television broadcasts of "entertainment shows," including game shows, dating shows, and celebrity talk shows. This has resulted in a reduction of 126 to only 38 "entertainment shows" broadcast in China per night. Some of the most popular ones, such as *If You Are the One*, were subsequently suspended as part of the government's effort to control television content deemed as "excessive entertainment" and harmful to society. This is part of a larger effort on the part of the Chinese government to bolster China's so-called "cultural security" [38] by increasing the government's ideological control of the production and distribution of media content.

SEX: PERFORMANCES OF COMMODITIZATION

Adolescence is typically a time of sexual development and exploration. Due to socio-economic disparities in China, the way that sex and sexuality function within youth culture is often related to socio-economic factors. The youth in China's largest cities, such as Shanghai, Beijing, and Shenzhen, as well as second-tier cities like Chengdu and Hangzhou, for example, have never before had so many venues for dating, including restaurants, karaoke clubs, night clubs, bars, and pool halls. As incomes in China continue to rise, disposable cash for youth—and particularly money spent on dating and clubbing—has never been higher. Some of the world's largest and most spectacular clubs are now located in China, and world-famous musical artists such as Avril Lavigne and the Black Eyed Peas as well as DJs such as Paul Oakenfeld and Diplo regularly visit China. A visit to just about any disco in China displays the blurry reality of sex and youth in China today. One question becomes immediately apparent: How can one differentiate the women who are partying from those who are working, or from those who are both playing and working? The stark reality is that according to some estimates, 10 percent of women between the ages of eighteen and twenty-eight periodically work as sex workers.

Consumerism is an important part of youth culture. Advertising aimed at the youth, and especially advertising that capitalizes on the image of youth, is substantial, and youth consumer trends are often adapted to advertising campaigns targeting expanded demographics.[39]

Demographics for Internet users have dramatically expanded from younger to older users. QQ, China's most popular IM portal, like Facebook, was originally the domain of the youth, but now a large segment of the general population appears to be addicted to a number of QQ Internet-based games, such as "Struggling against the Landlord" (*dou dizhu*) and "50 K" (*wushi K*). Online shopping on China's largest online retailer, Taobao

Figure 2.1. **Young Shoppers Amble Past *Men's Health* Billboard, Beijing. Photograph by Tong Lam.**

(similar to eBay), also spread from the youth to older demographics, as did the popularity of reality talent competition TV programs, like Hunan TV's *Super Girl* and Jiangxi TV's *Red Song Competition* (*Hongge sai*), as well as popular Korean TV dramas, including *Miss Mermaid* (*Renyu xiaojie*) and *Wife's Temptation* (*Qizi de youhuo*).

One issue deserving exploration in this context of rampant consumerism is the relationship between consumption and the marketing of the self. What are the motivations for consumption by youth? For example, when one purchases a Louis Vuitton purse, how is one's self-value perceived? Louis Vuitton's largest market in the world is China, and its youth, especially young women, appear to be fixated on the signature "LV" as well as other luxury brands. Is the consumption of these bags solely on account of their quality, or is there a social value to "owning" and "showing" that one possesses an LV bag. One may also think in performative terms about this process of consumption and marketing the self: (1) consumption represents one's performance in society; (2) the object of consumption develops into a prop for one's performance. What we observe in China is not only a substantial trend toward consumption by youth, but also a transfer from the act of consumption to the marketing of the self—or transferring a value onto the self, and then, in a sense, soliciting buyers.

The commoditization of the self is most poignantly represented by the normalization of commercial sex among China's youth. This can be observed at different levels—college women who sign up as part-time mistresses to the nouveau riche, or simply the expectation that sexual relations inherently involve a financial transaction, usually paid by the man to the woman. One may observe a vicious cycle of sorts in which consumerism by youth drives the commoditization of the self, even in its extreme form, as a sexual transaction. The selling of one's youth, in sexual terms, can result in the expanded ability to participate in the performance of consumerism and the commoditization of one's youth. Despite Internet monitoring, it is still relatively simple to connect with a young woman (or man) who is a "part-timer" (meaning one who offers sex for money as a sideline occupation) on Tencent's QQ, China's largest IM platform.

YOUTH CULTURE AND NATIONALISM

This essay began with the concept that youth is a category that was defined historically in political terms and has been protected to some extent under this definition. The political classification of China's youth continues, but it is intersected by (rather than contained by) processes of consumerism and commoditization, especially as mediated by cyberculture. The political organization of China's youth was related to the survival and fate of the Chinese nation in the early twentieth century. Youth were mobilized by Mao Zedong during the Cultural Revolution as the main engine for political movement (i.e., turmoil)—carrying out the class struggle, implementing the smashing of the Four Olds (*sijiu*, "old culture, old customs, old habits, old ideas"), denouncing the bad elements, and other actions. And it should not be forgotten that it was the youth that led the calls for democracy in 1978 and, most famously, in 1989.

Today bold demands for political change are made by older intellectuals, like Liu Xiaobo, and even octogenarians but not the younger generation. What has happened to the voice of the youth in politics? When they are politically engaged—and this is not all that often—youth are involved in protests that express antiforeign sentiment. For example, they led the public charge against NATO's accidental bombing of the Chinese embassy in Belgrade in 1999 and fomented anti-Japan riots across China in 2005 because of Japanese textbooks that were accused of hiding the truth about Japanese atrocities against China during World War II.[40] The youth spearheaded anti-Japanese protests again in October 2010 over Japan's seizing of a Chinese fishing boat captain in the disputed waters near the unoccupied islands in the East China Sea known as the Senkaku Islands by Japan and Diaoyutai by China.

RELIGION AND INTERCULTURAL EDUCATION

In general Chinese youth are becoming more engaged with religion and with churches: both in the official churches and in house churches and everything in between. As one commentator put it in reflecting on the changes of the last forty years, "China's youth once trundled across the countryside spreading communism. Now, they're spreading God's word."[41] There may well be many reasons for this, but I can think of three. First, the country's rapid change is prompting youth to find good luck via religion (educated and less educated alike) as they profess belief that the divine may ensure good luck—the kind of fortune that might make their lives easier and their success more likely. Some believe that "making money is literally doing God's work." Second, active involvement in religious activity offers an alternative form of social networking that stands outside the CCP and outside corporations. And third, many individuals who are concerned about materialism or who are from well-off families are looking to religion for a spiritual fulfillment and meaning beyond bourgeois comforts.

Clearly the country belongs to the youth of China, so how they are educated and how they think about China's role in the world will be critical. Still, India is currently and will be for some time more youthful than China, and this will prove significant in the coming years. The younger generation in China is facing some challenges—unemployment, an increasing proportion of retirees that they need to support, and an uncertain economy that will need to transform itself in the decades to come. More and more youth are leaving China to attend high school or college—whereas a generation ago it was mainly to attend graduate schools—in the United States, the United Kingdom, Australia, and other countries as well. Because this is a relatively new trend, it remains to be seen how the overseas educational experiences will affect this group of youth. Will they be China's future leaders? With China and the United States as "the most important bilateral relationship in the world" according to President Barack Obama, these students will certainly have opportunities to affect the future of the bilateral relationship and the future of China and the world. One of the objectives of this essay is to help students from China and students from around the world who are studying China reflect upon and challenge the points it raises. And I hope that in this way I might encourage greater dialogue and understanding between the youth of China and youth in the United States and around the world.

NOTES

1. "China's Communist Youth League Has 73.496 Million Members," *China Daily*, May 4, 2007, http://www.chinadaily.com.cn/china/2007-05/04/content _865669.htm.

2. For a list of sites blocked in China (including this Wikipedia site), see http://en.wikipedia.org/wiki/List_of_websites_blocked_in_the_People%27s_Republic_of_China.

3. Raymond Li, "Green Dam Dying for Lack of Cash," *South China Morning Post*, July 14, 2010.

4. Institute of International Education, "International Students: Leading Places of Origin," http://www.iie.org/en/Research-and-Publications/Open-Doors/Data/International-Students/Leading-Places-of-Origin.

5. Today's options for college students in China and the opportunity constraints for the college educated was a subject of debate on the *Room for Debate* blog of the *New York Times*. See "What Is a College Degree Worth in China?" December 2, 2010, http://www.nytimes.com/roomfordebate/2010/12/02/what-is-a-college-degree-worth-in-china?ref=education&gwh=6711CC172BEC5D3184A5BF9B0B01E8E0.

6. "China Home to 211 Million Floating Population," *China Daily*, July 13, 2010, http://www.china.org.cn/travel/expo2010shanghai/2010-07/13/content_20483664.htm.

7. Leslie T. Chang, *Factory Girls: From Village to City in a Changing China* (New York: Spiegel & Grau, 2009), provides an excellent account of the lives of female factory workers in Dongguan.

8. The 2008 iPhone photo of the Foxconn worker known as "iPhone Girl" may be seen at http://www.wired.com/gadgetlab/2008/08/factory-iphone/. Foxconn, located in Shenzhen, is the largest private employer in China. According to Joel Johnson, it accounts for nearly 40 percent of the $150 billion in total revenue of the world's consumer electronics industry. Conditions at the Longhua plant came under scrutiny in 2010 following a spate of suicides by workers who jumped from the roof of the massive complex. In the last five years seventeen workers have killed themselves. See Joel Johnson, "1 Million Workers. 90 Million iPhones. 17 Suicides. Who's to Blame?" *Wired*, February 28, 2011, http://www.wired.com/magazine/2011/02/ff_joelinchina/.

9. The test was given by the Paris-based Organization for Economic Cooperation and Development to fifteen-year-old students in sixty-five countries in 2009. For a report, analysis, and the rankings, see Sam Dillon, "Top Test Scores from Shanghai Stun Educators," *New York Times*, December 7, 2010, http://www.nytimes.com/2010/12/07/education/07education.html.

10. "2010 Forbes China Celebrity List," *China Hush*, April 29, 2010, http://www.chinahush.com/2010/04/29/2010-forbes-china-celebrity-list/.

11. In 2006 the name of the program changed to *2006 Happy China Mengniu Yoghurt Supergirl Voice* (*2006 kuaile Zhongguo mengniu suanru chaoji nusheng*).

12. In fact, in 2005, during the broadcast of *Supergirl*, Hunan TV had the second highest number of viewers of any television station, following CCTV's dozen channels. An estimated 400 million viewers watched the finals in 2005.

13. During the finals, on August 26, 2005, the winner received 3.52 million votes by text message. The top three finalists received nearly 9 million votes in 2005 and over 10 million votes in 2006.

14. Jim Yardley, "An Unlikely Pop Icon Worries China," *International Herald Tribune*, September 5, 2005, http://www.nytimes.com/2005/09/04/world/asia/04iht-super.html.

15. Requoted in Raymond Zhou, "Secret behind Idol-Making Super Girl Contest," *China Daily*, August 27, 2005, http://www.chinadaily.com.cn/english/doc/2005-08/27/content_472681.htm.

16. Posted on the online message board Xici Hutong on August 26, 2005.

17. Zhou, "Secret behind Idol-Making Super Girl."

18. "More to Democracy Than a Reality Show," *South China Morning Post*, August 28, 2005.

19. See http://www.zonaeuropa.com/20050829_1.htm.

20. See http://www.zonaeuropa.com/20050829_1.htm.

21. See http://www.zonaeuropa.com/20050829_1.htm.

22. See http://www.zonaeuropa.com/20050829_1.htm.

23. See Joel Martinsen, "The Cult of a Super Girl," *Danwei*, May 31, 2009, http://www.danwei.org/trends_and_buzz/believe_in_li_yuchun.php.

24. Joel Martinsen, "Hoax Dictionary Entries about Legendary Obscene Beasts," *Danwei*, February 11, 2009, http://www.danwei.org/humor/baidu_baike_fake_entries.php.

25. It is important for the U.S. reader to realize that the availability of media content, particularly on the Internet, is governed by commercial interests and so is not unrestricted. As well, the Federal Communications Commission (FCC) monitors and regulates all broadcasting to make certain that it fits within the guidelines of appropriateness.

26. "China's mobile phone users exceed 900 million: MIIT." http://www.gov.cn/english/2011-05/24/content_1870362.htm (May 24, 2011).

27. "China Internet Market Brief—2010," http://www.internetworldstats.com/asia/cn.htm. According to the *China Daily*, on November 23, 210, China had 830 million mobile phone subscribers. Jingting Shen and Yannan Tuo, "Mobile Users Allowed to Ring Changes," *China Daily*, November 23, 2010.

28. Haizhou Zhang and Chunyan Zhang, "China Prepare to Defend Administration of Net," *China Daily*, November 23, 2010.

29. "Breaching the Great Firewall: Home-grown Microblogs Are Succeeding Where Twitter Failed," *Economist*, October 28, 2010.

30. Blogging in China started in 2002 with CNBlog.org, China's first online forum about blogging technology and culture, and BlogChina.com, which covers China's IT industry. The term *boke*, literally meaning "vast guests," was coined as the Chinese translation of "blog."

31. At the end of October 2004, China had more than forty-five large blog-hosting services. Decentralization of the blogs made them initially more difficult to monitor by censors. However, sites that host blogs and microblogs continue to be either blocked or censored in China.

32. One can view the video at http://www.youtube.com/watch?v=AQZAcT1xaKk.

33. http://www.danwei.org/danwei_noon_report/post_13.php.

34. Hu Ge quoted in Jane Macartney, "E Gao Ergo Parody," at: http://www.zonaeuropa.com/culture/c20060108_1.htm.

35. The camp was the source of controversy and concern when it was reported in August 2009 that one Internet addict, Deng Senshan, fifteen, died while in treatment there. It seems that he had been beaten to death in the course of a scolding for running too slowly. See Zhu Yanping and Lan Tian, "Parents of Teen Who Died at

Internet Camp Want Answers," *China Daily*, August 5, 2009, http://www.chinadaily .com.cn/cndy/2009-08/05/content_8521689.htm.

36. Kevin Voigt, "China Banning Time Travel for TV?" *CNN.com*, April 14, 2009, http://business.blogs.cnn.com/2011/04/14/china-bans-time-travel-for-television/.

37. Edward Wong, "China TV Grows Racy, and Gets a Chaperon," *New York Times*, December 31, 2011.

38. Edward Wong, "Pushing China's Limits on Web, if Not on Paper," *New York Times*, November 6, 2011.

39. See, for example, the blog *China Youthology* (*Qingnian zhi*) (http:// chinayouthology.com/blog/), "a research-based consultancy for marketing, communication, and product design targeting youth in the China market."

40. Josh Kurlantzick, "China's Next-Generation Nationalists," *Los Angeles Times*, May 6, 2008, http://www.carnegieendowment.org/publications/index .cfm?fa=view&id=20095.

41. See the five-part report by Louisa Lim, "In the Land of Mao, a Rising Tide of Christianity," *National Public Radio*, the first of which aired on July 19, 2010, http:// www.npr.org/templates/story/story.php?storyId=128546334.

3

Dismantling the Socialist Welfare State: The Rise of Civil Society in China

Jessica C. Teets

On October 1, 2009, the People's Republic of China celebrated its sixtieth anniversary, and in the United States most of the media coverage focused on China as a communist country under repressive single-party rule. However, while repression under the Chinese Communist Party (CCP) persists, it also is necessary to recognize that the transformation of China under communist authority, while not ushering in a new era of democracy, has brought about meaningful change in the social and political life of most citizens, who are increasingly willing and able to engage in the collective organization that is a hallmark of civil society.

Civil society is commonly defined as the aggregation of voluntary civic and social organizations, such as charities, nongovernmental organizations (NGOs), community groups, professional associations, trade unions, business associations, and advocacy groups. These groups are formed by concerned citizens and create a space for citizens to collectively participate in politics for many purposes—to protect the environment, to promote better regulations, and sometimes, as Alexis de Tocqueville (1805–1859) described in the eighteenth-century United States, to defend against the tyranny of the state.[1] In fact, many scholars have attributed the fall of authoritarian regimes to the ability of civil society to mobilize opposition to the state, such as the late Václav Havel's literary group in the former Czechoslovakia.[2] Based on these historical experiences in Europe and the United States, the development of a civil society in China might serve as a democratizing influence that the CCP seeks to repress.

However, the emergence of a civil society in China where these voluntary citizen groups increasingly participate in a limited way in public policy is often represented as a schizophrenic one in Western media, with headlines ranging from "AIDS Activist Leaves China for U.S., Citing Pressure" to "China's Activist Groups Grow, Even without Official Blessing." The first story details how AIDS activist Wan Yanhai fled China due to continuing government harassment, and the second explains the rapid growth of civil society in China despite difficulties in registering as a nonprofit organization versus a for-profit organization. While both of these stories focus on the difficulties of advocacy in China, the second one also illustrates the increasing growth of this sector. How do we reconcile these two contradictory stories of a civil society in China that is simultaneously vigorous and controlled?

I contend that both of the perspectives presented above can be reconciled by understanding the nature of decision making in China. Given the large size of the country and perhaps traditional caution of the party leadership, decision making in China has often proceeded slowly by using local innovation to drive national change. For example, the decision-making philosophy used for economic reform is called "crossing the river by groping for stepping stones" (*mozhe shitou guo he*), which implies that change occurs by moving slowly from one stage to another after recalibrating the strategy to adjust for negative effects. This approach is also being used with political reform, especially the development of civil society. The government allows for a great deal of informal civil society activity and local innovation, ranging from online charities such as One Kilogram More and nonprofit incubators like NPI. These groups proliferate and often partner with local governments without legal status, if the local government agency trusts that the intentions of the group are not to challenge the political authority of the government.

This trust may be earned over time or through personal connections. The central government then may select certain groups and innovations to encourage all local governments to adopt as models or, conversely, repress any groups or innovations that might challenge social stability. This is the fundamental goal in government decision making: encouraging the ability of civil society groups to solve social problems without sacrificing political control, often discussed as "social stability." Since the early 2000s, stability maintenance, known as *weiwen* in Chinese, has become a primary policy goal involving multiple government agencies and local cadres. In fact, over the past few years, thousands of stability maintenance offices have opened and more than three hundred thousand government officials have been enlisted in "community service management." In this chapter, I describe the development of civil society over the last two decades and examine its changing relationship with the government as it tries to balance these two, often competing, goals of political reform in China.

THE DEVELOPMENT OF CIVIL SOCIETY IN CHINA

Since 1990 an associational revolution has been occurring in China, with the number of civil society groups and participation rates dramatically increasing. Civil society regulations require approval from the government, as I explain in more detail below, and increasing registration might indicate a desire for social control; however, it also indicates the government's awareness that people are forming voluntary associations rapidly. The Ministry of Civil Affairs reports that registered social groups have increased from fewer than five thousand in 1988 to over four hundred thousand in 2009, with unregistered groups greatly exceeding this number. This explosion of civil society initiated a debate in the early 1990s over the independence of these groups from the state. This focus on autonomy from the state derives from one of the most influential scholars of civil society, Jürgen Habermas, who in 1989 through historical analysis of the emergence of civil society in Western Europe defined civil society as composed of autonomous, voluntary associations acting in the public sphere.[3] In the Western literature, scholars theorized a normative connection between an autonomous civil society and a healthy democracy.[4]

Many scholars researching emergent civil society in China criticized the applicability of Western civil society theory as inappropriate to Chinese culture and history, and those who chose to use this theory found that an autonomous civil society simply did not exist in China.[5] For example, X. L. Ding suggests that civil society groups are parasitic on the state, meaning they formally are attached to official institutions and have overlapping responsibilities and staff with government institutions.[6] However, this use of autonomy as a defining characteristic of civil society engenders the problem of how to understand autonomy from the state. Is this a dichotomous category or a continuum of state-society relationships? If there is a spectrum ranging from complete independence to complete repression, how much autonomy is necessary for the component groups—nonprofits, nongovernmental organizations, social clubs, and associations—to be considered a "civil society"?

The experience of civil society groups in China illustrates that autonomy from the state is not a dichotomous relationship. Different groups in Chinese civil society have varying relationships with the state, ranging from complete autonomy matching an ideal Western conception to complete cooption closer to a state corporatism model. As a prominent Chinese researcher argues,

Due to funding sources and relationship with the government two models of NGOs exist: one from above to below and one from below to above. The first one usually serves as a branch of the government, sharing its functions, people

and funding. However, recently these groups have had conflict between serving as the government's assistant and the interests of the social groups they
serve. The other type of NGO has more autonomy, but less money and less
access points (mostly informal) to government.[7]

This theoretical reliance on a dichotomous understanding of autonomy
does not reflect the reality of civil society in many countries. Even in
Western countries, civil society is less autonomous from the state than our
theories prescribe. For example, Lester Salamon finds that most Western
governments fund NGOs at high levels—Western European NGOs receive
56 percent of their funding from the state.[8] As Gordon White has argued,
"in brief, the extent to which a specific social organization embodies the
defining qualities of 'civil society'—autonomy, separation and voluntari-
ness—is a question of degree rather than either/or."[9] Therefore, autonomy
should be understood as a continuum of state-society relationships, with
some groups closer to the state than others at different times. Depending
on the goals of civil society groups—opposing the state, revolution, policy
advocacy, or service delivery—the relationship with the state might differ.
In order to understand varying state–civil society relationships that might
be shifting, contested, and periodically accommodating or oppositional,
the relationship between civil society and the state should be part of the
research question rather than the definition, allowing us to better analyze
the dynamic interaction between state and society.

Analyzing government regulations on group activity, with respect to formation and fund-raising, illustrates the changing nature of the relationship
between state and civil society. As discussed above, the number and types
of Chinese civil society groups have dramatically increased since the mid-
1990s, consisting of social organizations, business and industry associations, charities, foundations, and nonprofits. In addition to the growth in
the number of domestic groups, Chinese branches of international nongovernmental organizations (INGOs) proliferated during this time period. For
example, the Nature Conservancy opened three offices in western China
and Beijing, in addition to multiple project offices, and Green Peace also
opened offices in Hong Kong, Yunnan, and Beijing. All types of civil society
groups are registered by the Ministry of Civil Affairs through a three-step
process known as the "dual management system" (*shuangchong guanli tizhi*):
groups register with the local Civil Affairs bureau, secure a government
agency as a sponsor, and undergo an annual review.

While many groups choose not to register and either act informally
or register as a for-profit enterprise, the ones that do register must place
themselves under the "professional management" of a state organ with
responsibilities in its area of work, in addition to being registered and
reviewed annually by Civil Affairs departments. The professional management agency holds a wide range of responsibilities, including supervising

the organizations' "ideological work," financial and personnel management, research activities, contacts with foreign organizations, and reception and use of donations from overseas, which is the primary funding source for larger groups. This system is so expensive and difficult for most groups to navigate that many simply register as a for-profit organization and pay taxes, or operate informally without any legal status. This is in contrast to the relatively straightforward process of registering as a nonprofit organization in the United States, where groups simply incorporate so as to be a legal entity and apply to the Internal Revenue Service for tax-exempt status.

This system results in great variation in the legal statuses of these associations; many register as social organizations with the Ministry of Civil Affairs, but also many are unofficially associated with a university or operate informally. Jude Howell contends that since the early 1990s, if the group appears to have political goals the state will repress the group, but if the group appears beneficial local officials especially will cast a blind eye toward registration.[10] In response to registration difficulties and subsequent large numbers of unregistered groups operating informally, since 2009 several local governments such as Beijing, Shanghai, and Shenzhen have been experimenting with reforming the registration process to only require that groups register with the local Civil Affairs Bureau and undergo an annual evaluation by the bureau.

Government regulation on fund-raising is also strict, with domestic fund-raising allowed only to government-organized charities like the China Red Cross Society and, since late 2010, to registered public foundations like the film and martial arts celebrity Jet Li's One Foundation. These restrictions mean that most organizations still have low capacity in domestic funding, staffing, and geographic reach. Currently, large groups and branch offices of INGOs receive the majority of funding in the form of international grants and transfers. Although INGOs and international foundations increasingly fund Chinese groups to help develop greater capacity, smaller grassroots groups complain that only larger groups that cover certain "hot" issues or branches of INGOs secure this type of funding.[11] Despite primarily funding larger groups, the impact of past international funding on the capacity and development of groups in China cannot be overstated. For example, the Ford Foundation initiated a capacity-building project in Yunnan in the mid-1980s that sent a number of volunteers to training sessions both inside and outside of China. When these volunteers returned, the majority established groups and received funding and additional capacity-building training from the Ford Foundation.[12] These organizations and the newer groups in which they helped build capacity compose the civil society community in Yunnan. However, INGOs face the same difficulties as smaller grassroots groups with registration, and the *Notice of the State Administration of Foreign Exchange* (SAFE) has since March 2010 required that groups receiving foreign funding clear additional administrative hurdles, making receiving these funds more difficult, but not impossible.[13]

Mass organizations, such as the Labor Federation, and other government-organized groups are most likely to secure funding from the government, although grassroots groups sometimes secure limited funding from their supervising units.[14] However, since the mid-1990s, even mass organizations such as the Women's Federation must seek increased member funding due to declining state funding.[15] Another source of funding is domestic fund-raising and member dues; but except for a few registered charities, groups cannot legally fund-raise inside of China. The restrictions on domestic fund-raising are due to many different reasons—concerns about suspicious groups like terrorist groups in Xinjiang receiving international funding, concerns about corruption and money laundering, and concerns about international democracy-promotion groups funding antistate organizations. Many groups raise funds illegally inside China, but such organizations only raise small amounts of money due to the need for low exposure of the fund-raising events or activities.[16] While membership dues increasingly constitute a larger portion of overall group funding, small memberships mean that this source alone cannot support most groups.

Although the statistics regarding civil society in China illustrate the rapid growth of these organizations in sheer numbers, participation, and diversity of issue area, it is also clear that these groups face significant challenges with capacity issues in that most groups are small, service-delivery-oriented organizations without secure legal status and restricted ability to fund-raise. In the next section, I address how the dismantling of the socialist economy resulted in the downsizing of the government's role in society and shifted the burden of public-goods provision to the local state, which created space for civil society to partner with local officials to solve social problems. While this analysis does not question the still powerful status of both central and local state in China, these reforms both intentionally and unintentionally have created legitimate space for civil society organizations as long as groups do not challenge party authority through social instability.

POLITICAL REFORM IN CHINA:
BALANCING DEVELOPMENT WITH SOCIAL STABILITY

As the economy grew rapidly in the late 1980s after the initiation of economic reform, the lack of effective channels for relaying the concerns and views of new socio-economic groups to the state meant that the government became increasingly out of touch with the changing needs of society and unable to negotiate and balance an increasingly diverse range of interests.[17] These challenges initiated a new approach to governance, one focused on creating a strong "regulatory state" (*youxian zhengfu*). This new model of governance introduced the idea of intermediary social organizations assisting the government with social welfare and the concept of an arms-length regulatory relationship with the state supervising society and market rather than directly controlling social activity and production. In response throughout the 1980s and 1990s the party leadership pursued both village elections and institutional reforms with the objective of "improving governance" (*shanzheng*) by creating a limited, regulatory state that departed radically from the Chinese state under Mao's leadership. Under Mao, the state provided cradle-to-grave social welfare and directed both society and the economy in all affairs. One of the most significant reforms under Deng Xiaoping's leadership was the "small state, big society" reforms in the late 1980s (*xiao zhengfu, da shehui*), which envisioned a substantial downsizing of the party-state apparatus accompanied by the rise of an autonomous sphere of associational life at the local level. Dali Yang argues that as the government began to focus its energies on a smaller number of major functions, especially the provision of public goods and infrastructure, more room for nongovernmental organizations was created, ranging from neighborhood committees to industrial associations and professional organizations.[18]

Thus far, most of the institutional reforms have emphasized a downsizing of the government's role in society, especially in the context of dismantling the former socialist system, which has had far-reaching consequences. One consequence of pursuing this regulatory state model is that the Chinese elite now appear to take it for granted that the power of government must be delimited, frequently referring to "administration in accordance with law" (*yifa xingzheng*) as shorthand for putting limits on what the government can do.[19] However, what this limited state is responsible for in practice is still contested between the central and local governments and between the local state and society. This process of transition to a new model of state governance is unresolved, ongoing, and full of tension.

Taken together, these reforms fundamentally alter the concept of governance to one of a more limited government allowing legitimate space for civil society activity. As I explain below, these reforms both intentionally and unintentionally encourage partnership between the local state and civil society groups. Although some civil society leaders prefer either a completely independent or even oppositional relationship with the state, and some local officials prefer either the nonexistence or complete subordination of civil society groups, the majority of local officials and group leaders have selected a relationship that falls between these absolute positions. For many local officials, partnering with civil society helps meet performance goals, thereby leading to promotion or bonuses, while the majority of groups seek to partner with local officials to gain access to a closed and nontransparent policy-making process.

The reforms initiated to dismantle the socialist system decentralized responsibility for public-goods provision to local government without providing enough revenue transfer to cover these additional duties, generating a gap between funding and responsibilities commonly known as "unfunded mandates." As seen in policy debates in the United States over public-goods provisions like No Child Left Behind legislation, creating unfunded mandates forces local governments to innovate in either generating more income or seeking private assistance to provide these goods. Transferring primary responsibility for the provision of public goods, such as education, health care, infrastructure, and social security programs like unemployment insurance, to local governments set goals difficult for local officials to meet, such as providing pensions for millions of workers laid off from former state-owned enterprises (SOEs).

In fact, with the demands on provincial and subprovincial governments increasing while fiscal transfers from the central government remain low, most provinces operate a budget deficit to fund an overwhelming number of social programs.[20] Local governments do not possess much fiscal autonomy to meet these responsibilities because the central government restricts the ability to tax local populations and to secure bonds or loans. However, local governments often borrow or tax illegally to generate extra-budgetary revenue.

These unfunded mandates also affect individual officials' careers through an evaluation system emphasizing economic development and social order.[21] In the 1980s the central government began a series of civil service reforms to replace the loyalty-based cadre system with one based on performance. After a number of revisions, the current civil service system uses a Target Management Responsibility System, which ranks performance-based targets. Leading cadres ranked as "excellent" receive bonuses, pay raises, medals, honorary titles, and merit records.[22] While promotion is not considered a reward under this system, officials who receive "excellent" evaluations for two or more years in a row are often promoted: "In short, today almost all Chinese local officials have been structured into a highly personalized, individualized incentive scheme."[23] Competition for promotion generates a number of adaptive strategies by local officials, common among them being partnering with civil society groups to either bridge the resource gap faced by many local governments or develop an innovative governance model, which can increase the likelihood that an official is recognized (and rewarded) by the central government within the large pool of eligible officials.

Civil society organizations help local officials meet economic and social promotion goals through running pilot programs to deliver public goods, generating research and policies for the use of local officials, and acquiring international funding and resources to use for government projects. In contradistinction to assisting local officials in meeting development goals, civil society groups can punish uncooperative officials through publicizing the behavior of cadres via public opinion mobilization or complaints to higher levels of government.[24] For example, in 2006 a group of laid-off workers organized by a retired cadre active in labor issues conducted a protest outside the government offices in Yunnan province while higher-level officials were visiting to publicize economic discontent, ultimately resulting in satisfying the workers' requests.[25] As one Yunnan official who witnessed these protests stated, "cadres' reputations are very important because reputation leads to the peoples' trust which leads to cooperation. Cooperation helps a cadre meet their goals."[26] Thus, local government officials depend on a good reputation in society to ensure voluntary compliance with rules, and a subsequent good performance record with supervisors to secure promotions.

In addition to the ability of groups to bridge the resource gap to help local officials meet promotion goals, civil society also helps develop innovative solutions to governance challenges such as the structural or endemic poverty afflicting both Yunnan and Sichuan provinces. Successful innovation often catches the attention of central government officials and party leaders, leading to rapid promotion, such as former Premier Zhao Ziyang's (1919–2005) pioneering of the Household Responsibility system in the late 1970s and early 1980s before being promoted to General Party Secretary. This policy-making methodology in China depends on decentralized policy experiments driven by local initiative with the formal or informal backing of higher-level policy makers. If judged to be an effective solution to targeted governance problems, these "model experiences" are extracted from the initial experiments by the central government and disseminated through extensive media coverage, high-profile conferences, visitation programs, and appeals for emulation to more regions and eventually integrated into national policies.[27] This process of policy making allows local officials to develop models, which if successfully diffused into national policy, elevates their status and aids in promotion.

During interviews I conducted, many local officials mentioned this technique to me as a reason to partner with civil society groups; not only do groups offer best practices in poverty alleviation, community participation, and environmental conservation, they also offer financial and technical resources to help implement these ideas.[28] In this way, the link generated by the policy-making process in China between decentralized experimentation and promotion encourages local government officials to partner with civil society groups in search of new models to address governance problems. As one cadre from the Health Bureau explained, the reason the local government seeks to partner with groups is because they can provide it with community networks, technology, and specialized knowledge (training, new models), and also can run pilots for the government to test new policy ideas.[29] In light of this strategy, many provincial governments create "innovation awards" to encourage policy innovation at lower levels that can then be tested and disseminated by provincial leaders. For example, in Beijing the head of one district formed a partnership with a grassroots group, Shining Stone Community Action, to develop a new model for integrating migrant families into new urban communities, which enabled him to win the "innovation in governance" award along with a cash reward and recognition from the mayor.[30]

Although civil society groups are increasingly assisting local government in solving development issues, this must be balanced with the other main goal of the Target Management Responsibility System—social order. Concerns with social stability, or perceived antistate activities, permeate the party leadership and all levels of government. Most officials describe this concern as a historical one originating from the chaos of foreign invasions in the late 1800s, the end of the dynastic system in the early 1900s, and the civil war overlaid with World War II in the 1940s. These were the historical defining moments forming the Communist Party and the People's Republic of China, and they engendered a profound desire for social order among the party leadership as well as many ordinary citizens. An official policy of stability maintenance (*weiwen*) developed in the late 1990s as China struggled with mass layoffs caused by the privatization of state-owned enterprises and accelerated in 2004 when the color revolutions deposed authoritarian leaders in the former Soviet republics. This policy became more important as the CCP reacted to a series of challenges, including rioting in Tibet before the 2008 Olympics and Xinjiang in 2009, and the Charter 08 petition calling for more democracy that led to the jailing of the drafting author, Liu Xiaobo, the 2010 Nobel Peace Prize winner.

Social stability or maintenance is the paramount goal of the party leadership and is broadly defined as preventing social unrest that might threaten economic development and the party's political hegemony. Statistics illustrate growing "mass incidents" of demonstrations, protests, and riots throughout the 2000s—totaling 87,000 in 2006, an increase of 6.6 percent from 2005. Since 2008 officials evidence rising concern about protests in the minority areas of both Tibet and Xinjiang in western China, as well as the possibility that rising income gaps and unemployment among the rural population and recent college graduates might trigger increasing unrest. This concern is also reflected in the discontinuation of the annual official reports on the numbers and kinds of mass incidents. The ability of civil society organizations to mobilize citizen action against the state is well understood in China in the wake of the color revolutions in the post-Soviet republics, where citizen protests forced democratization in Serbia in 2000, followed by the Ukraine, Kyrgyzstan, and Georgia. In China civil unrest in Shanghai in 2008 halted construction of the Maglev transit project and forced a chemical plant in Xiamen to close a new factory.

Local officials thus attempt to balance the benefits of partnership with concerns about social mobilization and instability. For example, even though the British INGO Oxfam has successfully worked with many local governments to undertake poverty alleviation programs, when it attempted to link college student volunteers with urban migrant workers, the Ministry of Education instructed all universities to stop collaborating with Oxfam. These are viewed as two sensitive populations given high unemployment rates, and the central government is concerned about joint mobilization, similar to concerns of the linkage of college students with urban workers during the Tiananmen protests in 1989. This example illustrates the balance that local governments strive to achieve between meeting development goals and maintaining social order, as required by the central government and party leaders. Oxfam in this instance was allowed to continue operating its poverty alleviation programs but was "encouraged" to stop its college volunteer program with migrant workers. The case demonstrates that, unlike many predictions that such groups would not be able to proliferate, civil society groups are expanding in size, scope, and significance; however, government control over these groups is increasingly nuanced. Although not completely shut down despite engaging in work the party leaders viewed as sensitive, indirect controls are used to push groups like Oxfam onto a more service-oriented path and away from anything potentially disruptive of social order. Analyzing the myriad pressures on local government allows us to understand how these seemingly disparate and incoherent decisions fit together into one decision-making frame. These challenges in providing social welfare motivate greater local government cooperation with civil society groups that can access international funding and innovative models to address these problems, a critical new development illustrated in a case study of Sichuan province based on interviews I conducted in 2008.

POVERTY ALLEVIATION IN SICHUAN: LOCAL STATE–CIVIL SOCIETY COLLABORATION

Sichuan is a geographically large and diverse province, covering an area roughly the same size as France and, before the city of Chongqing and its surrounding area was put under separate administrative status in 1997, China's most populous province (see figure 3.1). Over 90 percent of the province is classified as hilly or mountainous and thus has some of the highest rates of poverty in the country with a per capita GDP of 4,012 *renminbi* ($618 U.S.) in 1997—ranking twenty-second among thirty provinces in China. By 2000 Sichuan possessed 7 percent of the total 592 "poverty counties" designated as the poorest counties in China, which ranks it as the third poorest province. In addition to this endemic poverty, dismantling the central welfare state and decentralizing the provision of public goods pushed the responsibility for providing social welfare to this large, poor province to the local government. In response to the presence of these poor mountainous areas, many types of groups operate in Chengdu, the provincial capital of Sichuan province, most prevalently poverty-alleviation and environmental groups. As part of the local government apparatus, the Provincial Poverty Alleviation Bureau (PAB) conducts government-run pov-

Figure 3.1.   Sichuan Province—Active Site of Poverty Alleviation and Environmental Reform.

erty alleviation programs. Although the bureau did not have a reputation for seeking collaboration with outside parties, the problem of poverty in Sichuan soon overwhelmed local resources, leading to collaboration between the PAB and poverty-alleviation groups.

In the mid-1980s, a Chinese branch of a United States INGO established offices in China to address problems of poverty and sustainable development in rural areas. This group set up an office in Beijing to deal with policy advocacy and established project offices in the rural western provinces like Tibet and Sichuan to conduct poverty-alleviation projects. In the mid-1990s, the project office in Chengdu secured World Bank funding to initiate a pilot program for poverty alleviation based on a model of community participation. After securing international funding for this pilot program, the INGO branch leader, who formerly worked at a different local government agency, used his connections to have his former government colleagues introduce him to the relevant officials at the PAB. Next the group leader met with officials from PAB and offered to assist officials by sharing the group's unique skill set, which he described as conflict-resolution skills, participation models, technology, and funding, to reduce poverty in the mountainous regions. The PAB officials agreed to partner with the INGO to pilot this community-participation model advocated by INGOs and donor agencies as international best practice in poverty alleviation. The first pilot project was small in scale and only overseen by provincial officials so that if it was seen to be ineffective or socially disruptive, local officials could quickly and quietly shut down the pilot.

As the first step of this community-participation model, the group used staff from its Chengdu office and U.S. headquarters to conduct training sessions with community leaders and PAB officials on how to discover structural causes of poverty that might differ from community to community. Next the PAB met with these local leaders to discuss root causes of poverty in each community in sessions mediated by the INGO, and then incorporated that feedback into a poverty-alleviation plan rather than imposing a single PAB-developed plan on each community. The poverty-alleviation plan was then financed and managed by the provincial and subprovincial PAB offices, but it was executed by the local community leaders originally involved in the planning process. Due to the success of the original pilot in meeting poverty-alleviation goals established by the central government, PAB officials expanded this program to four additional counties in Sichuan.[31]

An official I interviewed from the PAB stated that, while originally skeptical of this bottom-up approach, he believes this model to be very effective, although the ability of community leaders to participate at high levels is still somewhat constrained.[32] Even though the process of influencing national-level policy is a long one—a "ten-year process"—beginning with a pilot site, then study tours for higher-level officials, and finally the policy "bubbles up" to the national level, he contends that it is the most effective way to change policy in China.[33] As discussed above, this system of decentralized innovation spurred the process of economic reform beginning in the late 1970s and continues to motivate governance innovation among local officials.

In response to this policy-making process, civil society groups in China increasingly seek to collaborate with local government to solve specific development problems. This model of first changing local government policy and then diffusing upward to the national level is called an "action-research" strategy, which consists of three stages.[34] First, the group asks either pilot-project partners from lower levels of government or personal connections in other branches of government to advocate for this policy to higher-level officials on behalf of the group. Second, the group leader invites targeted higher-level government officials to an onsite workshop to convince them of the benefits of this policy. Third, the group must demonstrate an external resource commitment if policy is adopted or expanded, usually in the form of a grant from a foreign foundation or an INGO headquarters. This strategy depends on a good demonstration site (i.e., large scale and with a long operation time), supporting research illustrating policy benefits, an understanding of government needs and policy processes, and the presence of trust between the government officials and group leader. Although this understanding and trust may be purchased by hiring a retired government official to serve as the government-management liaison, groups without government access may still develop this type of relationship with the local government through partnerships over time. However, this model obviously is most appropriate for larger groups with higher capacity and access to international funding.

The group goals for this strategy are twofold: first, policy diffusion or "bubble up" to higher levels of government; and second, securing access to a policy-making process normally closed to participation from parties outside the government. This group was successful in using a partnership with the local state to change the PAB's policy for creating poverty-alleviation plans from a top-down, one-size-fits-all process to a community-participation model that encourages indigenous knowledge and citizen participation. This successful case demonstrates the utility of this local state–civil society cooperation model for both civil society groups and local officials desiring additional funding and models to address stubborn development problems. In this area there is space for civil society groups to conduct service-delivery projects and, in an indirect way, influence policy. However, groups challenging party authority by venturing into political topics like human rights, or mobilizing angry citizens like the parents of the schoolchildren killed in the Sichuan earthquake, would not be allowed to continue these activities.

In fact, a few years earlier, this same INGO managed several similar projects in Tibet but, after harassing office visits and demands for documentation from local officials concerned that the group was trying to mobilize angry Tibetans against the regime, finally left the province to work in neighboring provinces of Yunnan and Sichuan that were considered less politically sensitive. Although many civil society groups work in Tibet, the balance of development and social stability for local government is perpetually tilted in favor of social stability, creating a much smaller space in which to act.

CONCLUSION: IMPROVING
GOVERNANCE WITHOUT DEMOCRATIZATION

In the beginning of this chapter I asked how we reconcile the two contradictory views of civil society in China—one that is simultaneously vigorous *and* controlled—and argued that a better understanding of local government's goals can help explain these contradictory outcomes. Since the 1990s, political reforms such as "small state, big society" and the decentralization of social-service delivery to ill-funded local governments have created space for the development of civil society groups in China. Simultaneously, improved access to international funding and innovative strategies to share with local governments increased the capacity and influence of these groups, which currently remain dependent on international donors. In this environment, civil society groups actively partner with local officials to gain indirect access to the policy process.

Although the local state is increasingly collaborating with service-delivery groups, most civil society groups still have low capacity and work in a contested and dynamic regulatory space. However, given the policy-advocacy and service-delivery roles these groups are beginning to play in China, civil society groups should not be considered insignificant simply because they do not conform to categories and definitions generated through the democratization literature and Western historical theories. Political participation in closed, nontransparent environments relies on access to, not autonomy from, decision makers. Therefore, a deeper understanding of the interaction between civil society strategies and local government decision making is necessary to fully analyze the impact of these groups on governance and any potential future democratization process beginning at the local level.

I contend that civil society collaboration with local government improves governance through increasing transparency, citizen participation, and public-goods provision; however, this collaboration cannot be accurately described as a process of democratization. As China transitions from a socialist state-centric governance model to a regulatory one with private firms active in the market and civil society groups in society, the civil society sector is changing rapidly. Even though these groups are still operating in an authoritarian country with little legal protection and thus subject to arbitrary closure or fines, these groups are proliferating and increasing participation in policy making. In fact, as two experts recently found, 2010 was the "year of grassroots organizing," and this changing civil society sector has lasting implications for governance in China.[35] These groups increase citizen participation in the policy process, deliver needed public goods and services, and are fundamentally helping to shift the governance model in China.

However, this is *not* a process of democratization. And even though many of the tools of social control have become more indirect and nuanced since Mao's rule, the space within which these groups are permitted to act is still delimited by the government in strict and controlled ways. While the freedom to organize and act publicly is still controlled, increasing group activity in the policy process—both policy formation and implementation—is liberalizing this process and legitimizing citizen participation at least through groups in policy making. While civil society development in China does not correspond to democratization, it does change the role both of citizens and state officials in policy making. Analyzing civil society development during this process of transition in China shows us that the relationship between civil society and political change, especially democratization, is more complicated than many thought. As explained in this chapter, local government's dual, and often conflicting, role of promoting economic development while maintaining social stability generates the simultaneous cooperation with and control of civil society represented in divergent news headlines about civil society in China.

SUGGESTIONS FOR FURTHER READING

Gold, Thomas. "The Resurgence of Civil Society in China." *Journal of Democracy* 1, no. 1 (2008): 18–31.
Ho, Peter. "Greening without Conflict? Environmentalism, NGOs and Civil Society in China." *Development and Change* 32, no. 5 (2001): 893–921.
Tanner, Murray Scot. "China Rethinks Unrest." *Washington Quarterly* 27 (Summer 2004): 137–156.

NOTES

1. Alexis de Tocqueville, *Democracy in America* (1835), ed. J. P. Mayer, trans. George Lawrence (New York: Harper & Row, 1969).

2. Vladimir Tismaneanu, *Reinventing Politics: Eastern Europe from Stalin to Havel* (New York: Free Press, 1992).

3. Jürgen Habermas, *The Structural Transformation of the Public Sphere: An Inquiry into a Category of Bourgeois Society*, trans. Thomas Burger (Cambridge, MA: MIT Press, 1989), 54.

4. Robert Putnam, *Making Democracy Work* (Princeton, NJ: Princeton University Press, 1993).

5. Philip Huang, "'Public Sphere'/'Civil Society' in China? The Third Realm Between State and Society," *Modern China* 19 (April 1993): 216–40; Francis Fukuyama, "Social Capital and the Global Economy: A Redrawn Map of the World," *Foreign Affairs*, September/October 1995; Heath Chamberlain, "Civil Society with Chinese Characteristics?" *China Journal* 39 (1998): 69–81.

6. X. L. Ding, "Institutional Amphibiousness and the Transition from Communism: The Case of China," *British Journal of Political Science* 24 (July 1994): 293–318.

7. Wang Ming, "China's NGO and Civil Society Development," *Caijing (Finance and Economy Magazine)* (2002): 350–52.

8. Lester M. Salamon, S. Wojciech Sokolowski, and Associates, *Global Civil Society: Dimensions of the Nonprofit Sector*, vol. 2 (Bloomfield, CT: Kumarian Press, 2004); Shaoguang Wang, "Money and Autonomy: Patterns of Civil Society Finance and Their Implications," *Studies in Comparative International Development* 40 (Winter 2006): 3–29.

9. Gordon White, Jude Howell, and Xiaoyuan Shang, *In Search of Civil Society* (Oxford: Clarendon Press, 1996), 6.

10. Jude Howell, "New Directions in Civil Society: Organizing around Marginalized Interests," in *Governance in China*, ed. Jude Howell (Lanham, MD: Rowman & Littlefield, 2004), 151.

11. Author interview with member of indigenous knowledge nonprofit organization (NPO), Lijiang, Yunnan, April 5, 2007.

12. Author interview with staff member of environmental INGO, Kunming, Yunnan, May 10, 2007.

13. Karla Simon, "Recent Developments in Chinese Law Affecting CSOs/NGOs," in *Reinvigorating Civil Society in China: A Socio-Legal Analysis* (Oxford: Oxford University Press, 2011).

14. Author interview with member of indigenous knowledge NPO, Lijiang, Yunnan, April 5, 2007.

15. Author interview with Women's Federation members, Simao, Yunnan, March 9, 2007.

16. Author interview with foreign volunteer for health-related NPO, Kunming, Yunnan, June 6, 2007.

17. Jude Howell, "Getting to the Roots: Governance Pathologies and Future Prospects," in *Governance in China*, ed. Jude Howell (Lanham, MD: Rowman & Littlefield, 2004), 231.

18. Dali Yang, *Remaking the Chinese Leviathan* (Stanford, CA: Stanford University Press, 2004), 57.

19. Dali Yang, "State Capacity on the Rebound," *Journal of Democracy* 14, no. 1 (January 2003): 43–50.

20. Christine Wong, "Budget Reform in China," *OECD Journal on Budgeting* (2007): 33–56.

21. Susan Whiting, *Power and Wealth in Rural China: The Political Economy of Institutional Change* (Cambridge: Cambridge University Press, 2001).

22. Maria Edin, "State Capacity and Local Agent Control in China: CCP Cadre Management from a Township Perspective," *China Quarterly* 173 (2003): 35–52.

23. Han Tian, ed., *Lingdao ganbu kaocha kaohe shiyong quanshu* (Practical Comprehensive Handbook of Reviewing and Evaluating Leading Cadres) (Beijing: China Personnel Press, 1999), 131, as cited in Shu-Yun Ma and Wai-Yin Chan, "The Provision of Public Goods by a Local Entrepreneurial State: The Case of Preservation of the Nanyue Relics in China," *Journal of Development Studies* 40, no. 1 (2003): 119–41.

24. Kevin O'Brien and Lianjiang Li, *Rightful Resistance in Rural China* (Cambridge: Cambridge University Press, 2006).

25. Series of five author interviews with government cadre in Simao, Yunnan, February 16, 2007.

26. Series of five author interviews with government cadre in Simao, Yunnan, February 16, 2007.

27. Sebastian Heilmann, "From Local Experiments to National Policy: The Origins of China's Distinctive Policy Process," *China Journal* 59 (January 2008): 1–30.

28. Author interview with local official, Chengdu, Sichuan, July 10, 2008.

29. Author interview with Health Bureau cadre, Kunming, Yunnan, June 6, 2007.

30. Author interview with staff member of community-participation NPO, Beijing, June 1, 2008.

31. Author interview with local official, Chengdu, Sichuan, July 10, 2008.

32. Author interview with local official, Chengdu, Sichuan, July 10, 2008.

33. Author interview with local official, Chengdu, Sichuan, July 10, 2008.

34. Author interview with staff member of an environmental INGO, Chengdu, Sichuan, July 3, 2008.

35. Shawn Shieh and Guosheng Deng, "An Emerging Civil Society: The Impact of the 2008 Sichuan Earthquake on Grass-Roots Associations in China," *China Journal* 65 (January 2011): 181–94.

4

Mutually Assured Destruction or Dependence? U.S. and Chinese Perspectives on China's Military Development

Andrew S. Erickson

> One can imagine a future in which China contemplates limited first strikes against an adversary's population centers or strategic forces. In such a violent world, we may dream of the days when China was only MAD [only pursued mutually assured destruction].
>
> —James Mulvenon, Center for Intelligence Research and Analysis

> The sustainable development of [the] two powers enables both to benefit from non-rival policies and that is why Sino-U.S. relations should be based on mutually assured dependence.
>
> —Xu Hui, China National Defense University

The National Intelligence Council is the U.S. intelligence community's center for midterm and long-term strategic projections, producing Global Briefings every four years between election and inauguration day. The most recent of these highlights China's rise as a great power with increasing influence on the global system. It indicates that while the United States retains its overall positioning in the world, it has lost leverage in relative terms:

> China is poised to have more impact on the world over the next 20 years than any other country. If current trends persist, by 2025 China will have the world's second largest economy [including the EU] and will be a leading military power. It also could be the largest importer of natural resources and the biggest polluter. Although the United States is likely to remain the single most powerful actor, the United States' relative strength—even in the military realm—will decline and US leverage will become more constrained.[1]

This analysis raises several key policy questions: What will U.S. policy be? What will China's be? What challenges and concerns will influence their evolving military relationship in the security realm? Will "mutually assured dependence" prevail over "mutually assured destruction"? These questions animate the chapter that follows, one that explores the mutual fears and concerns of the United States and China over each other's military objectives and capabilities as well as the prospects for their mitigation and even abatement.

FOREGROUNDING THE ANALYSIS

Adapting to an increasingly powerful China will be neither instantaneous nor easy. The United States and China will face particular challenges in their relations and positions in the world that, if not managed carefully, could cause considerable tensions. China's recent development suggests that its so-called Century of Humiliation (the period from roughly 1840 to 1945 when China was subject to crushing predation and subjugation by outside powers) was an aberration. Now it is returning to what it believes is its rightful place as a great power in the international system. But herein lies a challenge: this exceptional period of weakness in Chinese history corresponds with the duration of the United States' meteoric rise on the world stage. Never before has the world witnessed the simultaneous presence of a powerful United States and a powerful China, let alone their interaction. Nearly as exceptional is the phenomenon of two great powers in the international system with two very different cultures, political systems, geographic regions, and sets of national interests poised to avoid a great power war. It is time to reconsider the utility and effectiveness of the age-old scarcity narrative of the rise and fall of nations.

Although China is unlikely to eclipse the United States in overall power and influence in the near or distant future, the best example of the successful incorporation of a major rising power into the international system—the United States itself—may offer needed perspective on any analysis of China's "peaceful rise." The earlier history of the United States' emergence as a world power has been described as relatively "peaceful," largely because of the U.S. resemblance to Great Britain, which had itself been the preceding "greatest power." Even with such ties, these Euro-Atlantic powers fought two wars, one in which the future United States declared independence, and a second (the War of 1812) that included substantial naval combat, occupation of each other's territory, and the burning of Washington. The United States subsequently declared the Monroe Doctrine ("hands off the Americas"), and the Royal Navy enforced it, because both nations had a vital national interest in keeping other European powers from establishing footholds in the Western Hemisphere.

Moreover, while the United States was successful in avoiding great power conflict in the nineteenth century, its growth was hardly peaceful—as the indigenous peoples of the continent, the Mexicans, and the Spanish will attest. For that matter, the growth of the United States as a nation also included a civil war that killed 2 percent of its population. Lastly, the process by which the United States replaced Great Britain as the global hegemon was hardly peaceful: two world wars, in which Washington and London fought on the same side, were a significant part of that power transition. And whereas Great Britain was a small island nation with an unwieldy empire whose extraordinary global influence proved unsustainable, U.S. national power appears far more broad-based and durable—thereby obviating the possibility that Washington will assuage Beijing's concerns by relinquishing its preeminent status.

That status, however, hinges in part on a globe-girdling military presence that Britain never achieved, involving U.S. bases, staging areas, or troops on all continents save Antarctica. This extraordinary span of presence and power, particularly in areas surrounding China, worries Beijing, which is developing its own countervailing capabilities and wields increasing long-range presence and influence of its own. At the same time, the United States and China have shared interests and areas of interdependence. They have been engaging sporadically in military exchanges and joint meetings of commanders and officers, although this has been limited severely by differing notions of transparency and reciprocity. Against this backdrop, the United States and China will hope for the best, but continue to prepare for the worst.

This is the larger context of developing U.S.-China relations in the initial decades of the twenty-first century. Most fundamentally, the United States fears that China seeks to, and is increasingly capable of, undermining the U.S. preeminent position in world affairs achieved through its successful manner of governance and performance in World War II, subsequent construction of the postwar international system, and ongoing status as an indispensable provider of global public goods. China, for its part, fears that the United States and other Western powers will never accommodate its return to its hard-won position as an autonomous, moral, and powerful civilization with a preeminent regional role. This fear persists despite Beijing's abandonment of Maoist insurgencies and its new identity as a champion of the interests of developing nations in promoting a more diverse and equitable international system. The fears and aspirations of the United States and China draw on powerful currents of national identity and experience. Consequently, they are easy to reinforce and difficult to moderate. In coming years, driving factors, such as their constant development of new high-end military capabilities, are likely to become more significant. Given the military hardware already available to both sides, the costs of giving into those fears would be too devastating to contemplate.

CHINA'S GEOPOLITICAL IDENTITY AND TRAJECTORY

Over the past century China, like the United States, has been ideologically exceptionalist. Indeed, each centers its identity on a powerful and enduring idea. Whereas the United States sees its mission as that of the shining "city on a hill" and a purveyor of democratic capitalism, China has long viewed itself as an ancient "Middle Kingdom" whose meritocratic cultural superiority produced orderly society at home and respect abroad.

The U.S. vision of itself as a disseminator and a defender of capitalist democracy offers clear prescriptions for its role in the world, as evidenced by the continuing vigor—and even the periodic hubris (as seen in Vietnam and, most recently, Iraq)—of U.S. foreign policy. Ever since colonial incursions at the beginning of the nineteenth century, China, on the other hand, has battled an identity crisis. Indeed, to the extent that China was relatively insular during its early golden age of development and regional power, it maintained an imperial tributary system and never developed a robust *international* identity.

China's present grand strategy may be described as a multilevel process that seeks to restore and maintain territorial integrity, thereby ensuring peace for economic development, social stability, and the legitimacy of the Chinese Communist Party (CCP). Its members (more than 78 million) believe the party's leadership is essential to realizing these interrelated objectives and that China's recent success validates their approach. Strategic efforts focus in particular on resisting U.S. "containment" and opposing independence in any form for Taiwan. Economic efforts emphasize access to economic inputs and export markets, entailing major acquisitions of energy and minerals, often by entering into mutually profitable dependency-inducing relationships with the governments of developing nations. U.S. analysts debate the extent to which this is primarily an ad hoc process involving bottom-up demand "pulls" from a wide variety of actors or a coordinated top-down "push" strategy that amounts to a strategic shopping spree by China's government and state-owned enterprises (e.g., national oil companies) to exploit the current global economic crisis. In any case, China's government generally employs pragmatic experimentation, although bureaucratic interests and organizational impediments sometimes complicate this.

In Beijing's strategic sights, both U.S.-China relations and the question of Taiwan's status loom large. The Taiwan issue is particularly challenging for China's leaders because it is tied to China's economic development and, through it, to all their other major problems. If they can retain political power in the meantime, China's leaders would prefer to defer major international issues (and even the Taiwan question, if necessary) until they can achieve sustainable economic growth through domestic reform, thereby securing the basis for a long-term buildup of comprehensive national strength. The issue will probably intensify when China's economic and military power increase to the point where Beijing feels more able to assert its interests. Many U.S. strategists worry that this point is now arriving; I agree that some significant changes appear to be visible.

At a lower level of intensity, China's international efforts, while approved by elites in developing countries, face increasing local backlashes. Examples include Beijing's support of governments such as those of Sudan, Zimbabwe, and Zambia, whose policies are deeply unpopular with certain segments of the societies that they govern. China's strict conception of independence and respect for other nations' sovereignty, which has long included a vow not to station military forces abroad, has limited its willingness to use military means to protect and rescue its citizens overseas.[2] China's relevant power projection capability has heretofore been relatively limited. While I would argue that concerns about Chinese overseas military ambitions are exaggerated, many U.S. analysts fear that this is already in flux and could change dramatically over time.

NOT COMMUNIST BUT "TECHNONATIONALIST"

Since 1949 the leaders of the People's Republic of China (PRC) have promulgated ideology to guide society toward specific national goals. Chairman Mao Zedong called for class-based social revolution as the mobilizing principle for Chinese society. Following the disastrous failure of that utopian ideology, Chinese leaders, starting with Deng Xiaoping, seized on the idea that technological strength determines national power in a harshly competitive world. This "technonationalism" was seen as the best principle to modernize China to great power status. Technonationalism represents both a new ideological direction and a testament to historical continuity in Chinese political thought. As in the past, use of foreign technology is justified as a means of strengthening China and offers the prospect of finally reconciling two goals that have eluded China for over a century: national sovereignty and modernization.

By concentrating authority and privileging ideology, China's post-1949 political system brought the question of its international identity to the fore. Despite early ideological clashes that convulsed Chinese society, China's leaders have long articulated a set of principles that officially govern

China's international actions. The Five Principles of Peaceful Coexistence of 1954 emphasize "mutual respect for sovereignty and territorial integrity, mutual non-aggression, non-interference in each other's internal affairs, equality and mutual benefit, and peaceful coexistence."[3] These principles have led some scholars to draw parallels to China's imperial past as a "benevolent" regional hegemon.

These Five Principles, however, do not acknowledge the extent to which nations must engage in competitive activities, even war, to defend their national interests. Perhaps most importantly, they imply an egalitarian international system that is scarcely in keeping with China's notion of itself as a "great power" that demands deference even beyond that merited by its current material capabilities. For these reasons, it is doubtful that the Five Principles completely inform Beijing's foreign policy. Rather, they are a product of China's earlier dalliance with exporting world revolution and overcoming the Soviets as the best model for the nationalist uprisings in places like Southeast Asia and Africa.

This contradiction has led U.S. experts and others to explore other sources and manifestations of a "true" Chinese conception of international relations. Some (such as Harvard's Alastair Iain Johnston, a scholar of Chinese classical military texts) contend that, over centuries, leaders and bureaucratic elites have distilled China's historical experiences into a "strategic culture" that emphasizes both territorial integrity and selective and carefully calibrated use of force to address key national interests.

Domestic policy under Mao Zedong was highly ideological, even irrational, at least from the standpoint of popular welfare as opposed to individual or party political survival. For example, in 1967 the Central Committee recalled embassy personnel in stages to participate in the Cultural Revolution. According to former foreign minister Huang Hua, "nearly all the ambassadors and counselors of the Chinese embassies abroad were called back to China, and became the targets of criticism and attack." As a result, "the Foreign Ministry became a severely damaged department" and its work was "seriously impaired."[4]

With a few exceptions, Chinese foreign policy since 1949 has been both rational and professional. Under Mao's strategic thinking and Zhou Enlai's professional—and often moderating—implementation, PRC foreign policy was carefully attuned to changes in nations' relative power. This is evident in China's initial "leaning to one side" policy favoring the USSR (1949–1959), its subsequent championing of "nonaligned" nations to improve its own international position at the 1955 Bandung Conference, and its shift toward cooperation with the United States against the USSR in 1970.

Deng Xiaoping's ascent in 1978 brought realism even more consistently to the fore as a determinant of Chinese foreign and security policy. This can be seen in his termination of aid to foreign insurgencies and assumption of a more independent foreign policy for China as a third-power balancer in the 1980s. This trend continues in China's current efforts to position itself as an emerging great power, promoting a "multipolar" international system.

Close examination of China's diplomacy and military action since 1949 suggests that, despite communist rhetoric and internal turmoil, it has primarily followed a "realist" course of international relations for the past half century. Realism dictates husbanding national power and utilizing alliances to achieve maximum material benefit from an anarchic international system in which nations can only truly depend on themselves.

The question facing China's leaders today is not how to fulfill ancient cultural imperatives, or even how to develop a nebulous conception of ideological legitimacy. Communist ideology, however disastrous in application, was designed to serve specific material objectives. Instead, Beijing must determine how to maximize measured dimensions of national power in order to achieve its material interests in a competitive international system. Over the past half century, China has dramatically transformed the ideological basis on which to pursue this goal, abandoning Maoist "politics in command" in favor of science.

China's present leaders hope to coordinate a transformation that is more gradual but equally as dramatic as the one their party had originally sought after taking power in 1949. Beijing's methods may be new, but not their motivation: using authoritarianism to transform China into a great power, commanding order at home and respect abroad. Under the ideological aegis of technonationalism, China has surrendered collective activism in favor of economic and technological development.

Deng Xiaoping's consolidation of power in the late 1970s and the initiation of economic reforms heralded the rise of truly "expert" technocrats into China's leadership. While Deng also rehabilitated a number of party elders of Long March fame, their new role was primarily to provide continuity and legitimacy; a younger generation of technocrats supervised the actual reforms. The Long March revolutionaries were ultimately forced into lucrative retirement to allow technocrats to exert increased influence.

During the Tiananmen Crisis of 1989, Deng Xiaoping initiated Jiang Zemin's ascent to the Chairmanship, a process that culminated in Jiang's assumption of leadership after Deng's death in 1997. An archetypal technocratic leader, Jiang received his degree in electrical engineering. Thanks to his deft manipulation of bureaucratic politics, he advanced in Shanghai party leadership. Once at the top of the leadership structure, Jiang was surrounded by fellow technocrats, many of whom were engineers. Long before he consolidated power, Jiang emphasized that "China's security calculus should . . . incorporate economic, scientific, and technological dimensions." In 1992 he declared that post–Cold War geopolitical competition is, "in essence, a competition of overall national strength based on economic, scientific, and technological capabilities."[5]

Not only was China's third-generation leadership (after Mao and Deng) technocratic, it ceded power to a fourth generation under Hu Jintao (BS, hydraulic engineering) that is even more technocratic in its background and policy preferences. Starting in 2012, a fifth generation—led by Xi Jinping (PhD, chemical engineering)—will continue this tradition.

CHINA'S MILITARY DEVELOPMENT

China's rapid rise on the international stage has made the question of its military trajectory salient. Beijing is developing its military much in the same way that Deng developed China's market economy: by initiating modernization in the most pressing and promising areas and then attempting to extend this progress to the less-developed and less-crucial areas. China's overall military capabilities remain limited geographically, and it has yet to develop fully the wide range of platforms, weapons systems, and supporting infrastructure needed for large-scale, high-intensity power projection far beyond its immediate maritime periphery and lengthy land borders. Yet as part of a larger process of creating expanding "pockets of excellence," China has made great progress in developing certain strategic weapons. For example, China's People's Liberation Army (PLA) places strong emphasis on missiles (see figure 4.1). Its short-range conventional missiles have advanced quickly to become the world's most numerous. They have the capacity to target Taiwan, as well as various nations around

Figure 4.1.   PLA Mobile Missile Launcher. Lithograph by Samm Tyroler-Cooper Sacks.

China's periphery, and increasingly surface vessels as well. They even offer the potential for export to strategic allies, without threatening China's own security.

Evolving Regional Security Policy

As part of an ongoing revolution in military doctrine and hardware, Beijing is accruing a limited but growing capacity to project force beyond its immediate borders for the defense of its large maritime interests and burgeoning coastal development. China's Central Military Commission,[6] in part by devoting greater resources to the PLA Navy, is in the process of operationalizing a strategy that Deng originally proposed in 1979. Admiral Liu Huaqing further developed, articulated, and promoted a strategy of "Near Seas Defense," which he defined as covering the Yellow, East, and South China Seas. He also envisioned China's defensive capabilities eventually extending to the First Island Chain, the Second Island Chain, and beyond. This strategy—which was accepted in 1986—at present entails preparing to participate in limited-scale, high-tech, high-intensity, potentially operationally offensive conflicts on, under, and above the "near seas" and their approaches. China's construction of outposts on the Spratly and Paracel Islands that it captured in 1974 (in its longest distance opposed amphibious operation to date), 1988, and 1995, as well as its testing of ballistic missiles in the Strait of Taiwan on the eve of Taiwan's first presidential election in 1996 suggest that it is committed to defending its territorial claims and regional sphere of influence, which it believes should include Taiwan, other islands and maritime zones in the "near seas," and the potentially oil-rich shipping lanes of the South China Sea.

However, China's attempts to focus on its maritime periphery are complicated by its other border problems. It has been said that the United States' four greatest allies are Canada, Mexico, the Atlantic, and the Pacific; China lacks such peaceful and economically conducive surroundings. Although some areas remain unstable, China has settled virtually all its disputed land borders save for those with India and Bhutan. Moreover, it has resolved none of its maritime claims, leaving disputes with all of its sea neighbors: the Koreas, Japan, Vietnam, the Philippines, Malaysia, Indonesia, and Brunei.

As of late these have been a particular source of regional and international concern with Japan's arrest in disputed waters near the Pinnacle Islands (administered by Japan as the Senkakus, and claimed by China as the Diaoyus) of a Chinese fisherman. On September 7, 2010, the Chinese trawler *Minjinyu 5179* collided repeatedly with Japanese Coast Guard patrol boats, prompting detention of skipper Zhan Qixiong. A major diplomatic incident ensued, in which Beijing cancelled all bilateral meetings at the ministerial level and above, summoned the Japanese ambassador six times, and allegedly suspended rare earth shipments. In what was widely perceived as caving in to Chinese pressure, Japan released the trawler and fourteen of the crewmembers on September 13 and Zhan eleven days later.

Beijing regards Taiwan, which some in the U.S. view as a self-governing democracy, as its own wayward province. Gaining bilateral and cross-strait endorsement of the One China Policy has been a major, and largely successful, focus of PRC diplomacy since 1972. As Shirley Kan of the Congressional Research Service explains:

> Since 1971, U.S. Presidents—both secretly and publicly—have articulated a "one China" policy in understandings with the PRC. Congressional oversight has watched for any new agreements and any shift in the U.S. stance closer to that of Beijing's "one China" principle—on questions of sovereignty, arms sales, or dialogue. Not recognizing the PRC's claim over Taiwan or Taiwan as a sovereign state, U.S. policy has considered Taiwan's status as unsettled. With added conditions, U.S. policy leaves the Taiwan question to be resolved by the people on both sides of the Taiwan Strait: peacefully, with the assent of Taiwan's people, and without unilateral changes. In short, U.S. policy focuses on the process of resolution of the Taiwan question, not its outcome.[7]

Because the PRC is unable to achieve reunification with Taiwan but insists on pursuing its One-China Principle, Taiwan's status remains the most likely point of military conflict for Beijing, and for bringing Washington into conflict with Beijing. China maintains that Taiwan must commit to a process of reunification by an unspecified time in the near future. Beijing further insists that, if necessary, it will intervene militarily to prevent Taipei from declaring independence.

Recent Incidents

U.S.-China rapprochement had a military component from the start: Henry Kissinger shared intelligence on the Soviet military with Chinese counterparts in 1971. Military-to-military relations were initiated formally during Secretary of Defense Harold Brown's trip to Beijing in 1980. During the 1980s, the United States sold China many types of military and dual-use equipment, including helicopters and torpedoes, and there were plans to upgrade fighter avionics. But this ended abruptly with a Euro-American arms embargo following the 1989 Tiananmen Crisis.

The resulting discord, coupled with the Cold War's end, eroded the strategic rationale for military cooperation. Meanwhile, Taiwan's democratization since the late 1980s has raised the salience of its international status in Beijing's eyes. By the mid-1990s, the first significant U.S.-China security tensions since the Vietnam War emerged. During 1995 and 1996—in response to then Taiwan President Lee Teng-hui's series of antiunification statements culminating in a controversial address at Cornell University—the PLA conducted a series of live missile tests in the waters off Taiwan's ports. Beijing stopped this brinkmanship only when Washington dispatched two carrier battle groups toward the region and urged both sides to moderate their rhetoric.

Since then Sino-U.S. military incidents have occurred with disturbing frequency. On May 1, 2001, a Chinese J-8 fighter collided with a U.S. EP-3 signals reconnaissance aircraft that it had been intercepting over international waters approximately seventy nautical miles south of Hainan Island. The J-8 and its pilot crashed into the South China Sea, never to be seen again. The EP-3 made an emergency landing on nearby Hainan Island; there the crew was detained for two weeks. Their aircraft was confiscated, only to be returned *in pieces* later. At issue were fundamentally different perceptions of sovereignty and interpretations of international law. The United States and many other nations believe that it is permissible to conduct aerial surveillance in international airspace, that is, beyond twelve nautical miles from a nation's coastline. China disagrees and regularly sends military aircraft to intercept and monitor such missions, just as a variety of Chinese vessels routinely confront U.S. research vessels surveying high seas near (though never inside) China's territorial waters. Such encounters could readily produce an unanticipated and unwanted crisis in the future.

Although immediately after September 11, 2001, there was a convergence of U.S. and Chinese national interests resulting in counterterrorist intelligence sharing and joint financial monitoring working groups, by the mid-2000s this strategic respite had passed—overcome in part by Chinese convictions that the United States was mired in Iraq and Afghanistan even as China was rising rapidly in comprehensive national power. A series of incidents epitomize the problem of Chinese nontransparency and its impact on crisis management between the two nations. Not only have a number of recent events been murky in explanation, there have also been confusing signals about who was making various related decisions (China's central leadership, the PLA, the foreign ministry, or even Chinese civil maritime enforcement agencies). This lack of coordination raises worrying uncertainties about Chinese civil-military relations and bureaucratic coordination, and the PLA's policy influence.

A November 2004 incident in which a Chinese *Han*-class submarine was tracked by the Japan Maritime Self-Defense Force as the submarine passed submerged through Japanese territorial waters in the Ishigaki Strait was blamed on a navigational error in a manner that does not appear credible to naval experts. In October 2006 a Chinese diesel submarine reportedly surfaced unexpectedly within eight kilometers of the U.S. Navy's *Kitty Hawk* aircraft carrier as it was operating near Okinawa. China's January 11, 2007, antisatellite test, reportedly the single greatest human source of satellite-endangering debris in history, has still not been satisfactorily explained, despite repeated inquiries by the U.S. government; Beijing was only slightly more forthcoming regarding its January 11, 2010, antiballistic missile test.

And despite widespread evidence that China is developing and deploying an antiship ballistic missile—a potentially offensive and destabilizing technology because it creates incentives for a preemptive strike against associated targets—Beijing has made few official public statements in this regard. In November 2007 two U.S. minesweepers and the *Kitty Hawk* carrier strike group were denied permission, on separate occasions, to make port calls in Hong Kong. There may well be clear explanations for each of the above events, but unfortunately, with only a few partial exceptions, China's government has been unwilling to provide any.

The *Impeccable* incident of March 8, 2009, in which a group of Chinese civil maritime vessels and fishing trawlers harassed the surveillance ship USNS *Impeccable*, then operating some seventy-five miles south of Hainan Island, constituted perhaps the most serious crisis in U.S.-China military relations since the EP-3 incident. It also highlighted a relatively new (and ongoing) form of engagement: the use of civilian vessels. Subsequent U.S. offers to support Association of Southeast Asian Nations (ASEAN) members in efforts to "multilateralize" discussion of disputes over South China Sea claims, and Beijing's angry responses, threaten to make this a particular zone of future tension.

Lack of strategic transparency and understanding remains a major problem between China and the United States. Beijing has traditionally disclosed far less information about the most critical aspects of its military capabilities than has Washington; its strategists believe that as the weaker party it must use ambiguity to compensate for technological inferiority. This has been exacerbated by ongoing Chinese efforts to use the suspension of military-military relations as a means of expressing umbrage at U.S. policy; this has happened twice in two years (2008, 2010). While China's rising military strength increasingly incentivizes the PLA to engage in "selective transparency" in order to impress its populace and deter its U.S. competitor with improved capabilities, this remains insufficient to reassure Washington. Meanwhile, Beijing complains that Washington lacks "strategic transparency," or credible explanations, regarding its own intentions. This issue raises the larger question as to what degree military-to-military activities will be subject to ever-shifting political winds and strategic disagreement; or rather, if there is any hope that they will not be the first casualty of such challenges in the future.

Growing Resources for a Growing PLA

The PLA's official 2011 defense budget is $91.5 billion. Though widely believed by Western analysts to be understated, even this figure is well over twice that of India, and second only to that of the United States (roughly $700 billion in 2011). Since 1990 it has enjoyed double-digit growth, with the exception of 2003 (in which growth was 9.6 percent) and 2010 (7.5 percent). No major power is even approaching this level of defense spending growth. China's defense industry, while still uneven in efficiency and quality of output, is improving steadily. Together, these factors enable steady increases in overall PLA capabilities, with particularly rapid progress in selected areas.

U.S. analysts differ widely in their assessment of China's defense budget, in part because it is difficult to compare directly with those of Western industrial powers. Some believe there is now firm evidence that Beijing fully intends to challenge Washington for regional leadership in maritime East Asia and may even reach further to conduct extensive operations. Others have concluded from the extent and nature of recent budgets that China is simply pursuing military power commensurate with its economic strength and sufficient to facilitate reunification with Taiwan. Certainly the expenditures are higher than Beijing's official figure, which omits large hard-currency transactions such as China's recent purchases of Russian aircraft, submarines, and destroyers. Nevertheless, it is clear that China's defense investment has grown considerably and will continue to grow in the future.[8]

Bifurcated Military Development, at Home and Abroad

Close to home China's military capabilities are rapidly reaching a very high level. However, they are making much slower progress, from a lower baseline, further away. The most common source of error in Chinese and U.S. analyses of PLA development is the conflation of these two factors.

China's pattern of emerging military development clearly reflects its relative ranking of security concerns. Its military capabilities may be represented by a series of concentric circles, or "range rings," with the most advanced, potent, and numerous platforms and weapons systems concentrated on China's shores, in its territorial waters (up to twelve nautical miles from its shores), in its claimed exclusive economic zones (up to two hundred nautical miles from its shores), and in the South China Sea, which China claims virtually in its entirety, although it has not stated officially the specific basis for this claim. This is hardly surprising; the three "near seas" contain all China's maritime claims—disputed with all its maritime neighbors—as well as rich resources to which it seeks access. Here China's capabilities are advancing rapidly, and it is increasingly prepared to wage "local limited wars under high technology conditions."

Figure 4.2. Dual Canister Missile Launcher Engaged. Lithograph by Samm Tyroler-Cooper Sacks.

PLA development thus far has been focused largely on developing a variant of regional "anti-access/area denial" (A2/AD) to prevent Taiwan from declaring independence, in part by developing credible capabilities to thwart U.S. forces in the event of intervention. The PLA's current order of battle is based primarily on the world's foremost array of substrategic land-based mobile missiles (see figure 4.2); diesel submarines armed with cruise missiles, torpedoes, and sea mines; and improving variants of surface ships and aircraft likewise outfitted with increasingly capable missiles. Though already formidable in firepower, it remains clearly sized and shaped primarily for defending claims on China's disputed maritime periphery as opposed to conducting extraregional blue-water sea control operations. To assess related scenarios, one must compare the actual assets that relevant militaries could deploy; outright comparison of Chinese and U.S. forces is misleading unless one envisions an all-out global conflict between the two. This is virtually inconceivable.

Although concerns about Taiwan's status have played a prominent role in driving Chinese defense spending since at least the mid-1990s, the PLA's defense interests are now necessarily greater as its reliance on foreign resources, trade, and shipping lanes grows. Taiwan President Ma Ying-jeou's March 2008 landslide election and his pragmatic policies have greatly stabilized cross-strait relations. So with China continuing to grow as a global stakeholder, its navy is likely to supplement its previous approach. Its current naval platforms and weaponry largely support a Taiwan- and "near seas"–centric access-denial strategy. China will continue to develop these core capabilities but also add what the Office of Naval Intelligence terms "new but limited requirements for protection of the sea lanes beyond China's own waters, humanitarian assistance/disaster relief, and expanded naval diplomacy." China's capabilities are clearly growing, but its naval intentions—at least beyond asserting control over its claimed territorial waters to include Taiwan—remain unclear.

Further afield, in the Western Pacific and the Indian Ocean, China has not developed high-intensity military capabilities, instead projecting power in the form of recent peacetime deployments. The PLA now has much to be proud of and talk about in this area, having dispatched

- a frigate and military transport aircraft to safeguard the evacuation of Chinese citizens from Libya in February 2011;
- nine (and counting) task forces to escort over 4,000 ships and rescue 40 from attacks by pirates in the Gulf of Aden since December 2008;
- a hospital ship to treat over 15,500 in African and Indian Ocean nations in summer 2010; and
- a variety of aircraft, and vehicles, and personnel to assist the victims of two major earthquakes (Wenchuan, 2008; Yushu, 2010)—as well as other natural disasters—in China.

Although apparently constructive and peaceful in nature, such efforts are viewed by some as a prelude to more expansive maneuvers. Beijing already has the capability to augment its power projection capabilities, but this would require far greater investment in nuclear-powered submarines, deck aviation, auxiliary platforms, overall force structure, and training. Such preparations would be extremely visible to outside observers; thus far there are few indications that China is moving substantially in this direction.[9]

CLASH OF PERSPECTIVES

The yawning gulf between U.S. and Chinese strategic perceptions is salient in the latest reports produced by their respective militaries. China's latest Defense White Paper (2010) outlines a purely "defensive" national defense policy of "active defense." It vows that China will "never seek hegemony." Instead it intends to safeguard China's security situation by preventing "separatism," curbing U.S. arms sales to Taiwan, and increasing stability in the Asia-Pacific, despite U.S. attention thereto and what it views as promotion of strategic struggles therein. The PLA will achieve this by pursuing a three-step development strategy: (1) engaging in "informationalization," or the application of information technology and networks, as well as other technological progress, to achieve a revolution in military affairs and thereby leapfrog the earlier era of "mechanization"; (2) coordinating economic and defense development; and (3) deepening reform. The PLA is preparing for three major types of warfare: winning local wars in conditions of informationalization, deterring crises and wars, and increasing its capabilities to deal with nontraditional security threats.

Where the Chinese report focuses on intentions, policies, and history and gives virtually no details on China's current military capabilities, the U.S. Department of Defense (DoD) annual report on China's military power focuses on specific capabilities. The DoD engages in broad speculation about China's intentions but emphasizes that lack of transparency leaves significant uncertainty. Beijing's official spokespeople and media harshly denounce each year's DoD report, yet offer no specifics regarding which facts they consider wrong or what the correct information is.

Not surprisingly, the reports' differences are rooted in something much deeper than technical analyses. Several fundamental differences in viewpoint obscure U.S.-China security relations, posing major obstacles to mutual understanding, let alone cooperation. Their very different modern histories have produced a significant strategic cultural divide, as mentioned above.

The inability of Beijing and Washington to reach an understanding concerning Taiwan's status has long been the principal obstacle to improvements in U.S.–China relations. Since 1949 the PRC has consistently and clearly emphasized the vital importance of reunification with Taiwan as a central tenet of national policy. Beijing fully expects Washington to honor its commitment not to support Taiwan independence even as Washington also strives to honor its self-imposed responsibility to protect Taiwanese democracy amid massive cross-strait changes. Arguably, economic integration and rising Chinese military strength make the island increasingly indefensible militarily and complicate the previous status quo. Fortunately, since his election President Ma Ying-jeou has pursued a positive and practical policy of improving relations and economic links between Taiwan and mainland China.

Despite these recent improvements, however, Taiwan's status will remain sensitive. No U.S. president has the power to change a basic reality: the preservation of Taiwan's democracy is an issue of critical importance politically and morally to the United States and one that enjoys overwhelming congressional support, at least for now. The ability of Washington and Beijing to agree to disagree regarding their enduring strategic differences will determine the degree of their ability to cooperate to safeguard larger commercial, resource, homeland security, and maritime interests.

In addition to their concerns about the sensitive issues of Taiwan's status, political system, and international space, Chinese policy makers and analysts also believe that the United States unduly employs military means to address problems better addressed by other approaches. Ongoing Obama administration efforts to reinvigorate such organizations as the State Department and pursue manifold diplomatic initiatives to provide a broader range of public goods (broadly beneficial services) in the international system have received little acknowledgment from Beijing, which feels that the United States is continuing intolerable "business as usual" in China's "front yard" by approving yet another arms package for Taiwan and intervening in South China issues. Arguments by some U.S. pundits that extreme and divisive efforts should be made to prevent China's rise are neither realistic nor helpful. Unfortunately, some Chinese officials seem unwilling to recognize that the United States is home to diverse discussion and debate, and these perspectives are in no way mainstream views—yet are not subject to government control.

From the U.S. perspective, China's ongoing limitations in military transparency, both in terms of capabilities and intentions, coupled with its rapid increases in defense spending and wide-ranging military modernization, remain another source of great concern. This situation undermines U.S. cooperation initiatives—which are being attempted with increasing willingness—for fear that China is unwilling or unable to reciprocate equitably. A related concern is that China may attempt to exploit U.S. goodwill by imposing greater political demands. Under these conditions, the reality of prevailing politics and values in Washington (including deep-seated suspicions of Chinese capabilities and intentions that transcend partisan lines) circumscribes the evolution of better military-to-military relations with Beijing, something the latter does not seem to understand fully. Beijing's lack of transparency and reciprocity only strengthens the critics of cooperation, engendering wide speculation in the United States and elsewhere concerning China's intentions, much of it inaccurate, unsubstantiated, and worst-case in nature. Nonetheless, the lack of communication from Beijing unnecessarily helps feed this trend in Washington.

A degree of public clarification for China's major strategic actions would do much to allay U.S. concerns, even if it defends China's strategic reasoning, with which the United States may strongly disagree. While official explanations for China's military development and assertions of benign intent may fulfill domestic political and even cultural imperatives, they ultimately do not serve Beijing's interests vis-à-vis the United States. They are not persuasive, or in some cases even comprehensible, to a U.S. audience. A prime example is President Hu Jintao's invocation of the oft-repeated Chinese vow that "we do not engage in arms race[s] or pose a military threat to any country. China will never seek hegemony or pursue an expansionist policy."[10] Specific statements regarding the nature and scope of PLA development would be a far more effective way to reassure a U.S. audience.

The obstacles to strategic transparency are sobering. Breakdown of cooperation is often a problem of information; the lack of clear information can lead to mutual defection from agreements. Asymmetric information (more available to one party than to another) could be intentional or unintentional. It could stem from a lack of internal coordination (e.g., the military and diplomatic bureaucracies) or intentional mixed messages. Even the security dilemma could be driven by (mis)perceptions of information. This is especially important since national strategic trust is essential to a stable bilateral relationship and makes it even more hazardous to suspend repeatedly bilateral military-military relations. Thus the Chinese provision of vague, righteous descriptions of Beijing's strategic intentions that fail to explain key behaviors, coupled with a degree of military power and influence on the part of the United States that causes even its more detailed explanations of intent to be held in suspicion, makes it more difficult for the two sides to achieve a firm basis for robust security cooperation.

CONTEST FOR REGIONAL INFLUENCE?

Looking forward, can China's leaders achieve what an increasing number of U.S. strategists fear they may: hegemony in East Asia, thus challenging U.S. interests and its military presence there?

In order to assess the potential for such an attack on U.S. interests, one must first determine the options open to China's leadership. China's leaders will expend considerable energy and resources vis-à-vis Taiwan because they worry about national strength and territorial integrity, CCP popular legitimacy, and succession politics. The majority of current Western military analyses suggest that China lacks the capability to conduct a successful amphibious invasion of Taiwan, particularly if the United States elected to intervene. The most potent threat to Taiwan's democratic future might come from a PRC missile and air strike campaign combined with an air and naval blockade, which could devastate Taiwan's military capability and economy while affording China a defensive position.

In order to frustrate Chinese operations without dangerous escalation to general war with the mainland or nuclear exchange, a Taiwan-U.S. coalition would need to establish short-range local supremacy in the form of air and water dominance. Current force balances suggest that, absent U.S. assistance, Taiwan would be unlikely to prevail even in this scenario. Because ballistic missiles, strikes from attack aircraft employing standoff munitions, mines, and submarines are integral to the PLA's Joint Blockade Campaign, the significant PRC buildup of these armaments has altered the military balance in the mainland's favor.

Given China's growing but limited capacity to undermine successfully U.S. fundamental East Asian interests—with the possible exception of coerced reunification with Taiwan—it is reasonable to conclude that China will not achieve East Asian hegemony in the foreseeable future. However, several factors could complicate this. First, it is always possible that the United States might lose the will to maintain a strong, expensive presence in East Asia. Although this negative outcome is unlikely to take place given Washington's strong interests in the region, the fate of the United States' two most significant regional allies might affect its opportunity to do so. Were Japan to revise its constitution, develop a "normal" foreign policy and military, dissolve the U.S.-Japan Security Treaty, or otherwise force Washington to remove its troops from Okinawa and Honshu, U.S. presence in the region would be significantly compromised.

The Korean peninsula, the other division left over from the Cold War, looms as a particular geopolitical challenge for the region. It is difficult to imagine how North Korea's third-generation dynastic leader Kim Jong-un and any future successors could continue a totalitarian system into the mid-twenty-first century; yet it is also hard to see how they could implement meaningful economic reforms without risking their regime's overthrow. The National Intelligence Council sees "a unified Korea as likely by 2025—if not as a unitary state, then in some form of North-South confederation." China, in particular, is positioning itself to be a "powerbroker" with a veto over any future developments on the peninsula and opposes any measures that it fears could cause instability, even at the expense of supporting this repugnant regime. South Korea is in a particularly difficult position, and this is likely to weigh on its alliance with the United States in the future. China is hardly interested in a unified peninsula and will seek to exploit its leverage with both Koreas to wrest considerable concessions in the event of a move toward their consolidation.

Were the Koreas to reunify under a Beijing-brokered agreement, U.S. troops might have to restrict their operations on the Korean Peninsula or even leave it entirely. The presence of a new democratic regional power on China's border could further destabilize the region. However, both scenarios are unlikely to materialize overnight, and while they would almost certainly contribute to a decline in direct U.S. military influence in East Asia, they would work as well to prevent Chinese domination. Furthermore, the United States has striven to reduce its dependence on specific foreign bases in East Asia by building up Guam as a forward military logistics hub. A positive outcome for more than half a century of ruinous instability on the Korean peninsula would be to transform the Six Party Talks into a broader Northeast Asian security mechanism. This would give all key regional stakeholders a voice and help prevent Beijing from denying Washington a seat at the table regarding key Asia-Pacific affairs.

The rise of China and corresponding relative decline of U.S. influence in the East Asian region would be an event of tremendous significance in international relations. But while Pentagon analysts are charged with vigilantly preparing Washington for worst-case scenarios, the most extreme *global* projections already seem infeasible.

First, China appears disinclined to become an aggressive Soviet-style global superpower. Of course, China might attempt to resolve the Taiwan question in its favor at any time, and its military capabilities are gradually raising the potential cost of U.S. intervention. Still, such an intervention could be extremely costly to China's comprehensive national strength. Even were it prepared to pay a high price for its actions, China would have no guarantee of prevailing in such a conflict.

Second, China will not achieve hegemony even in East Asia, at least for the foreseeable future, because it will lack the capabilities and, to some extent the intention, to undermine U.S. interests in East Asia. Moreover, the intervening years of economic development in China *may* unleash sufficient democratization, rule of law, demographic transition, and environmental degradation to reduce (or at least constrain) Beijing's regional hegemonic capacity. China will consolidate its power in the region, however, and thereby permit the maintenance of a balance of power with the United States, its allies, and actors such as the ASEAN nations, which want no power to dominate the region. If the U.S.-China relationship is properly managed, great power confrontation in East Asia may be avoided, and the region could retain the relative stability necessary to foster strong economic growth and possibly the future development of institutions promoting regional security.

SHARED INTERESTS: REASON FOR HOPE

Despite their differences, Washington and Beijing must reach a new understanding regarding their respective roles in East Asia and the Asia-Pacific more broadly. The benefits of doing so could be substantial. In the unfortunate event of a U.S.-China conflict, maritime forces would be the most likely to be used; yet they are also the most likely to encounter each other and work together in peacetime. The two nations' navies and other maritime services have the opportunity, even the duty, to do what other services have not: establish a new and cooperative relationship. Given the unique nature of sea-based presence, port visits, diplomacy, and critical trade relations, maritime forces interact in peacetime differently from other services. For the U.S. and Chinese maritime forces, this generates many compatible and overlapping strategic priorities. Indeed, when seaborne bilateral trade is considered, the two nations already have a major maritime partnership, albeit one in which the military element lags far behind the commercial.

It is in the maritime dimension that the potential sources of conflict and cooperation must first be sought. For instance, improved cooperation would enable mutually beneficial moving of assets. In the case of their navies, this could involve shifting investment from platforms and weapons systems useful primarily for major combat operations to "shaping" assets facilitating diverse efforts against everything from substate actors to natural disasters. These are challenges likely to be even more pronounced in the world the National Intelligence Council envisions by 2025.

The United States and China must find the means to accept each other's perspectives and roles. Washington must accept the reality that Beijing is assuming an increasingly important and independent role in global affairs. The Chinese government must realize that its confusing signals do not lend themselves to strategic trust. This situation must be improved through increased transparency of strategic intent and capabilities and better crisis management. Both powers must accept that they will both have a significant presence in East Asia for the foreseeable future, and hence must achieve some form of "competitive coexistence" there.

Following two years of increasing tension, Sino-U.S. strategic relations experienced a welcome, if largely symbolic, recalibration in 2011, when U.S. Secretary of Defense Robert Gates visited Beijing between January 9 and 12 and President Hu Jintao subsequently visited Washington and Chicago on January 18 through 21. The civilian leadership on both sides clearly wanted to move beyond recent acrimony, yet together with economic interdependence, the complex contradictions and concerns that characterize the relationship were all on display, so substantive results remain uncertain.

Two days into Gates's visit, a new J-20 stealth aircraft prototype made a short test flight in Chengdu. Hu assured him that the timing was coincidental. Yet *Jane's* quoted Chinese sources as suggesting that "China may have accelerated the schedule for the J-20's maiden flight after the US Department of Defense finally agreed to modernise Taiwan's fleet of Lockheed Martin F-16A/B fighter aircraft."[11] The test thus resembled a muted strategic communication to an international audience, albeit not a formal one that might provoke diplomatic discord.

Both sides affirmed the importance of the relationship, and Gates visited the command base of China's Second Artillery (ground-based missile forces). Gates proposed a "strategic security dialogue—as part of a broader Strategic and Economic Dialogue—that covers nuclear, missile defense, space, and cyber issues." No substantive specifics were agreed on, however, and what will actually come out of the visit is another story. U.S. skeptics believe that the PLA has been compelled to participate to avoid disrupting

President Hu Jintao's subsequent state visit to Washington. They believe that the PLA's senior leadership has no intention of actually following through with substantive initiatives after Hu's visit, and they will be monitoring the situation closely.

President Hu's state visit to the United States encompassed a far broader and more positive set of subjects than the contentious military relationship. The trip was a success for him, as it proceeded largely without incident and he was treated as the leader of a great power with a vibrant economy. In contrast to his 2006 Washington visit, he was accorded a twenty-one-gun salute and a state dinner. Problems of U.S. concern, such as North Korea, trade, and human rights, were discussed, but no commitments were made. Nevertheless, Hu's visit was clearly designed to reassure U.S. interlocutors (such as President Obama and key officials in his administration), as contentious Chinese terms like "core interests" were conspicuously absent.

A TOP-LEVEL "RESET"?

At present this positive if merely symbolic dialogue and exchange is the best that can be hoped for among top leaders. Particularly important, given the unfortunate potential for misperception and miscalculation, as well as the potential for productive cooperation in such areas as counterterrorism and counterpiracy, is maintaining regular U.S.-China military dialogues and exchanges, including at high levels. These exchanges are not barometers of "who wants what more" and should not be severed to send a political message; U.S.-China military relations are simply too important for that, and that is not how responsible, mature powers conduct policy.

In order to move beyond their deep skepticism, the two sides must minimally agree to do more than "consider" each other's proposals. They must actually pursue substantive dialogues on key issues of strategic concern. Such discussions entail no preconditions to agree on any policy matters, so there is no reason not to make a good faith effort to begin. Alternatively, failure to discuss these critical areas—in which the PLA is making rapid progress—regularly and substantively will only enhance mistrust.

The United States and China are critically placed to shape the emerging international order. Yet their differences in national identity, culture, political system, and interests—which manifest themselves most dangerously regarding several key geopolitical, territorial, and maritime areas vis-à-vis East Asia—threaten to bring them into crisis and conflict. This remains true even as the two nations develop unprecedented mutual economic dependence and shared interests in a secure, prosperous global system.

Regardless of its exact parameters, building and sustaining a significant level of mutual trust and strategic cooperation will require substantial effort and patience. Washington and Beijing will have to live with considerable ambiguity and should expect occasional setbacks. For the foreseeable future, there will be significant differences in their military capabilities, political systems, and national interests. To guard against the threat of conflict as China, the rising power, gains on the United States, the dominant power today and for the foreseeable future, both sides will likely find it necessary to "hedge"—not only rhetorically, but also economically, politically, and even militarily.

Just as Chinese officials, analysts, and media constantly charge that many in Washington promote a "China threat theory," many in Beijing likewise promote a "U.S. threat theory," construing ulterior motives from virtually any U.S. action. Analysts and planners in the United States need to look at the big picture, which strongly suggests, arguably with some notable exceptions, an overall Chinese desire and need to cooperate with, rather than to challenge, the United States. And the renewed U.S. focus on humanitarian operations should be seen by Chinese for what it is, an opportunity for mutually beneficial cooperation and improved relations. Ongoing deployment of Chinese naval vessels to defend against piracy in the Gulf of Aden suggests the capability and intention to focus increasingly on humanitarian assistance and disaster relief. Such factors may support mission convergence and increase strategic space for Sino-U.S. maritime cooperation, although exploiting opportunities will require sailing into strong headwinds and taking the waves as they come. Perhaps in this way "mutually assured dependence" will prevail over tendencies toward "mutually assured destruction."

SUGGESTIONS FOR FURTHER READING

Chinese analyses in English on China defense and foreign policy issues are available from *China Security*, http://www.chinasecurity.us/.

Foreign analyses on these subjects, many written by U.S. researchers, are available from the following:

China Air and Naval Power, http://china-pla.blogspot.com/
China Analysis from Original Sources, www.andrewerickson.com
China Maritime Studies Institute (CMSI), http://www.usnwc.edu/cmsi
China SignPost, www.chinasignpost.com
China Military Power Mashup, http://www.china-defense-mashup.com/
China's Defence Today, www.sinodefence.com
CNA China Studies, http://www.cna.org/centers/china/publications
Jamestown *China Brief*, http://www.jamestown.org/programs/chinabrief/
Project 2049 Institute, http://project2049.net/

Some of the best sources on military and strategic issues that frequently cover China-related subjects include the following:

Center for Strategic and Budgetary Assessments, http://www.csbaonline
    .org/publications/all/
Information Dissemination, www.informationdissemination.net
National Bureau of Asian Research, www.nbr.org
Naval War College Review, http://www.usnwc.edu/Publications/Naval
    -War-College-Review.aspx
RAND Corporation, www.rand.org
The Diplomat, http://the-diplomat.com/

Relevant latest U.S. government reports include the following:

National Air and Space Intelligence Center. "Ballistic and Cruise Missile Threat."
    NASIC-1031-0985-09, Wright-Patterson Air Force Base, Ohio, April 2009, http://
    www.fas.org/programs/ssp/nukes/NASIC2009.pdf.
National Air and Space Intelligence Center. *People's Liberation Army Air Force 2010.*
    Wright-Patterson Air Force Base, Ohio, August 1, 2010, http://www.au.af.mil/au/
    awc/awcgate/nasic/pla_af_2010.pdf.
Office of the Secretary of Defense. "Military and Security Developments Involving
    the People's Republic of China 2010." Annual report to Congress, August 16,
    2010, http://www.defense.gov/pubs/pdfs/2010_CMPR_Final.pdf.
O'Rourke, Ronald. "China Naval Modernization: Implications for U.S. Navy Capa-
    bilities—Background and Issues for Congress." *Congressional Research Service,* July
    22, 2011, http://www.fas.org/sgp/crs/row/RL33153.pdf.
The People's Liberation Army Navy: A Modern Navy with Chinese Characteristics (Suit-
    land, MD: Office of Naval Intelligence, 2009), http://www.fas.org/irp/agency/
    oni/pla-navy.pdf.

NOTES

1. Office of the Director of National Intelligence, *Global Trends 2025: A Transformed World* (Washington, DC: National Intelligence Council, 2008), vi–vii.

2. Most recently, a notable exception to this isolationist practice occurred in
Libya when the Chinese government rescued Chinese nationals caught in the
middle of the conflict. Although China's government took credit for the evacuation,
they insisted on moderating media coverage to avoid inflating domestic expectations regarding future crises or to disclose the extent of popular opposition to the
Qaddafi regime.

3. Ministry of Foreign Affairs of the People's Republic of China, "China's Initiation of the Five Principles of Peaceful Co-Existence," November 17, 2000, http://
www.fmprc.gov.cn/eng/ziliao/3602/3604/t18053.htm.

4. Huang Hua, *Huang Hua Memoirs: Contemporary History and Diplomacy of China* (Beijing: Foreign Languages Press, 2008), 192–97, 280–83.

5. Yongjin Zhang, "China's Security Problematique: Critical Reflections," in *Power and Responsibility in Chinese Foreign Policy*, ed. Yongjin Zhang and Greg Austin (Canberra: Asia Pacific Press, 2001), 264.

6. This is the supreme military policy-making body, chaired by China's "paramount leader" and staffed by ten other top officials and military officers. It is usually the first official post to be secured in the quest for succession, as was demonstrated by both Deng Xiaoping and Jiang Zemin.

7. Shirley A. Kan, "China/Taiwan: Evolution of the 'One China' Policy—Key Statements from Washington, Beijing, and Taipei," *Congressional Research Service*, June 24, 2011, http://www.fas.org/sgp/crs/row/RL30341.pdf.

8. China's development of a modern strategic arsenal is part of a comprehensive and costly, though gradual, long-term and proportionally affordable military buildup. U.S. analysts believe that the extent and nature of Chinese defense spending suggests both the future status of China's military power and China's intentions as it continues military modernization.

9. The U.S. Department of Defense estimates that

> while remaining focused on Taiwan as a primary mission, China will, by 2020, lay the foundation for a force able to accomplish broader regional and global objectives. By the latter half of this decade, it is likely that China will be able to project and sustain a modest sized force—perhaps several battalions of ground forces or a naval flotilla of up to a dozen ships—in low-intensity operations far from China. It is unlikely, however, that China will be able to project and sustain large forces in high-intensity combat operations far from China until well into the following decade.

See Office of the Secretary of Defense, "Military and Security Developments Involving the People's Republic of China 2010," annual report to Congress, August 16, 2010, 29, http://www.defense.gov/pubs/pdfs/2010_CMPR_Final.pdf.

10. "Hu Jintao Says China Will Never Seek Hegemony," *China Daily*, January 21, 2011, usa.chinadaily.com.cn/video/2011-01/21/content_11908544.htm.

11. Reuben F. Johnson, "China's J-20 Makes Maiden Flight," *Jane's Defence Weekly*, January 12, 2011, http://www.janes.com/products/janes/defence-security -report.aspx?ID=1065929024.

5

China's Environmental Tipping Point

Alex L. Wang

China's remarkable economic rise over the last three decades has placed tremendous pressure on the environment, damaged natural resources, and increased risks to human health. To be sure, human activity has had significant impact on China's environment for thousands of years. Nonetheless, the pace of China's economic growth since "reform and opening" in the late 1970s—averaging 9 percent annually—and the role China has taken on in recent decades as the "factory to the world" have exacerbated the country's environmental challenges and created a host of new environmental problems. On the domestic front, China's environmental problems include pollution of air, water, and soil; water shortages; desertification and soil erosion; loss of biodiversity and habitat; and a range of other issues. At the international level, China is a major contributor to global environmental issues, such as climate change, ozone depletion, and trade in endangered species, as well as regional issues, such as trans-boundary air and water pollution.

Many of China's environmental problems are inextricably linked with its energy mix. China's energy overwhelmingly comes from coal, which is relatively cheap and abundantly available within China. Eighty percent of China's electricity is produced by coal-fired power plants, compared with 44.9 percent in the United States in 2010, and less than 30 percent for OECD Europe.[1] China's coal use has been a major contributor to air pollution and helped to make China, as of 2007, the world's leading emitter of greenhouse gases.[2] Moreover, China passed the United States in 2010 to become the world's largest energy consumer. The country's energy demand growth has led to an ever-increasing reliance on foreign supplies of oil, gas, and coal as China's domestic supplies have fallen short, exacerbating energy security concerns. On the positive side, from 1978 to 2000 China made unprecedented improvements in energy efficiency, decreasing energy intensity (i.e., energy per unit of economic output) by two-thirds. However, from 2001 to 2006, because of heavy investment in energy-intensive industries like steel, cement, and smelting, China's energy intensity reversed its long-term downward trend.

China's environmental and energy challenges have begun to draw a substantial response from the government and society at-large. The open question is whether this response will be adequate to the task.

IS CHINA'S ENVIRONMENT AT A TURNING POINT?

As of this writing in 2012, China's environment is arguably at a turning point. At the policy level, China has in just the space of a few years raised the priority of energy efficiency and the environment arguably to the highest it has ever been. As economic conditions improve and public environmental awareness grows, there is also now a wider range of public action on environmental protection than ever before, and the sophistication of actions by local communities, environmental groups, and other actors has grown by leaps and bounds. China's strong economic growth has also given it the ability, if willing, to devote significantly more resources to environmental protection than it has at any time in the past.

Much has been written about the severity of China's environmental and energy crisis in recent years. On the other hand, there has also been a great deal of media attention on China's "green tech revolution." But the story told to date is incomplete and fails to recognize the broader shifts occurring in Chinese society in response to the environmental pressures brought about by economic growth. China is indeed facing the most serious environmental challenges that any country has ever seen, but investment in "clean tech" alone will not be sufficient to meet them. The "clean tech" story is an important one, as many see China as the laboratory where these technologies can be tested cost-effectively and brought to market to compete eventually with traditional fossil fuels. Yet even with their tremendous growth rates, wind and solar are only expected to account for a few percent of China's energy mix decades from now, and dirtier fossil fuels will dominate for the foreseeable future.

In fact, a growing recognition of the tremendous economic, political, and human costs of China's environmental problems over the last decade, concerns about economic security and prospects for continued economic growth, and the pressures of stepping up to a larger role on the global stage have generated a wide-ranging response within China. On the government side, faced with the dramatic reversal in energy efficiency gains in the early years of the new millennium and with increased social unrest and public dissatisfaction from environmental pollution, China elevated the position of environment and energy in the country's eleventh Five-Year Plan, establishing high-priority national targets for energy intensity reduction and pollution reduction of sulfur dioxide and chemical oxygen demand, a measure of water pollution. This plan also included a slate of supporting policies and funding mechanisms. Moreover, China has instituted a series of governance reforms that have the potential to strengthen environmental protection. There is debate over the efficacy of these reforms, but they are, at a minimum, important first steps. And in the span of just a few years, China has indeed become a global leader in the development and manufacturing of clean energy technologies through heavy investment, as well as in the establishment of clear market signals and incentives for "green" energy technologies.

Any discussion of these reforms as "progress" must include a number of caveats. It would be a mistake to think that top-down government action is a panacea for China's environmental challenges. Despite what many commentators are saying, it is not true that "when China decides to do something, it can just do it." A variety of structural reasons, such as largely decentralized, local control of environmental management, have led to a system with notoriously weak environmental compliance and enforcement.

If it is to happen at all, public demand and advocacy will play a critical role in turning around China's environment. Given the political constraints on civic organizing in China today, there has been remarkable opportunity for the populace to speak up, mobilize, and even take to the streets on behalf of the environment. Formerly sensitive issues like transparency and public participation have received more—though still inadequate—government support in the environmental arena because they are viewed as helpful to government efforts to meet environmental goals. Local communities, environmental groups, lawyers, and others have played an important role in highlighting environmental injustice and have pushed for stronger implementation of environmental laws and policies. The public role remains weak, but in recent years there have been important openings in the way that citizens can engage on environmental issues in the public arena.

I previously worked in China for nearly six years with the U.S. environmental group the Natural Resources Defense Council (NRDC), partnering with various actors to improve environmental compliance and enforcement, rule of law, and public involvement in environmental protection to bring about a cleaner, healthier environment. Our goal was, in short, to look for ways to make laws on the books a reality on the ground. Over the years, my colleagues and I worked with Chinese environmental officials at the central and local levels, environmentalists, lawyers, journalists, and citizen groups around the country who were struggling against enormous odds to combat China's environmental problems. In particular, we partnered with government agencies to strengthen air pollution laws. We worked with local Chinese partners to empower citizens and environmental groups to participate in hearings, comment on draft laws and policies, and obtain environmental information. We collaborated with lawyers and judges seeking ways to use the law to stop pollution. This work in China gave me the chance to see firsthand the opportunities and challenges for environmental protection in China. The barriers to change are immense. But many of the ingredients necessary for China to turn the corner on its environmental and energy problems are beginning to fall into place.

This chapter will first examine the nature of China's environmental crisis. It will then turn to a discussion of the government response, which has given increasing attention to environmental protection and energy efficiency in recent years. It will then examine the public response, which is playing an indispensible role in pushing forward environmental protection in China.

CHINA'S ENVIRONMENTAL CRISIS—HOW SERIOUS IS THE PROBLEM?

It is by now well known that China's environment is under a tremendous amount of pressure. One need not repeat here the oft-cited litany of statistics about China having sixteen of the top twenty-five most polluted cities in the world; that China is the leading global emitter of greenhouse gases, sulfur dioxide, and a host of other pollutants; that more than 320 million Chinese people do not have access to clean drinking water; or that one-third of the water on the Yellow River is not fit even for industrial use.[3] The numerous headlines and magazine covers in recent years have conveyed to even the most casual observer the sense that China's environment is in serious trouble.

One might wonder, though, just how China's environmental problems compare to the state of the environment in the rest of the world. On a variety of fronts, pollution levels in China are comparatively much worse. Sulfur dioxide pollution in China, for example, is much worse than in the United States or Europe. The sulfur dioxide pollution in China is due in large part to the burning of high-sulfur coal in coal-fired power plants and other industrial sources, along with the lack of effective pollution control.

China is also the world's largest emitter of nitrogen dioxide pollution, a product largely of internal combustion engines (from rapidly increasing motorized vehicle use) and thermal (coal-fired) power plants. Nitrogen dioxide is a precursor to photochemical smog and ozone, both of which have serious impacts on human health.

At the global level, China is now the world leader in the greenhouse gas emissions causing global climate change. In 2009 China emitted 7.5 billion tons of carbon dioxide, 24 percent of the global total. The United States, the world's second largest emitter of carbon dioxide, released 5.9 billion tons of carbon dioxide in 2008. The United States' per capita carbon dioxide emissions, however, are still more than four times higher than China's, and the United States accounts for by far the largest percentage of historical greenhouse gas emissions. It is also worth considering that exports, according to one study, account for one-third of China's greenhouse gas emissions.[4]

These factors have caused China and other nations to raise equity and justice issues related to climate change in international negotiations and beyond. The interconnectedness of the global supply chain and the benefit that those around the world receive from China's manufacturing powerhouse in terms of cost savings and diversity of products raise questions about whether and how we all share in the responsibility for China's environmental challenges.

These are just a few data points among many. A survey of the environmental situation in China in just about every category imaginable shows that China's environment is in crisis.

THE IMPACT OF CHINA'S ENVIRONMENTAL PROBLEMS

The consequences of this environmental situation are severe. These include adverse effects on health, economic growth, and China's "social stability."

Health and Economic Costs

The immediate and long-term effects of China's environmental pollution are significant. The World Bank found that the health costs of just air and water pollution in China amounted to about 4.3 percent of China's gross domestic product (GDP) and that the total cost of air and water pollution (including nonhealth costs) was 5.8 percent of GDP.[5] One study found that one-tenth of birth defects in Jiangsu Province was due to environmental pollution.[6] Pollutants from coal-fired power plants in China have been shown to have serious neurobehavioral effects on the development of children.[7]

Social Stability

Rapid development and environmental degradation in China have driven a seemingly continuous stream of local protests and "mass incidents," in

Chinese government parlance. There have been highly publicized local protests over chemical factories, waste incinerators, high-voltage power lines, high-speed rail lines, heavy-metal poisoning, lead smelters, and battery factory chemical spills in local waterways. Farmers have lost their livelihoods to pollution, children have literally been poisoned by heavy metals, and "cancer villages" are believed to be sprouting up throughout China. Government estimates have noted that a major water pollution accident occurs in China more than once every two days. Many of these are accidents that close off water supplies for hundreds of thousands of people. In 2005 there were some 50,000 disputes over environmental pollution, according to State Environmental Protection Administration Minister Zhou Shengxian.[8] From 2001 to 2005 Chinese environmental authorities received more than 2.53 million letters and 430,000 visits by 597,000 petitioners seeking environmental redress.[9]

Beyond the statistics, China's environmental problems have serious, everyday consequences for Chinese people. Moreover, it is often the poorest and least privileged in society who bear the brunt of the problem. In recent years China has confronted a startlingly large number of heavy-metal poisonings, mostly involving children. In 2010 China's Center for Disease Control and Prevention (CDC) released preliminary results from a five-year study on the Huai River that found a causal connection between pollution and cancerous tumors.[10] More generally speaking, concerns about food safety and the impact of poor air and water quality on health are widespread among Chinese citizens.

At a workshop in Beijing in late 2010, one senior Chinese judge put it this way:

> We used to be a terribly poor country. When I was in school, there were no cars, we had no meat to eat, and our clothes were patched and of poor quality. Over the past three decades . . . China has become the second largest economy in the world. Last year we passed Germany, this year Japan. But this growth has brought about terrible environmental problems. If we have economic development that brings about such serious environmental problems, *is it really development?*

THE SOURCES OF CHINA'S ENVIRONMENTAL WOES

China's current environmental problems can be attributed to three major shifts:

1. China has become an industrial and manufacturing powerhouse—the "factory for the world."

2. Despite dramatic improvements in energy efficiency over much of the last three decades, the absolute energy consumption needed to power all of this economic activity in China is growing at an extraordinary rate. The overwhelming majority of this energy is produced by dirty coal.

3. China's own people have increasing purchasing power. Consumption—purchases of homes, cars, consumer goods, and the like—is growing exponentially.

It may come as a surprise that Walmart began to source its first product out of China only in 1993. Just two decades later, the "Made in China" label has become ubiquitous. Indeed, China makes 70 percent of the world's toys, 66 percent of its shoes, 50 percent of its color televisions and digital cameras, and 33 percent of the world's computers and refrigerators.[11] China also produces 49 percent of global flat glass, 48 percent of cement, 45 percent of the world's steel, 42 percent of lead, 28 percent of aluminum, and a major portion of the many materials that supply our infrastructure and the products that support our daily lives.[12]

The production of these modern-age commodities creates environmental degradation of all varieties. The dyeing of fabric for the clothes we wear creates water pollution, and many of China's factories still use hopelessly outmoded technologies. Chemical manufacturing produces an array of toxic materials. The production of steel, lead, rare-earth minerals, and cement requires the extraction of materials from the earth and the use of intense heat that produces significant pollution. As the developed world has gradually shifted its industry to China, these environmental impacts have shifted to China as well.

In the modern world of global supply chains, however, these problems are not China's alone. They have domestic *and* global impacts, and they are caused by domestic *and* global actions. This is not to absolve China for responsibility to control what goes on within its borders, but only to point out that consumer decisions outside of China can make a difference in increasing or reducing environmental degradation within China. For example, environmental and consumer advocacy groups are pressing for greater transparency regarding the environmental impacts of products manufactured in China and sold in the Chinese market and abroad. Indeed, a growing recognition of the interconnectedness of global supply chains has given rise to efforts to "green" supply chains and to uncover poor environmental performance among companies that produce products for export. Domestic Chinese organizations like the Institute of Public and Environmental Affairs and the Green Choice Alliance—and international organizations like NRDC, World Resources Institute, Conservation International, and others—have worked with major corporations like Walmart, Levi Strauss & Co., and H&M to reduce environmental impact.

All of China's rapidly expanding economic output must of course be powered by energy, the production of which produces pollution and other environmental impacts. In China energy largely means coal. Oil, natural gas, biomass, waste-to-heat, and other sources are also part of the energy mix, but in China over 70 percent of energy is still produced by coal—much of it high-sulfur and highly polluting. The extraction and transport of these materials result in significant environmental effects from open pit mining, mountaintop removal, oil pipelines, tailing discharge from mining operations, oil tanker and shipping spills, and coal mining accidents. The burning of these materials leads to more pollution.

Increasingly, China is turning to other forms of energy, including hydropower, nuclear, wind, and solar because it simply needs more energy in *any* form to continue growing. But coal (and fossil fuels more generally) will be king for the foreseeable future. Unless a price is placed on carbon that incorporates the cost of climate change and other environmental impacts, coal will continue to be simply too cheap and abundant to give up. The power sector is the leading producer of China's sulfur dioxide emissions. While there is no doubt that growth rates for wind, solar, and other forms of nonfossil energy will continue to be impressive, fossil-based energy is still expected to be about 85 percent of all energy in 2020.

At the same time, China's own domestic consumption is increasingly a major driver of environmental degradation. Increased incomes, massive migration from rural areas to urban centers, and an intense push to develop domestic infrastructure have spurred a construction boom and rapid construction of freeways and rail and driven skyrocketing vehicle ownership, among other things. As a matter of national policy, China has set a priority of increasing domestic demand and consumption in its twelfth Five-Year Plan. In 2009 China became the top producer and the leading market for automobiles in the world. China's inventory of motor vehicles reached 170 million, up twenty-five times from 1980 levels.[13] Domestic consumption will be an increasingly important aspect of China's energy use, although for now energy use in the residential, commercial, and transportation sectors account for just 12, 5, and 13 percent, respectively, of final energy consumption in China.[14] Industry still accounts for nearly 70 percent of China's energy use. But domestic consumption is only slated to increase and will have a growing impact on China's future environment. With respect to a variety of metrics (such as car ownership, energy use, meat consumption, and so on), per capita consumption in China is still much less than in the United States, but the sheer size of China's population means that in absolute terms it has surpassed the United States in many measures of consumption.

THE GOVERNMENT RESPONSE

The Chinese government is well aware of these environmental and energy challenges. However, for many years, their response was weak. Incentives to focus on economic development to the exclusion of other policy priorities, weak checks and balances, strong local protectionism of industrial polluters, insufficient investment in environmental protection, poor transparency, and inadequate public oversight all contributed to a seemingly intractable environmental crisis.

Increased Government Attention on the Environment

In the past Chinese decision makers have often cited the need to achieve economic development before focusing on environmental protection. However, in recent years China's environmental crisis has drawn an increasingly robust government response. There has been a clear evolution toward stronger government rhetoric in favor of environmental protection and energy efficiency over the last fifteen years or so.

China's leaders have issued a series of statements in recent years highlighting the need to elevate environmental protection and make it a priority on par with economic development. In December 2005 the State Council issued a "Decision on Implementing the Scientific Approach to Development and Strengthening Environmental Protection," which among other things called for strengthened enforcement of environmental laws and regulations, aggressive penalties for noncompliance, and utilization of legal mechanisms to compensate pollution victims. At a major national conference on environmental protection in 2006, Premier Wen Jiabao emphasized that China must transition "from a focus on economic growth to a system that places equal emphasis on environmental protection and economic growth."

Rhetoric alone would not be a cause for much optimism, given China's historical difficulties with environmental compliance and enforcement. However, China began to add more teeth to its environmental pronouncements in the lead up to and during its eleventh Five-Year Plan (2006–2010). These included governance reforms such as high-priority pollution-reduction and energy-efficiency targets, a range of new environmental mechanisms, a greater emphasis on transparency and public participation, and substantial investment in "green" energy technologies.

First, environmental priorities and targets were given the highest-level priority in China's eleventh Five-Year Plan. The most prominent targets were ones to reduce energy intensity (energy use per unit of gross domestic product) by 20 percent and pollution from chemical oxygen demand (COD) and sulfur dioxide by 10 percent each from 2005 levels. Most importantly, and in contrast to environmental targets in earlier Five-Year Plans, the eleventh Five-Year Plan targets were designated as high-priority "veto targets," meaning that failure to meet them would cause government officials to lose promotion and bonus opportunities automatically. This punitive treatment was a first.

China announced in 2011 that it had exceeded its eleventh Five-Year Plan targets for sulfur dioxide and COD emissions, and had "roughly met" its energy intensity reduction targets.[15] The energy targets were taken quite seriously because of the possible bureaucratic career consequences. They were accompanied by a series of implementing programs as well. These included the Top-1000 Enterprises Program, which involved signing agreements with China's top one thousand energy-consuming enterprises to improve energy efficiency.[16] Another major approach has been the shutdown of outdated production capacity in a wide range of sectors. These outdated facilities were among the most polluting and least energy efficient facilities and often did not contribute much to jobs or economic growth. Their shutdown is also consistent with China's policy to consolidate industries to make them more globally competitive and is viewed as supportive of China's goals to improve energy security.

In some places, government officials took the energy targets *too* seriously, so to speak. In the final year of the Five-Year Plan, as government officials rushed to complete their targets, stories of counties cutting power to hospitals, streetlights, and public heating began to emerge. In Anping County in Hebei Province, for example, the local government cut off power to hospitals and streetlights in an attempt to meet its energy-savings targets.[17] The central government scrambled to issue documents deeming such shutdown of public services illegal and anathema to the objective of the energy-intensity target (i.e., to improve energy efficiency), but the incidents highlighted the challenges of motivating behavior in a country the size of China.[18] There has also been concern about incentives to falsify reporting of data. Moreover, China's environmental targets were limited to just two pollutants and did not deal with the countless other pollutants (particulate matter, ozone, carbon monoxide, lead, cadmium, mercury, etc.) that harm human health. Ministry of Environmental Protection Vice Minister Zhang Lijun highlighted this issue in a 2010 press conference, saying in effect that China had won the battle in meeting its pollution targets but was losing the war as environmental quality in general continued to worsen.[19]

Second, China implemented a range of new environmental reforms and used existing authorities more aggressively. In 2005 China's State Environmental Protection Administration (SEPA), a notoriously weak government agency, commenced a so-called EIA storm, a campaign to shut down projects and facilities that had failed to conduct a legally required environmental impact assessment (EIA). Since then, the authority of the environmental agencies to approve EIA documents has increasingly been used in conjunction with China's energy policies to limit energy- and resource-intensive industrial development. SEPA also pressed for authority and in practice utilized "regional preapproval" (*quyu xianpi*), a process of limiting new development in areas that had seriously violated total emissions limits. In 2006 it also established regional offices in an attempt to improve supervision of local compliance (though such offices have been woefully understaffed). In 2008 SEPA was elevated from bureau to full ministry status and renamed the Ministry of Environmental Protection. The ultimate impact of these measures remains to be seen.

Third, the government took initial steps to open the door to greater environmental public participation and transparency. Among Chinese agencies, the central environmental authority has tended to be a stronger supporter of public involvement because the public's interests are viewed as aligned with agency interests and helpful for agency enforcement work. As in many other countries, public demand for stronger environmental enforcement in China can serve as a counterweight to pressure from companies and local governments for less-stringent enforcement. Official authorities for public participation and greater transparency include the Environmental Impact Assessment Law (2003) and national regulations on open government information and open environmental information.

In general, implementation of these rules has been poor. For example, the Institute of Public and Environmental Affairs, a Chinese NGO, and the Natural Resources Defense Council (NRDC) jointly developed a Pollution Information Transparency Index (PITI), which evaluated environmental transparency in 113 Chinese cities. In the first two years of evaluation, overall performance was just over thirty points of a possible one hundred, and response to public information requests in many cities was poor. Nonetheless, a number of cities performed relatively well on environmental disclosure, showing that good transparency practices are feasible at China's current stage of development.

The public is also increasingly turning to various dispute resolution mechanisms, such as lawsuits, letters and visits (*xinfang*), and the administrative reconsideration process; however, the level of public trust in these mechanisms is low. Thus, garnering the attention of the right government officials through media, protest, and other informal means is still viewed by most people as the most effective way to resolution of problems.

The ineffective implementation of these official public participation channels reflects in significant part government caution about opening the door too widely to public involvement and transparency. The robust, aggressive rollout of top-down government environmental and energy targets stands in stark contrast to the modest implementation of public participation channels. Nonetheless, these reforms mark a significant change from the past.

Finally, China has boosted its investment and policy support for clean energy technologies, making it, in a very short time, a world leader in the manufacture of solar, wind, and other renewable forms of energy. In 2009 China announced a 2020 target to obtain 15 percent of its energy from non-fossil sources[20] and that same year was the global leader in green technology investment—investing $34.6 billion in green technologies, compared to $18.6 billion for the United States.[21] In 2010 China added sixteen gigawatts (GW) of installed wind power capacity for a total installed capacity of 41.83 GW, overtaking the United States, which had 40.2 GW.[22] China's growth accounted for nearly half of the entire global increase in installed wind capacity (35.8 GW).[23] China is the world's leading manufacturer of solar panels, which are mostly for export. China's own installed solar PV capacity at the end of 2008 was less than one hundred megawatts, or 0.01 percent of China's entire installed capacity. China's target for installed solar capacity by 2020 was 1.8 GW, which experts believe China will far exceed (reaching 10 GW or more).

Can China be in the midst of an environmental crisis while also leading the world in green technology development? Though coal is expected to decline in the future as a percentage of China's energy mix, it is still likely to be as high as 74 percent in 2035. As such, cleaner energy technologies will help, but they will only provide a partial solution. Moreover, China's global leadership in "clean tech" is not only a reflection of China's tremendous need for all forms of energy, but partly an indication of how developed countries, particularly the United States, have failed to assign critical priority to fossil fuel alternatives. However, many of China's environmental troubles stem from the overwhelming portion of its energy sector that remains quite dirty, as well as from inefficient development and poor regulation of industrial facilities, a booming transportation sector, inefficient water use, and a host of other issues.

China's moves to become a leader in clean energy technologies, however, may ultimately prove to be a major benefit to the global environment. Its advantage in low-cost manufacturing and its heavy investment in renewable energy sources have the potential to drive down costs for cleaner energy technologies, one day making them cost-competitive with dirtier energy sources.

China's twelfth Five-Year Plan (2011–2015) expands on the initiatives of the preceding plan. Some have called this the greenest Five-Year Plan in China's history because of stated commitments to the development of environmental protection and clean energy industries, as well as additional pollution reduction and climate targets. State commitments include an energy-intensity reduction target of 16 percent, a carbon-intensity reduction target of 17 percent, and a target to increase nonfossil fuels as a percentage of the total energy mix to 11.4 percent (up from 8.3 percent). Seven additional pollutants will be added to the existing pollutants with targets, for example, sulfur dioxide and chemical oxygen demand. These also include nitrogen oxide, ammonia nitrogen, and five heavy metals (lead, mercury, chromium, cadmium, and arsenic).[24] China has also announced that it will provide significant investment and policy support for the development of "strategic emerging industries" in the new energy and environmental protection areas. Reportedly, it will also provide 4 trillion yuan ($600 billion) in financial support for these industries.[25] One Chinese expert from the Chinese Academy of Environmental Planning has predicted a doubling of China's overall investment in environmental protection in the twelfth Five-Year Plan.[26] Increased investment in environmental protection and energy efficiency and continued focus on improving performance on environmental and energy metrics are all positive signs for China's future. Critically, environmental and energy objectives in the latest central government plans are viewed as engines of future economic development, not barriers to economic prosperity.

THE PUBLIC RESPONSE

A government response alone, however, will not be enough to address China's environmental challenges. This is because, in the past, implementation of environmental priorities has been a persistent problem.

In recent years, growing public awareness of China's environmental problems and stronger public demand for better environmental quality has spurred a number of public responses. Local communities have organized to push back on undesirable projects or fought to stop ongoing pollution. Though as a group they are still weak, a number of Chinese environmental groups have matured and turned to more diverse, sophisticated advocacy approaches. Public demand has increased for greater transparency about environmental quality and performance of facilities. The proliferation of environmental laws has given the public a new tool for protecting itself from environmental harms, even as the law still suffers from infirmities that seriously hamper its effectiveness.

Local Community Response

The most aggressive, vigorous responses to environmental problems in China have come from local communities. Many of the cases that have garnered significant media attention have involved either local opposition to proposed large-scale development projects, such as chemical plants, waste incinerators, and high-speed rail projects, or opposition to ongoing pollution or environmental degradation that is either suspected of causing health problems or damage to personal property, such as crops or animal farming stocks. In the last few years, a trio of cases gained particularly widespread domestic and international attention, though there are many lesser-known cases like it around China. These were the Xiamen PX case, the Shanghai Maglev case, and the Panyu garbage incinerator case.[27]

In the Xiamen PX case, using web chat rooms and text messages, thousands of local residents famously organized a "stroll" (*sanbu*) through the streets of the southern city of Xiamen in an ultimately successful protest to stop the development of a Taiwanese chemical plant. The plant project was moved to a different city in Fujian in the end—an environmental success for locals in Xiamen, but an unresolved problem for residents of the city to which the project was relocated. The Shanghai Maglev case involved local concern about the health and environmental impacts of a high-speed rail line. The Panyu case reflected local concern about the pollution from a proposed waste incinerator project. These cases are not unique but rather reflect what appear to be a growing number of cases involving middle-class protestors with a mix of environmental, health, and economic concerns (e.g., impact on property values). The approach—revolving around organized protest—demonstrates a lack of faith in official participation or legal channels and the common knowledge among many in China that government officials are evaluated by the senior levels of government on their ability to maintain social stability. In practice, citizens have come to learn that protest is often an effective way of achieving goals and obtaining concessions.

Local protests have also occurred in the wake of severe pollution incidents. For example, in 2009 a series of cases involving heavy-metal poisoning of children cropped up throughout China.[28] Angry parents protested in an effort to stop the polluting factories and to obtain compensation and medical care. The spate of unrest drove a policy development process that culminated in a national plan to address heavy-metal pollution, including emissions reduction targets of 15 percent for five heavy metals, though the details of the plan remain secret. Anecdotal evidence suggest that there are countless other cases involving local communities concerned about their children's health, farmers who have faced crop damage or harm to animal stocks, homeowners concerned with how environmental degradation will affect local property values, and a seemingly endless range of other problems.

Environmental NGOs

Environmental NGOs have drawn a great deal of interest from Chinese citizens and the international community alike. Though still weak, environmental NGOs have played an important role in increasing environmental awareness and have in some cases started to engage in more sophisticated advocacy that is having a real impact.

China's environmental civil society started from simple beginnings but has grown markedly, particularly in the last five years. China's first registered nongovernmental environmental group, Friends of Nature (FON), was established in 1994. The number of environmental NGOs has grown significantly since then, reflecting the greater amount of political space for civil society groups to work on environmental issues in China. A 2008 survey by the All-China Environment Federation found that there were 3,539 environmental NGOs in China, up from 771 in 2005.[29] For the most part, these groups remain small, with nearly half having between one and five full-time staff and 29 percent with no full-time staff at all.

A number of China's environmental groups, which largely engaged in environmental education in the early years, have become increasingly sophisticated in their advocacy. Today such groups engage with multinational corporations to "green" their supply chains, participate in international climate negotiations, comment on legislation, initiate legal actions, and carry out complex, multichannel advocacy against often much more powerful polluting enterprises or development projects, such as hydropower projects.

The development of Friends of Nature over the last sixteen years is a prime example of this shift in China's environmental civil society. In addition to their traditional environmental education work, FON has moved toward more sophisticated policy and community activism, including helping communities to deal with environmental justice issues surrounding waste incinerators, advocating for greater transparency of listed companies in China, and setting up a rapid response team to review environmental impact assessments of major polluting projects. Moreover, FON has come to play a critical role in reaching out and serving as a resource to communities around the country, often where FON volunteer groups have formed.

But in addition to FON, there are now a surprising number of environmental groups around China that have developed a variety of approaches and continue to battle against unbelievable odds to improve China's environment. These include Ma Jun's Institute of Public and Environmental Affairs, Jin Jiaman's Global Environmental Institute, Wang Yongchen's Green Earth Volunteers, and countless others. Among these are important community-based or local-level groups that have carved out a niche monitoring and defending the local environment, such as Yun Jianli's Green Hanjiang in Hubei Province, Huo Daishan's Huai River Defenders in Anhui Province, Wu Dengming's Green Volunteer League of Chongqing, and more fledgling groups like Green Anhui and Green Camelbell in Gansu Province. In many cases, NGOs have played an important role in supporting local communities to achieve their goals.

Despite progress, China's environmental NGOs still face difficult odds some seventeen years after the establishment of FON. Antiquated government rules still limit fundraising, membership, and the range of activities. Onerous and unclear registration requirements limit groups' independence. Environmental groups have always had the most room to operate in China among NGOs, but it says something that FON still has only twenty staff as it nears the end of its second decade.

Public Participation, Transparency, and Environmental Law

Public participation, information transparency, and environmental law generally are playing a larger, though still limited, role in environmental advocacy efforts in China than ever before. The Chinese government, in an effort to identify potential disputes and provide a release valve for public opinion, has gradually opened the door to greater official channels for public involvement in environmental affairs. The 2003 Environmental Impact Assessment Law was an important first step in this regard, as the law set forth provisions regarding the right of the public to comment on proposed projects. Though the rules are imperfect, the law generated a great deal of interest from the public and environmental groups and raised public expectations about the ability to participate. In 2007 China's State Council passed national regulations on open government information. SEPA was the first agency to follow with agency implementing regulations. Its interest in the information disclosure regulations stemmed from a view that greater transparency could aid environmental officials in their enforcement work.

Increased government and company disclosure of environmental information, although still limited by developed country standards, has enabled civil society efforts such as the Water and Air Pollution Maps created by Ma Jun and the Institute of Public and Environmental Affairs (IPE). It has allowed environmental groups like IPE and NRDC to identify factories with poor environmental performance and work with multinational corporations that purchase from these factories to develop approaches to reducing pollution. The Pollution Information Transparency Index mentioned above—involving two environmental NGOs evaluating the level of environmental transparency at 113 municipal Chinese government bureaus—would have been unimaginable even just a few years earlier and has created a platform through which government agencies are affirmatively reaching out to NGOs to improve performance.

More generally, greater legal consciousness among the public has begun to take hold in China. Since as early as 2005, with the founding of Friends of Nature, sympathetic officials in different government agencies, academics, and other environmentalists have advocated the development of an environmental public-interest litigation system in China to allow agencies and citizens to bring public-interest suits against polluters and intransigent government agencies. Wang Canfa and the Center for Legal Assistance to Pollution Victims marked in 2010 its tenth anniversary of assisting pollution victims to obtain compensation and relief. Litigation is still not the preferred avenue and law remains difficult for the public to use in practice, but law is undoubtedly changing in positive ways the landscape upon which the public registers complaints.

The struggle to stop a chemical plant portrayed in the Academy Award–nominated documentary *The Warriors of Qiugang* demonstrates the promise of the law and the distance still left to travel for rule of law in China.[30] In this case, the law both failed and saved Qiugang Village. Zhang Gongli—the leader of the villagers and a farmer with only a middle school education—brought several lawsuits that proved unsuccessful despite seemingly clear violations of the law. Early lawsuits by other villagers were met with retaliation and beatings from company thugs. Petitions sent to the local government were lost and met with no response. The failure of official channels to respond to the villagers' complaints drove the villagers to take to the streets in protest and forced them to take their grievances to Beijing. Yet despite these failures in the legal system, the ability of the villagers to ground their grievances in the law proved to be a powerful weapon. There is a memorable scene in the film in which a villager holding a tattered official copy of a 2004 speech on the environment by China's President Hu Jintao points to a passage from the speech about the legal liability of officials who "connive to ruin and pollute the environment." The villager says, "President Hu Jintao's own words! We've got Hu Jintao on our side. What are we afraid of?"[31] The villagers repeatedly cited specific legal violations by the local factories. The law bolstered the legitimacy of the villagers' grievances, even as they were forced to take extralegal measures to have their grievances heard. The ability of the villagers to gain leverage by negotiating their grievances in the "shadow of the law" is an important development; one might hope that it marks a positive step among many in the effort to create a stronger rule of law in China.

CHINA'S ENVIRONMENTAL FUTURE

There are many reasons to believe China is beginning to head in a more environmentally responsible direction. In response to rising public dissatisfaction with environmental problems and greater recognition of the heavy economic and human costs of environmental degradation, pollution reduction has become a highly publicized government priority. China's policies to increase energy efficiency and develop a clean energy technology industry are aligned with the national interest in maintaining economic growth and developing global economic leadership. The designation of clean energy, energy efficiency, and environmental protection industries as "strategic emerging industries" is an important sign of how China has linked its future economic growth with sustainable development.

Nonetheless, China's past efforts to shift its industrial structure away from heavy, energy-intensive industry toward a larger service industry have largely failed. Moreover, while these efforts to support clean energy technology could go some way toward curing many of China's environmental ailments, there are a host of other environmental challenges (heavy-metal pollution, for example) that still depend on China significantly increasing its investment in environmental protection, reforming its environmental governance structures, elevating transparency and public participation, and breaking the hold of local protectionism. Whether initial positive reforms continue will depend on continued public attention and advocacy. Incidents like the Xiamen PX case and the thousands of similar cases that do not receive similar levels of media attention show that communities in China will aggressively advocate for their rights.

One has to wonder: Will these cases spill over into more widespread general advocacy for the environment in China? Will any of these cases be the equivalent of the famous U.S. case in the 1960s of the Cuyahoga River catching fire or Rachel Carson's seminal environmental book *Silent Spring,* or the Japanese cases regarding Minamata disease (a neurological disease due to mercury poisoning)? What might be the wake-up calls that mobilize public opinion and transform environmental and energy regulation? As China's economy booms and people are distracted by ever-increasing economic opportunities, massive pollution accidents that might have been expected to become tipping points in China's green movement, such as the 2005 Songhua River benzene spill that poured about one hundred tons of chemicals into a local river, or the 2010 Zijin Mining Group chemical spill that killed some two thousand tons of fish, have failed to ignite more widespread support. And yet, in August of 2011 upwards of 20,000 protesters in Dalian, who were confronted by a wall of police in riot gear, still succeeded in bringing about the closing of the Fujia Chemical Plant, which was to produce the toxic gas paraxylene (px).[32]

In many ways, the stars seem to be aligning for meaningful environmental improvement in China, but only time will tell whether it can move away from this ominous turning point in its challenging environmental history.

SUGGESTIONS FOR FURTHER READING

Internet

Switchboard, the Natural Resources Defense Council's staff blog (posts tagged for China), http://switchboard.nrdc.org/blogs/issues/greening _china/

Greenlaw China, NRDC's China law and policy blog, www.greenlawchina
.org

Alex Wang's Twitter feed on all matters related to China's environment
and energy future, www.twitter.com/greenlawchina

China Dialogue, a bilingual site covering China's environment, www
.chinadialogue.net

A site with information regarding China's low-carbon initiatives, organized by the World Resources Institute, www.chinafaqs.org

U.S. Environmental Protection Agency's China site, http://www.epa.gov/
ogc/china/initiative_home.htm

The website for China's Ministry of Environmental Protection (English
site available), www.mep.gov.cn

Film

The Warriors of Qiugang, an Academy Award–nominated short documentary by Ruby Yang and Tom Lennon. See "The Warriors of Qiugang:
A Chinese Village Fights Back," *Environment 360*, http://e360.yale.edu/
the_warriors_of_qiugang_a_chinese_village_fights_back; Alex Wang, "New
Documentary Follows the Struggle to Save China's Environment," *Huffington Post*, January 14, 2011, http://www.huffingtonpost.com/alex-wang/
the-warriors-of-qiugang-a_b_808382.html.

Books and Articles

Economy, Elizabeth. *The River Runs Black: The Environmental Challenge to China's
Future*. Ithaca, NY: Cornell University Press, 2004.

Ma Jun. *China's Water Crisis*. Norwalk, CT: Eastbridge, 2004.

Mertha, Andrew C. *China's Water Warriors: Citizen Action and Policy Change*. 2nd ed.
Ithaca, NY: Cornell University Press, 2008.

Van Rooij, Benjamin. *Regulating Land and Pollution in China, Lawmaking, Compliance,
and Enforcement: Theory and Cases*. Leiden: Leiden University Press, 2006.

Wang, Alex. "The Role of Law in Environmental Protection in China: Recent Developments." *Vermont Journal of Environmental Law* 8, no. 2 (2007): 195–223.

Watts, Jonathan. *When a Billion Chinese Jump: How China Will Save Mankind—or
Destroy It*. New York: Scribner, 2010.

NOTES

1. C. Fred Bergston et al., *China's Rise: Challenges and Opportunities* (Washington,
DC: Peter G. Peterson Institute for International Economics / Center for Strategic
and International Studies, 2008), 152; U.S. Energy Information Administration,
"Electric Power Monthly, March 2011," 1, http://www.eia.doe.gov/cneaf/electricity/

epm/02261103.pdf; U.S. Energy Information Administration, "International Energy Outlook 2010," http://www.eia.doe.gov/oiaf/ieo/electricity.html.

2. International Energy Agency, *World Energy Outlook 2007* (Paris: International Energy Agency, 2007), 313.

3. Chris Buckley, "China Says It Is World's Top Greenhouse Gas Emitter," *Reuters*, November 23, 2010, http://www.reuters.com/article/idUSTRE6AM1NG20101123; sulfur dioxide: "China's sulfur dioxide discharge tops world list," *Xinhua*, August 3, 2006, http://www.china.org.cn/english/2006/Aug/176872.htm; "China Eats the World," *Mother Jones*, December 10, 2007, http://motherjones.com/environment/2007/12/china-eats-world; "1/3 of China's Yellow River not even fit for industrial use," *Discover*, November 26, 2008, http://blogs.discovermagazine.com/80beats/2008/11/26/13-of-chinas-yellow-river-not-even-fit-for-industrial-use/.

4. See Buckley, "China Says It Is World's Top"; U.S. Environmental Protection Agency, "Inventory of U.S. Greenhouse Gas Emissions and Sinks: 1990–2008," April 2010, http://www.epa.gov/climatechange/emissions/downloads10/US-GHG-Inventory-2010_ExecutiveSummary.pdf; Adam Vaughn, "A History of CO2 Emissions,"*DataBlog, Guardian*, September 2, 2009, http://www.guardian.co.uk/environment/datablog/2009/sep/02/co2-emissions-historical; Ben Block, "Exports Account for One-Third of China's Emissions," *Worldchanging*, August 12, 2008, http://www.worldchanging.com/archives/008354.html.

5. World Bank, "Cost of Pollution in China: Economic Estimates of Physical Damage," http://web.worldbank.org/WBSITE/EXTERNAL/COUNTRIES/EASTASIAPACIFICEXT/EXTEAPREGTOPENVIRONMENT/0,,contentMDK:21252897~pagePK:34004173~piPK:34003707~theSitePK:502886,00.html.

6. Malcolm Moore, "China's Soaring Birth Defects Linked to Pollution," *Telegraph*, January 9, 2009, http://www.telegraph.co.uk/news/worldnews/asia/china/4209057/Chinas-soaring-birth-defects-linked-to-pollution.html.

7. Frederica Perera et al., "Benefits of Reducing Prenatal Exposure to Coal-Burning Pollutants to Children's Neurodevelopment in China," *Environmental Health Perspectives* 116 (2008): 1396–1400, http://ehp03.niehs.nih.gov/article/info%3Adoi%2F10.1289%2Fehp.11480.

8. SEPA is now known as the Ministry of Environmental Protection. Li Fangchao, "Environment Issues Addressed More Urgently," *China Daily*, May 4, 2006, http://www.chinadaily.com.cn/bizchina/2006-05/04/content_582631.htm.

9. Chinese Government White Paper, "Environmental Science and Technology, Industry, and Public Participation," http://www.china.org.cn/english/MATERIAL/170390.htm.

10. "CDC Finds Cancer Link to Huai River," *Global Times*, December 29, 2010, http://china.globaltimes.cn/society/2010-12/606525_2.html.

11. Institute of Public and Environmental Affairs, "The Green Choice Alliance for Responsible Supply Chain Management," August 2008, 2, http://www.ipe.org.cn/Upload//2010-08/7b2d7a8c07f1400a993cb55876c714eb.pdf.

12. For steel see "Global Steel Output Surges by 29 Percent: Trade Body," *China Post*, June 23, 2010, http://www.chinapost.com.tw/business/global-markets/2010/06/23/261844/Global-steel.htm; for lead see Doe Run Company, "Emerging Economies Driving Global Lead Market," press release, June 28, 2010, http://www

.doerun.com/EmergingEconomiesDrivingGlobalLeadMarket/tabid/179/language/
en-US/Default.aspx.

13. See Ministry of Environmental Protection of the People's Republic of China,
http://www.mep.gov.cn/gkml/hbb/qt/201011/t20101104_197140.htm.

14. Bergston, *China's Rise*, 111.

15. "Carbon Intensity Targets Unveiled," *Xinhua*, March 1, 2011, http://news
.xinhuanet.com/english2010/sci/2011-03/01/c_13755116.htm.

16. Lynn Price, Xuejun Wang, and Jiang Yun, "The Challenge of Reducing Energy
Consumption of the Top-1000 Largest Industrial Enterprises in China," *Energy Policy*
38, no. 11 (November 2010): 6485–98, http://china.lbl.gov/sites/china.lbl.gov/
files/Top-1000.Energy_Policy_November2010.pdf.

17. "Chinese County Uses Blackouts to Achieve Energy Saving Goal," *Eni-
gin News*, September 6, 2010, http://www.enigin.com/about/enigin-plc/news/-/
enigin-news-chinese-county-uses-blackouts-to-achieve-energy-saving-goal.

18. See Central Government, http://www.gov.cn/jrzg/2010-09/19/content
_1706054.htm.

19. See http://www.gov.cn/2010lh/govzhibo_20100310b.htm.

20. However, much of this is expected to come from hydropower (with the accompanying environmental and forced-migration issues) and nuclear power.

21. Pew Charitable Trust, "Who's Winning the Clean Energy Race?" http://
www.pewtrusts.org/uploadedFiles/wwwpewtrustsorg/Reports/Global_warming/
G-20%20Report.pdf.

22. Wind Turbines Manufacturer in China, "China Added 16 GW of Installed Wind Power Capacity in 2010," http://windturbines.china-windturbine
.com/2011/01/china-wind-power-capacity/.

23. "Wind Capacity Increases by 22% in 2010," *Commodities Now*, February
2011, http://www.commodities-now.com/reports/environmental-markets/4925
-wind-capacity-increases-by-22-in-2010.html.

24. The five heavy metal targets appear to be lower priority targets than the other
four pollution reduction targets, however.

25. Li Woke, "Spotlight Shines on New Energy Sector," *Global Times*, October 20,
2010, http://business.globaltimes.cn/china-economy/2010-10/583723.html.

26. "China Is Set to Lose 2% of GDP Cleaning Up Pollution," *Bloomberg News*,
September 17, 2010, http://www.businessweek.com/news/2010-09-17/china-is-set
-to-lose-2-of-gdp-cleaning-up-pollution.html.

27. Royston Chan and Sophie Taylor, "Hundreds Protest Shanghai Maglev Rail
Extension," *Reuters*, January 12, 2008, http://www.reuters.com/article/2008/01/12/
us-china-maglev-protest-idUSPEK32757920080112; "S China's Guangzhou Sus-
pends Incinerator Project until Environmental Assessments OK," *Xinhua*, November
23, 2009, http://news.xinhuanet.com/english/2009-11/23/content_12524614.htm.

28. "Angry Villagers Stage Lead Poisoning Protest," *China.org.cn*, http://www
.china.org.cn/health/2009-08/18/content_18352966.htm; "More Parents Protest
against Lead Poisoning in China," *Reuters*, August 20, 2009, http://www.reuters
.com/article/2009/08/20/idUSPEK183380; Li Xinran, "Hundreds of Chinese Villagers Protest Lead Poisoning," *Globalization Monitor*, September 18, 2009, http://www
.globalmon.org.hk/en/095environment/hundreds-of-chinese-villagers-protest-lead
-poisoning/.

29. "China's Environmental NGOs' Influence Increases as Total Doubles in 3 Years," *Xinhua*, October 31, 2008, http://news.xinhuanet.com/english/2008-10/31/content_10288246.htm.

30. Alex Wang, "New Documentary Follows the Struggle to Save China's Environment," *Huffington Post*, January 14, 2011, http://www.huffingtonpost.com/alex-wang/the-warriors-of-qiugang-a_b_808382.html.

31. A speech is, of course, not technically "law," but remarks from China's most senior leaders can have an important impact on the understanding of the law.

32. Citizens of Dalian were motivated by safety concerns occasioned by the location of the plant less than 60 meters from the waters of the East China Sea. Within a day of the protests on August 14, 2011, the municipal government ordered the plant to be closed immediately. By mid-January 2012, however, there were reports that the Fujia plant had quietly resumed operation.

6

China's Historic Urbanization: Explosive and Challenging

Timothy B. Weston

In 2011 and 2012 the dramatic challenge to, and even the overthrow of, long-entrenched authoritarian regimes by popular movements in North Africa and the Middle East has occasioned considerable discussion among pundits as to whether China's government might be the next to be toppled. Many have observed that China's massive internal security apparatus (the annual budget for which, as of March 2011, outpaced that of the country's military for the first time[1]) is far better prepared to manage and channel oppositional sentiment within society than were those of the fallen governments of Tunisia and Egypt (as well as those that remain under siege by their own people). However, the fundamental question at the heart of the comparison is this: Does the Chinese Communist Party (CCP) possess sufficient legitimacy to prevent discontent within society from boiling over and becoming a threat to the very survival of the Beijing government? Here the answer appears to be yes, the primary reason being that the CCP has presided over the most sustained and breathtaking economic expansion of modern times, something exemplified by the dramatic transformation of the country's urban landscape.

While the world's most developed economies have slogged through a deep economic trough in recent years, Chinese cities have boomed and the Chinese gross domestic product has continued to grow at the phenomenal rate of between 9 and 10 percent annually—a torrid pace that has been maintained for two decades running! So while many Chinese will criticize their government for many things and will lament that their society has become corrupt and perhaps soulless, they are also well aware that nearly half a billion of their fellow countrymen have been lifted out of poverty over the past several decades of communist rule. In other words, enough Chinese people feel they are enjoying upward social mobility or the prospect of it to make it highly unlikely that they would trade in the generally rosy status quo for an uncertain future.

All the same, lacking the legitimacy that comes with being elected at the ballot box, the Beijing government recognizes that it must continue to deliver on the Chinese people's desire for upward social mobility if it wishes to remain their preferred choice to govern the country. To do that, it has determined, the economy must maintain a growth rate of at least 8 percent annually in order to absorb the large number of workers entering the labor market; experts suspect that if growth falls below that rate, the country's unemployment problem could become severe enough to trigger serious political instability. Thus the CCP has wagered that ongoing political stability depends on its ability to go on being the goose that lays the golden egg. In this spirit, at the 17th Party Congress convened in Beijing in 2007—the eighteenth will occur in fall 2012—the communist government set an ambitious economic growth target of quadrupling the country's GDP from $1.08 trillion U.S. (the figure from the year 2000) to about $4.32 trillion by 2020.[2] If that target can be reached, the party should be able to persuade the Chinese people that its eggs indeed remain golden.

The CCP's ambitions for continued economic growth are tied directly to the country's stunningly rapid process of urbanization, for more than anything else it has been the astounding growth of cities over the past several decades that has accounted for China's high economic growth rates. As the authors of a respected and widely quoted recent report on Chinese cities have written, "urbanization and China's robust economic growth have gone hand in hand. Cities have been the major drivers of China's GDP growth over the past two decades and they will become even more so over the next 20 years." The report, prepared by McKinsey Global Institute and titled "Preparing for China's Urban Billion," notes that cities account for fully 75 percent of China's annual GDP at present and projects that by 2025 they will account for 95 percent of the country's annual GDP. Large cities attract more talent and investment than smaller ones and are typically at the hub of a network of smaller cities, which has the effect of increasing economic diversification and regional growth.[3]

Key figures in the Chinese capital are equally clear on the close relationship between urbanization and economic growth. Zheng Xinli, vice president for the China Center for International Economic Exchanges and a top adviser to the government, recently indicated that urbanization is "a key factor bolstering the country's growth" and "a significant contributor to the nation's gross domestic product during the twelfth Five-Year Plan (2011–2015), and in the longer term."[4] Certainly, China is not alone in relying on cities to promote economic advance. As J. Vernon Henderson writes, "Urbanization is an integral element of rapid income growth and industrialization throughout the world, as countries advance from low to higher income levels."[5] What all of this makes abundantly clear is that the fate of the Chinese economy, and perhaps that of the CCP as well, is closely linked to the nation's ongoing urbanization process.

CHINA'S URBAN TAKE OFF BY FEEL AND IN NUMBERS

That the story of China's modernization has been closely bound up with the transformation of its cities will come as no surprise to anyone who has visited there over the past quarter century—to those who, like myself, have watched China's cities molt their former skins and become wholly unrecognizable. In the 1980s even the largest, wealthiest, and most modern cities of Beijing and Shanghai felt quiet and sleepy. One knew one was surrounded by millions of people, but the pace of life was slow (bicycle speed), colors were muted, advertising hardly existed, public infrastructure was crude and relatively undeveloped, and modern conveniences were few and far between. In many ways China's biggest cities felt like massive villages lacking the urban feel to which I was accustomed from my experience in big U.S. cities.

To visit Beijing or Shanghai today is an entirely different experience: one feels as though one has traveled into the future unfolding. I distinctly recall standing on the Bund in Shanghai in the mid-1980s and looking across the Huangpu River. Rather than the now iconic, futuristic skyline of present-day Pudong, there were a few low-lying and completely nondescript buildings on the opposite shore (see figure 6.1). Likewise, twenty years ago when I was a foreign student, the Beijing Capital International Airport was a drab, utilitarian place and the road from the airport (it could not be called a highway) into the city was lined by earthen shoulders, ditches, and closely planted trees. Traffic moved slowly and conveyed an odd assortment of bicycles, buses, minibus taxis, trucks, three-wheeled tractor contraptions, and horse-drawn carriages. It felt like the countryside, not the immediate suburbs of the capital of the world's most populous nation. Today, when one's plane lands in Beijing, one disembarks at one of the largest and most modern airports in the world before being whisked into the gleaming, futuristic, and endlessly unfolding capital city on massive super highways crowded with internationally famous name-brand luxury cars and lined by high-rise office buildings sporting signs for multinational companies.

The speed at which Chinese cities are changing and the huge amount of money being spent on infrastructural improvement in the wealthiest Chinese cities far outpaces what is happening in U.S. cities, where municipal governments are broke and even maintenance of existing, outdated infra-

Figure 6.1. Pudong: Future in the Present. Photograph by Tong Lam.

structure is a very challenging problem. While many cities in the United States are crumbling, Chinese cities are being built and rebuilt along increasingly modern and eye-catching lines. Shenzhen, the city next to Hong Kong and China's fastest growing over the past several decades, is the best-known example of a massive urban area developing where there was only a fishing village thirty years ago (see figure 6.2). Today the population of greater Shenzhen—the central city and its suburbs—is close to nine million people. At that size, Shenzhen would qualify as the fourth largest city in the United States, behind only the New York, Los Angeles, and Chicago metro areas. In all of Europe there are thirty-five cities with populations over one million. By 2025 China is projected to have 221 cities with populations over one million, twenty-three of which will have more than five million residents.[6]

Still, one can be awed by what has happened in Beijing, Shanghai, Shenzhen, or any other Chinese city without fully appreciating what the transformations of those cities bespeak about the truly historic changes underway in China today. Seeing a few places up close over time—in my case, mainly Beijing and Shanghai—provides an invaluable sense of qualitative change across the decades but cannot illuminate the broader demographic transformation unfolding throughout the country as a whole. To begin to understand the scale of the transformation on a national level requires stepping back to consider the hard-to-fathom statistics that describe China's

Figure 6.2.   Shenzhen: From Village to Megalopolis. Photograph by Chris DeWolf.

population in relative terms. While the country's current 3.5 percent annual rate of urban population growth is not as rapid as the 5 to 6 percent rates experienced by other developing countries during times of economic take off, the absolute numbers of people in China make what is taking place there of global significance.[7]

To gain some appreciation for the meaning of China's current population of 1.3 billion people, which constitutes some 20 percent of the world's population, it is instructive to point out that the populations of single Chinese provinces are often as large as those of entire countries with which readers may have some familiarity. For example, the population of the eastern seaboard province of Shandong, at 84 million people, is larger than that of Germany, at 81 million; the central province of Hunan, with 64 million inhabitants, has a larger population than France; and the number of inhabitants in Guangdong in the far south, China's most populace province, which is just under 100 million people, is roughly equal to that of the Philippines, the twelfth most populous country in the world.[8]

As these numbers communicate the magnitude of China's population in global terms, it becomes possible to understand how it is that in terms of absolute numbers China's 3.5 percent annual rate of urbanization can translate into the fastest rate of urbanization in world history. For as long as there has been a China, the vast majority of the country's population has resided in villages and made its living off the land. But that basic and unchanging truth has recently become history. In January 2012 China's National Bureau of Statistics reported that in 2011 the country's urban population exceeded its rural one.[9] As demographer Wang Feng states, "China is for the first time crossing a historical landmark from a country that's dominated by people engaging in agriculture, living in the countryside, to an urbanized society."[10] This is a remarkable and momentous fact. Consider that in 1980, at the start of the Deng Xiaoping–led reforms, roughly 80 percent of China's 980 million people lived in the countryside and 20 percent in cities. In terms of actual numbers of people, that means that some 200 million Chinese lived in cities in 1980. According to the National Statistics Bureau in Beijing, the number today is over 690 million, while the number of rural-dwellers is about 656 million.[11]

In the space of thirty years China has gone from having an urban population equal to roughly two thirds of the current population of the United States (approximately 310 million) to one that is equal to twice the current population of the United States. By 2025 urban dwellers are expected to make up roughly 60 percent of the country's entire population, with some experts predicting that the number could climb closer to 70 percent (see figure 6.3). Those numbers will be historically high for China, of course, but still lower than in other parts of the world. Today, for example, 82 percent of the U.S. population lives in cities, while in Latin America and Europe the numbers are 79 percent and 73 percent, respectively.[12] Over the next fifteen years Chinese cities are expected to become home to an additional

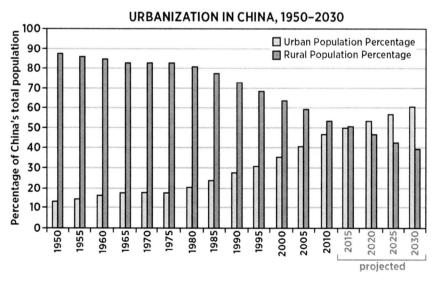

Figure 6.3.   The Upward Scale of China's Urbanism.

350 million people, raising the total number of city dwellers to about one billion. That means that roughly one out of eight people in the world will be a resident of a Chinese city by the year 2025. Between now and that year more people will be added to the urban population of China than exist in the entire United States today. The number of new people who will be added to China's urban population by 2025 will equal the combined populations of Germany, France, Britain, Italy, South Korea, South Africa, Spain, Poland, and Canada!

WHAT'S DRIVING CHINA'S URBAN EXPLOSION?

China's map is dotted with large urban areas, but most of the largest and wealthiest cities are located along or within a few hundred miles of the country's long eastern coastline. During the past several decades, foreign and domestic private-sector investment has been concentrated in urban centers and industrial zones located along the coast, helping to integrate those places into the global economy. It is coastal, urban China that has developed into the country's prosperous manufacturing center; indeed, the story of China as factory to the world is largely set in the cities of the coastal region, particularly those of the southeastern seaboard, although massive inland cities such as Chongqing and Wuhan also play a significant role. It is in such places that the vast majority of consumer goods upon which middle-class consumers across the globe have come to rely are produced.

The wealthiest places in China are urban centers along the coast, but it is in its midsize cities beyond the eastern seaboard where China's middle class is likely to grow the fastest over the next few decades.[13] The nation's growing middle classes are overwhelmingly concentrated in its urban areas, and the largest and wealthiest middle-class populations reside in the urban areas along the eastern seaboard. Those urban middle classes in turn fuel private consumption, which has emerged as a significant driver of economic expansion in its own right, accounting for over a quarter of China's GDP growth between 1990 and 2005. As with all other trend lines describing urbanization in China, those for urban consumption point steadily upward; by 2025 the urban consumption share of GDP is expected to reach 33 percent.[14]

China's urban growth and its contribution to the enrichment of the nation's economy is closely linked to the expansion of its middle class and to the money it can spend on goods and services. Rather than being new to the cities, China's emerging middle-class households, which, according to one measure, command an annual income of between $12,000 and $18,000 U.S., tend to have originated from within a population that has resided in urban areas for generations.[15] In general, the middle class is composed of people from smaller families (the one-child policy traditionally having been more strictly enforced in cities than in the countryside) who have benefited from the superior educational systems, social networks, and career opportunities available in urban areas. Such people have naturally filled white-collar positions within government, industry, and business, and in terms of their aspirations for material comfort and a degree of upward social mobility for their children in many ways resemble middle classes in other parts of the world.

As the Chinese middle class develops so too do the dreams of multinational corporations, which fantasize about supplying a seemingly endless number of consumers prepared to spend money on themselves and especially on their children. It is this prospect that has in recent years led Best Buy, Home Depot, Carrefour, IKEA, Walmart (which itself currently ranks as the seventh leading trading partner among *nations* with China!), and other companies catering to middle-class consumers to make aggressive pushes into the Chinese market, and the same prospect also accounts for the arrival in China of foreign automobile, insurance, banking, and luxury goods companies.[16]

But the story of China's urban growth and its contribution to the enrichment of the nation's economy is not principally centered on its expanding middle class. Instead, it is the influx into cities of migrant workers from the countryside that accounts for the huge boom in the populations of Chinese cities. In 2010 over 260 million Chinese were counted as migrants, that is, as people living and working outside their native villages, towns, or cities.[17] The number of China's migrants is thus fairly close to the total number of people who live in the United States. This massive internal migration of people from rural areas to the cities, world historical in terms of its speed and scale, explains how it is that the trend lines plotting the percentage of the nation's population that is rural versus the percentage that is urban have been converging and recently crossed, such that urban Chinese now outnumber rural Chinese for the first time in history.

The flood of rural migrants is the direct result of two key phenomena: first, the uneven nature of China's economic development since the reform period began in the late 1970s; and second, the government's decision to relax the household registration (*hukou*) system in order to increase labor mobility. I will briefly discuss each of these subjects in turn. The reform policies that Beijing has pursued since 1980, in addition to the positive effect of helping to lift millions of people out of poverty, have created a highly unequal society divided along regional as well as occupational lines. China becomes poorer and less developed the further west one travels from the coastline, and in particular the further one moves away from wealthy coastal cities. The wealthiest provinces in terms of overall GDP, Guangdong, Jiangsu, Shandong, and Zhejiang, are all located on the coast,

while the poorest ones, Tibet, Qinghai, Ningxia, and Gansu, are located far
to the west, in China's vast interior (see figure B). In terms of per capita
income, the same geographical pattern holds true. The wealthiest places
are the coastal cities of Shanghai, Beijing, and Tianjin (where per capita
incomes are roughly $20,000 U.S. per year), and those cities disproportion-
ately attract investment and skilled workers. As far as per capita income is
concerned, six of the top seven provinces, Jiangsu, Zhejiang, Guangdong,
Shandong, Liaoning, and Fujian, are located along the eastern seaboard
(the noncoastal province that makes it onto this list is Inner Mongolia). By
contrast, in terms of per capita income, six of the seven poorest provinces,
Guizhou, Gansu, Yunnan, Tibet, Guangxi, and Sichuan, are located far from
the coast (the one exception here being Anhui, which, while landlocked, is
located in eastern China).[18]

The wealth gap between urban and rural China has been visible and
growing for decades and today is the highest in Asia. This gap is largely
attributable to the fact that farming in China tends to have low rates of
productivity owing to underinvestment in the agriculture sector and a poor
ratio of land to peasant laborer, whereas worker productivity is far higher
in Chinese cities.[19] Between 2001 and 2005, the annual income of China's
urban dwellers nearly doubled; during those same years the economic
situation in most of the countryside, home to some 700 million people, remained stagnant. More recently the situation has improved somewhat, with
rural incomes beginning to rise in many parts of the country (a point to
which I will return below), but the rate of wealth accumulation in rural areas cannot compete with that in urban China. In 2009 the average income
of someone living in a Chinese city was about $2,500 U.S., in contrast to
$755 for someone living in the countryside.[20] Furthermore, while people in
cities have better access to quality education, schools in rural areas generally
remain backward even while the cost of enrollment has been rising.

The wealth and developmental gap between China's coast and much of
its interior regions is thus the major factor propelling people off farms and
into cities in search of better opportunities. Migrant laborers tend to work
in factory and construction jobs, as domestic servants, or in other service
trades. The work they do in these areas is critical to the country's economic
growth. Since the late 1980s, according to "a conservative estimate" from
UNESCO and the Chinese Academy of Social Sciences, "migrants have
contributed 16 percent of gross domestic product growth."[21] In the early
decades of the reform era, when migration to cities was still a new phenomenon, the majority of migrant workers spent a few years at most in cities
before returning to their villages in an improved economic position that
enabled them to provide better lives for their children and parents. This
pattern has not completely shifted today, since some of the jobs that migrants take are seasonal or of limited duration (such as construction jobs),

but as time has passed an ever-increasing number of migrants has sought ways to remain in the cities. This trend is related to the fact that well over half of today's migrants are under thirty years of age; such people are better able than their older counterparts to adjust to life in cities and to adopt the urban lifestyle as their own. They have no desire to return to their native villages, which they find isolated and dull after years spent in a city.

This point is captured in a recent news story featuring a twenty-year-old woman named Li Biying, who left her village in Sichuan at age fourteen and now works in an underwear factory in Dongguan, a Guangdong Province industrial city oriented toward the overseas export market. Li works at the factory with other young women from Sichuan and has no desire to return to her native village. "People my age think, what would I do in the countryside? I don't know how to do anything!" Li goes on to say, "I remember once we were growing wheat at home, it had just sprouted and it looked just like grass. I couldn't tell the difference so I pulled it out. My mom was so mad, she said, how could anyone not tell the difference between wheat and grass?" Li's comments make plain that a deep gap in lifestyle and expectations for the future has opened between her and her parents: "My parents say I've been working in the city for so long that I don't look like a country girl anymore. I tell them, people learn and they change. You want to become a better person and keep moving forward."

A survey conducted in 2008 by the China Youth Center found that among migrants under thirty some 56 percent planned to remain in the city where they work. One trade union official speaking to this trend noted of migrant laborers like Li Biying, who often dress in trendy ways that make it impossible to distinguish them from their urban counterparts, that "they are more accustomed to urban life than rural life. They've never been hungry, never felt the cold and never had to worry about food or clothing. They can't 'eat bitterness' like their parents."[22] Because so many migrant laborers have no intention of returning to their villages, in many rural areas the bulk of the working-age population is absent, off at work in a city and sending remittances home to support the small children and elderly who now make up the majority of many village populations. Like small towns in rural parts of the United States, which young people have also been leaving in droves in recent decades, many villages across China are dying, losing their economic and social vitality and fast becoming shells of their former selves.

The exodus of youth from the farm is not without a silver lining, however, for as young and middle-aged workers take themselves out of the rural labor pool they contribute to a labor shortage that in some rural areas is pushing up the wages of those who remain behind to do agricultural work. So while the children are off in cities or middle-sized towns earning wages they could not possibly command if they remained in the countryside, their parents' labor is becoming more valuable, contributing to the overall enrichment of the family. Nationwide per capita incomes in rural China are now rising, which is certainly a welcome development for those who live there, yet there is no denying that life in agricultural China remains far poorer than life in the country's cities. Su Hainan of the China Association for Labor Studies, a government think tank, recently stated, "In some regions, we have seen encouraging signs that farmers' incomes are rising quickly, but that doesn't mean the nationwide urban-rural wealth gap is narrowing." Su underlined the point that incomes in urban areas are three to four times higher than in the countryside, adding that it could take several decades before that gap is closed.[23]

Aside from the structural economic and developmental gap between rural and urban China, the other key factor that helps explain the tidal wave of rural Chinese into China's cities in recent decades has been the government's decision to relax the household registration (*hukou*) system as a means of promoting labor mobility. The communist government put the household registration system in place in the late 1950s as a key component of its command economy. That system worked as an internal passport, requiring people to remain tied to their place of birth for life, unable to move to other locations within the country without special and very difficult to get permission from the authorities. The essential bargain that the government struck with the Chinese people was to offer socialist benefits—guaranteed employment, subsidized housing, essentially free medical care and education, grain rations, and so forth—but only through the institution of the household registration system. People could only gain access to the benefits of socialism through compliance with the rule that they remain for life wherever their household registration was located. In this way the government was able to guarantee an adequate labor supply to meet the needs of the planned economy and to prevent peasants from flooding cities, where living conditions were better than in the countryside. The household registration system curtailed people's freedom to move and locked hundreds of millions of Chinese into permanent residence status in impoverished rural locales where the perks of the socialist system were far less in evidence than in urban areas, home to the more privileged urban working class and intelligentsia. While creating a profound quality-of-life gap between rural and urban China, from the government's perspective the *hukou* system was essential to the maintenance of social stability under a planned economic system.

Household registration formally remains in place in China today, but starting in the late 1970s and 1980s the communist government began to engineer a fundamental transition from state socialism to something more closely resembling market capitalism, a transition that necessitated the creation of far greater labor mobility. As the economic transformation began to take hold, it became apparent that new factories sprouting up along the coast could not count on a sufficient supply of workers unless the household registration system was relaxed, allowing rural Chinese to move to coastal cities to take up jobs on factory floors. Relaxation of the *hukou* system began in the 1980s with a relatively small number of mostly female migrant laborers being granted permission to leave their native places in order to work in urban factories, most of which were located in China's southern coastal provinces. Salaries and living and working conditions for these migrants were typically poor, but compared to life on the farms, factory work still presented better economic prospects.

What started as a trickle of migrants moving from the countryside in the early years of the reform era became over the course of the 1990s and the first decade of the new century, when the economy was heating up and the demand for labor skyrocketing, a raging torrent—very likely the largest internal migration in human history. Simply put, without the government's policy change, its willingness to relax strict enforcement of the household registration, the extraordinary economic takeoff that China has witnessed in a generation's time would not have been possible. Beijing clearly understands that continued torrid economic growth requires worker itinerancy and actively encourages private job-placement agencies to work with both municipal officials and employers to match rural dwellers with employment opportunities.[24]

THE GREAT CHALLENGES GOING FORWARD

Given the yawning wealth gap between urban and rural China, the foregoing discussion of the government's relaxation of the household registration system and the way that policy has unleashed a tidal wave of rural dwellers into cities draws attention to the double-edged nature of China's explosive urbanization and to the fluid and unresolved nature of government policy in response. Because migrants are unable to transfer their household registrations to the cities where they are working and instead remain registered in their native places, typically they are not able to avail themselves of government services—subsidized housing, income support, affordable education for their children—in the cities where they live and work. In this way they become second-class citizens in their own country, without the advantages of the social services that their urban-resident counterparts are able to count upon. What's more, urban residents rely on people from rural backgrounds to do difficult and dangerous work that they themselves are unwilling to do. Migrants dominate the "labor force in dirty and dangerous trades: 70 percent of construction workers, 68 percent of manufacturing employees, and 80 percent of coal miners are migrant workers."[25] Urbanites often look down on the poorer, less sophisticated, and less well educated migrant workers in their midst. This situation is not unlike that in the United States, where migrants without legal status provide much of the labor that U.S. residents are unwilling to perform while nevertheless facing discrimination from ordinary citizens and in the eyes of the law. Currently, there are tens of millions of migrant workers (compared to a little over twelve million in the United States) living in this legal limbo in Chinese cities; in Beijing alone, "about half the 460,000 children born over the past three years cannot be registered as official residents."[26]

Migrants are challenged by the high cost of living in cities. While China's urban middle class is becoming increasingly oriented to a consumer life-style and status consciousness pushes members of the middle class to purchase ever more expensive goods and services as a means of distinguishing themselves from those just below them on the social ladder, the urban poor, many of them migrant workers, are finding themselves unable to keep their heads above water. Municipal governments often contribute to this problem. Unable to raise revenue by issuing municipal bonds or through rapid tax increases, such governments often resort to selling real estate. "Across China, an estimated 40 to 60 percent of local government revenue is acquired in this way."[27] Seeking to boost revenue and their positions in the national urban economic pecking order, such governments often sell land to wealthy developers who then construct luxury towers and shopping centers that price those at the lower end of the economic spectrum out of the market.

This developer-led urban construction has contributed to a glut of luxury buildings and to a dangerous property bubble that has the potential to bring great harm to the Chinese economy.[28] The major barrier to fulfillment of the dream of many migrant workers—to move to cities on a permanent basis—is the rising cost of living in urban areas. The fact that their household registrations remain in their native villages and provide them with the guarantee of land to farm should they wish to return to the countryside provides migrant workers with a modicum of security.[29] As stated, however, many migrants have no wish to go back to the poor and often desolate places from which they came.

There is little doubt that China's economic takeoff has been largely dependent on the rapid growth of its cities, and that migrant workers have played a key role in this process. However, the influx of millions of people from the countryside poses challenges to municipal governments that must accommodate so many extra people in already crowded and polluted urban environments. It has not been uncommon for municipal security forces to support more restrictive in-migration policies out of the belief that migrants contribute to higher crime rates in cities and are harder to track and manage than official urban residents.[30] The filthy shantytown slums peopled by newcomers from rural backgrounds found in cities throughout the developing world do not exist in China, however. This is a consequence of the sale of land by municipal governments and their encouragement of building (as a means of raising revenue), as well as enforced requirements that employers provide workers with dormitories or other forms of housing.[31] Nevertheless, migrant workers tend to live in less-sanitary conditions than their urban-resident counterparts, and their housing is typically crowded and poorly integrated into the larger urban system. Most migrant workers also lack medical insurance and those who suffer from occupational disease in China are overwhelmingly migrant workers. To be sure, municipal governments recognize the indispensability of migrant workers and are seeking to improve conditions for such people by providing more job training, expanding health insurance, permitting nongovernmental organizations to offer them services, and providing the children of migrant workers with more affordable schooling.[32] Such efforts not withstanding, the massive number of migrant workers who populate Chinese cities will continue to pose complex problems for municipal governments into the foreseeable future. Today some 20 percent of China's urban population is made up of migrants, and experts predict that by 2030 the figure will rise to 50 percent.[33]

Indeed, the speed at which Chinese cities are growing is compounding a variety of problems. Municipal governments are hard pressed to build infrastructure fast enough to keep pace with the rate at which demand is growing. Pollution is a serious problem throughout urban China and poses serious health risks. The widespread use of dirty coal to generate electricity and the rapid rise in the number of automobiles have created grave air pollution problems in many Chinese cities and very high rates of respiratory disease. According to the World Bank, China endures 750,000 premature deaths annually due to air pollution and is home to sixteen of the twenty most air-polluted cities in the world.[34] As more people move to cities, use resources, and seek higher standards of living, they contribute directly to the pollution problem.

Even as rapid transit systems are being built in one city after another across the country, these are hardly able to offset the extraordinary speed at which surface streets and highways have become impossibly congested with the cars being purchased at an astounding rate by members of the country's increasingly affluent middle class. Over the past decade Chinese have begun their own love affair with private cars that rivals that of the United States. When I was a student in China in the late 1980s and early 1990s, private cars hardly existed: today most people I know in China own at least one car. As China becomes home to an ever-growing number of cars, its appetite for oil also increases, pressing on the finite supply of that natural resource and contributing to higher oil prices the world over.

Moreover, cars and the level of affluence they represent certainly are not available to everyone. As car society explodes, new roadways are being built across China at dizzying speed, gobbling up precious agricultural land while changing the experience of urban living both for those with means and for those whose incomes have not kept pace. As Beijing resident Xue Songlin, a member of the vast population of people who cannot afford a car and who still gets from place to place mostly by walking, states, "The road had been widened, but that is all for cars. Now I have to go a long distance to cross the road. . . . It's not convenient for walkers as before."[35] Suburbs built on the U.S. model are growing up on the outskirts of most Chinese cities, complete with large yards, two-car garages, and neighborhood golf courses.[36] Conspicuous consumption is prevalent in such neighborhoods, as wealthy families vie with one another to build the gaudiest homes or to drive the most expensive cars. Many of these neighborhoods are highly exclusive, often locked behind gates—the Chinese version of the gated community. Planned townships built to resemble European communities are a strange and noteworthy twist on the emerging Chinese suburban dream (see figure 6.4). Well-to-do Chinese interested in such places can now choose between communities named Thames Town and Italy Town, both located within the larger Shanghai region.

Another kind of suburbanization taking place is the movement of entire urban neighborhoods of people to newly built high-rise communities on the outskirts of town. Not infrequently this process is fraught with tension because municipal authorities sell the valuable land that makes up inner-

Figure 6.4. Real Imitation—Shanghai's Thames Town Community. Photograph by Tong Lam.

Figure 6.5.   Periurban "Instacity." Photograph by Tong Lam.

city neighborhoods to developers at high prices; those developers then force residents to move out of what is now their private property before proceeding to construct luxury homes and shopping malls that the former residents could not possible afford. This process can have the positive effect of relieving incredibly dense inner cities and of improving the material conditions of people's lives. At the same time, people are often forced to move against their will, and it is not uncommon for newly suburbanized residents to feel alienated in their new, antiseptic homes, far removed from the more community-focused way of life they formerly knew.

A related, highly peculiar phenomenon is the construction of entire cities in the vicinity of major metropolitan areas, or sometimes in quite remote places, that are entirely devoid of people. These "ghost towns" consist of huge neighborhoods of towering apartment buildings, government offices, wide boulevards, and even the infrastructure for mass transit systems. Developers who have purchased agricultural land from municipalities or other types of local authorities have built these spec cities. The goals of the municipal governments are twofold: first, the usual one of raising revenue—they can fetch a higher price for the land by selling it to developers than they can from leasing it to farmers; and second, the reduction of urban congestion by providing clean, well-planned suburban spaces that will induce urban residents to move out of city centers into surrounding regions. In some instances these spec cities have indeed attracted residents and have become living communities, but in other cases massive planned cities, in some instances intended to be home to over a million people, have sat deserted for years on end because of the high cost of the property in such places.[37] Here again the pace and method of urban and suburban development has contributed to a dangerous property bubble that threatens China's economy.

China's urban explosion shines a light on that country's growing wealth and sophistication and speaks to the opportunities for profits, continuing wealth production, and improved standards of living for ever more people into the foreseeable future. As the authors of the McKinsey Global Institute's "Preparing for China's Urban Billion" state, "For companies—in China and around the world—the scale of China's urbanization promises substantial new markets." That same report estimates that by 2025 China could well have paved 5 billion additional square meters of road, built 170 new mass-transit systems, and added 40 billion square meters of floor space in five million buildings, fifty thousand of which could be skyscrapers, "the equivalent of constructing up to ten New York cities." As already stated, China's rapid growth and the consumer mentality it is generating have inspired countless multinationals and smaller foreign companies to invest in the China market, both to sell goods to individual consumers and to gain contracts that enable them to participate in China's massive and endless number of infrastructure construction projects. All of this will lead to China's ongoing integration into the international economic system, pointing to the positive aspect of China's rapid urbanization for the Chinese people and for the global economy.

At the same time, we must also train our attention on the way China's fantastic pace of urbanization is contributing to growing socio-economic inequality both within cities and between urban areas and rural ones, to the disappearance of large amounts of arable land as cities sprawl outward, and to an insatiable hunger for natural resources such as water, coal, oil, wood for home construction, and so forth. According to the McKinsey report, by 2025, in order to "fuel its investment requirements, urban China will account for 20 percent of global energy consumption and up to one-quarter of growth in oil demand."[38] Can China's urbanization process, for which there is currently no end in sight, continue to take place while avoiding doing severe damage to an already highly stressed domestic and global environment?

Indeed, at the end of this chapter, I find that my own questions abound: Is it healthy for planet earth if ever more Chinese aspire to and begin to realize the U.S. standard of living and way of life? And for U.S. citizens and others who already enjoy such high standards of living, what are the moral implications of this question? Are we entitled to continue to live the way we do while at the same time criticizing China and other newly affluent societies around the world for seeking to live the same way? Does China have the capacity to urbanize and develop in a smarter and better-planned way than has the United States and much of the rest of the Western world? Will Beijing and China's municipal governments get out in front of the urbanization process quickly and effectively enough to design efficient, environmentally safe, people-friendly cities, or will the process continue to unfold haphazardly, according to the dictates of the private-profit motive, thereby resulting in poorly planned, environmentally wasteful cities that lack a human soul?

China's socialist ideology, while hardly dominant any longer in the minds of most Chinese citizens, suggests the possibility of a state-guided approach to the fastest urbanization in human history, one that could minimize the damaging effects of the process while maximizing the positives. By all appearances, the Chinese government thinks and plans according to a longer-term timeframe than does the U.S. government, which would seem to bode well for the chances that China will be able to urbanize in a reasonably intelligent and planned fashion. Yet the pace at which urbanization is unfolding in China, the still relatively low level of environmental consciousness in the country, the weak and often corrupted nature of China's legal system, and the extraordinary hunger for wealth on the part of so many people, especially property developers, suggest that the central government and lower-level governments will continue to have a difficult time managing the rapid rise of an urban-dominated Chinese society. The Chinese Communist Party finds itself caught in the vise of competing interests: on the one hand, it must encourage urbanization so as to continue to stimulate economic growth; on the other hand, it must guide the process such that China's cities are sufficiently comfortable as to appeal to the middle class's desire for a high quality of life. Extreme social inequality that increases social instability, terrible congestion, and life-threatening levels of pollution, all products of the same urbanization process that is fueling China's remarkable economic growth, have the real potential to seriously harm society and thereby to weaken the Chinese people's support for the Communist Party.

SUGGESTIONS FOR FURTHER READING

Campanella, Thomas J. *The Concrete Dragon: China's Urban Revolution and What It Means for the World*. New York: Princeton Architectural Press, 2008.

Hessler, Peter. *Country Driving: A Chinese Road Trip*. New York: Harper Perennial, 2011.

Meyer, Michael. *The Last Days of Old Beijing: Life in the Vanishing Backstreets of a City Transformed*. New York: Walker & Company, 2009.

Wasserstrom, Jeffrey N. *Global Shanghai, 1850–2010: A History in Fragments*. New York: Routledge, 2009.

NOTES

1. Chris Buckley, "China Internal Security Budget Jumps Past Army Budget," *Reuters*, March 5, 2011.

2. "China to Quadruple 2000 GDP by 2020," *Xinhua*, November 9, 2002.

3. Jonathan Woetzel et al., "Preparing for China's Urban Billion: Summary of Findings," McKinsey Global Institute, March 2008, 13, 27.

4. Chen Jia and Yang Ning, "Urbanization to Drive China's Growth," *China Daily*, March 26, 2011.

5. J. Vernon Henderson, "Urbanization in China: Policy Issues and Options," November 14, 2009, 1, http://www.econ.brown.edu/faculty/henderson/Final%20 Report%20format1109summary.doc.

6. Woetzel et al., "Preparing for China's Urban Billion," 9.

7. Henderson, "Urbanization in China," 1.

8. Much of this information and other fascinating comparative data can be found in "All the Parities in China," *Economist*, February 24, 2011, http://www .economist.com/content/all_parities_china.

9. Michael Wines, "Majority of Chinese Now Live in Cities," *The New York Times*, January 17, 2012.

10. Chris Buckley and Michael Martina, "China's Population Grows Older and More Urban," *Reuters*, April 28, 2011.

11. Michael Wines, "Majority of Chinese Now Live in Cities."

12. Daniel H. Rosen, "China's Urbanization and Overcapacity," *Wall Street Journal*, December 30, 2009.

13. Dianna Farrell, "China's Urbanization Means Rich Rewards for Business," *Bloomberg Businessweek*, September 12, 2008.

14. Woetzel et al., "Preparing for China's Urban Billion," 14.

15. Elaine Chow, "China's Middle Class Will Reach 700 Million by 2020," *Shanghaiist*, July 26, 2010, http://shanghaiist.com/2010/07/26/chinas_middle _class_will_reach_700.php.

16. Andrew Clark, "Wal-Mart, the US Retailer Taking Over the World by Stealth," *Guardian*, January 12, 2010, http://www.guardian.co.uk/business/2010/jan/12/ walmart-companies-to-shape-the-decade?INTCMP=SRCH.

17. Buckley and Martina, "China's Population Grows Older."

18. This information is drawn from "All the Parities in China."

19. Henderson, "Urbanization in China," 8.

20. This information is drawn from Visual Economics, an online site that presents economic data in visual forms: http://www.visualeconomics.com/chinas -growing-wealth-gap_2010-03-31/.

21. Alexandra Harney, "Migrants Are China's 'Factories without Smoke,'" *CNN. com*, February 3, 2008, http://edition.cnn.com/2008/WORLD/asiapcf/02/01/china .migrants/index.html.

22. Anita Chang, "Young Migrants Changing the Face of China's Cities," *Associated Press*, March 13, 2001.

23. Alan Wheatley, "Analysis: Shandong Postcard: Big Changes Sweep Rural China," *Reuters*, April 25, 2011.

24. "China Is on the Move," *Newsweek*, December 12, 2005, http://www.newsweek.com/2005/12/12/china-is-on-the-move.html.

25. Harney, "Migrants Are China's 'Factories without Smoke.'"

26. David Pilling, "Mismanaging China's Rural Exodus," *Financial Times*, March 10, 2010.

27. Peter Hessler, "Boomtowns," *National Geographic*, June 2007.

28. Rosen, "China's Urbanization and Overcapacity." For a good debate on the degree to which China's property bubble poses a threat to the country's economy, see "China's Scary Housing Bubble," *New York Times*, April 14, 2011.

29. "Urban China: Playground for the Rich?" *China Daily*, February 23, 2011; "Scholar Warns of Radical Urbanization in China," *China Daily*, March 20, 2010.

30. "China Is on the Move."

31. Diana Farrell et al., "Where Big Is Best," *Newsweek*, May 26, 2008.

32. Harney, "Migrants Are China's 'Factories without Smoke.'"

33. Dexter Roberts, "China Prepares for Urban Revolution," *Bloomberg Businessweek*, November 13, 2008.

34. Philip Kennicott, "Sizing Up a Mega-City," *Washington Post*, August 4, 2008; Louisa Lim, "Air Pollution Grows in Tandem with China's Economy," *National Public Radio*, May 22, 2007.

35. "Urban China: Playground for the Rich?"

36. For a photo essay on China's suburbs, see "Life in China's Suburbs," *Time*, http://www.time.com/time/photoessays/2007/china_suburbia_multimedia/.

37. For photographs and discussion of these "ghost towns," see Holly Krambeck, "Rise of the Chinese Ghost Town," World Bank, September 12, 2010, http://blogs.worldbank.org/transport/rise-of-the-chinese-ghost-town; and "The Ghost Towns of China: Amazing Satellite Images Show Cities Meant to Be Home to Millions Lying Deserted," *Daily Mail*, December 18, 2010, http://www.dailymail.co.uk/news/article-1339536/Ghost-towns-China-Satellite-images-cities-lying-completely-deserted.html.

38. Woetzel et al., "Preparing for China's Urban Billion," 16.

7

The Worlds of China's Intellectuals

Timothy Cheek

"If the Chinese people themselves didn't want to forget first, we would have never forced them to forget," he says innocently. "It was the Chinese people themselves that took the initiative to take the amnesia medicine."

—He Dongshang, character in Chan Koonchung's *The Fat Years*

"Because we are in such a system, we are always asking ourselves whether we are brainwashed," he said. "We are always eager to get other information from different channels." Then he added, "But when you are in a so-called free system you never think about whether you are brainwashed."

—Tang Jie, graduate student at Fudan University, Shanghai

China's intellectuals, those predominantly urban, educated Chinese who choose to engage in the issues of public life and culture, have always been an important part of Chinese society, whether as imperial scholar officials in the dynasties or as scholars, writers, artists, critics, and even revolutionaries in modern China. Today China's intellectuals are increasingly in the world, but not of it. That is, they increasingly travel and speak and write outside China, but their primary concern remains what Gloria Davies has captured as "worrying about China" (*youhuan*) and others have noted as the obsession with "China problems." Just as the proverbial "American in Paris" was more about New York than the Left Bank, so Chinese intellectuals enter the world—the globalized civilization now dominated by Western culture but increasingly reflecting the rise of China and all of Asia—but they do it mostly in order to work on what they see as China's problems. The challenge for U.S. citizens and other Westerners is to appreciate why it is entirely sensible for China's intellectuals to be focused on home—for the

154

problems in China are many. After all, from a Chinese perspective, many of the so-called global concerns of U.S. and European intellectuals appear similarly self-focused. The challenge for China's intellectuals is to bring the talents and experiences of such a huge intellectual world to bear on global problems, as well as Chinese problems.

The world of China's intellectuals has exploded over the past two decades, breaking out of conformity to (or tight negotiations with) the Communist Party. They have confronted the challenges of professional specialization (and thus a loss of public voice) and commercialization (threatening to reduce intellectual work to infotainment).[1] In many ways, the life of China's intellectuals parallels that of intellectuals in the United States, Europe, and the rest of this globalized world. Nonetheless, as academics, as media professionals, as artists who have to sell their art to survive, and as entrepreneurs, China's educated classes still experience very real limitations to the exercise of their intellect—the party-state in China can and does crack down on those spouting inconvenient truths.

We shall see that China's public sphere[2] is a *directed public sphere* and that despite the raucous commercialism of globalized brands and media in China, this directed public sphere is still managed and enforced by the Chinese Communist Party (CCP). How to make sense of this? China's intellectuals today continue to dance the dance of engagement that they have with Chinese governments over the past century: professing loyalty, trying to provide a loyal opposition in ideas if not in organization, and testing the limits of what is permissible to say. They continue to worry about China, but under new circumstances: the problem is not just the West, or Japan, or economic backwardness, but rather something more homegrown and more complicated than simply "it's all the Communist Party's fault."

It is the weight of these problems—corruption, pollution, unemployment, the fate of some 200 million migrant workers, as well as the health of China's vast rural areas (issues covered in other chapters in this volume)—that keeps the attention of China's intellectuals focused on China rather than on the world. China's problems today are the problems of a dynamic and growing economy, but they are problems nonetheless. And most of China's intellectuals feel compelled to address them to the exclusion of problems elsewhere. This is despite the global reach of the Chinese intellectual life in what I call the "Sinophone Sphere."

The Sinophone Sphere is the universe of Chinese-language speaking and writing. The key identity of *Chinese* intellectuals today no longer turns on face or place alone—being Chinese or being inside the People's Republic of China (PRC)—but on language, that is, the language of discussion, blogging, publishing, and public speaking. For intellectuals who are in China or concerned with Chinese audiences, this language is modern standard

Chinese, or Mandarin. This language is based on Chinese characters, and despite regional variations and dramatically different pronunciations across a dozen and more dialects, such that Cantonese, the spoken language around Hong Kong and Guangzhou, is unintelligible to listeners in Beijing and most other dialect areas of China, it is the shared written resource of Chinese characters that enables the communities of discourse that define Chinese intellectual debate, inside China and on the web internationally.

Until the 1990s, Chinese intellectuals—aside from a few exiles—operated almost exclusively inside China, Hong Kong, or Taiwan. Over the past two decades, the growth of Internet communications, the extensive migration of educated Chinese across the globe, and the rise of multiple identities, what Aiwa Ong calls "flexible citizenship,"[3] have allowed intellectuals concerned about China and interested in contributing to developments inside China to participate in communities of Chinese intellectuals built around the globalized institutions of commercial publishing, world-class universities, and a vigorous international network of web pages and blogs that defy the so-called Great Fire Wall of China.

The universe of China's intellectuals is not homogeneous; rather, there are a number of intellectual worlds in China and in the Sinophone Sphere of intellectual life today. These intellectual worlds are formed by social life in arenas of activity that have rules and expectations that participants follow, rules that often clash with those of other communities or, in our case, intellectual worlds.[4] In China today the life of intellectuals is first of all subject to the ground rules of the directed public sphere of the CCP, and beyond that it is enlivened by the value spheres of several intellectual worlds: the official world of public and political life; the academic world of universities and scholarship; the commercial world of making, buying, and selling; the associational worlds of public intellectuals, religious groups, Internet communities, nongovernmental organizations (NGOs), and other tolerated groups; and finally, the *waiyu* world of "foreign language communities" in China, particularly those competent in English or other major European languages. This range of intellectual worlds inside the universe of Chinese-language intellectual debate means there is naturally a range of opinions among various Chinese intellectuals, but at the same time, there are shared concerns, assumptions, and ways of being a Chinese intellectual.

The way educated people address a problem is significantly different in China's intellectual worlds versus the intellectual worlds of the readers of this English-language book. To communicate across cultural horizons, we will have to take more effort than global "winners" (members of dominant societies) have usually taken to understand the perspective of China's intellectuals. We need to do this not simply for the ethical goals of respectful mutual understanding necessary for treating each other with dignity, or for the self-interested purposes of defending our economy, but primarily because we, as humans on earth, are in a lot of trouble. We need to work together effectively with Chinese to address those problems now—or at the very least so as not to add to the problems of poverty and sustainability with needless confrontations based on mutual offense born of misunderstanding.

CHINA'S INTELLECTUAL WORLDS (AND SPHERES)

Intellectual life in China is defined by two things: the directed public sphere of the CCP and the ethos shared across the great variety of intellectuals in the Sinophone Sphere that the defining activity of a legitimate Chinese intellectual is to worry about China and Chinese problems. A better understanding of these spheres, and the worlds of intellectual life within them, is critical to an appreciation of how Chinese intellectual life today works.

China's Directed Public Sphere

The directed public sphere is the public arena as it exists in China today: the media, public institutions like universities and cultural associations, and the legal structure of associational life (i.e., the rules governing NGOs, religious groups, and other groups). The term *public sphere* immediately brings to mind ideas of Western civil society, particularly in the popularized writings of Jürgen Habermas, but it is important to understand how different China's public sphere is from the European model or U.S. experience.[5] The key difference is that China's public realm is *directed* by the powerful propaganda system of the CCP.[6] In many ways, we can say that the Party in China *is* civil society, and its propaganda system (*xuanjiao xitong*) is the public sphere. This reality is strikingly different from Habermas's model of an oppositional public sphere confronting the state through the legally independent institutions of his civil society.[7]

In China the institutions of civility and social publicity are organized and controlled by the propaganda system—the culture and education system led by a member of the CCP Central Committee. This system integrates under party leadership the current newspaper and media systems, as well as internal reporting systems, the Chinese Academy of Social Sciences, and all universities and research institutes. It was born in the revolutionary base areas founded by the CCP during World War II and has continued into the post-Mao period *and* has been substantially reinvigorated in the past five years under the Hu Jintao administration. The concept of "directed" comes from Victor Serge's description of "directed culture" in Stalin's Soviet Union, in which the state controlled art, ethic, and ideas "for the good of the people."[8] Because the propaganda and education system in China

includes the arts and universities, Chinese writers, professors, and researchers, as well as journalists, belong to that web that is under direct control of
the Central Propaganda Department of the CCP. In Mao's China there was
no other "space" in which to speak, and this was the directed public sphere
of socialist China.

The reforms of post-Mao China have only fitfully changed that monolith.
There is more latitude and more market pressure, but the residual strength
of the institutions of China's propaganda state have confounded our expectations that increased marketization would lead to a liberal public sphere.
There is certainly more intellectual freedom in China today compared to the
Cultural Revolution period (1966–1976)—at minimum the blessed freedom
to be silent, to avoid politics, and to just get on with your own business. The
CCP has learned to use market freedom to serve the goals of directed culture,
with entertainment to distract the masses and financial inducements to cor-
ral intellectual energy in academic professorships and grants, government-
funded research projects, and state-approved artistic ventures.[9] And for those
incorrigible souls bent on dissent, there remains the gun. Jeffrey Wasserstrom
has evocatively named this startling mix of commercial excess and political
regress as "China's Brave New World," where China has succeeded in achieving something of the vision of Aldous Huxley's *Brave New World*: "the stabil-
ity-crazed, pleasure-mad society of 'Year of Our Ford 634.'"[10]

The Sinophone Sphere and Worrying about China

China's intellectuals, understandably, mostly communicate in Chinese.
In addition to the requirements of the directed public sphere that one must
meet in order to publish legally in China—primarily not to question or to
challenge the rule of the CCP—Chinese intellectuals must meet the expectations of the worlds of Chinese-language, or Sinophone, discourse. There
are rules for those who want to publish in the *New Yorker* or *Le Monde*,
and so, too, there are shared expectations, reflected in the track record of
notable writings, that an aspiring Chinese intellectual must meet. We can
recognize Sinophone discourse even when it is translated into English.
The structure of a discourse, as Gloria Davies so carefully describes, is not
limited to linguistic family alone. It is the constellation of expectations,
assumptions, and agreed-upon rules for what constitutes a good argument
or the "so what?" in intellectual debate. Davies captures the heart of this
contemporary intellectual life:

> As a praxis, worrying about China carries the moral obligation of first identify-
> ing and then solving perceived Chinese problems (*Zhongguo wenti*), whether
> social, political, cultural, historical, or economic, in relation to the unified
> public cause of achieving China's national perfection.[11]

What does this intellectual "worrying" look like? Take, for example, the opening paragraph of this translation of an essay by Wang Hui—a contemporary Chinese academic and public intellectual who engages Western scholars and is also frequently translated:

> Inquiry into scientism in contemporary Chinese thought is intimately bound up with the cultural atmosphere of mainland China during the late 1980s. This kind of inquiry is not primarily focused on "knowledge." . . . [But] if one cannot relate critical thinking on the course of modern history to a critique of Nazism and Stalinism, then . . . one might even end up concealing the true origins of despotism in modern society.[12]

Wang Hui in this passage invokes the "Western intellectual perspective" but only to justify worrying about Chinese politics.

Sinophone discourse in China's intellectual worlds is also shaped by assumptions about *how* to do intellectual work. We can see three core characteristics of this thought work among contemporary public intellectuals in China today.[13] First, such thought work continues to *privilege thought*, and particularly the search for correct thought, as the foundation of effective public policy. Thus we see continuity as well as change in the Sinophone discourse of contemporary Chinese intellectuals. "Old habits" (the volatile mix of philosophical idealism, educational optimism, and the social pragmatism of Maoist, May Fourth, and Confucian thinking) can be identified in contemporary writings by Chinese intellectuals. This collection of intellectual habits assumes that thought (*sixiang*) paves the road to social solutions—just as Wang Hui, in the quote above, requires "critical thinking" to address despotism.

Second, such assumptions in Sinophone writings provide the *channels of change* through which selective adaptation of foreign thought and discourse proceeds. Through these cognitively familiar channels new sets of ideas, such as political liberalism, have been introduced to the center of legal public discussion. Yet the content and use of those ideas are quite different from Western ones. When the Chinese liberal academic Xu Jilin applies Western liberal theory, he concludes that public intellectuals in China are better off organizing the institutions of publicity, such as journals, newspapers, and websites, than in organizing independent political parties.

Third, the cultural identity of these public intellectuals is clear. They are Chinese because they were born Chinese *and* live and work in the PRC, and that identity does not require them to justify their use of Western theory on grounds other than utility. One result of this assumption is that Chinese scholars living outside China must establish an institutional position inside China if they want to be taken seriously by their compatriots. While Sinophone discourse spans the globe—and anyone can join in via one of thousands of Chinese-language web pages, blogs, and bulletin boards—in order to be an *authoritative* speaker in this intellectual universe, you must present yourself as a Chinese living in China (or temporarily absent for purposes of study). So whether one is actually in the PRC physically or not, one must identify with it, claim a sure footing inside the nation, and focus on its issues. Otherwise you are a foreign commentator.

THE MANY WORLDS OF CHINA'S INTELLECTUALS

Under the watchful eye of the party's directed public sphere and animated by the moral call of Sinophone communities to find correct thought to save China, intellectuals in China in fact operate in a variety of concrete arenas or professional social worlds that establish further norms and shape expectations. Thus, when we read or listen to this or that "Chinese intellectual," we would be wise to ask, "From which world are you speaking?" From the official world of the PRC government? The academic world of formal scholarship? The commercial world? Or one of a variety of social organizations? And is this writing or speaking originally directed to Sinophone worlds or already meant to engage the outside world? A brief tour of these various intellectual worlds will help us identify such speakers and remind us of the variety of intellectual voices in China.

Official World

This is the world of the Chinese government that is completely dominated by the Communist Party and its ideology. The two overriding norms of the official world are to uphold the Communist Party and its policies and to defend the interests and honor of China. The *People's Daily* is the official mouthpiece of the CCP and is an authoritative source for understanding PRC government policy.[14] Most Chinese do not participate in this government discourse directly, though a number of intellectuals do, especially in the Academies of Social Sciences and the Party Schools. Moreover, the official world shapes the media in China. Commercial newspapers, TV, and radio have to toe the line of the *People's Daily*, or at least avoid contradicting it explicitly. Intellectuals flout these rules at their own peril. Within these guardrails there is considerable latitude to get on with the business of your social circle.

Academic World

Second only to the official world, the academic world is the most important for intellectuals in China. Scholarship has long held public prestige in Chinese culture, and recent developments have only reinforced that status.

Chinese society, like other East Asian societies, holds university professors in high esteem. Since the late 1970s the PRC has revived its university system and modeled it on the Euro-U.S. research university. This has produced a commitment to university research and to educating greater numbers of university students, and thus *huge* amounts of money have been directed to China's university sector in the past twenty years. University jobs are increasing in number and attractiveness—a most reasonable career for those aspiring to middle-class life.[15]

The result has been specialization. This has contributed to a massive withdrawal of intellectual talent from the public arena, though a few remain engaged. But those who still speak up increasingly do so as *experts* in their field rather than as public intellectuals or social critics. Most academics follow the path of Western scholars and publish in specialized journals and monographs using the technical language of the natural or social sciences. These highly educated folk identify themselves as "scholars" (*xuezhe*) or as "readers" (*dushuren*) rather than as broad "intellectuals" (*zhishifenzi*).

Commercial World

This is the intellectually least interesting arena—except, perhaps, for scholars of popular culture—but it is worth remembering that probably the vast majority of intellectual energy in China is active in this social world—the commercial market, creating entertainment, and providing services for profit. While commerce hardly defines an intellectual world, it does have two important roles: First, it aligns the interests of many intellectuals with the institutions of global capitalism and the rules for international business since many intellectuals make their living in businesses and professional services in this market. Second, the ease of movement of people and information necessary for this global economy provides many avenues for intellectuals to "hitch a ride"—a method adopted by many associations in China. That is, religious groups or public intellectuals will use a commercial channel, such as the Facebook-like website A-la-shan (described below) to communicate "under the radar" of Chinese bureaucracies aimed at monitoring religious or publishing activities.

The commercial world also provides a hybrid institution for Chinese intellectuals: the press. There are now literally thousands of commercial newspapers and magazines published in China today, and many aim to provide reliable news coverage and even muckraking reporting. However, as we see in David Bandurski's chapter on "watchdog journalism," there are real limitations to a free press. In part this is because no publication in China is completely free of the directed public sphere of the CCP. Indeed, most newspapers are commercial wings of government or party newspapers. For example, the famous muckraking newspaper *Southern Weekend*

(*Nanfang zhoumou*) is owned by and operated under the supervision of the Guangdong Communist Party.

Associational Worlds

Alternative political parties are illegal in China, but social groups (*she-tuan*) are legal. They are highly regulated by the Ministry of Civil Affairs, but they are a dynamic part of life in China (see Alex Wang's and Jessica Teets's chapters in this volume on the environment and civil society in local government). Below the tip of the iceberg of environmental NGOs or the Charter 08 signers, the vast majority of Chinese associational life organizes local social and religious interests—and these activities engage the intellectual activities of many educated Chinese. For instance, there are more Buddhist organizations, writings, and websites in China than there are democratic ones.

Yet the cooperative pose of China's associations, and the intellectuals active in them, does not make them either politically conservative (i.e., supporting the government in all things) or irrelevant. Take two examples. The first is the case of using commercial networks to pursue broader intellectual aims: book publishing. One Shanghai bookshop owner has been publishing books on academics and thought for the past five years, on topics that rarely appear on major presses, and he does so by just such amphibious organizing.[16] First of all, he is not legally a publisher, but a "consultant," so his editorial work is subject to the enterprise law and not the depredations of the government's publishing controls. Second, he secures the manuscripts, edits them, and arranges for the printing, while he gets the all-important ISBN number from a minor or cash-strapped legal publisher who is not too fussy. Our entrepreneur gets his book out; the press gets a title that sells. Both make money.

There are some two hundred such small private "publishers" across China publishing from a dozen to a hundred books a year each. In truth, most of the titles our Shanghai entrepreneur publishes are cookbooks, novels, and pop books (such as a translation of *The Da Vinci Code*), but this supports a small line of serious books of social and cultural criticism. While all legally published books are subject to censorship, small regional presses in poor provinces are often less scrutinized than the major presses. This is a small doorway to de facto press liberalization. Indeed, our publisher uses the website of Alxa League (*A-la-shan lianmeng*), an environmental group, as a safe place to communicate with suppliers and buyers.[17]

The second example of associational life is the Liang Shuming Rural Reconstruction Center outside Beijing. In the rural suburbs west of the capital, near the Fragrant Hills, is a compound that houses this voluntary group dedicated to the renewal of China's rural society. It is a community-oriented organization but is registered under People's University in Beijing, which provides its mailing address. Building on the ideas of a charismatic professor, Wen Tiejun, the group aligns its goals not only with its namesake, the noted "last Confucian" and rural reformer of the 1920s and 1930s Liang Shuming, but with current PRC government rural policy, the *sannong* or "three agricultural issues" (villages, rural inhabitants, and rural society).[18] The organization is a startling hybrid of Maoist slogans ("serve the farmers"), YMCA volunteerism (university-age youth join up to lead teams to help local villages), and early twentieth-century Chinese anarchism (a commune of these volunteers lives in the suburban compound, raises organic vegetables, and studies together the rural reconstruction materials of the organization). There is even a songbook replete with a disconcerting mix of Cultural Revolution songs, Hong Kong–Taiwan pop tunes, and folk ballads. When I visited the compound in June 2010, a cheerful group of young volunteers led me, and my colleagues, in a rousing round of singing from this hymnal. This astonishing mix of cultural resources blends in a cheerful community of committed young people dedicated to helping the less fortunate in their society. This group represents a partnership between intellectual youth and some idealistic university professors and is not part of the CCP Youth League, and indeed, it harkens through Liang Shuming to the most notable noncommunist rural reconstruction effort in China. It stands as a vibrant example of how China can confound our expectations.

Virtual Worlds of the Internet

We often think of the fractious and contentious world of the Chinese Internet, particularly the "angry youth" who chime in regularly on China's perceived confrontations with Japan, the United States, or any outside power that appears to threaten or impugn the dignity of the Chinese nation. Western newspapers regularly quote outrageous statements from Chinese netizens. But the Internet mostly reflects the professional and social worlds we have already met: you can find web pages for the Chinese government—both for the central government and the thousands of local governments—for all sorts of academics and scholarly publications and forums, and of course, for endless commercial Chinese equivalents of eBay, Facebook, Amazon.com, travel agencies, banking services—the lot. And we find on the web the voices of China's wide range of associations, from environmental NGOs to religious groups (both legally registered religious organizations and informal groups), intellectual blogs, and even self-help or social-service groups like the Liang Shuming Rural Reconstruction Centre.

Some characteristics of the Chinese Internet are worth considering beyond the headlines on angry youth. First, the Chinese Internet is huge, varied, but still ultimately controlled. It is indubitably part of China's directed public sphere, and the troubles Google had with the central government in 2010 are just a reminder: when push comes to shove, the Chinese state can shut any provider down and track most any individual netizen to her or his home. For those who wish to understand the dynamic and tension-filled dance between diversity and "harmony" (the PRC state's term for controlled public life), one need only look to the web—but it does require the ability to read Chinese. Fortunately, a number of new books give English readers a pretty good sense of the Chinese Internet.[19]

The lesson to keep in mind when reading Western newspapers or listening to reports on CNN or the BBC is that the Chinese Internet, like Chinese society, is unified but not homogeneous.[20] It is united by the directed public sphere, shared patriotism, the norms of the Sinophone intellectual sphere to worry about China, and the pleasure-seeking distractions of Wasserstrom's "Brave New World." But the lives and interests reflected on the Chinese web are by no means homogeneous: there is not only the usual human diversity of good and bad intentions, clever and dull minds, energetic and lax efforts; there is also the reflection of the social and professional worlds we have seen (and of course, private worlds of friend networks, fantasy fiction, and yes, pornography). It is easy to mistake the uniformity of compliance with PRC rules of public discourse and anxious patriotism with some unanimity of values and intentions. Scholars have been saying this for decades, but it bears repeating: China is diverse.

Second, the Internet does highlight some voices over others. The voice of popular nationalism is particularly served by the organization of the Chinese Internet. Because "loving China" is something the directed public sphere's police cannot censor, extreme statements made in the name of patriotism pick up a huge audience. The international community, particularly Japan and the United States, regularly obliges with either gaffes or real conflicts of interest (from islands in the South China Sea to demands concerning the exchange rates of China's currency, the *renminbi*, or Yuan). The result, as several scholars have shown, is that China's foreign policy is driven in part by managing these angry voices on the net.[21]

We think of China's Communist Party as all-powerful, but it still has to cope with the volatile public opinion expressed on the Internet, which often spills out on university campuses and the streets of the major cities (Susan Blum's chapter explores the citizen blogging movement in China). Thus, while more regulated than the Internet in other countries, China's Internet is nonetheless volatile and shows the limits of control of even the Communist Party. For advocates of freedom, this sounds good. The sobering aspect is that the most "free" examples on the Chinese Internet are voices of xenophobic ultranationalism. Even the efforts of well-educated graduate students with experience in Europe or the United States and conversant with English or other languages can be surprising: the Tang Jie epigraph at the start of this chapter is such an example. During the 2008 Olympic Torch relay China's runners were heckled as they ran through Europe and the United States because of their government's harsh suppression of demonstrations in Tibet. In response, Tang Jie and his Fudan University classmates in Shanghai produced a short video, "China Stands Up 2008," that looks like typical CCP propaganda in its defense of national purpose and rejection of Western interference. However, Evan Osnos's interview with him shows that for Tang this reactionary video was a product of just the sort of intellectual freedom U.S. citizens embrace.[22]

Finally, as we have seen, the Chinese Internet serves and promotes the growth of independent associations and communities of Chinese people with a shared interest. These interests range from the proverbial bird fanciers and chess clubs, to public-service organizations and charities, to, as we have seen, intellectuals using the Internet to organize publishing in a way that gets around China's restrictive press laws and organizing an independent youth movement for rural renewal. However, these groups do not act like U.S. citizens. Indeed, Wenfang Tang's survey of local political activism confirms that even among nonparty or nonestablishment intellectuals, there is an acceptance that the most practical way to bring about concrete political improvement is to work with the CCP.[23]

Dissent

There are Chinese dissidents in China today, and there have always been. Sun Yat-sen tried to bring down the Qing Dynasty in the late nineteenth century, and Mao Zedong and his fellow communists started as radical students and dissidents in the 1910s.[24] Other chapters in this volume (such as chapters by Alex Wang, David Bandurski, and Susan Blum) highlight important instances of social mobilization and resistance to misrule at the local level. The import of this chapter is not to diminish the courage and dedication of China's small circle of outright dissidents, but to show why most Chinese intellectuals seek avenues other than confrontation with the state to carry out their resistance to what they feel is wrong. I hope I have shown how the spirit of dissent as we know it lives behind the headlines in China's many worlds of intellectual life.

CHINA'S INTELLECTUALS IN THE WORLD

China's intellectuals are important also for their active roles in the wider world. Of course, this is not new. A list of recipients of the Nobel Prizes and other international prizes turns up a substantial list of Chinese names—nine, in fact—most of whom are scientists in the United States or other countries who are of Chinese heritage.[25] This is true in all domains, from business to academics to the arts. These are but the latest generations in a centuries-old engagement of Chinese in the broader world as "overseas Chinese" (*huaqiao* or *haiwai Huaren*).[26] The personal engagement of Chinese outside China is both centuries old and across class; it is not limited to laborers and shopkeepers but includes scholars and professionals. Chinese arts and ideas have long had a role to play in Western societies from seventeenth-century *Chinoiserie* arts in Europe to U.S. fascination with Chinese philosophy as part of "Eastern Wisdom."

Today's version of this personal and intellectual engagement of Chinese with the world reflects the many worlds of China's intellectuals we have met in the first part of this chapter. Thus we can distinguish the official world in the form of some three hundred Confucius Institutes spread across the globe.[27] These language and culture centers resemble similar efforts such as the Goethe Institute for German, Cervantes Institute for Spanish, and Alliance Française for French, except that the government control of Confucius Institutes is much stronger; they are, simply, part of the PRC's soft diplomacy, peddling the legitimacy of the current government along with the glories of Chinese culture and the opportunity to learn a desirable business language. The official world of Chinese thought extends to government-supported academic scholarships and grants that require Chinese scholars studying in the West to conform to the broad outlines of the directed public sphere and China's current foreign policy themes. In this, China generally only differs from, for example, the U.S. government and its information organs in terms of degree of intensity. All governments do this to some degree; the question we might ask is can Chinese intellectuals opt out (like we can) if they want to.

They can and do. One merely needs to be a specialized academic who steers clear of politics. China's academic world is not synonymous with the official world any more than North America's universities are synonymous with the goals of the government funding for teaching and research that all our universities accept. Some Chinese academics choose to be explicit spokespersons for the government, working in the Academies of Social Sciences or similar government think tanks, but tens of thousands work in China's main universities and subscribe to international norms of academic rigor and intellectual freedom. Indeed, the commitment of China's academics to the professional norms of scholarship is so profound that it is considered a problem by some commentators in China—for drawing public intellectuals away from public policy and burying them in libraries, laboratories, and ponderous academic journals.[28]

This current version of academic life in China includes peer-review research and "publish or perish" tenure criteria, and the highest criterion is "international reputation," which means publishing in English and getting the attention and respect of academic circles in the United States, Europe, and the rest of the world. Chinese academics active in Western scholarly circles fall into two groups: Chinese who have chosen work in the sciences or fields not directly related to China, and Chinese who have chosen to contribute to China or Asian Studies, or the understanding of China in the West. To the degree that they contribute to international science and academics, they are appreciated as successful professionals (and praised in China), but they are not seen as Chinese intellectuals until they address China's problems and in Chinese. Many do, but their writings in Chinese generally do not count for much in the Western academy. The two worlds—worrying about China and the Western academy—are largely parallel universes that do not communicate.

When we think of Chinese intellectuals in the world then, we need to remember this far greater group of intellectual Chinese—university-educated Chinese and professionals in the West. Depending on your definition of "intellectuals" (advanced education vs. engagement with public issues as society's critics), these professionals may or may not fall within our story. I generally follow the Western definition, what in China is today called "public intellectuals" (*gonggong zhishifenzi*), but it is always worthwhile to keep in mind the broader intellectual world of professionals: those who while they may not focus their work on public life nonetheless contribute

Figure 7.1. **China in the World, Beijing's MAD Designed Absolute Condominiums, Mississauga, Ontario, 2010. Photograph by Tong Lam.**

significantly—in government, academics, commerce, or associations—to the shape of public life.

The Chinese intellectuals who turn up on our media screens are generally exceptions to the main trends of life in China. This does not make them any less significant, but it is important to see the bigger picture. I like much of what Noam Chomsky says about my society (he is a critic of commercial media), but I would not be accurate if I told my Chinese colleagues that Chomsky is representative of intellectual life in North America. Readers of Western media know all about Liu Xiaobo, the courageous and now imprisoned representative of the domestic Chinese democratic movement that produced Charter 08, and the buzz around his winning the 2010 Nobel Peace Prize. Those who follow Chinese affairs a bit more closely will recognize Harry Wu, former labor camp inmate and advocate for his still-imprisoned comrades. They may know the names of a few of the brave Chinese lawyers (such as Chen Guangcheng and Gao Zicheng) who have endured police brutality for defending Chinese farmers, urban residents, and minority groups against rapacious developers and local strongmen.[29] They may have read the Mao biography or many media events of Jung Chang, the Chinese-British writer whose research may be fatally flawed (according to academics who doubt her use of sources and regret her black-and-white tirade)[30] but who nonetheless represents the anger and resentment of a generation of Chinese who gave their lives to Mao's ruinous Cultural Revolution only to be used and discarded by China's leaders. Those with artistic and intellectual interests will know Gao Xingjian, the novelist who won the 2000 Nobel Prize for Literature, and those following the news worry about the fate of Ai Weiwi, the controversial artist arrested in 2011. And some may have read one of the several academic translations of Wang Hui's analyses of contemporary China in the *New Left Review* or through Harvard University Press.

These are all important people known in the West, but they do not represent the variety and diversity of China's intellectual worlds. We are unlikely to get much help from China's varied intellectual worlds. The official world is interested in promoting PRC foreign policy, the academic world is interested in fitting in with our professional norms and "beating Harvard" at its own game, the commercial world is interested in selling (and mostly to Chinese customers), and the associational worlds have their own interests, from local issues to religious salvation to global themes of environment, infectious disease control, or fair housing. But beyond the particular focus of each subworld, China's intellectuals are unlikely to help us very much in our quest to understand their world because our needs are secondary to their primary mission: addressing China's problems. That does not mean China's intellectuals do not or will not speak to us. Many do, including the notable figures I just mentioned. However, their engagement with us is mostly instrumental, to further their contribution to the analysis and resolution of China's problems. We are brought in when we might be able to help their agenda.

This is as it should be. After all, U.S. intellectuals are mostly concerned about U.S. problems. Western academics use China as an example for their research. Yet the challenge before us—each in our own society and each with our national identification—is that our problems are not simply our own. They are global and they are pressing. We need to work together. For that, we need to understand each other. It has been the goal of this chapter to emphasize that in order to work together we must have a reasonably accurate understanding of who our partners are and what is on their minds. If we can keep in view the many worlds of China's intellectuals, remember the pressures and opportunities of their public world (the directed public sphere), and appreciate the overriding moral imperative of Chinese problems in the Sinophone Sphere, then we can build sustainable partnerships with our Chinese colleagues and tap their considerable wisdom and skill in addressing the problems that plague us all.

SUGGESTIONS FOR FURTHER READING

Davies, Gloria. *Worrying about China: The Language of Chinese Critical Inquiry*. Cambridge, MA: Harvard University Press, 2007.

Fewsmith, Joseph. *China since Tiananmen: From Deng Xiaoping to Hu Jintao*. New York: Cambridge University Press, 2008.

Hao, Zhidong. *Intellectuals at a Crossroads: The Changing Politics of China's Knowledge Workers*. Albany: State University of New York Press, 2003

Wasserstrom, Jeffrey N. *China's Brave New World—and Other Tales for Global Times*. Bloomington: Indiana University Press, 2007.

Zhao, Yuezhi. *Communication in China: Political Economy, Power, and Conflict*. Lanham, MD: Rowman & Littlefield, 2008.

Voices from China: Translations

Chan, Koonchung. *The Fat Years*. New York: Doubleday, 2011.

Sang Ye. *China Candid: The People's Republic*. Edited by Geremie R. Barmé, with Miriam Lang. Berkeley: University of California Press, 2005.

Wang, Chaohua. *One China, Many Paths*. London: Verso, 2003.

Wang, Hui. *China's New Order: Society, Politics, and Economy in Transition*. Edited and translated by Theodore Huters. Cambridge, MA: Harvard University Press, 2003.

Useful Websites

The China Beat (www.thechinabeat.org), a lively commentary on contemporary China by Western academics and journalists

China Dialogue (www.chinadialogue.net), a bilingual website based in England that puts Chinese and English scholars, NGO activists, and intellectuals into conversation

People's Daily (http://english.peopledaily.com.cn/), an English-language window into the official world of the PRC

Social Sciences in China (http://www.tandf.co.uk/journals/titles/02529203 .asp), an English-language journal of the Chinese Academy of Social Sciences, now published by a UK press

Human Rights in China (www.hrichina.org), a bilingual website based in the West that provides a forum for Chinese human rights activists

NOTES

1. See Yuezhi Zhao, *Communication in China*, and Zhidong Hao, *Intellectuals at a Crossroads*, in "Suggestions for Further Reading."

2. For the purposes of this chapter, "public sphere" marks the public arena in which people speak and listen, read and write about public affairs. On the debate of using Habermas's concept to explain China, see Frederic Wakeman Jr., "The Civil Society and Public Sphere Debate," *Modern China* 19, no. 2 (April 1993): 108–38.

3. Aiwa Ong, *Flexible Citizenship: The Cultural Logics of Transnationality* (Durham, NC: Duke University Press, 1998), 6.

4. Such as the "value spheres" of political, economic, or aesthetic life that Max Weber suggests. See, Hans Gerth and C. Wright Mills, eds., *From Max Weber* (New York: Random House, 1946), 147, 323–57.

5. A sound and accessible account of the attractions and limits of Habermas's model is given in Timothy Brook and B. Michael Frolic, eds., *Civil Society in China* (Armonk, NY: M.E. Sharpe, 1997), esp. 3–18. See also note 2 above.

6. For studies of the contemporary propaganda system in China, see Anne-Marie Brady, *Marketing Dictatorship: Propaganda and Thought Work in Contemporary China* (Lanham, MD: Rowman & Littlefield, 2008); and David Shambaugh, *China's Communist Party: Atrophy and Adaptation* (Berkeley: University of California Press, 2009).

7. This section draws from Timothy Cheek, "From Market to Democracy: Gaps in the Civil Society Model," in *Market Economics & Political Change: Comparing China and Mexico*, ed. Juan T. Lindau and Timothy Cheek (Lanham, MD: Rowman & Littlefield, 1997), 237ff.

8. Victor Serge's ideas on "directed" thought and culture are developed by the Hungarian poet and sociologist Miklós Haraszti in *The Velvet Prison: Artists under State Socialism* (New York: Basic Books, 1987).

9. Zhao, *Communication in China*, 5–7.

10. Jeffrey N. Wasserstrom, *China's Brave New World—and Other Tales for Global Times* (Bloomington: Indiana University Press, 2007), esp. 125ff.

11. Gloria Davies, *Worrying about China: The Language of Chinese Critical Inquiry* (Cambridge, MA: Harvard University Press, 2007), 7. By "praxis" Davies means political action, action in the public realm taken to change social life.

12. Wang Hui, "On Scientism and Social Theory in Modern Chinese Thought," in *Voicing Concerns: Contemporary Chinese Critical Inquiry*, ed. and trans. Gloria Davies (Lanham, MD: Rowman & Littlefield, 2001), 135.

13. This section draws from Timothy Cheek, "Xu Jilin and the Thought Work of China's Public Intellectuals," *China Quarterly*, no. 186 (2006): 401–20.

14. *Renmin ribao* (*People's Daily*) is conveniently available online, and with an English edition, at http://english.peopledaily.com.cn/.

15. W. John Morgan and Wu Bin, eds., *Higher Education Reform in China* (London: Routledge, 2001).

16. This information comes from my interview with a bookshop owner and independent publisher in July of 2006. Given that his purpose is to avoid attention, his identity will remain undisclosed.

17. See www.alsyz.com. Another website, www.alsm.unzt.com, was shut down in 2010.

18. Indeed, the group's website evokes the *sannong*: www.3nong.org. The group publishes a newsletter, a journal (*Shijian* or "Practice"), and a series of books—printed in just the same size (and red color) of Mao's *Quotations* (including the song book from which we sang)—under the general title *Daxuesheng xiaxiang zhinong zhidao shouce* (Guidebooks for University Students Going Down to the Countryside to Help Agriculture), published by *Hainan chubanshe* in 2008.

19. Two of the best studies on the Chinese Internet are Guobin Yang, *The Power of the Internet in China: Citizen Activism Online* (New York: Columbia University Press, 2009), and Johan Lagerkvist, *After the Internet, Before Democracy: Competing Norms in Chinese Media and Society* (New York: Peter Lang, 2011).

20. This is how Philip Kuhn describes the Chinese culture of the eighteenth century, and the insight holds for today. See his *Soulstealers: The Chinese Sorcery Scare of 1768* (Cambridge, MA: Harvard University Press, 1990), 223.

21. Suisheng Zhao, *A Nation-State by Construction: Dynamics of Modern Chinese Nationalism* (Stanford: Stanford University Press, 2004); Peter Hays Gries, *China's New Nationalism: Pride, Politics, and Diplomacy* (Berkeley: University of California Press, 2004); and Yang, *Power of the Internet in China*.

22. Evan Osnos, "Angry Youth: The New Generation's Neocon Nationalists," *New Yorker*, July 28, 2008. Tang Jie's video can be viewed at http://www.youtube.com/watch?v=MSTYhYkASsA.

23. Wenfang Tang, *Public Opinion and Political Change in China* (Stanford: Stanford University Press, 2005), 187.

24. For a reliable study that focuses on dissent, see Merle Goldman, *From Comrade to Citizen: The Struggle for Political Rights in China* (Cambridge, MA: Harvard University Press, 2005).

25. See the listing of all ethnic Chinese Nobel Laureates on *Wikipedia*: http://en.wikipedia.org/wiki/List_of_Ethnic_Chinese_Nobel_laureates.

26. Wang Gungwu, *The Chinese Overseas: From Earthbound China to the Quest for Autonomy* (Cambridge, MA: Harvard University Press, 2000), and Philip A. Kuhn, *Chinese among Others: Emigration in Modern Times* (Lanham, MD: Rowman & Littlefield, 2008).

27. See Lionel Jensen's essay in this volume and Xiaolin Guo, *Repackaging Confucius: PRC Public Diplomacy and the Rise of Soft Power* (Stockholm: Institute for

Security and Development Policy, Asia Paper Series, 2008), http://www.isdp.eu/index.php?option=com_jombib&task=showbib&id=5154.

28. Xu Jilin, "The Fate of an Enlightenment: Twenty Years in the Chinese Intellectual Sphere (1978–1998)," in *Chinese Intellectuals Between State and Market*, ed. Edward Gu and Merle Goldman (London: Routledge, 2004), esp. 194ff.

29. The fate of these and other Chinese lawyers are tracked and supported by the international NGO Committee to Support Chinese Lawyers, *Zhongguo lushi zhi fan.* See http://www.csclawyers.org/cases/.

30. Gregor Benton and Lin Chun, eds., *Was Mao Really a Monster? The Academic Response to Chang and Halliday's* Mao: The Unknown Story (London: Routledge, 2010).

8

Why Does China Fear the Internet?

Susan D. Blum

> For someone to perform a task solely on the basis of his motives and not bother about its effect is equivalent to a doctor only being concerned with making out prescriptions and not caring whether his patients die as a result. . . .
>
> We judge . . . doctors by looking at their practice or their results, and the same is true of writers.
>
> —Mao Zedong, *Talks at the Yan'an Conference on Literature and Art*

> All countries censor, but all censor in their own way.
>
> —Paraphrasing and modifying Tolstoy

Will the Internet save China from autocracy?

Why did the Chinese jail the first Chinese citizen living in China who was awarded the Nobel Peace Prize and refuse to release him to receive the award?

Is there one global Internet, with a universal set of meanings and rights, or does each society have its own?

Why does China fear the Internet? Should it?

This chapter is already out of date.

Cyber matters change so rapidly that anything published on paper is certain to lag behind current events.

So why should you read it?

I've tried to present general principles, illustrated by specific facts and cases. The principles should be relevant for some time, since many of them extend from times before the existence of the Internet. The facts, though, are surely already superseded.

For example, the number of Internet users in China was estimated at 23 million in 2000, 250 million in 2008, and about 400 million in mid-2010. The rate of increase may slow down as the obvious users—urban, young, middle-class, educated—have already signed on, so it is not certain what the number will be by the time you hold this book in your hands.

But you can be sure of two things: that it will be higher, and that you have tools by means of which you can find out the answer.

That is all preliminary, though. The main point I want to make, no matter what the details to support it, is this: All governments control Internet use—and the circulation of information—to some extent, but China is among a handful of countries that are especially repressive of the Internet and other forms of expression. In its company are Iran, Saudi Arabia, and Tunisia.[1] Judgments regarding Internet control stem from deeply held beliefs—theories—about how media do and should function.

MEDIA THEORIES

Cyber-utopianism is the view that the Internet will inevitably bring freedom and democracy, contrasting with *cyber-pessimism*, that it will enable greater surveillance, control, repression, loss of privacy, bullying, and other unwelcome consequences. A third position—we can call it *cyber-culturalism*—regards the Internet as neutral: simply a tool that can be used for good or ill, depending on the ways particular individuals employ it. The first two viewpoints share *technological determinism*—they regard a given technology as possessing inevitable consequences—and the third is *social constructivist*—suggesting an interplay between the cultural context and the technology.

These theoretical positions apply to the study of any medium (plural *media*)—from writing to printing to mobile phones, radio, TV, film, and now computers. It is helpful in reading about the Internet to identify the basic assumptions of each writer, even if they don't tell you directly what they believe.

If you come from an English-speaking country, you probably feel that censorship is, generally speaking, undesirable.

Yet it is important to recognize, before you feel *too* smug, that all countries, even the freedom-loving United States, censor. The Chinese government censors and controls speech in some different and some similar ways, for both different and similar reasons. But the Internet is not the same everywhere, because people are not the same. So you need to know something about the society that the Internet enters in order to make sense of what it means, whether we are talking about the Internet in Montana, Monrovia, or Mozambique. Here our concern is China.

The Internet in China entered a society in which certain ideas were already held about the flow of information and speech. In discussions about whether certain instances of speech should be permitted, we often find a strong preference for *image, order,* and *stability,* while in the United States we often assume that *human rights* and *freedom* are inherently desirable, with an acceptable degree of disorder.

In this chapter you will see how censorship works in the case of China's Internet. I contrast some use of the Internet with the push and pull of rulers and ruled, some of whom actively resist overt repression. First, though, we have to look a little more carefully at the concept of censorship, so that we can be clear about what we mean when we use this familiar term.

CENSORSHIP, SELF-CENSORSHIP, AND SECRECY

Censorship is the omission, suppression, or deletion of relevant information because of pressure; another way to think about it is as the erasure, blockage, or failure to produce speech that would otherwise occur. ("Speech" includes all produced expression, whether written or spoken language or images.)

In a broad sense all humans censor, whether to suppress expression of boredom at a professor's long lecture or dislike of a friend's new haircut, or to keep quiet about, say, government-sanctioned torture in order to avoid punishment. It is evident that even "truth" cannot be and is not expressed with absolute freedom and without limits, even if it is clear what truth is.

Societies differ in their ideas about what speech is limited or permitted, whether through convention, socialization, or even law. In the United States we can't shout "Fire!" in a crowded theater, or joke about guns in the airport security line. Hate speech is illegal, but we limit unpopular speech not by law but by public reaction. Profanity is highly charged speech usually using colorful terms for sexuality, excrement, and divinity; it is *taboo*— powerful, used only by certain people in certain contexts.

We teach children to keep certain kinds of facts and truths to themselves, lest they wound someone else's feelings. Sometimes citizens welcome government regulation of speech: we want our laws to control child pornography, sedition, libel, and fraudulent commercial claims. Even in settings in which a dominant trope of "freedom" reigns, there are limits to that freedom, some of which are internalized. It is always true that the most effective censorship is self-censorship.

Self-censorship relies on knowing what is acceptable and what is not, whether or not authorities are literally poised at one's door. In 1997, when

Hong Kong was about to be handed back to China following a ninety-nine-year lease to Great Britain, people worried about whether the Hong Kong press and universities would retain their independence and speak freely, even in criticism of the People's Republic of China (PRC), or whether, knowing the dangers, they would refrain from excessive criticism. Most observers agree that the media have remained somewhat free from overt censorship but that a great deal of self-censorship has also occurred. In China the threat of difficulty is often sufficient to keep people from engaging in controversial speech, at least in public, whether on the Internet or not.

China has a long history of self-censorship. When I did anthropological fieldwork in Kunming in the 1990s, people told me many times that their parents rehearsed with them what kinds of information could be revealed in what circumstances. They were not taught that the whole truth was, in general, the best policy, but rather to consider their audience and the uses to which the information would be put.

The Chinese nation-state is associated with a sixty-year history of state-run efforts to shape information. Sometimes this is dismissed with the English term "propaganda," a rough—and loaded—translation of *xuanchuan*, which has associations with promulgation, or spreading. Advertising is a kind of *xuanchuan*, as is gossip.

Analysts often trace the beginnings of China's propaganda to the 1942 Yan'an (or Yenan) Forum on Literature and Art, where Mao Zedong criticized petty-bourgeois writers' focus on the "dark"—exposing the negative. Instead, he urged revolutionary writers and artists to take into account the consequences of their writing and other activities and to focus rather on the "bright," extolling the good. Mao emphasized the effects that writers' actions would provoke in others, treating verbal actions as consequential. This explicit principle—words have effects, and their effects should be considered prior to speaking—is involved in decisions about releasing information, both on- and offline.

China is often regarded as an authoritarian country with an unacceptable amount of censorship, especially in media. Reporters without Borders, Human Rights Watch, Human Rights in China, Amnesty International, PEN American Center, the United Nations Universal Periodic Review, and many other humanitarian groups identify China as one of the nations most repressive of journalistic freedom. China jails more "cyber-dissidents" than any other country—forty-nine in 2008, according to Reporters without Borders.

Repression and censorship are cousins of secrecy. Secrecy involves who has access to information. Formerly, just about all data and statistics in China were regarded as "state secrets," circulating in *neibu* ("internal circulation") form. By 2004, however, China's National Bureau of Statistics offered a plan for improved "openness," implicitly acknowledging that it had been anything but open in the past.

Censorship and self-censorship share the more widely prevailing social norms about language use in China. At the same time, they are not uniform. Some in China resist authoritarian repression, such as those who signed the Charter 08 call for greater democratic reform, issued on Human Rights Day (December 10) in 2008. Several of the signers of this document have been jailed, including most prominently Nobel Peace Prize winner Liu Xiaobo.

THE INTERNET GOES TO CHINA

Networked computers for scholarly and scientific purposes first entered China in 1987 and remained entirely educational and academic until 1993. At that point, the Ministry of Posts and Telecom (MPT), later the Ministry of Industry and Information Technology (MIIT), founded CHINAPAC (renamed ChinaNET in 1995) to promote the spread of information.

Various government ministries competed with each other, each hoping for profits from investing in rival networks. The MIIT maintains control over data networks, both for profit and for oversight of content. The MIIT regulates China Telecom, which owns ChinaNET, in turn leasing to various internet service providers (ISPs).

At first these networks were extremely expensive. For example, initially forty hours of online time cost 400 to 600 RMB a month ($50 to $75 U.S.)—a fortune in those days, when average monthly salaries may have been only 350 RMB. In 1994 only 1,600 people in the PRC used the Internet. By 1996 it was 80,000, and by 1998 2.1 million. In 1999 Premier Zhu Rongji became aware of the enormous expense of using the Internet and ordered the costs lowered.

It was not until the early 2000s that any noteworthy fraction of the population regularly used the Internet, with an estimated 23 million users in 2000, out of a population at the time of one billion. By the end of 2010 that figure had exceeded 400 million, of a total population of 1.3 billion. As in the United States, it was initially used predominantly by young, unmarried, college-educated men, but with each year it has been spreading outward from that cohort.

More important than absolute numbers of users, though, is the percentage of the population using the Internet. The China Internet Network Information Center tracks this, noting for instance that 2007 "Internet penetration"—the percentage of each group that uses the Internet—is 38.8 percent for people aged eighteen to twenty-four but only 2.5 percent for people above forty. This latter figure is sure to rise. Users of the Internet in 2007 were 58.3 percent male and 41.7 percent female. About four-fifths of Internet users are urban. Issues of equal access are of concern to a government that aims for a satisfied populace. China's government encourages increased access to the Internet in general.

The Internet is used in familiar ways in China. The China Internet Network Information Center provides information about most frequently used services or functions of the Internet (as of 2007). Table 8.1 shows this information (note that I have slightly modified the wording in a few cases).

Much of the flow of information would be expected in most countries—having to do with connecting people. Online commerce is lower in China than in the United States but has been increasing. Note the absence of "pornography" as a category. Chinese surveys regularly report strong support for the government's control of pornography, which is frequently discussed.

Table 8.1. Purposes of Internet Use in China

Purpose for Internet Use	Percentage of Users Who Use This Function
E-mail	56.1
News	53.5
Search engine	51.5
Obtaining information (inquire about information of products, services, jobs, healthcare, government, etc.)	41.0
Forum, BBS (bulletin board system), discussion groups, etc.	36.9
Watching/downloading video (online TV)	36.3
Instant messaging	34.5
Listening to or downloading music (online radio)	34.4
Downloading or uploading files (excluding music and video)	32.9
Internet games	26.6
School/classmates' BBS	25.6
Blog	25.3
Online shopping	23.6
Online recruiting	20.8
Online chat room	20.8
Personal homepage service	20.3
E-journal	17.1
Online education	14.3
Online sales (including online promotion and auction)	13.3
Internet telephone (IP telephone, PC to phone)	11.2
Online finance (banking and stock trading)	10.5
SMS (short message service) and MSM (multimedia short message)	9.7
Online reservation (hotel, ticket, registration)	8.6
E-governance (online complaining, examine/approving, supervising, etc.)	7.7
Friends/matchmaking, community club	6.4
Other	6.4

Source: "Statistical Survey Report on the Internet Development in China," China Internet Network Information Center, January 2007, www.cnnic.cn/uploadfiles/pdf/2009/3/23/153540.pdf.

According to Chris Hedges in *The Empire of Illusion: The End of Literacy and the Triumph of Spectacle*, worldwide Internet pornography revenue totaled more than the combined revenue of Microsoft, Google, Amazon, eBay, Yahoo!, Apple, Netflix, and EarthLink—$97 billion in 2006. Pornographic sites—often connected with violence and torture—constitute 12 percent of the number of websites worldwide; one-fourth of all Internet searches are for porn. Thus the Chinese government's target of pornography is not unjustified. Still, campaigns to control the Internet are usually phrased as protecting social values and tastes, which can then easily turn to more political targets.

Chinese Internet users do not fully trust the Internet, just as they do not fully trust television, radio, billboards, or newspapers. Trust has in fact plummeted in the last decade, as alarming incidents or scares have become widely circulated.

Many of the Internet functions with which U.S. citizens are familiar exist in China, but with Chinese versions. Popular websites include Sina, Sina Weibo (microblogging has become extremely popular), Sohu.com, Danwei.com, and Tianya.cn. The most-used search engine is Baidu, with about 70 percent of search engine traffic. Google entered the Chinese market in 2006, agreeing to censor searches on Google.cn, but withdrew from China in January 2010. A year later it began trying to figure out a role in China. Searches on Google.cn are redirected to a Hong Kong site—uncensored.

In addition to computers, many devices with Internet access are widely, and increasingly, used in China, including smart phones. By June 2007 more than 75 percent of Internet users used broadband, and more than 34 percent used wireless or mobile phone access. By July 2010 broadband reached 98.1 percent of Internet users, mobile phones were used by 65.9 percent of Internet users to access the Internet, and 33 percent of mobile phone users surfed the Internet.

SUPPORT FOR THE INTERNET

Though we often think of the Internet as somehow "just there," intangible, it requires an enormous investment in and maintenance of a physical infrastructure, and government is involved in this in every country. It is clear that the Chinese government has encouraged the use of the Internet for some purposes: commercial interactions, e-government (often propagandistic rather than service oriented), news, entertainment. It built, supports, and maintains the infrastructure that permits Chinese to connect to the Internet, and many independent government ministries seek to profit from it. Yet as Eric Harwit and Duncan Clark wrote in "Shaping the Internet in China" in 2001, "Central government control of access to foreign web pages remains schizophrenic"—fostering some economic and social uses while blocking many political ones.

The Chinese government has embraced the commercial aspects of the Internet. It is earnestly involved in studying, tracking, and promoting its use. In some cases it has encouraged or at least tolerated expression on the Internet of nationalistic zeal, as when in 2008, protests in Tibet were covered by Western journalists in ways that were considered objectionable in China. Ordinary Chinese created, for example, an "anti-CNN" website that attracted tens of thousands of supporters. When protests about the Olympic Torch prior to the 2008 Beijing Olympics broke out in Paris, boycotts of the Beijing branch of the French store Carrefour were organized online. Eventually the government urged people to call it off.

Overall, then, the Internet itself is a tool—a powerful tool. It functions within a particular context. And the potential for liberation or repression—or both—is in some sense still unclear.

While the government wants to harness the positive power of the Internet for increasing commerce and integration, it is firmly committed to reining in its unruly aspects, and especially those that challenge government power. To do that, it has many tools at its disposal, in an image usually expressed as "multilayered." Imagine trying to filter water: water treatment plants use rocks, charcoal, chemicals, natural processes, and filters of varying degrees of porousness. China aims, similarly, to keep out two kind of poisons: moral ills, on the one hand, but on the other, even more significantly, challenges to its autocratic rule. Such control takes many forms, from prohibiting mention of outlawed terms to the always-present threat of detection, intimidation, or incarceration.

THE LAYERS OF CONTROL:
THE "GREAT FIREWALL" AND BEYOND

Kill the chickens to scare the monkeys.

—Chinese proverb

The notorious Great Firewall of China (*Zhongguo Weida Fanghuoqiang*), officially the Golden Shield project (*jindun gongcheng*), was implemented in 2002–2003 to control, limit, and keep surveillance on Internet activities that are deemed "unhealthy," especially those that might challenge state interests. Relying on a complex combination of hardware, software, servers, filters, voluntary self-censoring, and an estimated 39,000 human monitors, this shield filters out undesirable material regarding sensitive political topics, especially those sometimes jokingly referred to as the 3 Ts (Tibet, Taiwan independence, the Tiananmen massacre), as well as "unhealthy" subjects, such as pornography. Pages can be blocked, connections can be severed, and other consequences can follow the discovery of Internet use violations. At its most severe, people charged as dissidents can be located and jailed, as was the case with Nobel Peace Laureate Liu Xiaobo.

All this is overseen by a confusing assortment of government bureaus, ultimately under the oversight of the Central Propaganda Department of the Chinese Communist Party (CCP), which has a web bureau. The State Council Information Office (SCIO) also has an Internet Affairs Bureau. Bloggers and others ironically refer to the detailed instructions regularly issued by these offices as "Directives from the Ministry of Truth"—one of many references to George Orwell's *1984*. China Digital Times regularly posts leaked directives in Chinese and English, with very detailed instructions about deletions, omissions, or specific ways of phrasing news or topics. As events unfold, directives immediately follow. Freedom House reports that between 1993 and 2007, Internet control was overseen by twenty-nine government agencies, which issued eighty-one ordinances. In 2010 a new agency, the Internet News Coordination Bureau, was formed to oversee Chinese web use.

In January and February 2011, protests and demonstrations—organized principally by Facebook—in Egypt and elsewhere in the Middle East led to the resignation and departure of Egyptian President Hosni Mubarak and spreading unrest throughout the region. This added to the cyber-optimists' view of the Internet's revolutionary potential (in Egypt, anyway). China's Ministry of Truth immediately issued tight regulations about how this news was to be handled. (When the protests initially occurred, a frequent comparison was with the Tiananmen protests of 1989—though in the Egyptian case the end was peaceful, not tragic.) Only the Xinhua agency would be permitted to relay information; no local news outlets could venture their own version, and Facebook and Twitter were especially blocked.

Later in February 2011, material circulated on the Internet about a call for protests in several Chinese cities on subsequent Sundays. Several hundred people, including hundreds of foreign journalists, showed up in a few places, usually to observe what they expected others to do.

While in Egypt and Tunisia the governments were blindsided by the substantial and adept youth use of social media such as Facebook, China, by contrast, was completely prepared. Police outnumbered alleged protesters by a substantial factor.

Because this was called a "Jasmine Revolution," the word *jasmine* was immediately blocked from Sina Weibo (the Chinese equivalent of Twitter) and the search engine Baidu, among other sites. To give a flavor of these directives, I include two of many sets of instructions from the week of February 17 through 24, 2011:

From the Central Propaganda Department: Media reports on the current changing situation in the Middle East must use standard copy sources. Reports cannot have the word "revolution" (geming). Regarding the reasons for the emergence of these mass protests, nothing can be reported regarding demands for democracy or increases in commodity prices. Reports also cannot draw connections between the political systems of Middle Eastern nations and the system in our country. In all media, when the names of the leaders of Egypt, Tunisia, Libya, and other countries are given, the names of Chinese leaders cannot appear next to them.

From the State Council Information Office: All websites are requested to conduct strict searches of interactive spaces such as online forums, blogs, micro-blogs, instant message tools, and text message services. Immediately delete the phrase "A nice bunch of jasmine" and related information.[2]

Note that specific platforms ("online forums, blogs, micro-blogs, instant message tools, and text message services") were targeted.

Beyond repression of certain platforms, China has many other means of controlling Internet use. Internet searches for forbidden terms result in messages that "the connection has been reset." This reminds me of the 1980s and 1990s, when Chinese censors occupied enormous rooms in the post offices, equipped with black marking pens. When outside magazines containing forbidden material were mailed to China, offending words were physically blocked out. The current automation makes it far easier to effectively block material—but in turn it means that slight deviations from the program can slip through, as you will see below.

In 2009 the government issued a regulation mandating that all computers bought in China have filtering software preinstalled. This "Green Dam Youth Escort" would filter undesirable content. The outcry—along with revelations about bugs in the software and security problems—was sufficient to delay, perhaps permanently, mandatory implementation. Other countries, though, including some Western democracies, are considering similar filtering to keep out pornography, gambling, hate speech, "Islamist" speech, and more.

Just prior to the 2008 Beijing Olympics, much was made of foreign reporters' need for free communication with the outside world. The situation became quite unstable; one day CNN, the BBC, the *New York Times*, or Voice of America was blocked and the next it was available. In the end, reporters did have the necessary access, but the situation in China was not fundamentally altered.

The architecture, or informational structure, of the Internet facilitates surveillance. All activities on the Internet can be traced to particular Internet protocol, or IP, addresses, which in turn can almost always be associated with specific locations. Users formerly could sign on anonymously in Internet cafes, but beginning in 2008 they had to be photographed and show their state-issued identification cards even in cafes. Some reports state that most people use pseudonyms. Even SIM cards for mobile phones are supposed to be registered, with users' real names. Text messages are increasingly intercepted by the Public Security Bureau.

It is not only the government that oversees Internet use. In 2006, for instance, five hundred students at Shanghai Normal University alone volunteered to "guide" fellow students' Internet use, turning them away from offensive or controversial topics and toward acceptable ones. They regarded this as their contribution toward building a "harmonious society." (Such work also gave them "points" in the patriotic and nationalistic—and careerist—game still operating within the Communist Party in China.)

The CIA issued a report on the "Student Informant System" in November 2010, using open-source information. The SIS builds on traditional spying and mutual surveillance techniques, established in the 1950s but made especially notorious during the Cultural Revolution (1966–1976). In this approach, people could report on their fellows for improper political *attitudes*, not only behavior. Such reports went into the secret "dossiers" that could not be seen by the persons whose lives were profiled within them. This was revived on college campuses after the 1989 Tiananmen Square "incident" ("massacre," protests) to root out forbidden sympathy with the protestors. This system relies more on intimidation than on actual arrest or prosecution, though these also endure. Seeking information about potentially subversive attitudes in the name of "stability," the police work with universities. A few well-publicized imprisonments or punishments can have the desired chilling effect. Students are sometimes punished for misdeeds as slight as an accused facial expression, as occurred when students at Beijing University were accused of expressions of undue happiness on the day in October 2010 that Liu Xiaobo's Nobel Prize was announced. They were threatened with scholarships being revoked and points deducted from assessments. Bloggers quickly labeled this "Facecrime"—yet another ironic nod to Orwell's shockingly fitting *1984*.

This carefully nurtured self-censorship, supported by a few incidents, means that many people simply opt out of political discourse. Junhua Zhang's study of six hundred blogs in 2007 noted that only one touched on the outlawed religious/martial arts group Falun Gong, and none mentioned 1989 or Tibet. It is simply safer to stay away from politics.

WHAT IS BLOCKED

It is not only websites that are scrutinized. Other forms of communication are overseen as well. For instance, the Voice over Internet (VoI) service Skype has a chat component, which, it was discovered, has been seeking messages containing sensitive terms such as "democracy," "Falun Gong," or "Taiwan independence." The complicity or resistance of foreign companies—including U.S. companies Yahoo!, Google, and eBay (former owner of Skype)—has become a tough issue with few easy answers. Following the arrest and sentencing to ten years' imprisonment of prodemocracy writer Shi Tao for an email he sent to the United States on Yahoo!, the U.S. Congress held hearings in 2006 about the role of U.S. companies colluding with the Chinese government to repress freedom of speech.

But even more than blocking specific sites (*New York Times,* Voice of America), the power of what is often called "Web 2.0"—in which users themselves generate, rather than simply consume, content—has made such applications increasingly the target of blockage. This occurs especially around certain events, such as every June, the anniversary of the Tiananmen massacre.

YouTube, Facebook, Flickr, and Twitter are frequently blocked for those using Chinese addresses, though there are Chinese equivalents and technological ways around this impediment. China is developing its own search engines, its own microblogging, and even an equivalent to Facebook (called Renren, "Everybody"). This gives Chinese Internet users a satisfying range of tools with which to occupy themselves. "Pure," Chinese, and uncontaminated by the outside world, they are easy to control and monitor, but this matters only to those who wish to challenge limits.

For many Chinese Internet users, their options are adequate. For others, though, who are not willing to comply or who are not thoroughly absorbed by practical economic goals, a fierce battle is underway.

ATTITUDES TOWARD CENSORSHIP

In a study of attitudes toward Internet control, Deborah Fallows reports that almost 84 percent of urban Chinese believe it should be managed, and that this should be done by the government. Westerners may expect great protests, but most ordinary Chinese are more concerned about feeding their families. That still, as in all things Chinese, leaves *millions* who are interested in political affairs.

Such Internet users cleverly attempt to elude the censors, employing everything from the technical use of proxy servers or deliberate misspellings to more subtle uses of sarcasm, parody, and humor. In the summer of 2007, the government shut down 18,401 websites, while countless others popped up. The government urges self-restraint on the Internet, a plea with which some Chinese citizens are willing to comply.

Savvy users in China and in other repressive countries sign on to proxy servers; the government has designed programs to chase them. Initially this took twenty-four hours, but by 2003 was down to about fifteen minutes.

By 2010 such proxy servers were an open secret. One website I discovered offered a dozen pages of possible servers, each existing for only a few hours or days. A huge commercial market for Internet "filtering circumvention tools" now exists.

THE PEOPLE'S INTERNET: THE POWER OF NUMBERS

Researcher Yang Guobin has tracked what he calls "activism" and "Internet incidents" on the Internet. He analyzes seven types of activism: (1) popular nationalism, (2) rights defense, (3) corruption and power abuse, (4) environment, (5) cultural contention, (6) muckraking, and (7) online charity. Some of these are encouraged by the government, and some are a source of concern, verging on paranoia.

For example, in 2008 following uprisings in Tibet and just before the opening of the Olympic Games, on May 12 an earthquake measuring 7.9 on the Richter scale devastated a part of rural Sichuan province, killing almost 87,000 people. Using the Internet, people sent money and assistance. The government encouraged this form of civilian kindness and generous spirit. But then some things happened:

Many of those who died were children, because the earthquake struck while they were in school, and many of the schools were built extremely poorly, using materials that were supposed to be adequate, but in fact corrupt officials and owners had often substituted poorer cement or had not followed regulations for earthquake-resistant building. The government attempted to settle with bereft parents, who would receive large payments as long as they dropped their lawsuits and never spoke publicly about this case. Many accused the government of "buying off" the mourners.

Activists Tan Zuoren and Huang Qi used the Internet to encourage investigation into the truth of the case. They were accused of endangering state security and possessing state secrets. Ai Weiwei, one of the architects of the "Bird's Nest" Olympic Stadium, supported their investigation, using his international fame to attract attention. He had an extremely popular blog—now defunct—that he used to create his Sichuan Earthquake Names Project, attracting volunteers to determine the precise number and identities of students killed, accusing the government of covering up names and numbers of victims and causes of the tragedy. He traveled to Wenchuan, the epicenter, to collect backpacks of the dead children for an art installation, where he was detained and beaten so badly that he needed brain surgery abroad. His Internet accounts were hacked. And in April 2011 Ai was "disappeared," taken into custody and eventually accused of the standard crime of tax fraud. His fame made this case notorious worldwide; he was not released for nearly three months despite enormous pressure from outside

China. Following his release, he was ordered to remain silent, yet through the last months of 2011 and the early months of 2012 he has been challenging his enforced repression by tweeting and giving limited, but candid, public interviews.

POPULAR ON THE BLOGOSPHERE

Internet users have increased rapidly in numbers, but the number of bloggers has erupted like a volcano, from 230,000 in 2002 to more than 7.6 million in 2006. Estimates are that one quarter of Chinese Internet users have blogs (*boke*), which would take the total to more than 100 million in 2010. While entertainment and silliness are just as common in China as elsewhere, a serious strain also exists. Things that somehow catch fire and "go viral" can affect the actual behavior of the government. The CIA tracks popular topics for bloggers, week by week. One finds a strong sense of social justice involved in many cases, as in December 2010 when word surfaced of twelve mentally retarded men who were sold into work slavery. Public outcry, much of it electronic, led the government to crack down on the perpetrators.

Another case was that of a Zhejiang village chief named Qian Yunhui who had been active in protesting about land disputes (as when a peasant's land is forcibly bought for a low price so that someone from outside the village can develop a business or extract resources at a great profit), leading to his arrest three times. In December 2010 he was crushed and decapitated by a truck. This image circulated widely, leading to claims that this was a deliberate murder by the government for Qian's political views. The official story was that this was an unfortunate accident. Netizens expressed such distrust of this version of the event that two or three investigative teams were sent, duly concluding as well that this was an unfortunate accident. So suspicious are many of government for frequent lying that many refuse to accept the findings. In any case, Qian is now known and referred to as a martyred hero who stood up to government corruption—emblematic of a "truth crisis." Clips of the funeral and police response are available on YouTube; they have been removed from Chinese video-sharing sites.

Given the increasing popularity of smart phones, which can videotape and post images almost immediately, and without detection, ordinary people are easily able to provide information to the public, whereas in the past it would have required professional journalists to get the story out— and they might well have been ordered not to attend to certain incidents. Cyber-optimists point to the power of such citizen journalists.

Another case of the intersection of the Internet with politics occurred in October 2010, when the son of a police official had a car accident that resulted in the death of a female student, Chen Xiaofeng. When police came to arrest the driver, Li Qiming, he shouted, "Go ahead. Sue me if you dare. My father is Li Gang!" Quickly the statement, "My father is Li Gang," became a rallying cry for those who deplore the misuse of connections and the evasion of justice for ordinary people.

RESISTANCE: SERIOUS PLAY

> The greatest enemy of authority . . . is contempt, and the surest way to undermine it is laughter.
>
> —Hannah Arendt

Viral videos have been responsible for initiating many of the most vivid, lively, and irrepressible forms of resistance to Internet censorship. For example, in 2009 a video showing a "grass-mud horse" (the three words, pronounced "*cao ni ma*," sound almost identical to an expression meaning "f*** your mother"). It is a visual image, which cannot easily be banned, and shows creativity, solidarity, and more with those who are angered by the limitations on speech (see figure 8.1).

As China Digital Times, which has been accumulating a "grass-mud horse" lexicon, states, "The Internet has become a quasi-public space where

Figure 8.1.   Grass-Mud Horse: Unambiguous Protest. Photograph by Tong Lam.

the CCP's dominance is being constantly exposed, ridiculed, and criticized, often in the form of political satire, jokes, videos, songs, popular poetry, jingles, fiction, Sci-Fi, code words, mockery, and euphemisms. . . . Within weeks, the 'grass-mud horse' became the de facto mascot of netizens in China fighting for free expression, inspiring poetry, photos and videos, artwork, lines of clothing, and more."[3]

The image of the imaginary grass-mud horse has in turn been depicted on material objects, used in speech and writing, and generally seen as a form of resistance that can be "plausibly denied."

Similarly, the term *hexie*, meaning "harmony," is punned using homophones for *he* ("peace" and "river"), *xie* ("even" and "crab"). So "river crab" is a term meaning, ironically, something has been "harmonized"—an Orwellian phrase suggesting eradication on the premise that it is somehow a danger to social harmony. It is a parody of China's leaders' "harmonious society" campaign, begun in the 2000s, to address the inequities between city and countryside, between coastal and inland provinces, between Han and minorities. This word, *hexie*, has become a code word for insisting on a facade of harmony. Those punished for violating this code, for speaking up about actual inequities, are talked about as being "harmonized."

The goofy *cao ni ma*, a parody of a llama, usually accompanied by childish music, attacks the *hexie*, the censors, depicted as dark, slimy, low crabs. Within a few years there will undoubtedly be other forms of resistance, but this demonstrates one collective, satirical attempt to express outrage at and defiance of official limitations.

HUMOR, PUNS, SATIRE, TECHNOLOGICAL EVASION

When literature-professor-turned-political-activist Liu Xiaobo was announced in October 2010 as that year's Nobel Peace Prize winner, he was serving an eleven-year sentence in jail for having cowritten the Charter 08 pledge for human rights. Liu first heard about the award from his jailers. Some reports are that the jailers treated him kindly, as if to demonstrate support. His wife, Liu Xia, has been under house arrest ever since (as of 2012).

Liu's name was immediately prohibited. Thereupon ensued what appears to be a gleeful attempt to circumvent the censors. *Language Log* lists several pages of terms that sound like Liu's name or have similar meanings, sometimes in other dialects of Chinese. This resembles the play on words that followed the taboos on emperors' names after their death, though now the play is multilingual. The linguistic features of Chinese—filled with words that sound alike (homophones) or written characters that look alike (homonyms)—make this an enjoyable form of word play and impossible to forbid. Such play had occurred with the Tiananmen Massacre of June 4, 1989. Obviously "June 4" cannot be entirely outlawed, but each year near the anniversary, it is. So people resort to terms like "May 35" to make their meaning clear—though in June 2011 even this was prohibited. For Liu Xiaobo, for example, the Romanized Cantonese pronunciation *Lau Xin-bo* is used, or a combination of English sound-and-sense play is substituted to create "Mini Ball Liu." *Xiao* meaning "dawn" is turned into a homophone also pronounced *xiao* but meaning "small." *Bo* sounds like English *ball.* Hence "Mini Ball."

OPEN NET? OPEN QUESTIONS

In the next several years, the Internet and its successor technologies are certain to play significant roles in political and cultural affairs. One issue that will be increasingly discussed is whether the Internet is singular or multiple: Given that the Internet exists within social, cultural, and philosophical contexts, as well as in disembodied, boundary-free "cyberspace," is it more accurate to imagine a world filled with different forms of the Internet or to regard it as singular?

In June 2010 China issued a "white paper" (an official government position paper) on what it termed its Internet sovereignty—the first nation to claim a unique version of the Internet, in contrast to a global, universal Internet. This document claimed the right to enforce regulations unique to China in the name of cybersecurity—pointing not only to national security but also to social stability (as challenged by pornography, for example). U.S. Secretary of State Hillary Rodham Clinton spoke in February 2011 about the universal right to Internet freedom, which China immediately protested. Ian Buruma described China's dismissal of U.S. ideals of universal human rights as a fight against "information imperialism"—a deliberate appeal to memories of nineteenth-century imperialism—comparing the current battle over information freedom, human rights, and democracy to prior encounters between China and the West. For hundreds of years, China has been trying to import "practical knowledge" (*yong*) without changing its "essential" culture (*ti*)—an unresolved tension. Outside pressure, he reminds us, has never been welcome or effective.

In coming years, we will all confront the following questions: Who has access to computers? Where and how is this access provided? This provides clues as to how it can be controlled and traced. Whose interests are served by the Internet? Business? Politicians? "Citizens"? And which ones? In which aspects of their lives? What are the limits of privacy? Who wants the control? Why? How do Internet "speech," ideas of privacy, control, embarrassment, or face compare with these ideas "offline," as media, assembly, and speech? How is the Internet like and how is it unlike other forms of communication and expression or other media? How do the technological dimensions of the Internet determine both its possibilities and its limitations?

Within each society one finds contrasting and opposing forces, some governmental, some individual, some corporate. (In the United States, corporate control of the Internet is the coming question—as in the issue of "net neutrality" and how the Google algorithm is affected by money.)

We may face wars about who gets to decide Internet freedom and control.

In the end, you should reflect on which side has it right: the cyber-optimists or the cyber-pessimists?

Will the Internet determine and shape the world? Or will individuals, in harmony with or in opposition to their governments and other powerful elites, be in control?

However we see this unfold, China's Internet will play a prominent role. Meanwhile, China fears the power of the Internet. Should it?

SUGGESTIONS FOR FURTHER READING

Websites

Amnesty International (AIUK Human Rights for China), http://www
.amnesty.org.uk/content.asp?CategoryID=10498
Berkman Center for Internet & Society, http://cyber.law.harvard.edu/
China Digital Times, http://chinadigitaltimes.net/
China Geeks, http://chinageeks.org/
Freedom House, http://freedomhouse.org/template.cfm?page=1
Global Integrity Commons, http://commons.globalintegrity.org/
Human Rights in China, www.hrichina.org
Human Rights Watch, www.hrw.org
OpenNet Initiative, http://opennet.net/
PEN American Center, www.pen.org
Pew Internet & American Life Project, www.pewinternet.org
Reporters without Borders, http://en.rsf.org/
United Nations Human Rights, Universal Periodic Review, http://www
.ohchr.org/en/hrbodies/upr/pages/uprmain.aspx

Books and Articles

Blum, Susan D. *Lies That Bind: Chinese Truth, Other Truths.* Lanham, MD: Rowman
& Littlefield, 2007.
Buruma, Ian. "Battling the Information Barbarians." *Wall Street Journal,* January 29,
2010.

Calingaert, Daniel. "Authoritarianism vs. the Internet," *Policy Review*, no. 160 (April/ May 2010): 63–75.

Deibert, Ronald J. "Dark Guests and Great Firewalls: The Internet and Chinese Security Policy." *Journal of Social Issues* 58, no. 1 (2002): 143–59.

Elgin, Ben, and Bruce Einhorn. "The Great Firewall of China." *Business Week*, January 12, 2006, http://www.businessweek.com/technology/content/jan2006/ tc20060112_434051.htm.

Fallows, Deborah. "Most Chinese Say They Approve of Government Internet Control." Pew Internet and American Life Project, March 27, 2008, http://www .pewinternet.org/pdfs/PIP_China_Internet_2008.pdf.

Fallows, James. "The Connection Has Been Reset." *Atlantic*, March 2008.

———. "Penetrating the Great Firewall." *Atlantic*, February 19, 2008, http://www .theatlantic.com/doc/200802u/fallows-china-censorship.

French, Howard W. "Chinese Censors and Web Users Match Wits." *New York Times*, March 4, 2005, http://www.nytimes.com/2005/03/04/international/ asia/04censor.html.

———. "As Chinese Students Go Online, Little Sister Is Watching." *New York Times*, May 9, 2006, www.nytimes.com/2006/05/09/world/asia/09internet.html.

He Qinglian, *The Fog of Censorship: Media Control in China.* New York: Human Rights in China, 2008.

Kalathil, Shanthi, and Taylor C. Boas, *Open Networks, Closed Regimes.* Washington, DC: Carnegie Endowment for International Peace, 2003.

Lessig, Lawrence. *Code and Other Laws of Cyberspace.* New York: Basic Books, 1999.

———. *Free Culture: The Nature and Future of Creativity.* New York: Penguin Books, 2004.

———. *Code Version 2.0.* New York: Basic Books, 2006.

Link, Perry. "The Anaconda in the Chandelier: Censorship in China Today." *New York Review of Books*, April 11, 2002, http://www.uscc.gov/textonly/txlink.htm.

Simons, Craig. "Groundswell of Sarcastic Humor Undermining China's Censors." Truth about China, March 11, 2007, http://archives.truthaboutchina .com/2007/03/groundswell-of-sarcastic-humor.html.

Tsui, Lokman. "The Panopticon as the Antithesis of a Space of Freedom: Control and Regulation of the Internet in China." *China Information* 17, no. 2 (2003): 65–82.

Yang Guobin. "The Internet and the Rise of a Transnational Chinese Cultural Sphere." *Media, Culture & Society* 25 (2003): 469–90.

———. "The Internet as Cultural Form: Technology and the Human Condition in China." *Knowledge, Technology, and Policy* 22 (2009): 109–55.

Zittrain, Jonathan, and Benjamin Edelman. "Empirical Analysis of Internet Filtering in China." Berkman Center for Internet & Society, Harvard Law School, December 3, 2002, http://cyber.law.harvard.edu/filtering/china.

NOTES

This chapter draws on my Kellogg Institute Working Paper, "Happy News: Censorship, Nationalism, and Language Ideology in China." I am grateful to the Helen

Kellogg Institute for International Studies at the University of Notre Dame and to Elizabeth Rankin for helping prod my thinking about this topic. I have benefited from interactions with Lionel Jensen, Victoria Tin-bor Hui, Xiao Qiang, Cynthia Mahmood, and Perry Link, though they cannot be held responsible for my interpretations. I appreciate the work of Tim Weston in helping me improve this chapter.

1. Many of the websites listed at the end of this chapter have special reports on the current situation in China.

2. "Latest Directives From the Ministry of Truth, February 17–24, 2011," China Digital Times, http://chinadigitaltimes.net/2011/02/latest-directives-from-the -ministry-of-truth-february-17-21-2011/.

3. "Introduction to the Grass-Mud Horse Lexicon," China Digital Times, http:// chinadigitaltimes.net/space/Introduction_to_the_Grass-Mud_Horse_Lexicon.

II

BEYOND THE HEADLINES

Photograph by Tong Lam.

9

Producing Exemplary Consumers: Tourism and Leisure Culture in China's Nation-Building Project

Travis Klingberg and Tim Oakes

On February 16, 2010, the Empire State Building was closed to the public for two hours for a special gathering of over one thousand Chinese tourists celebrating the lunar New Year. Chinese Consul General of New York Peng Keyu was on hand to light the building in red and yellow and to greet what Chinese national media called the biggest Chinese tour group in history.[1] China's state newspaper, *People's Daily*, wrote that the Chinese tourists were "warmly welcomed in New York City"[2] during the joint promotion by the New York City tourism board, Continental Airlines, and Macy's Department Store. The *People's Daily* claimed that the thousand-person tour group had pumped $6 million into the U.S. economy, an astonishing $6,000 per tourist expenditure.[3] The newspaper claimed that the group brought "vigor to the US east coast business, which [has been] quite depressed in the past two years." The lesson from New York? Chinese tourists carried bulging wallets; China's new global purchasing power had arrived on Fifth Avenue.

The thousand-tourist shopping trip was reported in the Chinese press as a story of China's *xiaofeili*—consumer power. The *People's Daily* went so far as to write that, "despite elevated government tension between China and the US regarding arms sales to Taiwan, the Dalai Lama's visit to the US, and trade disputes, the relationship between the two nations' people continues to be warm, especially in terms of tourism."[4] Even with the political tension between governments, the economic and social relationship between China and the United States is downright warm because of the consumer power of tourists. Something significant has happened here. China, the world's greatest producer of consumer goods, seems on track to become one of the world's greatest consumers as well, and tourism is at the leading edge of this change. What the story of the thousand-tourist group in

Manhattan leaves out, however, is the fact that changing consumer behavior in China is not simply a spontaneous effect of economic growth.

Although consumer habits often seem to reflect true freedom of choice, especially in advertising and marketing messages, there are many ways that consumption is guided by social norms, industrial priorities, and government policies.[5] Consumers who spend have become model citizens in China, and not only for the way they help "depressed" foreign economies. They are more prized by the Chinese government for their value in the domestic economy, relied upon to spur economic growth in hard times. Stable economic growth is one of the most important goals of the Chinese government, and as the story of the thousand-person tour group in New York illustrates, tourism can have a significant economic impact. Tourism has become a key part of China's domestic economy, and producing exemplary consumers of tourism is as important to the Chinese government as developing tourism infrastructure.

While China still remains one of the world's powerful producers of consumer goods, less attention has been paid to the fact that the Chinese are also becoming a nation of consumers and are being encouraged in this regard by their government. While Beijing's efforts to stimulate consumption have focused on things like expanding social security and subsidizing health care, giving households less reason to save money, tourism and leisure are also being heavily promoted among a growing urban middle class. Between 1996 and 2006 the number of domestic tourist trips in China grew by 54 percent. Despite a worldwide recession between 2008 and 2011, China's domestic tourism industry grew 9 percent in 2009 alone, reaching total revenues of 1.26 trillion yuan ($190 billion U.S.). In 2010 total tourism receipts were expected to grow another 14 percent to 1.44 trillion yuan ($218 billion).[6]

In less than twenty years, domestic tourism has become a central part of contemporary life in China. By the late 1990s, most urban professionals and so-called white-collar workers enjoyed a government-mandated two-day weekend, and since 2000 these workers have been given extended "Golden Week" holidays each year in a deliberate effort to encourage more shopping and travel.[7] In 2008 the traditional Midautumn, Dragon Boat, and Qingming festivals became official holidays, adding still more leisure time to the annual calendar. As urban Chinese middle-class consumers travel more often, tourism and leisure have been promoted as a way of life even for those who never leave their hometown.

Daily life in urban China is increasingly geared toward the kinds of leisure activities typically associated with tourism: visiting scenic, historic, and leisure sites, shopping, and dining out. And new suburban residential developments seek to convey a touristic lifestyle of leisure and culture in attracting new buyers. These deliberate strategies to stimulate domestic consumption have not only spurred fast economic growth, but have also served to produce a new kind of exemplary consumer, one the Chinese state depends on to drive economic growth. It is increasingly apparent in China that tourism is important not simply because it rakes in profits from a limited set of tourist sites and activities. Tourism has become something bigger, something that exerts an organizing force on contemporary Chinese society, something similar to, in Adrian Franklin's words, "other socio-technical structuring processes, such as nationalism, consumerism or even capitalism."[8]

In this chapter, we argue that Chinese government-initiated strategies of tourism development have produced the structures of a tourism industry (a transportation infrastructure, scenic or heritage site development, travel services, and management of leisure-culture industries) as well as exemplary consumers of tourism: modern Chinese citizens who seek tourism experiences dependably enough to drive sustained economic growth. At the heart of our argument lie three "tourist development" strategies implemented by the Chinese state that have produced exemplary consumers, namely, *naturalizing* tourism as a normal part of contemporary life, *speeding* tourism consumption by its citizens, and *building* tourism into the bricks and mortar of China's fast-changing cities. Through these strategies, tourism can be seen as an active social force in China, an integral part of social and economic life that should be recognized for its influence on contemporary notions of belonging and citizenship in China. We take the case of Chengdu, the capital of Sichuan Province (see figure 3.1), as a case example of the ways that tourism has reordered daily life in many Chinese cities.

MAKING TOURISM NATURAL

While it may seem unremarkable that tourism has become a "natural" part of life in urban China, a brief overview of tourism over the past century reveals that it has been anything but natural for modern China. In fact, a great deal of work has gone into *making* tourism normal—transforming it from an exotic symbol of early twentieth-century colonialism to a reluctant tool of China's post-Mao reforms, and eventually to an ordinary part of everyday life in China, as it is today. Tourism in China today no longer has the exotic, Western connotations it had even twenty years ago. Rather, most Chinese now view tourism as a normal and desirable part of modern life. This did not happen by accident, and it did not happen simply by opening China's economy to global capitalism. It happened—and it happened *fast*—because the government wanted it that way.

China's government itself had to accept tourism as natural before it could begin promoting it as such to the Chinese people. And that took some time.

Throughout much of the 1980s, tourism was regarded as a necessary evil, a relatively easy means of accumulating foreign currency, but one that carried the risk of "cultural pollution" from the decadent West. The government was, after all, managing a transition from decades of ideological control often critical of the West to a period of more open but still acceptably "Chinese" society. By the 1990s, however, the government could not ignore the fact that the greatest demand in tourism came not from the decadent West but from its own citizens. The 1990s thus saw a spectacular rise in domestic tourism, as local governments all over the country began to adopt new policies for attracting tourists from the booming coastal cities. Domestic tourism came to be seen as one of the most visible markers of China's booming economy and of the government's post-Mao promise to bring modernization and improve dramatically the quality of life for China's people.

This was not, however, China's first encounter with tourism. Many of the issues that the Chinese government faced in the 1990s regarding domestic tourism had been confronted during the previous consumer boom in China, in the late 1920s and 1930s Republican-era heyday of Shanghai. Shanghai at the time was the cosmopolitan center of China, a place where Chinese and foreigners mixed and where the first modern forms of domestic tourism in China originated. Taking their cue from foreign residents, Shanghai residents were the first to popularize leisure travel in China. In the early 1930s, tourism was viewed by some Shanghai elites as exemplary of a sophisticated cosmopolitan modernity, something that those elites sought to cultivate. Madeleine Yue Dong has documented this attitude in her history of Shanghai's *China Traveler* magazine, a China Travel Service publication that ran uninterrupted from 1927 until 1952.[9] In addition to articles about international destinations, *China Traveler* featured stories about travel in the rural hinterlands of Shanghai, trips up the Yangtze River and the Three Gorges, and treks to China's sacred mountains. Travel to these relatively accessible destinations for leisure was promoted by the magazine as a healthy form of consumption, in contrast to the sorts of debauched consumer practices Shanghai had become infamous for by the 1930s.

China Traveler, according to Dong, pointed out that "leisure-time escapes to the Chinese countryside [were] not . . . a traditionally Chinese habit. Repeatedly its pages highlighted the contrast between Europeans and Americans, who enjoyed traveling, and the Chinese, who tended to stay home."[10] In contrast to Germans, who, for example, loved music, liked to go outdoors, and traveled to faraway places, the Chinese were said to like to "drink and play mahjong to kill time."[11] These were viewed as unhealthy leisure practices that exemplified China's colonial status as the so-called sick man of Asia. In the 1930s tourism was a way to present a different China, both to the imperialist powers of the world and more importantly to China's citizens themselves. But tourism was not something that simply bubbled up once all the necessary infrastructural arrangements were made. The desire to travel, and a sense of pleasurability in travel, had to be cultivated. Tourists with a particular outlook on the world, in other words, had to be produced, and *China Traveler* was just one of many agents engaged in producing them.

This early exemplary Chinese consumer was more often represented as a "citizen of the world" rather than, say, a Chinese nationalist. Shanghai elites in the 1930s tended to view tourism not as an extension of imperialism and colonialism but as a "politically neutral and modern form of cosmopolitanism."[12] As such, tourism was something for modern Chinese to embrace and emulate without fear of betraying their national loyalties. Tourism might have become popular nationally had China not confronted nearly two decades of foreign invasion and civil war. It wasn't until the founding of the People's Republic in 1949 that stability returned. But by then the new communist ideology framed tourism as an activity of the capitalist elite, the very class the revolution sought to eliminate. The Chinese Communist Party sought to sweep away all vestiges of colonial modernity from China's "Westernized" cities—especially Shanghai. The tourist was no revolutionary, and tourism was soon viewed, like all social phenomena, as fundamentally political. Tourism—and the leisure time and disposable income to support it—was viewed, in short, as a product of bourgeois exploitation of the working class. Tourism had no place in a nation newly liberated from feudal landlords and foreign oppressors.

Mass leisure travel, and indeed leisure culture more generally, largely ceased during the Mao era, from 1949 to the early 1980s. Under Mao, China was governed with an emphasis on production at all costs. Leisure time was minimized in order to reduce consumer demand and save limited resources for reinvestment in production. Low wages also minimized consumption, and there was little for people to buy, even if they had the time and money. Yet touristic behavior did continue in some limited and distorted ways. Leisure travel was permitted as a reward for model workers and officials during the Mao era, and seaside resorts became famous sites for annual summer retreats of high-level officials. And in the late 1960s, during the Cultural Revolution, when the nation's higher-education system was largely shut down, hundreds of thousands of "Red Guards" were encouraged to take pilgrimages to China's revolutionary sites.

In 1979, once the Cultural Revolution fervor died and economic reforms began to be implemented, tourism reemerged, though at first only as a strategy for economic development. China embarked on a path to modernization that featured strategic engagement with, rather than self-imposed seclusion from, global capitalism. Global capital was invited to finance and profit from China's new openness, but strictly on China's terms and on a limited scale, such as in Special Economic Zones established along the southeastern coast.

In this environment, building an inbound international tourism industry was an additional tool for bringing foreign currency into the economy and for demonstrating China's newly opened door to the outside world.[13] International-standard joint-venture hotels were encouraged in major cities like Beijing and Shanghai, along with other cities determined to have particular appeal to foreign tourists, like Xi'an, Suzhou, or Hangzhou. Even as foreign tourists poured into China in the 1980s, the government did little to cultivate a new touristic sensibility among its own citizens.

Throughout the 1980s, despite the state focus on inbound tourism by foreigners, a domestic tourism industry began to form. This was partly due to the impressive entrepreneurship of the Chinese people, who chipped away at the state's exclusive control and were inspired by the new openness and the leisure-time examples set by foreign travelers. The spread of tourism domestically can also be explained in a more abstract sense by recognizing that tourism is much more than an isolated economic activity. Tourism can also be seen as an active social process, one that has "unintended consequences, failure, unforeseen agency, and promiscuous enrollment."[14] Adrian Franklin thus highlights the unpredictable qualities of tourism development, especially tourism's networklike qualities through which it spreads into other realms of social and cultural life. By the 1990s the government recognized the economic potential of developing a domestic tourism industry and began to order and actively encourage the growing interest in tourism by Chinese.

Through a series of changes in the 1990s, the government effectively "naturalized" tourism, molding it into a normal and acceptable part of modern Chinese life. First, with the uncertainty and general malaise following the Tiananmen crackdown of 1989, the government sought to speed economic growth and increasingly turned to consumption as a means of driving that growth. At the same time, the Party signaled its willingness to tolerate regional economic disparities as short-term costs of rapid growth. Thus the government cleared a path—ideologically and politically—for a new middle class of consumers. Second, the government made a few socially significant policy decisions that laid the foundation for a boom in leisure activity. The state standardized work hours in 1995, creating a forty-hour workweek and a two-day weekend. The state also implemented an annual national holiday schedule in 1999, allowing three major "Golden Week" holidays. Third, the government encouraged the development of a leisure cultural economy, in which "culture" became a major resource for development. Fourth, the broad adoption of new products and technologies by consumers put new hardware, software, and information in the hands of many more people than ever before. Through this process, new leisure practices and a cultural economy were incorporated into social relationships and built into the urban landscape.

The state's naturalization of tourism is clear at the scale of the nation, especially through historical changes in ideology and national policy. The National Tourism Administration estimates that nationally in 2008 Chinese made 1.7 billion domestic person-trips. And China's State Council—the central administrative government body of China, currently led by Premier Wen Jiabao—hopes that number will grow to over two billion person-trips by 2015.[15] This growth, like all urban growth in China, will depend more on changes happening in China's inland provinces than on further development of its largest coastal cities.[16] The development of inland cities is a key part of China's continued national growth (see chapter 6 by Timothy Weston), and the development of exemplary consumers that sustain a national economy likewise depends on changes happening in the inland provinces. And as the case of Chengdu shows, tourism is an integral part of China's future (see figure 9.1).

SPEEDING TOURISM

Since the early 1990s, domestic tourism has been knitted into the urban experience by the state through specific development strategies. Explicit state goals in 1993 aimed to integrate tourism with broader economic and social development goals, and to develop a well-managed domestic tourism market.[17] Between 1993 and 2008, as China's national economy grew at a 10 percent average each year, the domestic tourism industry grew even faster, averaging 16 percent each year.[18] In that time, the domestic tourism industry grew to generate over 4 percent of China's national economic output, and the central government wants that to grow to over 5 percent in the next five years. Now that tourism has been established as a key part of the economy, "speed" has become the dominant metaphor.

Speed shows up in tourism development plans from the national scale down to that of China's counties and townships. The State Council recently reported that speeding the development of the tourism industry is important to a broad range of economic and social development needs, including optimizing China's economic structure, strengthening China's soft power, promoting the social cohesion of China's ethnic groups, and improving the lives of the Chinese people.[19] The state is making an explicit connection between tourism development and broader goals of economic and social development, and as national policy is translated into regional and local action, the main discourse concerns speed.

The efforts to accelerate tourism development can be seen at work in recent years in the city of Chengdu. In the past ten years, Chengdu has become one of China's top commercial cities, boasting consumer markets as important as anywhere else in the country. The tourism industry is

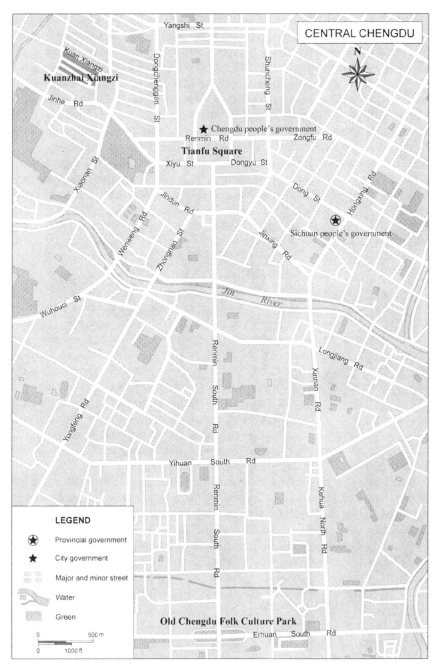

Figure 9.1. Chengdu, Provincial Capital and Capital of Developmental Tourism.

especially important in this city of nearly twelve million people. Tourism grew from less than 1 percent of the city's economy in 1993 to over 12 percent of the economy in 2007.[20] On one hand, tourism growth seems focused primarily on tourists and tourist experiences. The industry's growth is in fact measured this way by the government, through aggregated revenues of travel agencies, tourist sites, hotels, and other related businesses. The industry's growth is also apparent in the material changes that have taken place in Chengdu, with the rapid improvement of transportation infrastructure, diversifying lodging options, and new, accessible tourism services. The past decade of economic and material change in Chengdu is a testament to the 1990s goals of bringing tourism into the core of the national economy.

The development of Chengdu's tourism industry has had an impact well beyond the economic and material aspects of tourism. Daily life has been increasingly punctuated by tourism and travel, and Chengdu residents are as caught up in the tourism industry as visitors are. The improved transportation system has benefited everyone, not only tourists. New expressways and light rail make it possible to live in the suburbs and commute into the city for work. The airport bus remains one of the cheapest ways into the city, even if it comes with a sales pitch and a tourist map. A city tourist bus—designed like a San Francisco streetcar—offers some residents the best route to work. Tourism marketing and promotions are a constant backdrop in the city, filling backlit bus stop signs and weekend newspaper ad space. The driver's test curriculum, besides testing for recognition of stop signs and traffic lights, includes questions on how to recognize a tourist site: a road sign in brown instead of green or blue. Even in daily conversation, overheard at teahouses and restaurants, leisure travel is a common topic.

The spread of tourism into other parts of contemporary life in China is also apparent in "everyday" spaces of consumption—large shopping or entertainment areas, for example—that have taken on the scale and feel of tourist attractions. Chunxi Lu, for example, the main shopping district in the city, was transformed in the early 2000s from a tangle of street stalls and low-end retail stores into a slick pedestrian zone lined by national chains, bright lights, and international celebrities smiling down from billboard ads. To walk in many of Chengdu's remade districts is to confront the commercialization of nearly everything, and eating, shopping, and socializing in these spaces is often indistinguishable from that of a tourist. Just as there are many nontouristic ways of using all the "stuff" of the tourism industry, there are touristic ways of using everyday space. Tourism and commercial development have both taken hold of Chengdu, often playing off one another in ways that blur the distinction between tourism and everyday life.

The Chengdu, Sichuan, and central governments have each been concerned with speeding tourism, and the transformation of the city bears witness to the intensity of tourism development. This reached a peak in 2007, the best tourism year of the decade, contributing 41 billion yuan ($6.1 billion U.S.) to the local economy.[21] However, even as tourism became a normal part of contemporary life in Chengdu, the industry remains sensitive to external events. In 2008 Chengdu's tourism industry was hit by two major crises: the global financial crisis was beginning to strain the Chinese economy, and the Wenchuan earthquake happened in May, leaving eighty thousand dead in suburban and rural areas northwest of Chengdu. The local tourism industry was hit hard as tourists stayed away; tourism revenue for Sichuan Province dropped 40 percent from the previous year.[22] In the context of this slowdown, it became clear that tourism since the 1980s had become so normal, and such an important part of the economy, that it was now the *lack* of tourism that seemed out of the ordinary. Tourism, once undesirable, eventually acceptable, was now indispensable, so important to the local economy that the industry needed intervention. It needed speeding in a new way.

When the 2008 financial crisis began to affect China, the central government stepped in with a new priority. On the heels of a global crisis and fears of a domestic economic downturn, *xiaofei*—"spending" or "consumption"—became a buzzword. It was seen by some as a way out of the financial crisis, and by others as an entirely new economic model for China. The central government announced an economic stimulus of 400 billion yuan ($60 billion U.S.), and much of this money funded infrastructure development projects around the country. Cities responded with stimulus strategies of their own: Hangzhou distributed "shopping vouchers" to 500,000 residents each worth 20 yuan.[23] In Chengdu, the city government distributed 100-yuan consumer vouchers—about $15 each—to 379,000 of the city's neediest residents.

Speeding tourism in the face of a downturn did not only mean incentivizing regional and local governments to develop their tourism industries. Beginning in 2008, speeding tourism also meant local governments took action to incentivize tourists. As tourist numbers dropped, tourism promotions became a central strategy of speeding tourism locally. In 2007 the Chengdu city government and the city tourism bureau established an umbrella company to coordinate local tourism development. The Chengdu Culture and Tourism Group—known locally by its abbreviated form, Wenlu—is state funded, with $73 million in its coffers and a fifteen-point mission to develop culture and tourism in Chengdu. Wenlu's mission statement indicates its intended role to propel planning, push implementation, forge tourism projects, and speed tourism. The establishment of Wenlu before the 2008 crises indicates how important tourism already was to the city, and Wenlu's role would become even more important in the post-2008 recovery. In surveying the local tourism industry, which was characteristically fragmented between a large number of government and private institutions, Chengdu realized it could promote tourism by dropping entry fees on popular tourist sites. Only 5 percent of the city's tourism revenue came from those fees, and the system was one of the few parts of the industry that the city itself could control.

In March 2009, Wenlu implemented the Panda Card program, a discount card (see figure 9.2) sold for one yuan that offered free or half-price entry to eleven tourist sites under the management of the Chengdu Tourism Bureau, including the Giant Panda Research Base, the Dujiangyan irrigation project, and the Jinsha Museum. Local residents as well as tourists from outside the city and province became the target market, and the program was a popular success, with nearly ten million cards issued during the nine-month promotion. Four and a half million Silver Panda Cards (good for half-price entry for Sichuan residents) and about five million Golden Panda Cards (good for free entry for visitors from outside the province) were issued.

While it is difficult to analyze the exact impact of the Panda Card program on Chengdu's tourism recovery, the sheer number of people using the card was impressive. A Wenlu manager said, "Early in the promotion, there was a lot of trouble just handling all the people arriving to register and use their cards. We got it cleared up eventually, but the system couldn't initially handle the number of people."[24] As for its impact on tourism recovery, Sichuan Tourism Bureau director Zhang Gu made the following general assessment in mid-2010: "Sichuan's tourism has already recovered to pre-earthquake levels, and the numbers from the first half of 2010 bode well in restoring the confidence in Sichuan's tourism."[25] Looking back on the Panda Card promotion, the Wenlu manager made a similar assessment: "Chengdu's tourism revenue in 2009 had recovered to where it was in 2007. This would not have happened as fast without the Panda Card."

Figure 9.2. Wenlu's Panda Card (2009). Photograph by Travis Klingberg.

National stimulus money aimed at spurring consumption, local consumption vouchers, and tourist promotions are all examples of how the state at various scales has spurred consumption. For Chengdu, speeding tourism has been a priority, both as an ongoing strategy of economic development and as a strategy to stimulate leisure travel desires in the Chinese population. Speeding tourism is a flexible, multipurpose government strategy to develop the tourism industry, one that works both in the boom times and the crises. It results in measurable investments in tourism infrastructure, as well as in the creation of a specific sort of awareness in the Chinese population, a desire for and valuing of touristic experiences. The Panda Card played a central role in repositioning Chengdu as a top domestic tourist destination, and the local population was just as much a target market as visitors. The efforts by the state to speed tourism were a strategy of ordering (and restoring order to) the economy, as well as creating and encouraging touristic desire in the Chinese population.

BUILT-IN TOURISM

By the time tourists began returning to Chengdu in 2009, the city had long been one of China's most famous tourist cities—it was named "Top Tourist City in China" in an online poll in 2007, known for its Giant Pandas, archaeological treasures, and a rich cultural history ranging from food to poetry. However, for much of its history, Chengdu was not the intense consumer environment it is today. The city, once enclosed by a wall, had an imperial compound in its center, surrounded by warrens of low-rise buildings along mixed-use streets and alleys. Photos from as recently as 1960 show the imperial gate strung with revolutionary slogans, much like Tiananmen Gate in Beijing is today. Most of the city wall was torn down during the Cultural Revolution, replaced by open boulevards and new buildings signaling Chengdu's arrival in the modern era. The commercial transformation of the city that began slowly in the 1980s intensified in the late 1990s. In the past decade, the urban landscape of Chengdu has radically changed, with the development of gated residential complexes, widened roads and overpasses, skyscrapers, cutting-edge architecture, and at the street level with impressive numbers of shopping centers, luxury stores, computer markets, and entertainment districts.

As tourism has become a naturalized and incentivized part of contemporary life in China, so too it has been built into China's urban landscape (see figure 9.1). One of the most visible examples of this is Tianfu Square, Chengdu's central public square that was redesigned in 2007—*rebranded* might be a better word, as it is now something more like a theme park. The theme is Chengdu history: Twelve pillars along the square's edge present interpretive descriptions of Chengdu culture. Part of the square was recessed into the ground to resemble an archaeological dig suggestive of the local ancient civilizations of Sanxingdui and Jinsha. At the center of the square, gleaming in the occasional Sichuan sun, sits the Jinsha Sun-bird, the logo of the Chengdu tourism bureau, and a replica of the delicate, pounded-gold disc discovered at the city's famous Jinsha archaeological site. Here, at the symbolic heart of the city, sits tourism and culture.

Culture has also been built into unexpected corners of Chengdu. One of the city's largest roadway flyovers, a flattened cloverleaf interchange on the southern second ring road, was "culturalized" in 2006, its medians and empty underbelly transformed into the Old Chengdu Folk Culture Park. This sort of space is often dead, used for parking lots or maintenance sheds, or just filled in with shrubs and trees that quickly become covered in the gray dust of passing traffic. But the remade culture park features teahouses, art stores, public exercise stations, and an extensive exhibit of Chengdu's cultural history. A canal flows through the park, crossed by footbridges named for the most famous bridges that span the Jinjiang River, which flows through the city. Life-size bronze sculptures depict Chengdu residents of the past working and playing in "traditional" ways—a key maker, an ear picker, children playing dice. Interpretive displays of Chengdu's culture include maps of the city through time, etchings of daily life practices, and descriptions of Chengdu's traditional way of life. The columns that support the overpasses display relief sculptures of iconic city sites and scenes: streets, temples, old homes, and famous alleys. The city itself has become the museum, and despite the touristic feel, the culture park is so far off the tourist path that it is used mostly by local residents, who sometimes study the cultural displays but more often favor conversation, studying, or napping. As the culture park illustrates, Chengdu's "intangible" cultural heritage—its leisure practices, traditions, and unique "way of life"—has been transformed by the local government into a tangible cultural product, a built environment tailored to tourism and exactly the sort of space in which consumer habits can be encouraged.

One of the relief sculptures in the culture park is an image of Chengdu's most famous alley, named *Kuan xiangzi*—the Broad Alley. The alley appears on Qing Dynasty maps and likely dates at least to the Ming Dynasty, an era that has largely been erased from the urban landscape. Even into the late 2000s, the Kuan xiangzi *felt* like the remnant of an imperial past. It was a little shabby, but was lined with courtyard homes, covered by an apse of trees, and most importantly walked through by residents and occasional visitors. It was a quiet, lived-in corner of the city.

In 2005 Chengdu began work on a major transformation of Kuan xiangzi and two parallel alleys. Wenlu, the tourism developer behind the Panda Card, had formed a development company that repackaged the alleys as

Kuan zhai xiangzi, a new "cultural history protection area" that has since become one of the city's most popular tourist sites. The Kuan zhai xiangzi area had largely escaped the commercial development that has claimed huge parts of the city, at least until this project began to reinscribe the old neighborhood upon the new one. The crumbling old structures were refaced or completely rebuilt. Maps and signage were installed. Many of the old shops and residents were removed to make way for restaurants, teahouses, retail shops, and bars. Kuan zhai xiangzi became a brand, and it quickly came to symbolize the best of Chengdu's cultural history. A promotional booklet for the area opened with a reference to a 2007 *Time* magazine article, which called Chengdu "China's China." Extending the metaphor, the booklet proposed, "If Chengdu is China's China, Kuan zhai xiangzi is Chengdu's Chengdu."

The work of building culture into the city is by no means unique to Wenlu. In fact, the cultural "themeing" of Kuan zhai xiangzi reflects similar installations of culture in other Chinese cities. Two well-known predecessors are Shanghai's Xintiandi neighborhood and the Qianmen area of Beijing.[26] Like these projects, Kuan zhai xiangzi mixes the development of new consumer space with local culture and history. A Cultural History Wall, built along one of the alleys, frames Kuan zhai xiangzi's past as emblematic of the entire city's history, proceeding from maps and descriptions of the building materials used in the old city walls, moving through the mid-twentieth-century construction of the Science and Technology Museum, and finally to a series of trompe l'oeil exhibits based on historical photographs of Kuan zhai xiangzi. One relief sculpture of a pile of potatoes blends into a photo of a man selling potatoes from the back of his cart. A real wall blends into a fake wall that blends into a photographic view into a teahouse. A photo of men playing cards, their birdcages hanging above them, is accompanied by real birdcages placed to match those in the image (see figure 9.3). Along this wall, Chengdu's cultural history is not simply a generalized, ancient past; it is a stylized form of a life gone by, scenes that push out of the past into the space of the present.

Kuan zhai xiangzi, unlike similar projects in other cities, is intended to preserve not only the physical space and its accompanying historical narrative but also the entire way of life seen as an essential quality of Chengdu. It attempts to define and preserve the leisurely lifestyle that Chengdu is famous for and present to visitors a commoditized form of that lifestyle. And in an unexpected way, it works. Part of the magic of Kuan zhai xiangzi— magic at least in comparison to many mass tourism sites—is the possibility to wander, to stop, to eat meals or snack, to photograph artifacts from the neighborhood's history, or to ignore the spectacle and just read a newspaper. The alleys invite visitors to do something on their own and at leisure. The expected trappings of tourism are still here—the bus parking lot, tour

Figure 9.3. Everyday Life as a Tourist Site: Kuan zhai xiangzi. Photograph by Travis Klingberg.

guide services, gift shops, and recommended walking routes marked on easy-to-find maps. But there is no expensive entry ticket to buy, and the area is more like a bazaar to be experienced than a single sight to be seen and photographed. Kuan zhai xiangzi is easily navigable, yet still holds surprises: There is the unmarked shortcut between lanes. Many restaurants and teahouses are hidden behind narrow courtyard archways; stepping through them can feel like making a discovery. Half-opened doors give a view into the private spaces of residents, which look as well used and lived-in as the photos of old alley life.

Chengdu, in many ways *because* of its commercial transformation, is famous among Chinese as a city of leisure and idling. Kuan zhai xiangzi capitalizes on that history by creating an inviting space for tourists to experience that way of life. However, the lack of an entry gate to Kuan zhai xiangzi means that the "real" way of life of Chengdu residents spills out into the "fabricated" way of life presented in the tourist development. The area is as inviting to tourists keen on photography as it is to local dog walkers and retirees caring for their grandchildren. On a typical day, most people on their feet seem to be tourists, eyes constantly scanning the physical environment. But there are just as many sitting down on the many benches and teahouse chairs. And at the end of one alley, at lunchtimes on a school day, the Cultural History Wall is swarmed with schoolchildren who ignore it completely. There are very few spaces in China that blend tourism development with a local community in a way that they can coexist.

The everyday character of Kuan zhai xiangzi, the way it is "lived in" by tourists and locals alike, marks just how significantly consumerism, tourism, and the routines of everyday life have merged in Chengdu. It is, in short, an exemplary space of touristic consumption that cultivates the desire to journey through history, to linger in a space that feels familiar, and to appreciate Chengdu in a way that requires leisure time and disposable income. The result is unlike almost any other site in China. Kuan zhai xiangzi was constructed as a culturalized space for tourism, and yet there was a real, if inevitably flawed, attempt to preserve the local architecture and the livelihoods of local residents. Kuan zhai xiangzi is at once a touristic encounter of everyday Chengdu and an everyday encounter of Chengdu as a tourist site. Everyday life here is the realm of the exemplary consumer, the person for whom the practices of tourism come naturally, are encouraged by the state, and are built into the space of the city.

THE ARC OF THE EXEMPLARY

Kuan zhai xiangzi offers a chance to appreciate the full arc of tourism development in China. It is a place where we can see the results of decades-long government efforts to naturalize and speed tourism and to build tourism and culture into the national landscape. It is a place where we can see the ways the state has produced exemplary consumer-citizens who perfectly play out their "role": they flood into tourist sites and spend money, especially with incentives like the Panda Card. Unencumbered by Marxist ideology, they are apparently apolitical, pursuing a form of leisure perfectly suited to fulfilling both state goals and personal desires. They are as often local residents as they are visitors from other places.

The Chinese state exerts unmatched power in ordering tourist space and producing exemplary consumers, and in many ways Kuan zhai xiangzi is as much a product of orderly development as it is a mechanism for it, a means of bringing everyday life closer to tourism and installing tourism into everyday life. But as the Chinese government has produced tourist sites and good consumer-citizens, it is clear that this is not a simple story of control and obedience. While the American press sometimes presents China's central government as having unified, top-down control over its population, the reality is of course more complex. In some cases, the government does exert direct control through policy decisions, but in many more cases the government's influence on Chinese people comes obliquely, and sometimes in ways much like the marketing and public relations strategies of large corporations and governments in the West. And even despite the best government efforts to order the entire tourist experience, things fall apart.

The Cultural History Wall is overgrown with weeds, and the birdcages are breaking apart. Many visitors to Kuan zhai xiangzi sit with laptops, play cards or video games, rock their grandchildren in prams, or talk with old friends on new benches—they don't spend a dime. Some people move slowly with the bearing of a flaneur; others carrying groceries move quickly through the crowd toward home. There are rhythms here that a more "purely" ordered tourist space lacks. The "sights" are built into the site, woven together in a way that invites visitors to ignore the few interpretive signs, the smartly uniformed staff, and the signage and get caught up in walking, eating, and socializing.

The dominant model of tourism development in China continues to be mass tourism, and the state over the past twenty years has sustained this model through repeated efforts to standardize, centralize, and integrate the industry (in the same way that Lionel Jensen in chapter 13 demonstrates that Confucius Institutes have standardized culture). At the same time this model has brought tourism closer to the everyday lives of the Chinese people through policy, promotion, and urban reconstruction. China's new tourists are exemplary consumers not only because they serve an important role in the country's economic growth, but also because they are living lives full of desires and choices and finding a landscape in which they can fulfill those desires. These consumers are exemplary of being modern, of being successful, of being Chinese.

The exemplary consumer in China, then, is not simply dominated, never completely captured by the political ordering of the party-state's socialist vision of a modern China, nor by the economic ordering of pervasive market capitalism, both of which prize docile bodies as reliable cogs in the political-economic gears that sustain a system. Seen in this light, the arrival of Chinese tourists on New York City's Fifth Avenue is more complicated than it appears at first. While the "thousand-person" tour showcased China's exemplary consumers to both Chinese people back home and the world beyond, it also marked a much broader social process in China, the outcomes of which remain uncertain. As changes in the city of Chengdu illustrate, social life throughout much of China is being reordered around the touristic consumption of things, places, and experiences. And while the tourist's role in this reordering is deeply entangled with the government's efforts to produce exemplary Chinese consumer-citizens, innumerable chances remain—even on a trip with a thousand shoppers—to do what many people do in the new tourist spaces of Chengdu: to ignore the spectacle, to play or read, to walk through, and perhaps even leave the cash in that bulging wallet.

SUGGESTIONS FOR FURTHER READING

Jia Zhangke. *24 City*. Cinema Guild, 2008. (Film)

Kuan zhai xiangzi website, www.kzxz.com.cn/english/index.asp.

Meyer, Michael. *The Last Days of Old Beijing*. New York: Walker & Co., 2008.

Nyiri, Pal. *Mobility and Cultural Authority in Contemporary China*. Seattle and London: University of Washington Press, 2010.

Tomba, Luigi. "Of Quality, Harmony, and Community: Civilization and the Middle Class in Urban China." *Positions: East Asia Cultures Critique* 17, no. 3 (2009): 591–616.

Wang Di, "Entering the Bottom of the City: Revisiting Chinese Urban History through Chengdu." *Chinese Historical Review* 12, no. 1 (2009): 35–69.

Winter, Tim, Peggy Teo, and T. C. Chang, eds., *Asia on Tour: Exploring the Rise of Asian Tourism*. London and New York: Routledge, 2009.

NOTES

1. "Niuyue huanying qianming Zhongguo lüketuan" (New York Welcomes 1000 Chinese Tour Group), *Sohu.com*, February 18, 2010, http://women.sohu.com/20100218/n270285548.shtml.

2. "Chinese become most generous tourists in New York," *People's Daily*, February 23, 2010, http://english.peopledaily.com.cn/90001/90778/90860/6900057.html.

3. The newspaper perhaps made this calculation based on 2007 data. For that year, 400,000 Chinese tourists visiting the United States spent over $2.5 billion.

4. "Zhongguo qianren lüxingtuan fumei guo Chunjie; Diguo Daxia teshe zhuanchang" (1000 Chinese Tour Group Goes to the United States, Celebrates the Spring Festival with a Special Performance at the Empire State Building), *Sina.com.cn*, February 12, 2010, http://news.sina.com.cn/c/2010-02-12/053319680247.shtml.

5. See, for example, Robert Foster, "The Commercial Construction of 'New Nations,'" *Journal of Material Culture* 4, no. 3 (1999): 263–82. For China specifically, see Patricia Thornton, "From Liberating Production to Unleashing Consumption: Mapping Landscapes of Power in Beijing," *Political Geography* 29, no. 6 (2010): 302–10; and Ngai Pun, "Subsumption or Consumption? The Phantom of Consumer Revolution in 'Globalizing' China," *Cultural Anthropology* 18, no. 4 (2003): 469–92.

6. Emily Rauhala, "China's New Travelers Aren't Far from Home," *New York Times*, February 1, 2010, http://www.nytimes.com/2010/02/02/business/global/02tourist.html.

7. Jing Wang, "Culture as Leisure and Culture as Capital," *Positions: East Asia Cultures Critique* 9, no. 1 (Fall 2001): 69–104.

8. Adrian Franklin, "The Tourism Ordering: Taking Tourism More Seriously as a Globalising Ordering," *Civilisations* 57, nos. 1/2 (2008): 25–39, esp. 30.

9. Madeleine Yue Dong, "Shanghai's *China Traveler*," in *Everyday Modernity in China*, ed. M. Y. Dong and J. Goldstein (Seattle: University of Washington Press, 2006), 195–226.

10. Dong, "Shanghai's *China Traveler*," 204.

11. Dong, "Shanghai's *China Traveler*," 205.

12. Dong, "Shanghai's *China Traveler*," 220.

13. On the growth of tourism in China in the 1980s, see Virginie Oudiette, "International Tourism in China," *Annals of Tourism Research* 17 (1990): 123–32; and Alan Lew and Lawrence Ye, eds., *Tourism in China: Geographic, Political, and Economic Perspectives* (Boulder, CO: Westview Press, 1995).

14. Franklin, "Tourism Ordering," 31.

15. State Council Research Department, *Xin shiqi zhongguo lüyouye fazhan zhanüe* (New China Tourism Industry Development Strategy), 2009, 44.

16. Laurence Ma and Fulong Wu, eds., *Restructuring the Chinese City: Changing Society, Economy and Space* (London: Routledge, 2005).

17. State Council, *Guanyu jiji fazhan guonei lüyouye de yijian* (On the Idea of Vigorously Developing the Domestic Tourism Industry), 1993.

18. State Council Research Department, *Xin shiqi zhongguo lüyouye fazhan zhanüe* (New China Tourism Industry Development Strategy), 2009, 7.

19. State Council Research Department, *Xin shiqi zhongguo lüyouye fazhan zhanüe*, 33–37.

20. Chengdu Bureau of Statistics, 2008 (Beijing: Zhongguo tongji, 2008); Chengdu Bureau of Statistics, 1994 (Beijing: Zhongguo tongji, 1994).

21. Chengdu Bureau of Statistics, 2008 (Beijing: Zhongguo tongji, 2009), 263.

22. Huang Zhiling and Luo Xianyu, "Sichuan Reopens to Tourists, Full Recovery by 2010," *China Daily*, June 15, 2008, http://www.chinadaily.com.cn/china/2008-06/15/content_6761484.htm.

23. "Hangzhou jiangxiang waidi lüke paisong 4000 wanyuan lüyou xiaofeiquan," February 5, 2009: http://www.hangzhou.gov.cn/main/zwdt/bmdt/lm/T276810.shtml

24. Interview by Travis Klingberg, Chengdu, Sichuan, August 6, 2010.

25. "Chengdu jiakuai lüyou chanye zhuanxing shengji budai—Chengdu lüxingshe zixun," July 29, 2010, http://www.028ly.net/news18/news-18-125600.html.

26. See Thomas Campanella, *The Concrete Dragon: China's Urban Revolution and What It Means for the World* (New York: Princeton Architectural Press, 2008).

10

Professionals and Populists: The Paradoxes of China's Legal Reforms

Benjamin L. Liebman

Over the past fifteen years, China's Communist Party leadership has embraced law to an unprecedented degree. China's leaders view the creation of a fair and effective legal system as crucial to their own legitimacy. In a society in which few true believers in communism remain, and in which the sole ideology often appears to be economic growth at any cost, strengthening the legal system has become an important tool used by leaders to curb abuses, to address inequalities within China, and to confirm China's place as a major international power. Legal reforms have not only served the state's interests; they have also empowered individuals. Law has become an important tool for individuals fighting injustice or seeking redress.

China appears to be creating a form of authoritarian justice that is largely unprecedented. China's legal system mixes professionalism and populism. The system serves the state's interests in political control at the same time that it encourages individuals to use law to protect their rights. Law today is also an important baseline used to evaluate the state's conduct. The legal system has drawn heavily on Western experience at the same time as it continues to use tools developed during China's revolutionary past. This chapter will begin with an examination of two cases that help to highlight important current trends and then will turn to a discussion of the progress made and problems in China's legal reform efforts.

BACKGROUND: TWO CASES

Media coverage made Zhao Zuohai a celebrity and may have saved his life. Zhao's case became a national sensation in the spring of 2010, but his saga started twelve years earlier, in 1998, when he was questioned and then released by police in connection with the disappearance of fellow villager Zhao Zhenshang in his native Henan province. The two Zhaos were not related, although rumors circulated that they had both had affairs with the same woman. Zhao Zuohai's real trouble started a year later, on May 8, 1999, when a decomposed headless body turned up during the drilling of a well in the village. Local police arrested Zhao Zuohai the next day on suspicion of killing Zhao Zhenshang. The police claimed that Zhao Zuohai confessed to the killing on nine separate occasions over the next six weeks.

Zhao Zuohai might well have been dead had it not been for the role of the municipal procuratorate, which had jurisdiction over the case. Instead of moving forward promptly for what in most cases would have been a routine murder conviction, the procuratorate, which was responsible for bringing charges, sat on the case for two years. The procuratorate was apparently troubled by the lack of DNA evidence showing the corpse was that of the missing Zhao Zhenshang. But the procuratorate was unable to resist pressure from local Communist Party officials to resolve the case. During the summer of 2002 the Political-Legal Committee of Shangqiu Municipality—the party body that coordinates legal and police work—met and ordered the procuratorate to bring charges within twenty days. In October 2002 the municipal procuratorate charged Zhao with murder. He was tried in November and convicted in December. Yet the three judges who heard the case did not sentence Zhao to death, as would generally be routine in a case of intentional murder without mitigating circumstances. Instead, Zhao received a suspended death sentence, the functional equivalent of a life sentence—perhaps a signal from the judges that they recognized problems with the case. Zhao was defended in court by a trainee lawyer who lacked a license and who had never tried a criminal case. Zhao never appealed, but the provincial high court reviewed the sentence, as was required of all death sentences, and affirmed the decision in a 161-character opinion.

On April 30, 2010, Zhao Zhenshang, the murder victim, reappeared in the village after an eleven-year hiatus. Far from being dead, he claimed that he had spent the past eleven years as an itinerant seller of watermelon seeds and other goods, having fled the village fearing he had killed Zhao Zuohai in a fight. One week later, as local and provincial authorities were discussing how to handle the case, the *Dahe News*, a popular daily in the provincial capital of Zhengzhou, ran a lengthy article on Zhao Zhengshang's reappearance under the headline "Aren't You Dead? How Come You Are Alive?" A media frenzy ensued, with publications and broadcasters nationwide, ranging from municipal tabloids to *People's Daily* and China Central Television, rushing to cover the case. The next day, on May 7, the Intermediate People's Court of Shangqiu Municipality submitted evidence to the provincial high court confirming Zhao Zhenshang's identity. On May 8 the provincial high court overturned Zhao Zuohai's conviction. The court declared him innocent and stated that a plan would be developed to compensate him. Zhao Zuohai was released from prison on May 9; media reports provided gripping accounts of his release, describing his uncontrollable tears as he walked free. Four days later the provincial high court announced that Zhao Zuohai would receive 650,000 yuan (roughly $100,000 U.S.) in compensation for the wrongful conviction. Media accounts detailed officials' apologies in person to Zhao, which invariably were accompanied by additional cash payments. Subsequently, local authorities also constructed new homes for Zhao and for his eldest son.

On May 14 the police identified the headless body through a DNA match with the victim's father, who lived in another local village. Police also arrested one of three suspects; two more suspects were arrested later the same month. Police reported that the three had confessed and had pinpointed the correct location of a human skull that matched the headless body. Police announced that this time they had videotaped all of the confessions.

Zhao's case touched off widespread media discussion of the use of torture by Chinese police after he recounted in media interviews the interrogation techniques used by the police. Zhao displayed scars on his head that he said came from being repeatedly pistol-whipped. He described being knocked unconscious by police blows to the head, how the police had exploded firecrackers next to his head, and how the police had handcuffed him to a bench for thirty days to prevent him from sleeping. He said he confessed after concluding it would be better to be executed than to continue being tortured. Zhao's former wife, who divorced him after he was convicted, likewise recounted being detained in a factory warehouse and tortured in order to procure testimony against Zhao. Media coverage also turned to exposing other wrongfully convicted defendants.

On June 1 the three judges who handled Zhao's trial were suspended—despite the fact that Zhao's conviction was almost certainly the result of a decision by the municipal party political-legal committee and not the court. Indeed the case was striking in part because both the procuratorate and the court signaled their recognition of possible problems with evidence in the case, the procuratorate by delaying filing charges and the court by giving a suspended death sentence. Court officials announced that May 9, the day on which Zhao Zuohai was released from prison, would subsequently be "Wrongful Conviction Reflection Day" in the Henan Province court system, a day set aside to ensure that there are no more incorrectly decided cases.

On June 25 five police officers were criminally charged with torture, although only two of the charged officers were detained. The deputy county police chief who had overseen the case was dismissed and charged with dereliction of duty. After two months in the limelight, however, Zhao stated in July 2010 that he had been instructed not to discuss the case with the media further—though he subsequently raised a claim for an additional 650,000 yuan in compensation for the emotional distress suffered during his confinement.

Commentary in the Chinese media, and in particular on websites and in blogs, on Zhao's case focused not only on the widespread use of torture by Chinese police, but also on other factors that lead Zhao and others to be wrongfully convicted: tremendous popular and political pressure on local authorities to solve crimes; weak rules governing the admission of evidence in criminal trials; high conviction rates; the close coordination of work between the police, procuracy, and courts; and rapid trials in which courts often take police allegations as fact. Reports also noted the lack of negative repercussions for wrongful convictions: it is extremely rare for such cases to be uncovered, and blame is often assigned to low-ranking police, procurators, and judges. Yet many reports, in particular in official party mouthpiece media outlets, were also careful to praise the rapid intervention of officials in solving Zhao's case, noting that such quick actions "saved the reputation of the court system among the masses" and received approval from China's top leaders. In May and July 2010 the Supreme People's Court issued new rules explicitly limiting the use of evidence obtained by torture. The rules had been under discussion for nearly two years, but they were nevertheless perceived to be in part a response to the Zhao Zuohai case and resulting media outcry.

In contrast to Zhao Zuohai, Zhang Qiang's legal struggle never made the headlines. Like Zhao Zuohai's case, however, it provides insights into some of the most important trends in China's legal system. In March 2002 Zhang's son's nose was injured in a fight with another child while at school. Zhang Qiang sued the child who had hit his son and the school. Less than three months after the incident a local court in Zhang's hometown in northeast China issued a decision assigning 80 percent of responsibility to the two defendants and 20 percent to Zhang's son. The court ordered the two defendants each to pay 2,100 yuan in compensation. Zhang appealed, arguing that compensation was too low and that the assignment of 20 percent liability to his son was unfair. Zhang contended that his son should have been awarded damages for emotional harm and for disability in addition to what the court had granted. The appellate court upheld the original verdict.

Zhang's case did not end with the final judgment from the appellate court. Following the decision, Zhang began a long campaign of petitioning—following a tradition of individuals who appeal directly to the state for redress of grievances. China's letters-and-visits, or petitioning, system operates through state letters-and-visits offices that exist at each level of the party-state. These letters-and-visits offices are designed to receive and respond to popular complaints filed in writing or in person. Many other party-state institutions, including the courts and people's congresses, also have their own letters-and-visits offices at each level. The system dates to the earliest days of the PRC and draws on imperial traditions of individuals seeking redress through direct appeals to the emperor.

Over the past two decades petitions and protests concerning court decisions have increased dramatically, resulting in extensive pressure on the courts. In response, courts have devoted significant resources to preventing protests and petitions. Most courts in China now have specialized offices responsible for handling and responding to petitions, but litigants also frequently file complaints regarding the courts to state letters-and-visits offices or to other party-state entities.

Within six months of the appellate court's decision, Zhang went in person to file his complaint with the letters-and-visits offices of his local district and municipal governments and the national letters-and-visits office in Beijing. He also filed complaints with his local municipal people's congress. He was told that his petition should be first filed with the court. But the court rejected his request to reopen the case, and Zhang resumed his campaign of petitioning and protest, repeatedly traveling to Beijing to file complaints both with the national letters-and-visits bureau and with the Supreme People's Court.

Zhang also escalated his campaign against the court decision by organizing petitioners from his hometown to join together and travel to Beijing to petition collectively. The effort had an immediate effect, reflecting state sensitivities regarding collective petitions: the state is concerned that collective petitions may escalate into unrest. In 2004 local authorities classified his case as a major petitioning case worthy of emphasis, and the intermediate court issued a decision withdrawing the prior judgment and ordering the trial court to rehear the case.

The court clearly hoped that by rehearing and changing the case they would pacify Zhang. Zhang, however, saw the retreat of the court as an opportunity: he raised his compensation demand to 220,000 yuan and demanded a new set of medical evaluations for his son, including for emotional distress. On rehearing the case the court assigned all liability to the two defendants and ordered them to pay Zhang a total of 6,792 yuan. Zhang's appeal was again rejected.

Although Zhang's petitioning had succeeded in pressuring the court to change its decision, he did not view his struggle as finished. He continued petitioning, now demanding 60,000 yuan in compensation, primarily for his son's alleged disability and for emotional harm. In May 2006 Zhang again organized a group of petitioners from his hometown to petition to Beijing—some with grievances against the courts and some with complaints against other government departments. The group unfurled banners outside the offices of the Central Discipline Commission of the Communist Party in Beijing. They were detained by Beijing police and sent home. The fact that a group of petitioners had protested at the central discipline office in Beijing resulted in increased pressure on local court officials to resolve Zhang's case. Institutions and individual officials and judges are evaluated in part based on the volume of complaints raised about their work, and the number of petitions to Beijing is an important metric used to evaluate whether local governments and courts are performing their jobs adequately. Significant volumes of complaints or protests can affect the careers of court leaders and of individual judges, regardless of the merits of the underlying grievances.

Court officials eventually decided to agree to pay Zhang 30,000 yuan, half of his demand, classifying the compensation as economic assistance to assist Zhang and his family, not compensation for the court decision. At the same time, they informed Zhang that any further petitioning would result in his immediate detention and sentencing to reeducation through labor. Zhang's case reflected a common characteristic of petitioning cases: petitioners and protestors are often treated leniently at first but face greater risk of being detained as they escalate their complaints.

Zhang refused to accept the compensation from the court and instead continued petitioning. The court subsequently refused to handle Zhang's complaint, instead transferring responsibility for the case to the local government—which in the end paid Zhang an undisclosed amount in exchange for his agreement to stop petitioning.

Zhang's and Zhao's cases both involved ordinary citizens who inadvertently stumbled into the formal legal system and who in the end won redress largely through extralegal procedures. The two cases provide insights into both the progress made in and problems that continue to undermine China's legal reforms as they enter their fourth decade: the powerful but also episodic role of the media in exposing injustice and in pushing for improvements to the legal system, serious attention to addressing some of the most egregious problems in the legal system, growing popular legal consciousness, widespread public discussion of problems in the legal system, and the continued importance and legitimacy of party intervention in court decisions. The two cases highlight how local authorities often face pressure to resolve cases rapidly or to meet targets in a range of areas, including solving crimes and reducing the number of complaints. The two cases also help to show some important trends in the Chinese legal system, and in particular in China's courts, that Western assessments of China's legal reforms often overlook.

CHINA'S LEGAL EVOLUTION

Before elaborating on current trends that the Zhao and Zhang cases reflect, it is important to reflect on what China has accomplished thus far. In the thirty-three years since China began its legal reforms in 1978, China has undergone perhaps the most rapid development of any legal system in world history. China has tried over the past three decades to accomplish a level of lawmaking and legal development that occurred over centuries in most Western nations. China had no functioning legal system as it emerged from the Cultural Revolution and began opening to the outside world in 1978. The lack of a legal system during the Cultural Revolution was particularly striking given that for much of the past two thousand years China had one of the most sophisticated legal systems in the world. Realizing how far China has come adds perspective that is important for understanding current developments and also why many in China bristle at Western criticism of China's legal system.

Since 1978 the changes have been remarkable. There were three thousand lawyers in China in 1978, virtually all of whom had been trained in the 1950s or earlier. Today there are approximately 166,000 lawyers, making the Chinese legal profession the third largest in the world. In 2009 alone, 353,000 people took the Chinese bar exam, with approximately fifty thousand passing. China's law schools began accepting students again in 1977 and 1978; all but one law school closed during the Cultural Revolution. Today there are more than six hundred law schools and law departments in China (roughly triple the number in the United States), with hundreds of thousands of students studying law at the undergraduate and graduate level. Large numbers of Chinese lawyers and law professors and increasing numbers of judges have spent significant periods studying in the U.S. or Europe.

There were few laws on the books in the late 1970s. China created legal institutions and began the process of drafting major law in the 1950s, modeling its legal system on that of the Soviet Union. But China suspended work on new laws, including a civil and criminal code, in the early 1960s and did not resume this work until 1978. Over the past thirty years China has drafted thousands of laws and regulations. Initially, law drafting focused on creating a basic framework for economic development, particularly matters most relevant to trade and investment. During the past decade, the scope of lawmaking has expanded greatly, with new laws addressing a wide range of topics, including not just corporate law and contracts but also environmental regulation, labor, women's and children's rights, administrative regulation, and administrative litigation.

Some of the most important changes in the Chinese legal system have been very recent. For much of the reform era most Chinese judges had little, if any, formal legal training. Today all new judges must be university graduates and pass the bar exam. Older judges have gradually either been removed from hearing cases or have been forced to pursue law degrees. In 2005 official reports stated that for the first time more than 50 percent of China's judges and procurators were university graduates, double the percentage of the early 1990s. Courts have in recent years devoted significant resources to creating oversight systems that reduce the risk of corruption and other forms of malfeasance, and a number of high-profile prosecutions of senior judges have been used to send a message that corruption will not be tolerated.

Civil litigation was virtually irrelevant in 1978. Today there are nearly six million civil cases annually. The range of claims has expanded so that courts today hear not only family law and contract cases but also personal injury cases, housing and land disputes, environmental lawsuits, defamation claims, and even a small number of discrimination cases. The number of labor cases has skyrocketed in recent years, reflecting both new labor laws and increased legal consciousness among workers. Ordinary people are using the system in new and creative ways, in some cases in ways that central party-state authorities have a difficult time controlling.

Weaknesses in China's criminal procedure law and in actual practice undermine the fairness of China's criminal justice system. The Supreme People's Court has also in recent years taken significant steps to improve oversight in capital cases, resulting in a significant drop in the frequency with which defendants are sentenced to death and executed. Nevertheless, although the number of executions each year remains a state secret, most estimates put the number of annual executions in the thousands, by far more than any other country in the world.

Chinese courts also hear approximately 121,000 cases a year against the government through administrative litigation. Claims against the police are common. Plaintiffs in China may not always get a fair hearing of their cases, but individuals nevertheless increasingly voice their grievances in the language of law.

Chinese courts have also shown willingness to innovate. Thus, for example, Chinese courts have adopted the equivalent of a public-person standard in some defamation cases, holding that persons in the public eye such as celebrities must be able to withstand a higher level of criticism than ordinary people, despite the absence of such a standard in Chinese law. In another case a judge in Henan Province invalidated a local regulation because it conflicted with national law—a radical step in a system in which courts do not have the power to interpret law or invalidate legislation. Courts routinely create new legal rules in less controversial areas.

The Internet is facilitating court development. Just a few years ago judges had little access to information about how cases were decided elsewhere.

Faced with a new legal question, they would generally seek guidance from superior courts. Today judges confronting new legal issues turn to the Internet to learn how courts elsewhere in China, or even overseas, have dealt with similar issues. This suggests there may be more room for courts to develop within the confines of the current political system than previously realized.

China has tolerated the creation of public-interest and activist lawyering. State legal aid institutions are now well established, and a wide range of functionally autonomous public-interest law institutions work to address a range of social problems, from the rights of children and migrant workers to environmental justice to women's rights. A small number of "rights protection lawyers" actively engage more directly in sensitive human rights work. The state has attempted to rein in such activism. In early 2011 dozens of rights lawyers were detained in the wake of revolutions in the Arab world and online calls for a "Jasmine Revolution" in China. Many were detained outside the criminal justice system, with no access to even the limited rights allowed suspects in the formal system. Public-interest lawyers working in less controversial areas also came under renewed scrutiny.

Yet public-interest lawyering is now well established in China, a significant development given that the terms *public-interest lawyering* and *rights protection lawyers* were virtually unknown fifteen years ago. Public-interest organizations with only loose ties to the state remain active in a range of subject areas. The state has encouraged public participation in the legal system through other mechanisms as well, including the use of public hearings and the solicitation of public comments on draft legislation.

POPULISM AND PROFESSIONALISM

Acknowledging progress is not intended to deny the many problems and abuses that continue to plague the effectiveness of law in China, many of which were evident in the Zhao Zuohai case. Courts remain subject to party oversight and control and are subject to a range of external pressures, including from officials, from the Chinese media, and as the Zhang Qiang case shows, from petitioners and protesters. Intervention into cases by party officials continues to be condoned, meaning that local officials often pressure courts to resolve sensitive cases in ways that serve powerful political and economic interests. This was made clear in the Zhao case both by the party political legal committee's order to procurators that the case should proceed and also by party officials intervening to resolve Zhao's case after news emerged that his victim had reappeared.

Yet even if intervention in cases continues—and is often praised by official party media outlets—such intervention is increasingly being challenged. This was made clear in July 2010 by the online reaction to news of a case brought by a frog farmer in Chongqing. Fu Qing started raising frogs in a pond near his hometown of Peiling in 2007. In June 2008 local authorities notified him that his frog pond was within the border of a planned new industrial park and thus would be condemned. Local authorities offered him 6,700 yuan per acre for his 1.5 acre pond. Some other local farmers accepted the offered compensation, but Fu refused, arguing that he was raising a more expensive variety of frog. A stalemate ensued between Fu and local authorities.

A few months later, in November 2008, construction began on the site near Fu's pond. Fu sued, arguing that the blasting and other work on the site resulted in the deaths of nearly three hundred frogs worth two million yuan. A court-ordered examination found that the defendants had caused the harm and that Fu had suffered 600,000 yuan in losses, but the court awarded Fu only 300,000 yuan in damages.

The trial court's hearing of the case had been characterized by repeated delays, allegations of official interference and police intimidation, and claims by the defendants that Fu was an ex-convict who was up to no good. On appeal the case became even more intriguing when Fu's lawyer uncovered an official document from the government entity in charge of the industrial park to the district court. The document had been placed in the court's files. Rather than focusing on Fu's legal claims, the document instead stated that the court should reject Fu's claim so as to avoid encouraging future litigation, both by Fu and by other farmers. The letter concluded that if the court failed to do so, "the court will not want to see the grave results." The letter was a threat that unrest would follow if the court ruled for Fu—and that the court would be responsible. Handwritten comments on the letter from the court vice president stated that the letter should be forwarded to the trial court judge responsible for the case, signaling that the judge should take account of the letter in making a decision.

Fu's lawyer posted the letter to the Internet, and news of the letter quickly spread. Some netizens characterized the letter as "the coolest government letter in history" because it provided such a clear example of official intervention. Commentators used discussion of the letter to condemn official intervention in cases and abuses of power: one news report highlighted a comment by a local official that "if even farmers can take advantage of the law, it will become more difficult for the government to operate according to the law."

News of other similar interventions also spread, including two cases in Shaanxi Province's Yulin Municipality involving disputes over mining rights. Both cases involved attempts by a local land bureau to avoid court decisions invalidating the transfer of ownership rights to apparently well-connected persons. In one case reports revealed a letter from provincial authorities to the Supreme People's Court that admonished the provincial high court for misunderstanding official policy and warned that enforcing the provincial court decision would have "grave impact on social stability and on the roadmap for development of Shaanxi Province." In both cases the news of official interference in the courts drew widespread condemnation, both online and in official party newspapers. The cases demonstrate that courts and lawyers are increasingly willing to push back against perceived inappropriate intervention.

The cases also underscore the lack of finality of court decisions. Litigants, be they ordinary parties like Zhang Qiang, local governments, or well-connected businesses, view court decisions as just one step—not the final step—in struggles to protect their interests. This sometimes is helpful to aggrieved petitioners, as it was to Zhang Qiang. But it also undermines the ability of courts to assume a role as a final arbiter of disputes or to ensure that court decisions are enforced. Indeed, some media reports have recounted how judges themselves have become petitioners, appealing to higher levels of the party-state after local authorities or locally connected enterprises have ignored court decisions.

Courts themselves often take the blame when things go wrong, even if judges and courts rarely have final authority over sensitive cases. This was evident in the Zhao Zuohai case, where the judges who heard the case were removed from office—despite the fact that the decision to proceed against Zhao had come from party superiors and the fact that the court's decision to issue a suspended death penalty may well have saved Zhao's life. When compensation was paid to Zhao it was the courts, not the police or procuratorate, that took the lead in apologizing and making payments to Zhao. Likewise, in Zhang Qiang's case the court was forced to change its opinion and to compensate Zhang despite judges' strong view that Zhang's claim for additional compensation had no legal merit. In the view of party-state superiors, however, the fact that Zhang was petitioning to Beijing suggested that the local courts had not taken sufficient steps to resolve the case.

Chinese judges are not unique in lacking life tenure or in being subject to external pressures: the majority of American state court judges are elected. But the evaluation system in China is extensive and reveals both the party-state's stability concerns and how law may become of secondary importance for judges seeking to resolve cases that involve a risk of protest. Evaluation of judges is based in part on whether they get their decisions right in the eyes of their superiors. Yet getting a decision right may mean issuing a decision that satisfies public or official opinion rather than legal standards. Judges are in some locations penalized if a litigant petitions or protests regarding a case—regardless of the merits of such complaints. Judges today are being instructed to "*anjie, shiliao*," meaning they must both decide the case and resolve the matter before them. The focus on resolving disputes can also cause courts to reopen closed cases or pay litigants themselves, as the court did in Zhang's case, to buy silence from litigants. Many courts (and governments) in China have established dedicated "compensation funds" to be used to pay petitioners to convince them to stop petitioning—because petitioners are viewed as a threat to both social stability and the legitimacy of the state. One consequence of the focus on "resolving the matter" in full has been a return to emphasis on mediation. Mediated cases are viewed as less likely to result in unrest. Many courts have set specific targets for judges to mediate a high percentage of cases.

In a system in which the greatest fear of the leadership is instability, the incentives to align decisions with public opinion or the demands of individual protestors are strong. Populist pressure can be beneficial, as it was in Zhao Zuohai's case and the subsequent attention to police torture. Yet in other cases populist pressures can lead to rushed decisions or to harsh treatment of less-popular defendants. China is not unique in experiencing extensive and sometimes excessive media coverage of high-profile cases or in there being allegations of "trial by the media." But the weak position of the courts, the continued legitimacy of official interference in court cases, and the Chinese media's traditional role as the eyes and ears as well as the mouthpiece of the party-state combine to make the media particularly influential in China.

The impact of populism is also manifest in the surge in court-related petitions and protests since the late 1990s. Petitioners, and some officials, argue that the rise of litigation reflects problems in the courts. Judges, not surprisingly, argue that petitioning reflects the weak position of China's courts and lack of respect for legal institutions and procedures. Petitioning is a rational choice for aggrieved individuals regardless of whether their complaints have merit: many petitioners have few other sources of financial support, and petitioning at least sometimes works, as it did for Zhang Qiang.

As the Zhao Zuohai case demonstrated, there is serious debate about the future path of China's legal reforms and widespread recognition and discussion of problems in the legal system. Yet addressing such problems has proven difficult. Often problems are addressed through political campaigns that focus on resolving the problem in and for a specific time rather than on institutional reforms that ensure problems do not recur. Part of the difficulty is one of resources: legal institutions may lack the resources (political, personal, or financial) to address such problems on an ongoing basis. Issues are addressed only when political mobilization comes from higher authorities. Yet the resort to campaigns also suggests an unwillingness to alter incentive systems for local officials or the authority of legal institutions in ways that align them more fundamentally with the avowed goals of such campaigns. Such campaigns can also have unintended consequences: the political-legal committee's decision to prosecute Zhao Zuohai was itself partly the product of a campaign to address the large number of persons held without trial, a recognized human rights problem known as "extended detention." A national campaign at the time resulted in pressure on local authorities to resolve all extended detention cases in their jurisdictions. The consequence, at least in Zhao's case, was not to release Zhao but rather to shift his status from being detained without charge to being wrongfully convicted.

Problems of wrongful conviction or political interference in court proceedings or pressure on local police to crack high-profile crimes are not unique to China. Indeed, in the months following the Zhao Zuohai case, some in the Chinese media appeared to delight in describing "American Zhao Zuohais." Yet the institutional dynamics and incentives that produced Zhao's conviction may be distinct to China. Such dynamics and incentives also lead courts to be responsive even to individual petitioners such as Zhang Qiang: pressure from higher-ups to resolve cases quickly and completely, obsession regarding instability, and inability or unwillingness to allow courts to become more autonomous or authoritative.

THE PARADOX OF AUTHORITARIAN LEGALITY

Both Zhao's and Zhang's cases also highlight the uniqueness of and the paradox inherent in China's legal reforms. The uniqueness stems from the fact that there are few precedents for a single-party authoritarian state creating a legal system on the scale China has done thus far. Chinese courts today handle eleven million cases a year, most of them routine and likely not subject to external influence. China has embraced not only rule-of-law rhetoric but also real institutional change—ranging from the establishment of an administrative law framework that regulates state actors to the creation of rights for individuals enforceable through the courts in a range of substantive areas. The Chinese party-state is now constrained by law even if legal rules are at times ignored in practice. China's legal reforms have included extensive study of foreign legal systems, and in many areas China has drawn on foreign experience as it has reformed its laws.

China has reformed while maintaining an authoritarian political system and continuing to use governance tools from the revolutionary period. In the courts such tactics are reflected in the persistent use of campaigns and populist rhetoric, in continued emphasis on mediation, in pressure on courts to resolve disputes in ways that are consistent with party policies and popular views, and in continued emphasis on popular input into the legal system. The paradox of China's legal reforms thus is manifest not only in tension between avowed commitment to the rule of law and the maintenance of single-party rule, but also in tension between legal reforms and political and legal institutions that continue to be extremely sensitive to populist views.

It is in the state's interests to have a legal system that serves as a forum for resolving individual grievances. It is far preferable for farmers to bring suit in court than to protest. Having such cases heard and resolved in the courts also sends a message that the legal system can be used to address rights-based claims of individuals. Yet creating incentives for more disputes to be brought into the formal legal system is a workable plan only if people feel that the system serves their interests. Too often the system is perceived as being fundamentally unjust.

China has devoted significant resources to legal education. Such efforts have worked—perhaps too well. Widespread legal education has created expectations that the system should protect ordinary people. There is risk, however, that interaction with the formal legal system may increase disillusionment, thus undermining the legitimacy of both law and the party-state.

Despite the progress in the Chinese legal system since 1978, many of the most difficult reforms remain to be undertaken. Again this was made clear in the Zhao case: it is difficult to see how fundamental changes can be made to police practices without both realignment of police incentives and a significant increase in public oversight. Within China there is widespread recognition that there are limits to what can be done in the current system, where courts lack authority and are subject to a range of influences that limit their ability to act independently. Far too often, party policies and the interests of individual officials trump legal norms and procedures, especially at the local level. Courts have begun a range of initiatives that are designed to improve both popular access to and confidence in the courts, including placing opinions online to holding hearings in villages to requiring judges to respond to litigants' questions within specified timeframes. Yet reformers in China recognize that if the role of law itself is to be strengthened, the focus of legal reform efforts in China must broaden. Such reforms would include reducing courts' links to local governments, making court finances independent, and reducing the ability of party-state officials to intervene in cases. These steps would help to strengthen the autonomy and quality of courts in China, even within the confines of overall leadership by the Communist Party.

The problem facing China's leaders today is that this next step of legal reform—in particular those reforms that are most necessary for curbing the worst abuses in the system—require structural reforms. Many of these problems are at least in part the product of China's particular political and institutional structure, one in which the party retains overall power, courts have limited powers even formally, and incentives favor stability above all else. China's leadership appears conscious of the risks inherent in continuing a system that, for example, encourages dissatisfied litigants to protest. Yet to date most efforts to address such problems have focused on pressuring local authorities to curtail protests, not on encouraging local authorities to respect court decisions.

CONCLUSION: CHINA'S
EXPERIMENT IN CONTROLLED TRANSPARENCY

Commentators in both China and the West have in recent years suggested that China's legal reforms are moving backward or have encountered new difficulties, the consequence of a new, more conservative leadership, in particular in the courts. The project of law reform has become more difficult since the middle of 2010, with the party-state taking a range of steps to rein in and restrict those seeking faster political and legal change. The most visible steps have been the detention of numerous activists. National and local governments have, however, also taken a range of steps designed to curtail even nonactivist lawyers and those involved in legal reform projects. These new restrictions reflect state fears of direct political challenges following the democracy movements that spread in the Middle Eeast in early 2011. But these steps also appear to reflect fundamental unease about the role of lawyers and law. Top leadership appears at best ambiguous about the value of following law and legal procedures in resolving contentious social issues. Views within China on the long-term impact of recent developments are mixed. Optimists view recent developments as a bump leading up to a sensitive political transition in 2012; others argue that China is experiencing the consequences of a fundamental change in how top leadership views law and the legal system.

Yet both Zhao's and Zhang's cases suggest that the evolution of the Chinese legal system is not merely the product of the views and intent of top party-state leadership. New technology and increased popular legal consciousness make it far more difficult than even a few years ago to cover up wrongdoing. The legal system has become surprisingly reactive to public opinion, for good and ill. Significant progress continues to be made in a range of substantive areas, as was evidenced by the Supreme People's Court's move to reduce the use of confessions obtained through torture. The project of law-drafting has continued. The courts devote significant resources to improving the training of judges. Yet Zhang's and Zhao's cases also show many ways in which the legal system has not changed despite thirty years of reform. Put differently, problems in China's legal system that have drawn widespread attention in recent years may be less reflective of a decision to slow down or turn back legal reforms than they are of continuities with China's prereform legal and governance system.

China's leaders are not ignorant of the risks of failing to reform. The need for greater transparency and reform is acknowledged by China's leadership, but it is also viewed with trepidation. Hence the state has tolerated and even encouraged recent efforts to strengthen administrative law, to have a greater role for public views in law-drafting, and to have an active role for the commercialized (but still state-controlled) media in curbing abuses. Recognition of the need for courts to play a greater role in resolving conflicts also helps explain tolerance of innovation by the courts in some cases. But there have also been efforts to ensure that none of these developments leads to challenges to party authority.

The Chinese party-state appears to be seeking to establish a system of controlled transparency in which oversight by a range of state and quasi-state actors is encouraged, but in which the role of nonstate actors and activists remains limited. Creating a vibrant and largely fair legal system that is able to resolve both commercial disputes and individual grievances remains an important element of this effort, even as authorities have engaged in the broadest political crackdown in years. Yet there are few, if any, examples of other authoritarian states developing sophisticated and fair legal systems that combine emphases on both professionalism and populist views of justice.

It remains far too early to determine whether this strategy will succeed. One thing that is clear, however, is that China's future legal and political development is likely to follow a trajectory that is unique to China. China today is an increasingly pluralistic society, one in which the greatest forces pushing legal development forward are the expectations of ordinary citizens about how the system should function. Individuals expect the legal system to protect their interests—and make their views known when it does not do so. New technologies make it both vastly harder to cover up injustices than just a few years ago and also easier for those seeking change to network and share experiences. Popular demands for justice helped free Zhao Zuohai. Yet, as the Zhang Qiang case demonstrates, there remains significant distrust of legal institutions.

The Chinese legal system is evolving in many different directions, and the role of law itself is increasingly contested. The Chinese legal system is developing from the ground up, as opposed to exclusively from the top down, in ways that neither outside observers nor China's leaders can predict. Law may come to play a transformative role in China, but the evidence to date cautions against predicting such an outcome, particularly in light of the steady disappearance in 2011 of some of the country's most prominent human rights attorneys, not to mention the severe house arrest of Chen Guangcheng. The paradox of the Chinese legal system is that growing use and importance of law may serve both to empower individuals and to reinforce party-state authority.

SUGGESTIONS FOR FURTHER READING

Gallagher, Mary, and Margaret Woo, eds. *Chinese Justice: Civil Dispute Resolution in Post-Reform China*. Cambridge: Cambridge University Press, 2011.

Liebman, Benjamin L. "Watchdog or Demagogue? The Media in the Chinese Legal System." *Columbia Law Review* 105, no. 1 (2005): 1–157.

——. "Innovation through Intimidation? An Empirical Account of Defamation Litigation in China." *Harvard International Law Journal* 47, no. 1 (2006): 33–178.

——. "China's Courts: Restricted Reform." *China Quarterly* 191 (2007): 620–38.

Liebman, Benjamin L., and Tim Wu. "Chinese Network Justice." *Chicago Journal of International Law* 8 (2007): 257–321.

Perry, Elizabeth, and Sebastian Heilmann, eds. *Mao's Invisible Hand*. Cambridge, MA: Harvard University Press, 2011.

Shirk, Susan, ed. *Changing Media, Changing China*. New York: Oxford University Press, 2010.

11

The Decriminalization and Depathologization of Homosexuality in China

Wenqing Kang

Homosexuality in China, like in other countries around the world, can be a very sensitive concern, often taken as a threat to conventional society and, in far too many cases, a cause for violent repression, incarceration, and even death. Although China has had a very long history of same-sex relations and erotica, much of which was widely documented in imperial times, the Communist Revolution brought a moralizing denunciation of homosexuality as perverse that was only ambiguously and contradictorily written into the criminal codes and medical diagnosis manuals. However, with the reforms of the last decades Chinese society has become more open and accepting of this sexual orientation, in keeping with its official decriminalization by the state.

While lesbian and gay life in contemporary China is improving, problems do remain. A visible queer culture has emerged in many cities. Gay bars, gay saunas, and gay parks, for instance, appear in the country's larger, more cosmopolitan urban centers. Websites are on the rise that report lesbian- and gay-related news and provide forums on queer issues as well as Internet dating services. Lesbian and gay film and cultural festivals, gay pageantry, and gay pride month are held in big cosmopolitan cities such as Beijing and Shanghai. Lesbian support groups and gay rights organizations in the name of AIDS prevention have formed in many cities, and the National Chinese Male Tongzhi Alliance was established in 2009.[1]

Many young people today come out as gay and lesbian, and some of their parents even become vocal supporters of gay rights. Evidence of acceptance has reached a point where same-sex marriage ceremonies are held symbolically on the streets of central Beijing and in other public and private locations in other cities. Still, the rise of a visible queer culture in China has been met with regulations and interference. Police intervention in gay social activities such as the interruption of gay pageantry in January 2010 and the recent raid on Mudanyan, a public park where gay people meet in Beijing, in September 2010 continue to appear in the media. Moreover, prostitution seems to have become a very prominent and troublesome issue for Chinese gay culture.

Exactly how should the public understand and react to contemporary queer culture in China? Simple answers such as "there must be more toler-ance" or "there must be more repression" cannot describe the complexity of the situation. When the media present a rosy picture of lesbian and gay life in China now, they usually provide two important pieces of background in-formation: homosexuality was decriminalized in 1997, and it was officially taken out of the category of mental illness in 2001. But how do we reconcile these legal facts with continuing police harassment?

To come to terms with this contradiction will require us to understand when and how homosexuality was officially criminalized and when and how it was pathologized in the PRC. These critical matters still remain unclear. Little research on the history of homosexuality in the PRC has been done or published in English.[2] By examining the history of official portraits of homosexuality in the PRC as either pathological or normal, I hope to shed some light on this shadowed subject. Furthermore, by revealing what still remains in contemporary Chinese law that could be applied to homosexual activities and how the medical profession defines homosexuality today, this essay will account for the difficulty of present-ing a straightforward description of contemporary Chinese gay culture.

DECRIMINALIZATION

Hailed as a legal milestone, the decriminalization of homosexuality in the 1997 Criminal Law of the PRC was actually a secondary consequence of two distinct changes in the existing criminal code. First, the provision on hooliganism (*liumang*) was eliminated. Second, the provision that "all crimes must be expressly prescribed by the law" (*zuixing fading*) was rein-stated so that no one would be criminalized for any conduct that was not officially prohibited in the law. These two changes were important revisions to the first Criminal Law of the PRC, promulgated in 1979, a few years after Mao's death and the end of the Cultural Revolution. Because sex between men was not clearly proscribed but was criminalized after being interpreted as a type of hooliganism under the old 1979 Law, these two changes in the new law amounted to the decriminalization of homosexuality.

Hooligans and Hooliganism

No stipulations that explicitly address homosexuality are found in the 1979 Criminal Law. Provision 160, on the "Crimes of Hooliganism," specified gang fights, provoking fights and stirring up trouble, sexual assault on women or other hooligan activities, and the disruption of public order. Provision 79, called the analogy clause by legal experts, says that "crimes not clearly stipulated in the provisions of this law may be sentenced by using the most similar provisions in the law with the approval of the Supreme People's Court."[3] According to Guo Xiaofei, one of the few scholars specializing in homosexuality-related legal issues in China, it was exactly these two provisions in the 1979 Criminal Law that made the criminalization of homosexuality possible. Anal sex between men could be punished as "other hooligan activities" under Provision 160 in official judiciary interpretations, which was made possible by the analogy clause.[4]

The meaning of "hooligan" (*liumang*) has constantly changed in China in modern times. One late-Qing writer described *liumang* as "those jobless migrants who were likely to create unnecessary conflicts in society."[5] According to Zhou Dan, an openly gay attorney and legal scholar writing in contemporary China, "hooliganism" was neither a legal term nor the name of a crime in the imperial and Republican periods. It was not until the 1950s under the Chinese communist regime that "hooligan" began to enter political and legal documents. Zhou traces the authoritative definition of *liumang* to the Chinese translation of Karl Marx's *Communist Manifesto*, in which the German term *lumpenproletariat* was rendered into *liumang wuchanzhe*, "hooligan proletariat," in Chinese. In the *Communist Manifesto*, the *lumpenproletariat* was described as "the social scum, that passively rotting mass thrown off by the lowest layers of the old society, [who] may, here and there, be swept into the movement by a proletarian revolution; its conditions of life, however, prepare it far more for the part of a bribed tool of reactionary intrigue."[6] This description of *liumang wuchanzhe* gave a new meaning to the term *hooligan* in the context of socialist China.[7]

Subscribing to Marxism, the communist state held that hooligans represented remnants of the old society and thus were to be subjected to socialist education and reform in the new China. Those who refused to change and continued to disrupt the social order would be punished by the state. It was in this context that gang fights, provoking fights and stirring up trouble, sexual assaults on women, and the disruption of the public order were listed as hooligan activities. Sex between men was also considered as a kind of hooligan activity but was not an openly discussed issue. Efforts to promulgate a new criminal code under the communist regime were made after the founding of the PRC, but the new laws were not formalized until 1979, in the wake of the Cultural Revolution, in an effort to enhance the socialist legal system.[8]

Jijian (Sodomy or Anal Sex between Males)

In twentieth-century China homosexuality could be narrowly understood as *jijian* (anal sex between men). In the sixteenth century, according to Matthew Sommer, the Ming-dynasty legal code punished anal sex between men through an analogy clause, stipulating that "whoever inserts his penis into anther man's anus for lascivious play shall receive 100 blows of the heavy bamboo, in application by analogy of the statute 'pouring foul material into the mouth of another person.'" As Sommer points out, "the statute quoted above never mentions *jijian* at all." *Jijian* as a legal term later appeared in the Qing law.[9]

Jijian can be translated as "sodomy," or "buggery." In Chinese, *ji* can refer to the penis, and *jian* may also refer to illicit sex between a man and woman. The word also carries the connotation that when a man has sexual intercourse with a married woman who is not his wife, he could potentially derail the patriline of the woman's husband's family by begetting an illegitimate son who could inherit the property of the woman's husband.[10] Since sex between men could not achieve this effect, the term *jijian* has departed from the original meaning of *jian*. When *ji* and *jian* are put together to mean anal sex between men, the term *jijian* becomes an oxymoron. Nevertheless, under a 1734 Qing law, anal sex between men—whether forced or consensual—was criminalized in the name of *jijian* through an analogy clause. The category of sexual offenses between men was modeled after the preexisting classification of illicit sex between men and women, and the act was punished accordingly.[11]

In one of its last efforts to modernize China, the Qing-dynasty government rewrote its legal code before its fall in 1911. One of the important features in the 1907 Qing legal code was the abolition of the aforementioned analogy clause. As a result, the statute on anal sex between men disappeared. Under the Republican government (1912–1949) following the fall of the Qing, no effort was made to criminalize sex between men, and the legal rule of "all crimes must be expressly prescribed by the law" also became a norm.

After the founding of the PRC in 1949, several drafts of the criminal code were written as policies and guidelines for tackling criminal activities, but no formal laws were promulgated until 1979. Except for a 1950 draft law that included forced sodomy (*jijian*) between male adults under the category of rape, the issue of sex between men did not appear in the legal documents of the central government.[12] Yet the issue of sex between men was constantly raised by local law enforcement personnel anxious for clarification and direction from the central state apparatus. The Heilongjiang Provincial High People's Court, for instance, in a letter dated March 19, 1957, asked the National Supreme People's Court for instructions in a case of consensual anal sex between two men who were held in a local labor reform camp. This correspondence between the two levels of government offices is a rare historical document that addressed the issue of homosexuality during the Mao era and is worth quoting at length. The Heilongjiang letter reads as follows:

> Serial Number 139
> Supreme People's Court,
> In Huling County, two labor reform convicts, Li and Li, had consensual sexual intercourse [sodomy, *jijian*]. The Middle Level People's Court of Mudanjian District in our province, which is in charge of the county, asked whether their behavior constitutes a crime that should be held accountable as a criminal offense.
> One argument is that consensual sodomy [*ziyuan jijian*] is a behavior that severely violates the social moral norm. In addition, this behavior occurred during their labor reform period, which exerted a very bad influence over other labor reform convicts. Therefore, both of them should be held accountable for a criminal offense.
> Another argument is that this type of consensual sex between men, although having a bad influence, is an issue of social norms. [They] should be disciplined administratively, but not be held accountable for a criminal offense.
> After discussion, we think that this is a kind of moral corruption detrimental to the social norm, and a behavior that violates the human body's physiology and function. Therefore, those who sodomize others by force should be sentenced to punishment. But as for whether the mutual behavior between two consenting persons constitutes a criminal offense, the central government has not had a regulation. According to Provision 154 of the Soviet Union Criminal Code, a man who has sexual intercourse with another man should be sentenced to three to five years of loss of freedom. What is the correct way to understand this provision? How do we understand whether the punishment also applies to consensual behavior? We don't have any basis or confidence to deal with this case and therefore specially ask the instruction of the Supreme People's Court.

The National Supreme People's Court responded on April 29, 1957, as follows:

> [We] have received the inquiry from your court numbered 139 of March 19. Regarding the question whether sodomy between two consenting adults constitutes a crime, a legislative solution is needed in the future. Before a clear provision is made in the law, we think it appropriate not to treat the case your court mentioned as a criminal offense.[13]

In this internal government correspondence, the writer of the Heilongjiang letter used the term *sodomy* (*jijian*) for both consensual and forced sex between men. While the Heilongjiang authorities seemed to know that forced sodomy constituted a crime, they found it difficult to deal with consensual sodomy. The letter from the National Supreme People's Court was clear that the current law carried no exact stipulation on consensual *jijian* and suggested that the local government should not criminalize this kind of act. It remained silent on the issue of forced sodomy.

The problem of lack of exact stipulations from the central government on sex between men, consensual or forced, persisted into the period after the promulgation of the 1979 Criminal Law. The problem was partially solved with the pronouncement of *The Answer to the Questions on How to Deal with Current Hooligan Cases* by the National Supreme People's Court and the National Supreme People's Procurator on November 2, 1984. It was in this document that *jijian* was clearly listed under "other hooligan activities" of Provision 160 of the 1979 Criminal Law. Among the six kinds of "other hooligan activities that are severe and constitute the crime of hooliganism" were "sodomizing young children, sodomizing adolescents by force, or severe cases of using violence and coercion to commit sodomy repeatedly."[14] In this important government document, although forced sex between men is clearly criminalized, the question of whether anal sex between consenting male adults should be considered hooliganism still remained unanswered.

Beyond the Realm of Formal Law

By law, anal sex between consenting male adults did not constitute a crime, or at least the 1979 Criminal Law and the 1984 interpretation of the crime of "other hooligan activities" did not mention consensual sodomy. In everyday life, however, men could be punished outside the formal legal system for engaging in anal sex during the Maoist and post-Mao reform period. Members of the Communist Party who engaged in consensual male-male sex could be disciplined with a warning within the party or have their party membership revoked. Nonparty members could lose their jobs, be detained without trial for a short period of time, or be sent to labor reform for longer durations.[15]

Moreover, although the 1984 interpretation only made clear that sodomy with minors and forced sodomy were severe cases of the hooligan crime, the police could still argue that anal sex between men both in public and in private was a type of general hooligan activity and thus they would make arrests accordingly. In those arrests, whether or not anal sex was involved was an important basis for disciplinary detention. One victim remembered that he was caught in bed naked with a male friend in his work unit dormitory by the police in 1994. During the interrogation, they were beaten into confessing that they had anal sex and were sentenced to fifteen days of detention. Afterward, a sympathetic police officer told them that they would not be detained had they not admitted to having anal sex. This piece of advice was backed up by what he had heard from other homosexual friends.[16]

THE 1997 CRIMINAL LAW

A new Criminal Law of the PRC was promulgated in 1997 (still in effect today), and the Criminal Law of 1979 was invalidated at the same time. In the new 1997 Criminal Law, the provision on hooliganism was deleted. Some of the crimes listed under the provision on hooliganism were rephrased and stipulated more specifically under different provisions, including acting indecently toward or assaulting a woman sexually by force, threats and any other similar means, and indecent conduct with a minor (Provision 237); gang fighting (Provision 292); provoking a fight and stirring up trouble (Provision 293); and engaging in licentious group activities (Provision 301).[17] No provision on sodomy was written into the new Criminal Law. In addition, Provision 3 of the new law clearly stipulates that "an act which is expressly defined by law as a criminal act shall be grounds for conviction and sentencing in accordance with law; if it is not expressly defined by law as a criminal act, it may not be considered grounds for conviction and sentencing." Theoretically, as a result of these changes, the 1984 interpretation of "other hooligan activities" was now invalidated. The story, however, does not end here.

THE PUBLIC ORDER ADMINISTRATIVE
PENALTY REGULATION OF THE PRC

In the PRC, the People's Republic of China Public Order Administrative Penalty Regulation (*Zhonghua remin gongheguo zhi'an guanli chufa tiaoli*) has been in place since 1957, and a new version was issued in 1987 only to be revised again in 1994. The 1994 regulation's stated function is as follows:

> Criminal acts as defined by the Criminal Law of the PRC, such as disrupting the social order, impairing the public security, infringing on the rights of other citizens, and exploiting or destroying public and private property are to be held accountable by law. Perpetrators who commit similar acts but less severe than those defined in the Criminal Law should be punished for the disruption of the social order according to this Regulation.

In Article 19 of the 1994 Regulation, "other hooligan activities," which could include consensual sex between men as understood through free interpretation by the police, were stipulated as behaviors disrupting public order, and men arrested under this article were subject to detention, fines, or warning.[18] In fact, most men found by the police engaging in consensual sex with other men were arrested exactly in the name of disrupting the social order, presumably based on this regulation. The regulation was in place until March 1, 2006, when it was replaced by the Public Order Administrative Penalty Law of the PRC, in which the term "hooligan" does not appear.

WAS THERE A DECRIMINALIZATION OF HOMOSEXUALITY IN 1997?

As the preceding discussion shows (through the 1984 legal interpretation of the "other hooligan activities" that was stipulated in the 1979 Criminal Law), men who had anal sex with minors in any case or with male adults by force could be held in criminal offense for anal sex. Men who engaged in consensual sex were subject to arrest by the police, and penalties could be applied to those who had anal sex, presumably according to the 1984 interpretation and the 1994 regulation. Therefore, it is safe to say that it is "anal sex between men" (*jijian*), not homosexuality in general, that was criminalized under the Criminal Law, at least from 1979 to 1997. With the changes in the 1997 law, no legal stipulations support the criminalization of anal sex between men anymore. This circumstance of law and practice has been interpreted as the "decriminalization of homosexuality."

The term *tongxinglian* (same-sex love), however, never appeared in any official Chinese legal document, and moreover, sex between women has not been a legal issue in the PRC. The much-reported 1991 "homosexuality" case in Wuwei County, Anhui Province, made these facts widely known. A father accused his daughter and her girlfriend of "committing homosexuality" and asked the local police to "strictly punish the ugly phenomenon" between "the two hooligans." The county public security division reported the case to the Chao Hu district, which again reported to the provincial level for advice. The case in turn reached the National Ministry of Public Security. Chao Hu district received this response from the Anhui Provincial Public Security Department:

> Regarding the Wuwei County homosexuality case that you reported, we have consulted with the Ministry of Public Security, and the answer is as follows: Currently, the law of our country does not have a clear stipulation on what homosexuality is and its legal status. In light of this situation, in principle, the case you reported should not be accepted. It is also inappropriate to treat the case as a kind of hooligan behavior and penalize [the people involved] for disrupting the social order. As for how to handle this particular case, you should consult related departments such as the procurators' offices and the judicial court.[19]

This 1991 document demonstrates a clear position by the National Ministry of Public Security on the issue of homosexuality. The ministry did not make any connection between *tongxinglian* and anal sex between men, *jijian.* While anal sex between men was understood as a type of hooligan activity and could be penalized under the Criminal Law and the 1994 regulation, homosexuality was neither a crime nor could it be explained as a type of hooligan activity appropriate for penalization. In other words, love between people of the same sex was not made illegal, but anal sex between consenting adult males potentially remained a criminal behavior.

In *Homosexuality in the Purview of Chinese Law*, Guo Xiaofei argues that no "decriminalization of homosexuality" has ever really occurred: "In the 1997 revision of the 1979 Criminal Law, the changes on the question [of hooliganism] had nothing to do with [the issue of] of homosexuality in terms of the motivation on the part of the lawmakers, and the connection made [between the new law and the result of] decriminalization of anal sex between men is also an 'interpretation after the event.'"[20] Guo's central argument is that the issue of homosexuality has not really been within the purview of Chinese legal thought, especially since the founding of the PRC. The legal code is dominated by heterosexist assumptions.[21] Specifically, the reinstatement of the principle of "all crimes must be expressly prescribed by the law" made the ambiguous "other hooligan activities" impossible to include in the new 1997 law, and that is why the crime of hooliganism had to be dissolved into different specific crimes, along with the annulment of the 1984 interpretation.

As an unintended consequence of the reinstatement of these legal principles, sex between consenting male adults was decriminalized. Although forced sex between a man and a male minor can be punished under the provision of indecent conduct with a minor, sex between and among adult men by force cannot be found anywhere in the new law.[22] That the issue of coercion has not been adequately addressed has led many legal specialists to complain about the failure of "the decriminalization of sodomy." For Guo, this situation exactly proves that the issue of homosexuality has been persistently outside the purview of Chinese lawmakers, and the so-called "decriminalization of homosexuality" has come about not intentionally but as an "unintended result."[23]

SEX BETWEEN MEN UNDER THE 1997 CRIMINAL LAW

The crime of forcing *women* into prostitution (*maiyin*) in the 1979 Criminal Law was changed to the crime of organizing or forcing *others* into prostitution (Provision 358) in the new 1997 Criminal Law.[24] Provision 359 also includes the crime of seducing or introducing others into prostitution, or providing others with places for prostitution. Under these provisions in the new law, sex between men could be criminalized as a form of male prostitution.

The famous 2004 Nanjing "homosexual prostitution case" (*tongxinglian maiyin an*) set the precedent. According to the procurator's indictment, brought in January 2003, Li Ning, who colluded with a certain Liu and a certain Leng, placed newspaper advertisements in the name of recruiting "male public relations personnel," as a front for hiring and organizing many young men to engage in prostitution with male consumers at his three different bars. From the seven confirmed cases of organized prostitution, Li profited 124,700 yuan.

At first, the procurator's office declined the police request for an arrest warrant, based on the legal interpretation that Provision 358 on "organizing others for prostitution" does not have a clear stipulation on organizing same-sex prostitution and the rule that "all crimes must be expressly prescribed by the law." Upon receiving this response, the police in Nanjing asked the procurator's office to reconsider this case. Meanwhile they released Li, since he already had been detained for thirty days, which is the maximum legal detention period. The procurator's office, however, sustained their earlier decision after their first reconsideration.

In caution, both the procurator's office and the police decided to refer the case to the provincial level. Following deliberation, the judicial department of Jiangsu Province, to which the city of Nanjing is administratively subject, decided to refer the case to the National Supreme People's Court for instruction. The Supreme People's Court in turn remanded the case to the Standing Committee of the National People's Congress, which eventually offered an oral response: use the provision on the crime of organizing prostitution to punish those who organize young men to sell sex to men. On the basis of this oral response, the court interpreted the "others" in the provision as referring to both male and female. Li Ning was summoned again in October 2003 and in February 2004 was sentenced to eight years in prison plus a 60,000 yuan fine for organizing prostitution.[25]

Victims of blackmail, along with the perpetrators, can also be punished by the police for engaging in prostitution. Thus the net of deterrent threat is widened. But with the intensification of economic inequality in China, many poor young men resort to homosexual prostitution and become what is known as "money boys." Some of them simply engage in blackmail by taking advantage of closeted gay men who are looking for anonymous sex. In one case that was reported in two mainstream Tianjin newspapers, Liu, a married man over forty who lives in the city and works for a company, admitted a long history of homosexual tendencies. On August 18, 2002, Liu, via a gay website, became acquainted with Xiaoqiang, and the two decided to meet later that night. After they met, Liu brought Xiaoqiang and his friend, another young man, to the dormitory of his company, and the three of them had sex there. Afterward, the two young men demanded 1,500 yuan from Liu. Following an hour of failed negotiations, Liu sneaked out and called the police for help, accusing Xiaoqiang and his friend of blackmail. However, once the police determined what had happened, they detained all three, fining them 5,000 yuan each. According to the police, the three had engaged in prostitution as described in the Public Order Administrative Penalty Regulation.[26]

That the police could charge blackmail victims with homosexual sex on the grounds that they were engaging in prostitution suggests that many men feel insecure, if not threatened, when having casual sex with other men. Although recently the situation has improved for blackmail victims, these men may be punished for engaging in group sex (*juzhong yinluan*) under the current law. This provision against group sex clearly does not aim at homosexuals but could certainly be applied to this group of people. This troubling legal ambiguity is one of the reasons that the famous sociologist, gay rights advocate, and authoritative scholar on homosexuality in China, Li Yinhe, is openly campaigning for the abolition of the 1997 Criminal Law's provision on group sex.

DEPATHOLOGIZATION

Like the criminalization and subsequent decriminalization of homosexuality, its official pathologization and depathologization also occurred after the end of the Mao era. Unlike the decriminalization process, which was only a side effect of the promulgation of the new Criminal Law, depathologization was clearly a result of efforts on the part of medical experts and gay rights advocates.

Pathologization: A Post-Mao Phenomenon

While some people, as shown in the 1957 Heilongjiang letter to the Supreme People's Court, may have believed homosexuality to be a mental illness, it was not until the 1980s that it was officially categorized as such in the PRC. Official classifications of mental disorders and diagnostic criteria were not employed in the first half of the twentieth century, before the communists took power. In 1958 the Ministry of Health drafted a classification of mental disorders for the first national conference on the prevention of mental illness, but in the end this draft was never officially released.[27]

After the Cultural Revolution, several versions of mental disorder classification were drafted and revised between 1978 and 1984. The 1981 version was the first official one and was named *Chinese Classification of Mental Disorders* (CCMD). Subsequently, the CCMD was recommended to doctors all over the country who were working with mental illness. This preliminary taxonomy was expanded in 1984 with the formulation of specific diagnostic criteria. Over a four-year period, the criteria for three general types of mental disorders were released separately. According to Yang Desen, who wrote a brief history of the classification and criteria-making process, a very important additional task undertaken by the doctors and experts was the translation of the most up-to-date draft version of the "Mental and Behavioral Disorders" chapter of the *International Statistical Classification of Diseases and Related Health Problems, 10th Revision* (ICD-10), by the World Health Organization (WHO) and the third edition of the *Diagnostic and Statistical Manual of Mental Disorders* (DSM-III) by the American Psychiatric Association. These two documents served as "necessary reference materials" for the formulation of the comprehensive Chinese diagnostic criteria that were first drafted in 1988.[28]

In April 1989 the first completed draft including both the classification and diagnostic criteria of mental disorders was finalized at an extended conference of the standing committee of the Chinese Society of Psychiatry held in Xi'an. In order to acknowledge the earlier efforts to formulate explicit criteria, the first combined and complete version of *Chinese Classification and Diagnostic Criteria of Mental Disorders* was named the second edition (CCMD-2).[29] In the CCMD-2 that was adopted by the Chinese Society of Psychiatry and issued to the public in 1989, homosexuality was listed as a type of psychosexual disorder (*xingxinli zhang'ai*) and was officially pathologized.

In treating homosexuality as a type of psychosexual disorder, the Chinese Society of Psychiatry seemed to have followed not the DSM-III, which had taken homosexuality off the list of mental illnesses, but the ninth revision of the *International Statistical Classification of Diseases*, in which homosexuality remained among the two pieces of "necessary reference materials" on the list of mental disorders. In 1990, however, the WHO passed the tenth edition of the ICD, which came into use in WHO member states from 1994. Chapter 5 of ICD-10 clearly states that "sexual orientation by itself is not to be regarded as a disorder."

In 1994 the Chinese Society of Psychiatry revised the CCMD-2 and began to implement the CCMD-2-R. With respect to the CCMD-2-R, the committee undertaking revisions "still listed homosexuality as a 'sexual perversion' [*xingbiantai*], [deciding] not to adopt the method practiced in foreign countries that removes homosexuality from the disease classification system and considers it as absolutely normal." According to CCMD-2 and CCMD-2-R, both those who accept their sexual orientation (egosyntonic homosexuals) and those who want to change their sexual orientation (egodystonic homosexuals) were diagnosed as suffering from the mental disorder.

Wan Yanhai, a public health expert and gay rights advocate, actively campaigned for the depathologization of homosexuality during the second half of the 1990s and also wrote an account of the process. According to Wan, the reason that in 1994 some medical experts insisted on keep homosexuality on the list of mental illnesses was that they believed a "patient" status could sometimes protect homosexuals from police arrests. However, there were others who supported the pathologization because they believed that homosexuality violated social norms and law and that the psychiatric profession had the responsibility to reform and control it. The pathologization of homosexuality at that time could be used as an excuse both to protect and to prosecute homosexuals.[30]

The Making of the CCMD-3

Chinese medical experts have persistently claimed that they want to create a system for classifying mental disorders that is suitable for Chinese particularities while also meeting international standards. Facing the discrepancy between the newly changed international standard of the ICD-10 and the Chinese criteria of the CCMD-2-R, the Chinese Society of Psychiatry established a committee of medical experts to put together CCMD-3 in September 1996. Immediately afterward, an activist group called Aizhi ("Loving Knowledge") Action Project, organized by Wan Yanhai, began to campaign for the depathologization of homosexuality.

One thing that the Aizhi Action Project did was to focus Chinese medical experts' attention on the recent depathologization of homosexuality around the world, especially in the United States. This work triggered a debate among medical experts. Between August 1997 and February 1998, eleven articles appeared in the *Psychiatric Health News* (*Jingshen weisheng tongxun*), a professional journal published by the Zhejiang Psychiatric Health Institute. Some proposed that China should adopt the standard of DSM-4 and ICD-10 that eliminates homosexuality from the classification of mental disorders. Others insisted that homosexuality be classified as an abnormal sexual behavior, unacceptable according to Chinese social norms. Still others recommended compromises, such as not classifying homosexuality as a disorder but still calling for a cure, or still considering homosexual attraction as an illness but finding another name for it.[31]

In addition to affecting the discussion, another important achievement of the Aizhi Action Project was bringing the medical experts and the gay community together. In the past, the medical experts could only meet homosexuals who believed their sexual orientation to be problematic and sought their assistance. With the gay community involved, the doctors met many gay people who were entirely comfortable with their sexual orientation. Again, according to Wan, this kind of communication contributed tremendously to the change in how the medical experts viewed homosexuality and the later depathologization of homosexuality.[32]

In April 2001 the Chinese Society of Psychiatry published the third edition of the *Chinese Classification and Diagnostic Criteria of Mental Disorders* (CCMD-3). In the CCMD-3, homosexuality is still listed as a sexual orientation disorder (*xingzhixiang zhang'ai*) under the category of psychosexual disorders. It reads as follows:

62.3 Sexual Orientation Disorder
It refers to a disorder caused by various kinds of sexual maturation and the development of sexual orientation, which is not necessarily abnormal from the perspective of sexual love [*xing'ai*] per se. But, along with the sexual maturation and the development of sexual orientation, some people might develop a mental disorder. For instance, the individual does not wish to be or hesitates to act in a certain way, and is anxious about, depressed, or agonized by [his sexual orientation]. Some of them attempt to find treatment in order to change. This is the main reason that CCMD-3 includes homosexuality and bisexuality [on its list].
62.31 Homosexuality
[Diagnosing criteria]
   1. Fits the definition of sexual orientation disorder.
   2. Under a normal living condition, from adolescence, [an individual] has begun to show persistent sexual love interest toward members of the same sex, including thoughts, feelings, and sexual behaviors.
   3. Although able to have normal sex with members of the opposite sex, [the individual] has difficulties in establishing and maintaining a family relationship with a member of the opposite sex due to obviously declining or lack of sexual interest.

What has become evidence for the official depathologization of homosexuality in China is the statement that "[sexual orientation] is not necessarily abnormal from the perspective of sexual love per se." It is a compromised way of saying that "sexual orientation by itself is not to be regarded as a disorder," as stated in ICD-10. As later explained by medical experts and journalists, the important message in this statement is that the medical authority simply does not consider homosexuality abnormal, even though "homosexuality" is still listed under the category of "sexual orientation disorder." According to the CCMD-3, only those who cannot adapt themselves to their homosexual orientation are still defined as suffering from such a disorder, although the criteria for diagnosing homosexuality do not seem to support this interpretation.

This kind of ambiguity could be a result of the twin guidelines for the making of the CCMD-3, that is, meeting international standards while also preserving Chinese characteristics. Following the ICD-10, the CCMD-3 writers suggest that homosexual orientation is not a disorder. Maintaining the notion of *Zhongguo tese*, "Chinese characteristics," they create a concept of sexual love, which seems different from the notion of sexual orientation.

Because the concept of sexual love is never clearly defined in these materials and sexual love is deemed "not necessarily abnormal," the difference between sexual orientation and sexual love remains unclear. There is still much that must change before the complexities of the human heart can be accounted for even in a more enlightened age.

As this short account shows, both the official criminalization and pathologization occurred in the post-Mao period, as part of an effort to standardize the Chinese legal system and medical profession after the end of the Cultural Revolution. The decriminalization of homosexuality was only a side effect of the promulgation of the new 1997 Criminal Law of the PRC, when the Chinese government further strengthened its legal system in light of the social and economic changes occurring since the promulgation of the 1979 Criminal Law. The revision and final release of the CCMD-3 in 2001, which intentionally depathologized homosexuality, was clearly a gesture on the part of Chinese psychiatric professionals to meet international standards of medical practice, albeit incompletely.

Both Western and Chinese media tend to characterize the Mao era as a dark period of political oppression and the post-Mao period as a moment of liberation when social control loosened up, and they assume, explicitly and implicitly, that it was the Maoist regime that made homosexuality both a crime and a mental illness. This chapter does not argue that the Mao era was not repressive for homosexuals in China, and it is clear that further research needs to be done on the history of homosexuality during this period. What I hope my critical investigation into the history of the medical and political representation of homosexuality may have accomplished is to demonstrate how the focus on one issue "beyond the headlines" can permit us to understand the historical transition from China's "communist" past to its "reformist" present.

SUGGESTIONS FOR FURTHER READING

Books

Guo Xiaofei. *Zhongguofa shiya xiade tongxinglian* (Homosexuality in the Purview of Chinese Law). Beijing: Zhishi chanquan chubanshe, 2007.
Kong, Travis S. K. *Chinese Male Homosexualities: Memba, Tongzhi and Gold Boy*. New York: Routledge, 2010.
Martin, Fran. *Backward Glances: Contemporary Chinese Cultures and the Female Homoerotic Imaginary*. Durham, NC: Duke University Press, 2010.
Muhlhahn, Klaus. *Criminal Justice in China: A History*. Cambridge, MA: Harvard University Press, 2009.
Sang, Tze-lan D. *The Emerging Lesbian: Female Same-Sex Desire in Modern China*. Chicago: University of Chicago Press, 2003.

Sommer, Matthew. *Sex, Law, and Society in Late Imperial China*. Stanford: Stanford University Press, 2000.

Wenqing, Kang. *Obsession: Male Same-Sex Relations in China, 1900-1950*. Hong Kong: Hong Kong University Press, 2009.

Wing Wa Ho, Loretta. *Gay and Lesbian Subculture in Urban China*. New York: Routledge, 2009.

Yang Yifan, Chen Hanfeng, and Zhang Qun, eds. *Zhonghua renmin gongheguo fazhishi* (The Legal History of the People's Republic of China). Beijing: Shehui kexue wenxian chubanshe, 2010.

Zhou Dan. *Aiyue yu guixun: Zhongguo xiandaixing zhong tongxing yuwan de fali xiangxiang* (Pleasure and Discipline: Jurisprudential Imagination of Same-Sex Desire in Chinese Modernity). Guilin: Guangxi shifan daxue chubanshe, 2009.

Films

Chunfeng chenzui de yewan (Spring Fever), 2009. Directed by Lou Ye.
Zhi Tongzhi (Queer China), 2008. Directed by Cui Zi'en.

NOTES

I am indebted to Gail Hershatter, Lionel Jensen, Lisa Rofel, Jeremy Tai, and Timothy Weston for their invaluable comments on and careful editing of this article, as well as Guo Xiaofei and Zhou Dan for sharing their research. I would also like to thank Timothy Weston and the "China in and beyond the Headlines" conference participants for the opportunity to present this paper at the University of Colorado at Boulder in April 2010.

1. *Tongzhi*, "comrade," was the most common term of familiarity for men and women in postrevolutionary China; however, with the eclipse of comrade as a meaningful term in a nation of economic class and wealth, *tongzhi* has become the favored term of address for gay men.

2. But for a 1990s snapshot of actual attitudes and practices, see Dalin Liu, Man Lun Ng, Li Ping Zhou, and Irwin J. Haeberle, *Sexual Behavior in Modern China: Report on the Nationwide Survey of 20,000 Men and Women*, trans. Man Lun Ng and Irwin J. Haeberle (New York: Continuum Books, 1997). See also Susan D. Blum and Lionel M. Jensen, *China Off Center: Mapping the Margins of the Middle Kingdom* (Honolulu: University of Hawai'i Press, 2002), 219–37.

3. Quoted in Guo Xiaofei, *Zhongguofa shiye xiade tongxinglian* (Homosexuality in the Purview of Chinese Law) (Beijing: Zhishi chenquan chubanshe, 2007), 61.

4. Guo Xiaofei, *Zhongguofa shiye xiade tongxinglian*.

5. Quoted in Zhou Dan, *Aiyue yu guixun: Zhongguo xiandaixing zhong tongxing yuwang de fali xiangxiang* (Pleasure and Discipline: Jurisprudential Imagination of Same-Sex Desire in Chinese Modernity) (Gulin: Guangxi shifan daxue chubanshe, 2009), 209.

6. Karl Marx and Frederick Engels, *Communist Manifesto*, ed. Frederick Engels (New York: International Publishers, 1948), 20.

7. Zhou Dan, *Aiyue yu guixun*, 209–10.

8. Yang Yifan, Chen Hanfeng, and Zhang Qun, eds., *Zhonghuo renmin gongheguo fazhishi* (The Legal History of the People's Republic of China) (Shehui kexue wenxian chubanshe, 2010), 123–34. For a history of the Criminal Law and the Chinese legal system of the PRC in English, see Harold M. Tanner, *Strike Hard! Anti-Crime Campaigns and Chinese Criminal Justice, 1979–1985* (Ithaca, NY: Cornell University, East Asian Program, 1999).

9. Matthew Sommer, *Sex, Law, and Society in Late Imperial China* (Stanford: Stanford University Press, 2000), 119–20. Wenqing Kang, *Obsession: Male Same-Sex Relations in China, 1900–1950* (Hong Kong: Hong University Press, 2009), 93–94.

10. Kang, *Obsession*, 93.

11. For details, see Sommer, *Sex, Law, and Society*, 124–25.

12. Guo Xiaofei, *Zhongguofa shiye xiade tongxinglian*, 60.

13. Quoted in Guo Xiaofei, *Zhongguofa shiye xiade tongxinglian*, 63, and in Zhou Dan, *Aiyue yu guixun*, 185–86.

14. Quoted in Guo Xiaofei, *Zhongguofa shiye xiade tongxinglian*, 61–62.

15. Guo Xiaofei, *Zhongguofa shiye xiade tongxinglian*, 95.

16. Guo Xiaofei, *Zhongguofa shiye xiade tongxinglian*, 95–96.

17. Guo Xiaofei, *Zhongguofa shiye xiade tongxinglian*, 85.

18. See Zhou Dan, *Aiyue yu guixun*, 227.

19. Quoted in Zhou Dan, *Aiyue yu guixun*, 201.

20. Guo Xiaofei, *Zhongguofa shiye xiade tongxinglian*, 85–86. Also quoted in Zhou Dan, *Aiyue yu guixun*, 227.

21. See Guo Xiaofei, *Zhongguofa shiye xiade tongxinglian*.

22. According to Zhou Dan, this kind of situation has changed since the promulgation in 2006 of the Public Order Administrative Penalty Law, which lists acting indecently toward others as behaviors of violating personal rights (Provision 44). As Zhou points out, since "others" could be both male and female, sex between men by force could be criminalized according to this provision. Zhou Dan, *Aiyue yu guixun*, 227–28.

23. Guo Xiaofei, *Zhongguofa shiye xiade tongxinglian*, 85–93.

24. Guo Xiaofei, *Zhongguofa shiye xiade tongxinglian*, 110; Zhou Dan, *Aiyue yu guixun*, 229.

25. Guo Xiaofei, *Zhongguofa shiye xiade tongxinglian*, 104–5. A similar case that occurred in Chengdu, Sichuan Province, in 1998 was closed without a lawsuit for lack of a clear legal stipulation. After the intervention of the People's Congress in the Nanjing case, two other similar cases happened in Beijing and Shanghai, and the accused were found guilty and sentenced. Guo Xiaofei, *Zhongguofa shiye xiade tongxinglian*, 117 and Li Qing, "Nanjing Tongxinglian Maiyin An" [Nanjing homosexual prostitution case] in *Fenghuang zhoukan* [Phoenix Weekly]. No. 141, March 2004, 40–2.

26. As reported in *Meiri xinbao*, Tianjin, August 20, 2002, and *Jinwan bao*, Tianjin, August 20, 2002.

27. Yang Deshen, "Zhongguo jingshen jibing fenlei fang'an yu zhenduan biaozhun zhiding gongzuo de lishi yu xianzhuang" (The History and Current State of

the Formulation of the Chinese Classification and Diagnostic Criteria of Mental Disorders), *Shanghai jingshen yixue* (Shanghai Psychiatry) (1989): 10.

28. Yang Deshen, "Zhongguo jingshen jibing fenlei fang'an yu zhenduan biaozhun zhiding gongzuo de lishi yu xianzhuang," 11.

29. Yang Deshen, "Zhongguo jingshen jibing fenlei fang'an yu zhenduan biaozhun zhiding gongzuo de lishi yu xianzhuang," 11–12.

30. Wan Yanhai, "Zhongguo tongxinlian zuoxiang zhengchang" (Chinese Homosexuals Are Becoming Normal), in *Tongxinglian feibinglihua yiji xiangguang wenjian* (Depathologization of Homosexuality and Related Documents) (Beijing, Beijing Aizhixing yanjiusuo, 2001), 4.

31. Wan Yanhai, "Zhongguo tongxinlian," 8–10. For more details on the debate, see Zhou Dan, *Aiyue yu guixun*, 121–24.

32. Wan Yanhai, "Zhongguo tongxinlian," 6–8 and 10–11.

12

The Evolution of Chinese Authoritarianism: Lessons from the "Arab Spring"

Orion A. Lewis

> Political democracy is the wave of history; it is the inevitable trend for all nations of the world to move toward democracy, but the timing and speed of the development of democracy and the choice of the form and system of democracy are conditional. . . . In that sense, democratic politics is a political art.
>
> > —Yu Keping, deputy director of the Central Committee's Compilation and Translation Bureau, 2006

> As it stands, our political structure is not adapted to the current situation. Political restructuring . . . should be regarded as the hallmark of progress. . . . We must streamline the administration, delegate real powers to lower levels, and broaden the scope of socialist democracy, so as to bring into play the initiative of the masses and grassroots organizations.
>
> > —Deng Xiaoping, 1986

In early 2011, the Middle East—a region of the world known for durable authoritarian regimes—erupted with popular uprisings against long-standing dictatorships. In Tunisia, the twenty-four-year dictatorship of president Zine El Abidine Ben Ali came to an end in a mere eighteen days of largely nonviolent protest. This singular event changed Arab and international perceptions of the nature of authoritarian power and set off a wave of similar uprisings. Soon populations were protesting authoritarian rule, corruption, and lack of economic opportunities from Libya to Egypt, Jordan, and Syria. In February the thirty-year rule of Egyptian president Hosni Mubarak ended after an intense struggle between protestors, government thugs, and the military resulted in his stepping down from power, going into internal exile, and eventually, along with his inner circle, being arrested.

Taken together these dramatic events constitute the third "wave" of democratization that has occurred since 1989. Based on the work of Samuel Huntington, a wave of democratization is understood as a series of popular uprisings and authoritarian collapses that are interconnected due in part to the prevalence of global communications and the common inspiration drawn from other successful movements.[1] The Arab spring of 2011 followed the wave of revolutions that swept away Leninist regimes in the Soviet bloc in 1989 and the USSR itself a few years later, as well as the second wave of "color" revolutions that toppled autocratic regimes in central Asia during the previous decade.

Despite the government's control of information and society, history has shown that China is not immune to international trends. In retrospect, the Tiananmen Square protests in 1989 were the opening salvo in a series of challenges to authoritarian rule throughout the communist world. As veteran China analyst David Shambaugh has pointed out, the Chinese Communist Party (CCP) was "shaken to its core" by the Tiananmen crackdown and subsequently "watched in shock and trepidation" as the Leninist parties of the Soviet bloc were swept from power later that year.[2] Thus, Shambaugh reasoned, understanding how the Chinese leadership perceived these waves of democratization, diagnosed their causes, and drew lessons on how to avoid a similar fate can explain a lot about how the CCP attempts to maintain its rule in an age of democratization.

Given the interconnectedness of popular uprisings, it is not surprising that western media attention soon turned to whether China would also witness a "jasmine" revolution, inspired by the name given to the Tunisian uprising. Following the events in Tunisia and Egypt, some Chinese citizens did call for their own protests and tried to organize "strolls"—a popular protest tactic in China—to silently push for democratic reform. Consistent with their actions toward the uprising in Xinjiang in 2009, the party-state moved swiftly to repress these protests to prevent them from getting out of their control. They did so by utilizing the standard tools of repression: censoring the Internet for usage of the term *jasmine*, forcefully breaking up and cordoning off areas designated for protest, roughing up foreign journalists, and arresting and detaining high-profile critics of the regime who they perceived as potential troublemakers.

In the context of detentions and disappearances of prominent human rights lawyers, journalists, and activists, one arrest stood out: on April 3, 2011, prominent artist and frequent government critic Ai Weiwei was detained while boarding a flight. The son of one of China's most famous poets, Ai Qing (1910–1996), and designer of the internationally renowned Bird's Nest Olympic stadium, Ai had previously seemed untouchable because of his family's socialist credentials and his personal fame. These facts allowed him to say and do things that might have landed most other Chinese citizens in jail. Most recently he had run afoul of regional authorities for collecting the names of the nearly five thousand school children who died in the Wenchuan earthquake of 2008 due to shoddy public school construction. Ai's "public investigation" into the identities of the children caused him to be detained and beaten in 2009 by local Sichuan authorities.

Just as Ai Weiwei's ability to dissent was indicative of a gradually more tolerant and pluralistic regime (as pointed out by Ben Liebman in his discussion of law in chapter 10 of this volume), his arrest provoked wide international protest because it represents a reversal of free expression and the reemergence of the more authoritarian and repressive state that characterized the Maoist period and the Tiananmen crackdown. As commentator Jeffery Wasserstromn noted, the degree of repression used against potential instigators of social unrest seemed incongruous with the common view of an increasingly strong, economically successful, and confident authoritarian regime that is more "tolerant of varieties of opinion."[3] Instead, what has emerged is an image of an overly nervous party-state reacting with excessive force and repression to minor challenges. These events raise a number of important questions. How do we understand this reversion to repression? What has been the historical interaction between basic ideas of authoritarian repression and political reform? And how does this help us understand the long-term evolution of the CCP?

This chapter addresses these questions through a comparative analysis of how the CCP has responded to previous "waves" of democratization. Much of the reaction of the Chinese government to the Arab uprisings can be understood through the lens of factional politics within the Communist Party itself as it approaches its 2012 leadership transition. Instead of viewing the CCP as a monolith, it is useful to understand the different, varied, and often opposing ideas within the party and the ongoing debate over how the regime should respond to political and social discontent.[4] While somewhat oversimplified, researchers have characterized the ruling elite (as it characterized itself in the polemics of the Cultural Revolution) as being composed of both a hard-line conservative faction and a more liberal reformist faction—the classic "two-line" struggle.[5] In general, conservatives are extremely wary of political liberalization and seek to aggressively and swiftly assert authoritarian control during periods of heightened sensitivity and unrest. They are currently referred to as the "stability maintenance faction." In contrast, the reformist right is generally more tolerant of gradually greater freedom of discourse and supportive of political efforts to downsize and reform the role of government in society—essentially arguing for a more ideologically flexible regulatory state. In this view, the best way to solve unrest is not simply crackdown but also reforming political institutions to deal with the root grievances that drive it.

Understanding the different, sometimes conflicting political preferences in China helps us assess how the party-state deals with social unrest. Each of these factions draws different conclusions from democratic revolutions elsewhere and advocates different policy responses. These factional differences help explain the seemingly contradictory efforts by the regime to move both forward and backward on reform simultaneously. While overt repression is often used to suppress the proximate causes of revolution—protests and demonstrations—many reformers recognize repression alone will not keep the CCP in power in the long run. Instead, they argue, it must also address the grievances—poverty, unemployment, income inequality, injustice, corruption, and environmental degradation—that are the root causes of revolution.

Prominent reformist intellectual Yu Keping argues that political development in China requires developing mechanisms for "good governance." In this view, citizen participation provides a check on the concentration of power, limits corruption, and allows the authoritarian state to understand better the interests, aspirations, and grievances of its population. Reformist Premiere Wen Jiabao has expressed similar sentiments recently in public comments abroad, yet conservative propaganda authorities censored them, illustrating the tensions and debate within the regime over the issue. Because the government and its ruling political party are *not* monolithic, one cannot reduce CCP preferences to a singular desire for control. A more nuanced view of regime preferences recognizes that most government actors want *both* regime durability and "social stability." However, there are a variety of policy ideas about the best means to achieve these ends.

As a mature single-party regime, the government is composed of multiple factions at once. Inherent frictions within it explain why repressive actions in the short run have not prevented gradual liberalizing reforms in the long run. Political reform in China often seems conflicted and contradictory because the relative political clout of political factions shifts in response to periods of international crisis or domestic unrest. During those periods elites are fairly unified behind stability maintenance. As one official told CNN's Jamie FlorCruz, "stability trumps everything." Yet even during times of increased repression, political reforms and change often continue to take place simultaneously.[6] Despite the current round of authoritarian crackdown, the government has also invited online comments on a draft income tax law and is preparing major revisions to the regulation and normalization of NGOs.

Authoritarian durability is not just about repression but also about the ability to accommodate and incorporate the allegiance of a sufficiently broad segment of society. In a country of more than a billion people, this is a significant constituency. Electronic governance and media reform can be a facade of concern for citizen input, but such activities do represent a degree of elite deliberation. There is an important difference between a regime that cares only about buying off narrow groups of elites, such as that of Ben Ali or Muammar Qaddafi, and one that has a degree of concern for public legitimacy. Ongoing institutional change and political reform often represents the basic idea that the government must change in order to perform better and respond to grievances. As the classic Chinese idiom states, the government is a ship on the sea of citizen support. While the "sea can support the ship, it can also overwhelm it" (*shui neng zai zhou, yi neng fu zhou*).

Based on its own recent experience with major uprisings in the restive minority regions of Tibet (2008) and Xinjiang (2009), the Chinese leadership has learned to act swiftly and forcefully on any sign of significant popular uprising to prevent it from spreading. The existing social science literature suggests that a "jasmine revolution" is unlikely to occur in China soon, but it does explain why the CCP must continue to change regardless. Looking back on the past twenty-five years of reform in China shows that repression exists alongside gradual reform, accommodation of new interests, and efforts to satisfy at least enough public demands to maintain legitimacy and endure. The CCP's historical responses to democratization waves outlined below make the case for why we should expect ongoing reform and adaptation. Failure to learn the lessons of its own history, however, would greatly increase China's likelihood of revolution.

WAVES OF DEMOCRATIZATION AND THEIR IMPACT ON THE CCP

One way to grasp the impact of the Arab uprisings on political reform in China is to look at the ways the CCP has assessed and reacted to recent episodes of unrest. In 1989 the brutally violent repression of the Tiananmen protests coincided with the ouster of the party's primary liberal reformer, General Secretary Zhao Ziyang, and the ascendance of the conservative faction, headed by Vice Premier Li Peng. Conservatives were ascendant from the period immediately following Tiananmen until Deng Xiaoping's pro-reform "southern tour" in 1992. Many of Zhao's allies were ousted, coupled with aggressive suppression of debate via greater control of propaganda and some reversal of 1980s reforms. As Minxin Pei argues, the weakening of the liberal faction during this period had a chilling effect on political reform and fostered a number of illiberal policies that emphasized social control.[7] In the official CCP analysis that emerged, Zhao had erred in allowing too much freedom of expression and not suppressing the protests more quickly, the combination of which allowed the protests to spiral out of control, forcing the regime into a position of violent suppression.

This conservative view was only reinforced by external events: Europe in the fall of 1989, and the Soviet Union in 1991. Within CCP circles, the official analysis of the Soviet collapse was that Gorbachev's policy of dramatically liberalizing freedom of expression, *glasnost,* was risky and too quickly enacted. As well, they believed that Gorbachev failed because he allowed unrest to spread by not doing enough to suppress it quickly. The widespread view was that the regime needed to maintain the primary levers of authoritarian control—the party, the press, and the security forces.[8]

The policy implications of this assessment are clear. Social stability and control is primary, while political reform is of secondary or tertiary importance. The CCP subsequently sought to avoid the perceived mistakes of the USSR by continuing to change and adapt to shifting domestic and international conditions. It sought to rejuvenate itself by co-opting new segments of the elite, such as private entrepreneurs, and ensuring that party recruits are simply the most educated and capable talent. More recently, the party has sought to rebuild its outreach capacity by reintroducing work units where they had previously receded, such as in domestic and foreign corporations.

In terms of the press, numerous analysts in this volume and elsewhere have detailed how the government maintains tight control over political discussion, even in the context of rapid technological development and commercialization of the press. As media scholar Yuezhi Zhao has observed, "though the reform period has generally been characterized as an era of neoliberal downsizing of the government, captured by the 'small government, big society' slogan, the same period has seen a steady increase in the number of government departments and bureaus in the communication field."[9]

Thirdly, the government has invested heavily in its most critical pillar of control—the security apparatus. Already a substantial portion of the state budget prior to the unrest of 2011, recently released official figures show that spending on internal security has now surpassed the defense budget.

Tactically, the cumulative lessons of Tiananmen, the fall of the Soviet bloc, the color revolutions, and their own recent struggles with unrest in its west are evident in China's overbearing response to even nascent calls for revolution. The state has responded with overwhelming force in order to prevent unrest from gaining momentum, even in recent events that resembled more of a flash mob in concept and execution. In the end, there were many more members of the Chinese and foreign press along with the police at these gatherings. This also explains the detention of Ai Weiwei and others like him. Why would a single outspoken artist threaten one of the most durable authoritarian regimes in modern history? In his work *The*

Power of the Powerless, Czech dissident and former president Václav Havel explains the threat of dissent to authoritarian regimes:

> By breaking the rules of the game, [the dissident] has disrupted the game. . . . He has shattered the world of appearances, the fundamental pillar of the system. . . . He has broken through the exalted facade of the system and exposed the real, base foundations of power. . . . He has shown everyone that it is possible to live within the truth. Living within the lie can constitute the system only if it is universal. . . . There are no terms whatsoever on which it can co-exist with living within the truth, and therefore everyone who steps out of line denies it in principle and threatens it in its entirety.[10]

Given China's increasingly networked society, alternative ideas can spread more rapidly than ever before. If authoritarian control relies on the "universal" perception of power, then the regime cannot allow a single dissident to stand outside the boundaries of their framework. Ai Weiwei's detention was to make a point about the universality of regime power.

Repression though is only part of the story of how the CCP has learned from waves of democratization. As the literature on social mobilization and revolutions highlights, revolutions are often driven by two sets of factors: opportunity and grievance. Opportunity-based analysis focuses on how regimes constrain the actions of potential protesters and limit the options available for opposition. In this regard, the Chinese government has invested heavily in limiting the opportunities for criticizing the regime, and its physical repression of nascent movements is designed to limit opportunities for coordination. Grievance-based approaches, on the other hand, focus on the root causes of revolution—the problems, inequalities, and injustices that motivate people to rebel. In this regard, the CCP's understanding of the role of grievances in previous waves has also played an important role in its adaptation.

As David Shambaugh notes, the CCP's assessment of these collapses became increasingly sophisticated throughout the 1990s as it had more time to reflect on the differences between itself and other authoritarian regimes. In particular, he points to two themes that emerge in Chinese writing on the role of grievance: first, in the view of Chinese analysts, Soviet bloc countries failed to deliver economically; and secondly, these regimes were too authoritarian and divorced from the needs and interests of the populace.[11] In terms of economic development, the Soviet-style command economy failed to deliver substantial increases in standards of living; development was too unbalanced, overly reliant on heavy industry, and did not produce enough consumer goods. Coupled with additional economic problems such as rising inflation and debt, these economic failings were seen as important drivers of social dissatisfaction. On the political side, Chinese analysts saw Soviet-bloc countries as overly totalitarian, meaning that pervasive fear and intimidation had suppressed the population to the extent that it had no other way out than to topple the existing regime.[12] The corollaries of this basic problem were that many of these regimes had overly centralized leaderships that were too reliant upon corrupt dictators and divorced from the average citizen.

These were also the takeaway lessons of the "color revolutions," the general name given to the wave of revolutions in former Soviet Central Asian countries, consisting primarily of the "rose" revolution in Georgia (2003), the "orange" revolution in the Ukraine (2004), and the "tulip" revolution in Kyrgyzstan (2005). As Titus C. Chen has shown, scholars at Fudan University's Center for Russian and Central Asian Studies viewed domestic grievances—generated by poor economic performance, corruption, and inequality—as the most important causes of the revolutions. In an early analysis, its director, Zhao Huasheng, argued that the "most decisive" cause of the revolutions was the fact that economic performance in these countries was still below the level achieved prior to the collapse of the USSR. Similar to earlier analyses of the Soviet bloc, Zhao argued that pervasive economic inequality was due to official corruption.[13] Once again, Chinese analysts painted a picture of an economically stagnant and corrupt regime that failed to meet the fundamental interests and aspirations of its population. These grievances were the fuel that drove people to pack public squares in protest despite efforts at repression.

Clearly, a grievance-based assessment of revolution has the policy implication of encouraging the CCP to continue to engage in reform and institutional modernization in order to effectively respond to and mitigate social grievances. Representation of the broad masses of society has long been the basis of the concept of "socialist democracy" in the PRC, but the responsiveness of government to the people was a principle often ignored during the totalitarian Maoist period. It has taken on added significance in the reform era with an emerging and increasingly active middle class.

It is perhaps too early to fully understand the causes of the Arab Spring uprisings, but many of the economic and political causes of grievance appear in those countries as well: inflation, high levels of unemployment among the youth, corruption, and dictatorial regimes that appeared blind to the basic needs of the population as a whole. In contrast, rapid economic growth in China has provided tangible benefits to many citizens and has lifted hundred of millions out of poverty. At the same time, modernization has had a number of negative consequences that greatly impact large segments of the population—rural residents, migrant workers, unemployed students, and the poor countryside. Many of the issues that have driven change elsewhere, including income inequality, corruption, weak rule of law, and environmental degradation, are real and present dangers in China today. Indeed, these problems have led to significant unrest and numerous, sometimes violent protests at the local level over the past decade. Official tallies of "mass events" were seen to be on the rise before the government stopped releasing official statistics on them.

Another tactic of control is to "localize" unrest so as to keep it from spreading. In contrast to the heavy-handedness in the regime's suppression of jasmine-inspired unrest and uprisings in Tibet and Xinjiang, some local governments, primarily in the developed eastern provinces, have accommodated numerous local-level protests. The difference, Hong Kong political scientist David Zweig explains, is that "they are challenges to specific issues rather than ideologically driven, cross-regional organized events. . . . They are citizens' protests, not political actions aimed at changing the regime or forcing political reform on the regime."[14]

Given these political concerns, the CCP has consistently pursued social, economic, and political reform to a lesser degree, as a means of preserving its longevity. Conservative tendencies toward repression in the early post-Tiananmen years eventually gave way to a renewed emphasis on economic growth as the best means to meet the interests of the people. Deng Xiaoping's "southern tour" to Guangdong Province in 1992 was intended to be a catalyst for pushing forward with economic reforms. By the end of decade, China had witnessed another prolonged period of double-digit economic growth and had even joined the World Trade Organization, a change that had seemed unthinkable in the immediate aftermath of the crackdown that had made the country an international pariah in 1989.

A similar pattern appeared following the color revolutions. As with the revolutions in the Soviet bloc, the color revolutions provoked an immediate tightening of controls on societal organizations and the press in the period during and immediately after the wave. Once again, reformists did not back away from pushing forward. One of the primary critiques of the Jiang Zemin era of the 1990s was that the regime was overly focused on rapid economic growth at the expense of other important social issues such as inequality and social welfare provision. In light of ongoing debates about the role of these problems in driving unrest elsewhere, it is not surprising that "building a harmonious society" has become the party-speak framework for addressing grievances that might cause disharmony.

Thus we find that the CCP has often adopted a two-pronged strategy for dealing with societal unrest. First, it has sought to control opposition movements at the point of inception rather than allowing them to gain momentum. These efforts have been institutionalized and developed under the government's "stability maintenance" (*weiwen*) program. Government officials often travel to Beijing to receive training on how to disrupt protests with police, offer talks, and censor and manipulate Internet information—known as "channeling public opinion." The regime even pays thousands of people—known as the "50 cent gang"—to post favorable comments in online forums to influence discussion. While the first prong of this strategy receives the most attention from international observers, the second prong is equally important for long-term legitimacy—gradual institutional reform. Chinese strategists argue economic growth has given them "performance legitimacy" with the people, despite the lack of Western means of political legitimation such as elections. However, the concept of performance legitimacy has generally focused primarily on *economic* performance and ignored the political dimensions of the equation.

Increasingly, though, the party-state has begun to recognize that economic performance must also be coupled with better governance. In his review of Chinese scholarship on the issue, Chen points out that many scholars have argued for the need to move beyond a discussion of performance legitimacy and "incorporate issues of social justice in the policy-making equation," because "legitimacy was contingent upon societal recognition . . . [of] those socioeconomic groups that were relatively disadvantaged in the market economy."[15] In this regard many CCP leaders have been pragmatic in recognizing that political legitimacy comes from multiple sources: nationalism, economic growth, good governance, and social liberalization. China specialist Vivienne Shue highlights the fact that deeply historical conceptions of authoritarian legitimacy, known as "the mandate of heaven," had multiple components: "glory" (i.e., nationalism), "truth" (i.e., scientific knowledge), and "benevolence" (i.e., good governance).[16] Much of the discussion about a "China model" of authoritarian capitalism emphasizes the first two pillars of party-state legitimacy in the wake of Tiananmen: economic development and nationalism. Less attention has been given to the ideals of "good governance" that may also play a role in how the party-state has evolved.

This trend continued in 2010 when Fudan University's Institute for Advanced Study of Social Sciences held an international conference on government legitimacy. This meeting was noteworthy for its focus on a topic that remains politically sensitive, going to the core of the government's durability. Giving the keynote speech for the proceedings, Yu Keping made the argument that irrespective of ideological differences between Westerners and Chinese regarding the meaning of democracy, everybody should be able to agree that "good governance" should be the ultimate goal of any regime. How can a single-party regime achieve good governance in the absence of formal checks and balances and elections? He suggested that the CCP might develop institutions, such as a more developed judiciary, mechanisms for greater transparency and accountability within the CCP itself, and a variety of channels for "societal feedback." Feedback mechanisms are any avenue that allows citizens an opportunity to voice their concerns, share information with the state, and better scrutinize powerful elites. Many reformists thus view the gradual expansion of societal participation as an important means to achieve better governance within the single-party system. In this regard, Yu suggested that the CCP should be creative in developing an expanded role for "civic participation," a point he echoed in a recent op-ed amid the current crackdown.

In sum, the conventional wisdom that international waves of democratization have *only* caused a reversion to repression in China is not accurate. Instead, the CCP and Chinese analysts have drawn diverse lessons from the collapse of similar regimes, each with its own political implications. To be sure, the tools of control and repression remain important parts of the authoritarian toolkit, but they are but one outgrowth of international waves. Just as important is the fact that heightened domestic insecurity can be a catalyst for further reform. Somewhat paradoxically, repression and liberalization are two sides of the same coin of CCP durability.

In the long run, though, more than thirty years of "reform and opening to the world" has shown unmistakably that the overall trend in China is toward gradual reform, liberalization, and change. This gradual evolution of authoritarian rule has been a consistent feature of Chinese politics, despite periodic attempts at rollback. This reformist path does not mean that the party-state is slowly moving toward Western-style electoral democracy anytime soon, but it does mean there will still be opportunities for reformists to advance their agenda in the future.

Repression and liberalization are interconnected for another important reason: institutional reforms often have unintended consequences. Even if political liberalization is not the intended goal of specific reform measures, it is often the result. For example, the regime largely embraced Internet connectivity for the economic benefits but continuously tries to cope with its political consequences. The following section on cyber-nationalism provides an example of this. Additionally, the process of economic modernization also generates new pressures for change from within. The emergence of an educated middle class means there are hundreds of millions with the tools and motivations to challenge existing rules and creatively adapt to, or push back against, an overconcentration of power.

REFORM AS A CAUSE OF AUTHORITARIAN EVOLUTION

Politically, the party-state has sought to streamline, modernize, and "rationalize" its governing system without dismantling single-party control.[17] The 1990s were characterized by a push to downsize the state bureaucracy and reduce its role in managing every facet of daily life. This phase, characterized by the paradigm of "small state, big society," was also followed by a push to make government more effective. Political scientist Dali Yang argues that reformers transitioned from a focus on downsizing to one that sought to change the functions of government by developing a "program to curb government discretion, boost transparency, and promote government as service."[18]

In both the economic and political spheres, the CCP has faced a "dictator's dilemma," where the desire for reform often conflicts with authoritarian control. Economically, the regime has sought to build a market-driven system while downplaying the contradictions and negative consequences inherent in such a transition. Similarly, political reforms have generated a need to create policy feedback mechanisms that make governance more effective and legitimate, without losing single-party control. To cope with these conflicting tendencies, the party-state has sought new ways to improve its public support by modernizing its control over information technology, the media, and nongovernmental organizations while developing new, savvier means of engaging in public relations and spin.

In particular, the regime has emphasized nationalism as the primary means of establishing its legitimacy in the post-Tiananmen era. Following the disaster of the Cultural Revolution and repeated Maoist upheavals, communism has been greatly weakened as a unifying framework for legitimacy, a crisis further exacerbated by the Tiananmen crackdown of 1989. In response, the regime has emphasized nationalism and "patriotic education" (see Lionel Jensen's chapter in this volume) as a means of improving its public support. In this narrative, the CCP remains at the forefront of the long-term goal of national rejuvenation. Despite dismantling many of the structures of the socialist command economy, the current regime has made the case that it is still carrying out Mao's vision by making China a strong, developed country.

However, as James C. Scott has argued, claims to legitimacy often "contain the raw material for contradiction and conflict." He states, "the very process of attempting to legitimate a social order by idealizing it . . . provides its subjects with the means, the symbolic tools, the very ideas for a critique."[19] This is also true for nationalist discourse in China, which has interacted with rapid technological development. The proliferating chat rooms and blogs constitute a relatively liberalized public space for communication among citizens, providing new avenues for promoting nationalist ideas. The best-known source of online nationalist commentary has been the Strong Nation Forum (*Qiangguo luntan*) hosted by the official People's Daily Group (a government controlled media conglomerate), but this forum is also known for displays of critical popular expression. This phenomenon has also facilitated new forms of virtual activism, as nationalist activism online, due to its greater legitimacy, has become more widespread than "political" activism. [20] This growing array of communication outlets has important implications for how nationalism evolves because it alters who can participate in public discourse and creates opportunities for societal feedback. This generates a broader marketplace of ideas than that found in the traditional state-dominated news media. Thus new media have expanded both the variation in ideas and the interactivity of nationalist discourse. This determines the "evolvability" of the system, because the more citizens are able to interact, the greater the likelihood that people change their ideas.

In short, technological development creates opportunities for new societal actors to become adept at pushing forward and challenging censorship boundaries—this is why the Egyptian revolution was also dubbed the Facebook revolution. Instead of viewing China as governed solely from the top down by the regime, it is important to view the political system as a complex adaptive system. Top-down reforms pursued by the CCP are obviously central to political change, but a complete view also accounts for citizens and individuals impacting political change from the bottom up. Indeed, much of the most interesting work on Chinese politics today analyzes the variations in political preferences within the regime and the plethora of ways that citizens respond to, adapt to, and try to change political institutions over time.

This interactive dynamic between rising popular nationalism and a new media environment began to emerge following the large-scale popular protests against the U.S.'s bombing of the Chinese embassy in Belgrade in 1999. The vehemence and spontaneity of these protests has been highlighted as the clearest warning sign of how popular nationalist passions can boil over and threaten government control.[21] These trends only accelerated with the rapid growth of the Internet, as new waves of "cyber-nationalists" utilized the opportunities afforded them to criticize official foreign policy. In terms of foreign policy, official efforts toward a "responsible" foreign policy have often conflicted with the views of popular nationalists who seek a more confrontational stance, particularly with respect to Japan.[22]

In terms of domestic policy, cyber-nationalists have challenged both economic and political reform policies of the state. On the conservative side, the past decade has witnessed the rise of "New Left" intellectuals—a name given to those who use the government's own socialist and nationalist rhetoric to critique the direction of market reforms and argue for a greater emphasis on the "socialist" roots of the PRC. New Left thinkers have argued that economic reforms have gone too far in dismantling the socialist welfare state. Framing their positions as consistent with the nationalist project of building a strong and stable country, as well as the Maoist nationalism of the past, they argue that the government should return to socialist values and better address the grievances of disadvantaged groups. Initially, these intellectuals were largely shut out of mainstream avenues of expression in the traditional media, so they often utilized online postings to promote their ideas.

This variation clearly illustrates the complexities of nation building in a global media environment. No longer can the regime easily control how its policies are perceived domestically. Instead, it must now contend with more nationalist views of both the conservative and liberal varieties. For example, communications scholar Yuezhi Zhao points to the seminal role of the Internet in catalyzing debate during the "Lang Xianping storm" of 2004. Economist Lang Xianping gained public attention for criticizing the government's policy of privatizing state-owned companies. Not only did Lang circulate many of his ideas online, but the Internet "served as a distribution outlet for the earliest newspaper stories about Lang's lecture, and later, major portals circulated Lang's talks, press articles, and served as exclusive outlets for the views of many participating economists."[23] In the end, Zhao contends, the Internet helped promote a deeper debate over these critical ideas. As indicated above, the New Left's emphasis on social equality over rapid economic growth has been increasingly reflected in government pronouncements about developing a more robust welfare state and maintaining government intervention in the economy.

The rise of the New Left has also coincided with the emergence of the "angry youth" (fenqing)—a new generation of technologically savvy youth unhappy with a number of social ills generated by rapid economic development, such as income inequality and environmental pollution. Ironically, despite having come of age in relative material prosperity and international stability, this generation of angry youth have also utilized the opportunities afforded by online media outlets to become vociferous critics of perceived slights to China's image abroad as well as foreign policy positions deemed too weak at home.[24] For example, these cyber-nationalists pushed back virtually against Western media portrayals of China during the Tibetan protests of 2008 by posting videos to YouTube pointing out factual errors in Western media reports and vociferously defending the government's claim that Tibet was a historical part of China.

Not all strains of nationalist thinking are conservative in their orientation. In his expert analysis of the complexities of nationalist discourse in China, Zhao Suisheng points out that "liberal nationalism" advocates national rejuvenation through greater emphasis on individual rights and rule of law. Similar to other varieties of nationalism, liberal nationalists also advocate a strong defense of national interests, but they diverge from others in their view that the government should expand social freedoms and allow for greater political participation. These views were most prominent during the "liberal '80s" and helped influence the Tiananmen protests. Since then, these ideas have not been as prevalent, nor have they received as much attention, but they are nevertheless still present online and elsewhere. Zhao points out that liberal nationalists were present in online calls for anti-Japanese protests in 2005 in response to discussion of Japan taking a seat on the UN Security Council, and again during the counterprotests to international criticism during China's Olympic torch relay in 2008.[25]

The overarching framework of state-led nationalism has thus facilitated the emergence of a wide variety of nationalist discourses at the grassroots level. This has been enabled and facilitated by the development of information technology, providing cyber-nationalists of all stripes with the opportunity and the means to critique various aspects of state policy. Clearly, not all of these cyber-nationalists agree on what needs to be done to build a strong China, and many actors simply use the broad framework of nationalist discourse as a shield to advocate very specific policies. In this regard, reform has clearly allowed for greater societal feedback and interaction on major policy issues. Elsewhere I have termed this development "pluralized authoritarianism," which is defined by a greater diversity of voices engaging in critical deliberation within the overall boundaries enforced by the single-party state. Make no mistake: pluralized debate is not a mass phenomenon in China but a fundamentally elitist one, based on the judicious use of broad CCP policy frameworks as a shield to push for changes to official policy.

As has been the case with the New Left and the angry youth, public-sphere pluralism online can impact government policy. In 2010, for instance, the PRC reacted with exceptional ferocity after Japanese authorities detained a Chinese boat captain who had sailed to territorially contested islands. This aggressive response again seemed incongruous with the severity of the issue, but it is more readily understood as an effort to appear "strong" to its domestic nationalist constituency. Although it is impossible to measure precisely the extent to which such views impact policy choices, it is clear that the growth of popular nationalist discourse online is a concern to the regime. The Internet has also played a major role in organizing a series of anti-Japanese protests over the years. Thus, as one prominent Chinese foreign policy analyst noted, government officials play close attention to online public opinion with respect to foreign policy positions.[26] Both President Hu Jintao and Premier Wen Jiabao have acknowledged the importance of online discourse by engaging in online chats with Chinese citizens. This form of online popular opinion has become an important means of gauging the public mood, because the differences between online anonymity and in-person surveys means there are still many political obstacles to acquiring clear and accurate public-opinion polling.

Nationalism, as many observers have long noted, is a double-edged sword that can bolster support for the regime but also be turned against it. During anti-Japanese protests in 2005, it was clear that the regime was quite worried that the protests could spill out of control and that demonstrations could be used as a forum for diverse nationalist voices to critique the government. These popular nationalist demonstrations were organized largely online without the urging of officials, resulting in large-scale mobilization. In Shanghai alone an estimated twenty to fifty thousand people turned out in the streets. The government's nervousness that the protests could turn against the regime was evidenced by the fact that it ultimately sought to quell them. The regime sent out mass text messages warning citizens against "spreading false rumors" and stationed riot police outside the Japanese embassy. An official newspaper in Shanghai even warned of an "evil conspiracy" to bring down the Chinese government.[27]

WILL CHINA BE NEXT?

Authoritarian durability in China is not simply about whether the regime can suppress calls for change but also about the extent to which it can accommodate and incorporate them. As the previous section has shown, efforts by the party-state to meet the needs and desires of the people through economic reform, as well as efforts to reframe the nationalist project, often generate further calls for change. Recognizing the complex dynamics between repression and accommodation has important implications for understanding durability and change within authoritarian systems. Although many people rightly lament the continued repressive aspects of the PRC and its many challenges, it is also important to recognize, as many of the chapters in this volume do, the remarkable changes that have occurred over time. Current repression in China is not always a proactive strategy to prevent advancing freedoms; indeed, it is often a reaction to liberalizing changes that have already occurred.

The Arab Spring caused many analysts to question whether China will be the next country to witness a fundamental challenge to the regime. As the political scientist Scott Kennedy has argued, China scholars have often erroneously turned into political prognosticators rather than trying to explain the change and dynamism that is occurring in China today. Indeed, if the regime is successful in its goals, the process of democratic change might be a long and gradual one instead of a dramatic upheaval. If the Chinese government fails to continue to adapt to societal grievances, then pressure could build up and explode.

Will China be the next authoritarian regime to fall? No one can really answer this question, but we can take stock of the factors that are known to cause revolutions. In terms of opportunity, there are clearly many more avenues for dissent and criticism than before due to technological development. Cyber-nationalists of all varieties have utilized these opportunities and the basic rhetorical framework of nationalism to discuss issues, such as the government's foreign policy, which would have been strictly off limits a decade or two before. However, the opportunity to criticize is not the same as the opportunity to organize. Clearly, the regime's biggest fear is that disparate groups of protestors will band together to challenge the regime and that, once they do so, these movements will spiral out of its control. This is why the regime has invested in Internet censorship that focuses heavily on opposition groups with calls for regime change, as well as in the security apparatus to suppress any efforts at physical organization. For example, the banned Falun Gong organization has been able to disseminate its critique of the regime virtually inside of China by making judicious use of email, websites, and other online tools. However, attempts to organize physically are often met with harsh punishment. Indeed, the reason Falun Gong was originally banned was not because of dissenting political views but because it was able to mobilize thousands of people to turn out for a demonstration without the regime's knowledge in the late 1990s. As the events of this year have shown, the CCP is willing to pay a high price in terms of its international image in order to ensure that it does not give any opposition movement a chance to gain momentum.

In terms of societal grievances, China is in a much better position than most other authoritarian regimes because thirty years of growth has delivered tangible benefits to broad segments of society, not just a narrow ruling elite. However, with rising incomes come rising expectations. Throughout both the emerging middle class and the relatively disadvantaged groups in Chinese society, there is growing frustration with income inequality, corruption, and environmental pollution. Many in the countryside acknowledge that their standard of living has increased, but they now often come face-to-face with the fact that the wealth of many others has increased far more. Given the dramatic and glaring disparities between the developed coastal provinces and the underdeveloped inland provinces, or between developed urban centers and poor rural areas, it is safe to assume that this inequality will be a major source of grievance for some time to come. As the CCP's own analysts have argued, these types of economic imbalances were fatal to some Soviet-bloc regimes. Whether the regime's current efforts to address these inequalities and developmental imbalances will be enforced and effective enough remains an open question.

Despite the buildup of these grievances, it remains unlikely that a sufficiently wide segment of the population would mobilize for overall regime change. The stagnant power holders that ruled in the Soviet bloc or the Middle East often refused to fundamentally change their approach to economics or politics, thereby forcing critics to mobilize for change outside of existing institutions. In contrast, the CCP has been a reformist regime for over thirty years. This means that, even if someone is particularly aggrieved and willing to mobilize for change, they must ask themselves whether it is better to seek complete regime change or work through existing institutions, however imperfect.

In fact, there is considerable evidence that reforms have generated significant public support for the regime. In the Chinese context, democratic progress is not measured in absolute terms but instead is often viewed as relative to the past. In his survey of Chinese views of democracy and democratic progress, political scientist Shi Tianjian finds that a large percentage of respondents viewed the Chinese regime in 2007 as significantly more democratic than the government was in the mid-1990s, and far more democratic than it was in the late-1970s. Whereas only 22 percent of respondents rated the 1970s regime as "somewhat democratic" or "very democratic," 63 percent of respondents viewed the current regime this way. Amazingly, only 12 percent viewed the government as "somewhat dictatorial" or "very dictatorial," whereas 47 percent classified the 1970s regime this way. As Shi argues, this shift in views is reflective, "first, of their own conceptions of democracy, and second, of the baseline against which they measure change. . . . For many Chinese a paternalistic government that denies political competition is consistent with their view of democracy . . . for many, the limited increase in freedom they have enjoyed since Mao's death marks a real improvement from the past." [28]

This does not mean that the CCP can afford to be complacent. One of the major obstacles to reform is the fact that liberal gains often remain tenuous and subject to reversal, especially at the local level where officials have much greater discretion. Reformist leaders can often only tacitly support changes at the same time that others oppose reform and repress their area. Only greater institutionalization of an independent judiciary and fairer rule of law can really prevent corrupt officials from undermining regime legitimacy. As an editorial in the outspoken news weekly *Caixin* argued, "We fully agreed with the Politburo which once declared that the rule of law is the foundation of governance. The rule of law—unlike the rule by law—runs contrary to the idea of rulership by a handful of leaders. The rule of law is based on effective protection of civil liberties and human rights, as well as the effective restraint on state power." [29]

As the discussion of cyber-nationalism indicates, the CCP must now compete in the marketplace of ideas against an increasing variety of voices. No longer can policy be made behind closed doors and in back rooms without a modicum of public scrutiny. Instead, increased societal feedback continues to place pressure on the party-state to accommodate diverse societal interests, or at least pay lip service to them. This more interactive relationship between state and society will force the regime to continue to reform and adapt in order to survive.

Perhaps the biggest danger to the regime is the lingering assumption that repression alone will be sufficient to prevent unrest. Given the substantial crackdown of 2011, as well as similar tendencies toward brute force in Tibet and Xinjiang in recent years, many Western observers are fearful that these trends represent a long-term reversion to heavy-handed authoritarianism. As the *Economist* recently opined, "the latest freeze casts this widespread hope [for liberalization] into doubt."[30] However, pessimists should remember that there are still many Chinese elites—both inside and outside the government—who understand the danger of excessive repression. Repression can shape the opportunity structure for dissent and suppress nascent movements, yet it is often *simultaneously* a source of new grievance. Chinese public intellectuals have also expressed these views. In his blog posting "Where Does Chinese People's Resentment Come From?" prominent reformist economist Mao Yushi argues that it is not simply the usual suspects of income inequality and corruption. Instead, he makes the case that excessive use of indiscriminate force and lack of political reform are the root causes: "Although every society has some unreasonable individuals, China features a government that rarely listens to individuals or upholds justice; this, as a result, has translated into public resentment."[31]

As of this writing, security officials have released prominent human rights lawyer Jiang Tianyong. The same day, another prominent lawyer was taken into custody, followed by two more two weeks later. Ai Weiwei was eventually released in June 2011, and in another example of how new media have changed contentious politics, Chinese netizens helped to raise a considerable sum of money for him to legally challenge government-levied fines for tax issues. What do the revolving doors of the detention centers in China tell us about the government's response to the Arab Spring? First, that as with previous waves of democratization, repression of individuals is not likely to be permanent but is a short-term response designed to deter them from mobilizing others during a period of crisis or heightened unrest. Second, it indicates that the regime itself is conflicted about the extent to which it should employ repression and against whom. Factional politics play an important role in determining the exact nature and outcomes of the "stability maintenance" program. This helps to explain both the regime's style of repression and, perhaps, the eventual release of many of those detained.

Indeed, in the run-up to a key power transition in 2012, all factions are acutely aware of the stakes in terms of how China deals with unrest at home and abroad. Domestically, while China did not witness the emergence of a revolutionary movement in the wake of the Arab Spring, social unrest has nevertheless risen. According to leaked information reported by the U.S. Council on Foreign Relations, 2010 witnessed some 180,000 "mass events," a substantial increase from previous figures. 2011 continued this trend anecdotally with prominent cases of social protest in localities such as Dalian and Wukan.[32]

How to deal with this unrest has sparked significant factional debate in party circles and public discourse. This debate has also played out internationally in China's foreign policy approach to ongoing conflict in the

Middle East. In early 2011, China surprised some when it voted in favor of a UN resolution authorizing sanctions against Muammar Qaddafi's Libya and then abstained from vetoing the resolution that authorized international use of force. If these actions illustrated a more internationally engaged and "responsible" China, these hopes were quickly contradicted in 2012. China recently vetoed a resolution calling for the end of the Assad regime in Syria after considerable violence against its people. Nationalist hardliners have been quick to hail the government's willingness to assert its voice internationally and push back against efforts toward intervention in other authoritarian regimes. What type of regime will emerge after the transfer of power at the 18th Party Congress—one driven by responsible reformists or one controlled by repressive hardliners? The outcome will be crucial for determining whether the country continues on a path of gradual institutional evolution, or grievances are suppressed and build toward revolution.

SUGGESTIONS FOR FURTHER READING

Fewsmith, Joseph. *China since Tiananmen: From Deng Xiaoping to Hu Jintao.* New York: Cambridge University Press, 2008.

Heilmann, Sebastian, and Elizabeth J. Perry. *Mao's Invisible Hand: The Political Foundations of Adaptive Governance in China.* Cambridge, MA: Harvard University Asia Center, 2011.

Li, Cheng, ed. *China's Changing Political Landscape: Prospects for Democracy.* Washington, DC: Brookings Institution, 2008.

O'Brien, Kevin J. *Popular Protest in China.* Cambridge, MA: Harvard University Press, 2008.

Shirk, Susan L. *China: Fragile Superpower.* New York: Oxford University Press, 2007.

Zhiyue, Bo. *China's Elite Politics: Governance and Democratization.* Hackensack, NJ: World Scientific, 2010.

NOTES

1. Samuel P. Huntington, *The Third Wave: Democratization in the Late Twentieth Century* (Norman: University of Oklahoma Press, 1991).

2. David L. Shambaugh, *China's Communist Party: Atrophy and Adaptation* (Berkeley: University of California Press, 2008).

3. Louisa Lim, "China Cracks Down on Reporters, Potential Protesters," *National Public Radio Morning Edition,* March 14, 2011.

4. For an example of factional discourse in the public sphere, see David Bandurski, "What's Up with the People's Daily?" *China Media Project,* May 27, 2011.

5. In contrast to western democracies that often measure political preferences ranging from the liberal left to conservative right, China's hard-left Marxist founda-

tions have flipped the political spectrum, making reform of the socialist status quo the political "right." Those who support the preservation of, or return to, more socialist policies are known as the "left." In recent decades new generations of thinkers of both factions—and thus variants thereof—have emerged.

6. George J. Gilboy and Benjamin L. Read, "Political and Social Reform in China: Alive and Walking," *Washington Quarterly* 31, no. 3 (2008): 143–64.

7. Minxin Pei, *China's Trapped Transition: The Limits of Developmental Autocracy* (Cambridge, MA: Harvard University Press, 2006), 56–57.

8. Susan L. Shirk, *China: Fragile Superpower* (New York: Oxford University Press, 2007).

9. Yuezhi Zhao, *Communication in China: Political Economy, Power, and Conflict* (Lanham, MD: Rowman & Littlefield, 2008), 22.

10. Václav Havel and John Keane, *The Power of the Powerless: Citizens against the State in Central-Eastern Europe* (Armonk, NY: M. E. Sharpe, 1985), 39–40.

11. Shambaugh, *China's Communist Party*, 50.

12. Shambaugh, *China's Communist Party*, 65.

13. Titus C. Chen, "China's Reaction to the Colored Revolutions: Adaptive Authoritarianism in Full Swing," *Asian Perspectives* 34, no. 2 (2010): 5–51.

14. Cited in Jamie FlorCruz, "China Yields to Protests When Stability Matters," *CNN.com*, May 1, 2011.

15. Chen, "China's Reaction to the Colored Revolutions, 16–17.

16. Vivienne Shue, "Legitimacy Crisis in China?" in *Chinese Politics: State, Society and the Market*, ed. Peter Hays Gries and Stanley Rosen (New York: Routledge, 2010).

17. Dali L. Yang, *Remaking the Chinese Leviathan: Market Transition and the Politics of Governance in China* (Stanford: Stanford University Press, 2004).

18. Yang, *Remaking the Chinese Leviathan*, 150.

19. James C. Scott, *Weapons of the Weak: Everyday Forms of Peasant Resistance* (New Haven, CT: Yale University Press, 1985), 338.

20. Guobin Yang, *The Power of the Internet in China: Citizen Activism Online* (New York: Columbia University Press, 2009).

21. Zhao Suisheng, "China's Pragmatic Nationalism: Is It Manageable?" *Washington Quarterly* 29, no. 1 (2005): 131.

22. See Shirk, *China*.

23. Yuezhi Zhao, *Communication in China*, 302.

24. Evan Osnos, "Angry Youth: The New Generation's Neocon Nationalists," *New Yorker*, July 28, 2008.

25. Zhao Suisheng, "The Olympics and Chinese Nationalism," *China Security* 4, no. 3 (2008): 48–57.

26. Interview with international relations professor, Beijing, September 3, 2006.

27. Zhao Suisheng, "The Olympics and Chinese Nationalism," 141.

28. Shi Tianjian, "Democratic Values Supporting an Authoritarian System," in *How East Asians View Democracy*, ed. Yun-han Chu, Larry Diamond, Andrew J. Nathan, and Doh Chull Shin (New York: Columbia University Press, 2008), xv, 219–21.

29. Century Weekly Editorial, "Social Signs Point China to the Rule of Law," *Caixin Weekly Online*, June 13, 2011.

30. "China's Crackdown," *Economist*, April 16, 2011.

31. Mao Yushi, "Where Does Chinese People's Resentment Come From?" *China Elections and Governance Blog*, May 18, 2010.

32. Following tactics that emerged in the city of Xiamen in 2007, largely non-violent mass protests in the northeastern city of Dalian in August 2011 illustrated the ability of local citizens to successfully advocate the closure of a local chemical factory. Between late December 2011 and early January 2012, in the southern city of Wukan, local residents aggressively took over government headquarters and, after a tense standoff with security forces and local leaders, eventually negotiated for the removal of corrupt local leaders. See "A Dangerous Year: Economic Conditions and Social Media Are Making Protest More Common in China—at a Delicate Time for the Country's Rulers," *The Economist*, January 28, 2012.

13

Culture Industry, Power, and the Spectacle of China's "Confucius Institutes"

Lionel M. Jensen

> The building of Chinese soft power has occurred at the juncture of U.S. soft power declining as a consequence of the Iraq War. The medium that China has chosen to boost its soft power is, interestingly, akin to that of the American one through culture—albeit not in the form of moving pictures, but rather in the form of language teaching that has the name of Confucius written all over it.
>
> —Xiaolin Guo

No one watching the first televised event of the 2008 Summer Olympics can forget that night. Amid an enveloping haze and a dizzying array of colored lights, historical pageantry, projected images, and imaginative pyrotechnics, the city of Beijing gave the world the most spectacular opening ceremonies of the modern Olympiad. More than fifteen thousand performers, among them 2,008 drummers for the first sequence alone, made this the largest costumed entertainment in Olympic history. A program conceived and reconceived over two years by the filmmaker Zhang Yimou, this overture to the multiple movements of the Olympics' 302 competitions was a visually breathtaking celebration of China's "5000 years of continuous culture." More than this, however, the essential "Chineseness" of the pageant was thematically choreographed with video images of numberless faces from around the world that appeared on stadium screens. The audience of 91,000 and the millions who later watched on tape delay were awestruck.

The world audience should not have been surprised. Even with the many logistical challenges posed by orchestrating this one event, not to mention the futuristic architectural transformation of the Beijing cityscape, spectacle is something China does especially well. Think of lifting nearly three hundred million people out of absolute poverty in the last two decades, or the construction of the Three Gorges Dam, or the creation of the State Internet Information Office, or the completion of the South to North water transfer project that may ensure greater availability of water for the parched inhabitants of Beijing. China itself is a spectacle, and it enjoys global prominence as such. Since that memorable opening event, the country has gone on to host the most successful and visionary World Expo in Shanghai while becoming the second leading economy in the world and making Confucius (Kongzi) the global icon of Chinese culture and language learning in more than 660 Confucius Institute and Confucius Classroom sites across the planet.

This chapter will examine China's $10 billion export "culture industry" of Confucius Institutes and their role in strategic public relations, one linked directly to the exercise of political power yet also consonant with domestic cultural developments. These institutes are the cornerstones of an ambitious international rebranding enterprise by the Chinese government built from a diplomatic strategy reminiscent of one employed effectively by the United States for many decades. Moreover, much to the disquiet of its cash-strapped global competitors, it appears to be working. Its most visible cultural symbol is Kongzi, since 1687 better known as "Confucius." The significance of this symbol for its official Communist Party handlers, however, is not a settled matter, if one may judge from the recent placement and relocation of a thirty-one-foot bronze image of the sage at Tiananmen Square. So even as the figure of Confucius is uniformly exported to the world as a symbol of intercultural communication, what it symbolizes is a subject of political debate at home (see figure 13.1).

GLOBAL SHIFTS: PERPLEXITY AND U.S.-CHINA DEPENDENCE

For the last seven years the Chinese government has reconfigured and managed its international image through handsome investment in the culture industry.[1] At the 2007 17th Party Congress, President Hu Jintao emphasized that the Communist Party must "enhance culture as part of the soft power of our country to better guarantee the people's cultural rights and interests."[2] Culture, here, is the conduit of soft power; indeed, it is what makes it "soft." And China and the Communist Party, "in accord with . . . our nation's fundamental righteousness, the Chinese people's peace loving historical and cultural tradition, and the historical tide of human progress, [will] insistently follow the path of peaceful development," he waxed poetically.[3] Here domestic and international concerns are joined by culture in the very framework of the party's "socialism with Chinese characteristics,"

Figure 13.1 Kongzi in Exile within an Inner Courtyard of the National Museum, April 30, 2011. Photograph by Arif Dirlik.

which imagines a new role for China as an international persuader and provider.

Although intended to mitigate a backlash against China's success, these efforts to persuade by politeness can still produce the very reactions they wish to avoid. Under the influence of the soft-power research group at Beijing University, party leadership has shown sensitivity to this prospect by shifting the focus of its new engagement with the world from "peaceful rise" (*heping jueqi*) to "peaceful development" (*heping fazhan*). Nonetheless, winning hearts and minds through culture and commerce in this way—that is, by way of "authoritarian capitalism"—challenges the G7 economic model. China has become a credible competitor and to some seems poised to overtake the United States as the world's dominant economic and political force.

The persistent financial difficulties of the United States have brought it closer to China in a way that few could have anticipated before the former's misadventures in war and the world financial crisis of 2008 to 2009. Until recently, the most prominent—and very expensive—aspects of the U.S. global agenda have been the defeat of terrorism, countering the radicalization of Islam, and securing more allies in these quests as it prosecutes war on two very public fronts in Afghanistan and Iraq. Meanwhile, the People's Republic of China (PRC) was differently engaged: pursuing its quiet, persistent, persuasive, and contrasting foreign policy of peaceful development, a prominent aspect of which was the founding of *Kongzi xueyuan*, "Confucius Institutes" (CIs).

With this grand initiative in support of "cultural understanding," the Chinese government dramatically lessened the distance between the United States and China by providing Chinese-language learning and culture programs in schools, universities, and urban communities lacking the resources to do so on their own. In a time of drastic state and federal budget cutting, China's largesse has answered a critical need. As such, the satisfaction of this need is likely, in the view of the Chinese government promoters of the institutes, to lead to greater knowledge about today's China. The hope is that this will in turn condition a greater receptivity to China's public diplomacy. These expected consequences are not axiomatic. Invariably, the opening of each Confucius Institute, whether in Australia, Canada, Europe, or the United States, is met with a measure of anxiety engendered by the possible effects of political ties on programming. The politics of China's intentions were the cause for a hearing on Capitol Hill early in the Obama administration.

In February of 2010, seated at a Senate Foreign Relations Committee hearing on the establishment of U.S. public diplomacy centers abroad, Secretary of State Hillary Rodham Clinton was asked by Senator Richard Lugar, a Republican from Indiana, why the United States did not undertake in China a cultural mission similar to that of the Confucius Institutes, which he noted in astonishment had in just a few years set up sixty such sites in the United States. She replied, "On the Confucius Centers. The Chinese government provides each center with a million dollars to launch, plus they cover operating expenses that exceed $200,000 per year. We don't have that kind of money in the budget." With an unanticipated candor, the Senator got his answer: we cannot compete because we're short of cash.

Today the United States does provide underwriting for Radio Free Asia, Voice of America (only through 2012), Radio Martí, and other such information conduits that do not expressly advocate on its behalf. But they do act as recognized sources for current events in Asia (including China) and other parts of the world where they fall under the radar of censors. Although the United States Information Agency (USIA) has been dissolved, the government still allots approximately $750 million annually for international broadcasting. At the above-mentioned hearing the State Department requested $14.5 million for 2011 to open eight to ten cultural centers around the world. Even as the funding was approved, it was already known that the Office of Chinese Language Council International had already invested hundreds of millions of dollars on the global outreach programs of the Confucius Institutes, nearly seventy of which had been established in the United States by 2010.

The investment gap is massive, but so are the challenges China faces in attempting to alter its "brand." In fact, the reason for the hearing was the concern of the Foreign Relations Committee members, particularly Lugar, that the Chinese government would only permit the U.S. Department of State to establish four public diplomacy centers in China. This gap is not only an economic issue but a *political* one. It revealed the even greater chasm separating the policies of a multiparty democracy and those of a single-party dictatorship, especially one with sufficient lucre to dictate conditions of bilateral relations with any and all partners. For China's current leadership, soft power is aligned with hard power even when exercised in the name of the copyrighted commercial icon of harmony, "Confucius."

KONGZI REVIVAL: CULTURE FEVER AND NATIONALISM AT HOME

One significant dimension of China's peaceful development is the government's ideological emphasis on harmony at home as well as abroad. This emphasis, which has been reiterated by party officials with such mind-numbing frequency that it is now a common source of popular parody on the Internet (see chapter 8), is part of a shift away from the "hard power" of violent repression, confrontation, and threat seen for much of the 1980s and 1990s to the "soft power" of capital, compromise, and conversation in China's relations with the outside world. (However, in the wake of the popular revolts in Egypt, Libya, Syria, Tunisia, and Yemen, the Chinese government has returned to its relentless application of force as a means of exercising control over its population.)

In China from the 1950s through the 1970s, Kongzi/Confucius was a symbol of everything bad—a traditionalist, an elitist, the paragon of "old China." There were political campaigns—some quite violent—organized around criticizing the old sage and destroying any vestige of the tradition for which he stood. And then everything changed. Chinese material life advanced steadily; an academic and then later a popular passion for fundamental (meaning prerevolutionary) cultural values brought about the return of Confucius to a prominent place in daily life. A little over twenty-five years ago, the *Zhonghua Kongzi yanjiusuo*, or China Confucius Research Institute, was founded in Beijing. Its opening in the mid-1980s occurred during a period of widespread national enthusiasm, when rural and urban incomes were rising, people's diets improved, households were made responsible for their own profit, private property was restored, and getting rich was "glorious."

In China's cities, among intellectuals, party members, students, and writers, this time (late 1984 through early 1985) was commonly known as *wenhua re* ("culture fever"). The reappearance of Kongzi coincided with an extensive cultural discussion of "roots searching" (*xungen*), the revival of traditional martial arts and meditation practices (including the now outlawed spiritual discipline, Falun Gong), and the reassessment of what it meant to be Chinese. Within this popular zeal was a smaller, but no less intense "national studies fever" (*guoxue re*), a broad cultural front of several dimensions, some government sponsored, others independent. Of course, the many representatives of this front each had different agendas—academic Confucians with financial objectives, capitalist Confucians, "New Confucians," cultural entrepreneurs, universities, and even the party-state. What drew these manifold interests together was a political opportunity to accentuate, even publicize the significance of Chinese tradition, over and against the "spiritual pollution" of the West. Scholars and party bureaucrats found themselves aligned in a complex of nationalist collaboration that persists to this day.

From the very start, the operations of the China Confucius Research Institute were underwritten by the government's Ministry of Culture. The institute's members were academics who sought legitimacy for a revival of Confucian studies under the banner of "New Confucianism" (*xinruxue*). And of the multiple cultural exuberances of this anxious era, New Confucianism, perhaps because of its alignment with the party-state, was one of the few that survived the massacre at Tiananmen and the government's subsequent campaign against bourgeois liberalism. New Confucianism endured and became a discourse with multiple constituencies.

The coemergence of this cultural revival and China's accelerated economic growth convinced many observers (domestic and international) that it was no accident. To them cause and effect were linked: the Chinese people's recuperation of traditional values of family, hard work, respect for authority, and commitment to education was responsible for China's rapid expansion. This chronology makes clear the steady recovery of Confucian prominence, and by the mid-1990s the academic promotion of Confucius had become decisively more political. The ideological conditions for a new cultural nationalism had developed in China's accelerated march away from the humiliation of Tiananmen toward the admiration of a new global economic order dependent upon cheap goods, cheap labor, and new markets.

In the fall of 1993 the government advanced another step in the politicization of culture through strategic traditional symbols. The CCP launched a national educational program in patriotism and citizenship calling special attention to what it termed "socialist spiritual civilization." This *guoqing jiaoyu*, or "state of the nation education," campaign was intended to join patriotism and socialism into the "common spiritual pillar" of the Chinese people as it reinforced the core values of the party's "socialism with Chinese characteristics." The former president Jiang Zemin believed that these values were not communist per se, but traditional—those taught by Kongzi—and so a principal focus of schooling was the genius and glory of Chinese civilization. All schools were to erect small figures of Kongzi and to pay homage to him as the exemplar of the country's enduring values.

The Confucian-focused instruction was complemented with mandatory classes in modern history and the role the Communist Party played in bringing about the overthrow of colonial powers, the liberation of the country, and the economic reforms and opening. A few years later these diverse emphases were reflected in an editorial in *Renmin ribao* (*People's Daily*) that went so far as to proclaim that "Confucianism's rule of virtues and code of ethics and authority" were "the soul of the modern enterprise culture and the key to gaining market share and attracting customers." Politics and culture were good—and good for—business!

In most parts of the world Confucius, a revered symbol of integrity, tradition, honesty, and cultural distinction, has long been a household name. He is familiar as a figure of wisdom, even if he has been the subject of lampoon or caricature. There is nothing explicitly "Confucian" in "modern enterprise culture," but the technicians of such propaganda presume that the timeless grandeur of Chinese culture and civilization lingers along with the echoes of Kongzi's name. However, the presumption is meaningless because the symbolic range of this figure is unbounded. And, of course, that is the point. With such a universal symbol, anything can be attributed to it. In fact, the many manifestations of Confucius and Confucianism cover a panorama of contradictory representations and disclose the powerful presence of Confucian studies amid this popular national enthusiasm.

For example, Professor Deng Yajun of the Beijing Institute of Genomics of the Chinese Academy of Sciences recently promoted the establishment of a "Kongzi-DNA database," offering organic evidence of family distinction. Chinese claiming Kongzi for an ancestor can now use a genetic test to prove a direct blood connection to the great ancestor of Chinese social mores. "The fifth-century BCE social philosopher's ideas of filial piety and deference to elders influence Chinese society and politics even today." According to a report in the *Shanghai Morning Post*, Professor Deng's "countrymen can establish a genetic link in a test that will cost just a little more than 1,000 yuan (\$159 U.S.)."[4] The prominence—indeed, ubiquity—of the symbol Kongzi/Confucius conveys stature; although, one might wonder how Chinese scientists have obtained the Kong clan DNA from which they could assess the genetic claims of potential descendants. This is really not so important because what we are dealing with here is not reality but a myth of cultural status and national pride, specifically abetted by the government's culture and education ministries. In fact, this myth is the generative core of the Confucius culture industry at home and abroad.

In the spring of 2006 Guo Shipeng, reporting for Reuters on the pop culture mania of contemporary China, described the phenomenon of the academic pop icon and "third most beautiful woman in China" Yu Dan with the headline, "Anxiety, Emptiness Fuel Confucius Craze in China." The author of *The Heart of the Analects* (*Lunyu xinde*), Yu Dan was catapulted to national and international celebrity on the basis of her explanation on television of what the *Analects* of Confucius means to her. (It didn't hurt that she identified herself as "apolitical" and had the formidable backing of the party's official media.) Her book's orientation is self-help: armchair philosophy rather than philosophy. But it has exerted a powerful pull on the contemporary imagination as evident in sales of the book made from these lectures; over ten million copies have been purchased and pirated.

At roughly the same time that the "Yu Dan phenomenon" (*Yu Dan xianxiang*, as she is derisively called) was on her book and lecture tour in support of *Lunyu xinde* in 2006 and 2007, China's official news agency *Xinhua* made a startling announcement:

The China Confucius Foundation (CCF) will publish a standard portrait of the ancient philosopher in September in order to give him a single, recognizable identity around the world. The CCF unveiled a draft sculpture of Confucius yesterday in Jinan, capital of east China's Shandong Province, to solicit suggestions for the final version of the portrait. "A symbol of Chinese history and culture, Confucius is widely known around the world. A standard portrait is needed so that different countries could have the same image of him," said CCF General Secretary Zhang Shuhua. The new portrait would set the standard criteria for the image of Confucius, who had been represented in different ways when Chinese were presenting statues in foreign countries, said Zhang. Relief sculptures and portraits will be produced according to the finished sculpture.[5]

The final image was revealed in September of 2006 at the commemoration of the 2,557th anniversary of Kongzi's birth and is now supposedly displayed at the approach to all of the nation's local temples to Confucius (*Kongmiao*).[6] The direct involvement of the government in the sculpture competition preceding the selection of the official image was considerable and included a directive from the CCP Central Propaganda Department that the figure's features be "moderate but strict, authoritative but not fierce, reverent and peaceful."[7] Again, what stands out is the familiar refrain of culture, image, and the force of politics, in harmony with the sound of the mass production of sameness and stability.

A reader might ask: Why should one care about a Confucian cultural revitalization ten thousand miles from the United States? First, because this phenomenon is more than a fad; Kongzi is a sensation. Many believe that Confucianism's new popularity reflects a larger social need for a morally meaningful alternative to the competitive chaos of everyday life in China. Second, because, as is evident in the ongoing government campaign to build a "harmonious society," Kongzi has become the symbol of a new national moralism. Although it is uncommon for party luminaries to invoke Kongzi openly in speaking of policy, Hu Jintao was nevertheless quoted in 2005 as saying, "Kongzi said, 'Harmony is to be cherished.'" Here, as often happens in these kinds of canned speeches, politics outran the facts: there is no such saying in the *Analects*. Third, because Kongzi and Confucianism will soon be appearing at a college, elementary school, high school, or university very near you—*every six days* another Confucius Institute is opened.

THE CONFUCIUS INSTITUTE PHENOMENON

In 2004 the Office of Chinese Language Council International (more commonly known as Hanban) announced its launch of an ambitious international cultural initiative. This government-funded program was intended to "enhance understanding of Chinese language and culture among foreigners, develop friendly relations between China and other countries, foster development of multiculturalism and contribute to the building of a harmonious world."[8] There are two different creation myths:

Version A: It began modestly that same year with the opening of the first "Confucius Institute" as a pilot program in Tashkent, Uzbekistan. The timing of the launch of this program virtually coincided with the PRC's significantly improved bilateral relations with Uzbekistan (including a new joint venture with the oil giant Sinopec), suggesting that the application of power was soft but effective.

Version B: The Foreign Ministry signaled the success of its tireless diplomatic work of the first years of the twenty-first century by announcing the founding of the inaugural *Kongzi xueyuan* in Seoul, Korea, in November 2004.[9] By placing the first institute in South Korea—but it must be noted, not in partnership with the nation's flagship institutions, Seoul National and Yonsei Universities (both declined)—the Chinese government made a strategic overture to a nation that reveres Confucianism. The timing of the announcement was also quite suitable, coming at a time when the Six-Party Talks on nuclear disarmament in North Korea were fitful rather than smooth.

Both origin stories demonstrate targeted marketing in which culture and state act as designated complements of a wider arc of international engagement; indeed, a great number of the earliest Confucius Institutes opened outside of China were similarly coordinated with commercial or diplomatic overtures. Nevertheless, there is no questioning the spectacular proliferation of these institutes that have become so familiar in the United States that they were the subjects of parody on a segment of Jon Stewart's *The Daily Show*.[10]

By 2005 there would be forty such institutes, nineteen of them in the United States. So began the implementation of a vision for intercultural communication dedicated to global familiarization with the Chinese language. According to the most recent count, there are 322 Confucius Institutes and 369 Confucius Classrooms[11] in ninety-six countries with approximately 250,000 to 400,000 enrolled students—a sign of the popularity of this outreach program for the host cities and countries, not to mention the financial largesse of the Chinese government. In fact, if one were to simply assume a standard investment of $100,000 to $250,000 per annum over a five-year period, the total expenditure for the Confucius Institutes alone would be upwards of more than a billion dollars! According to a report by the BBC published in 2006, the Chinese government had initially committed $10 billion for the global dissemination of this soft-power program.

Measured by numbers alone, the success of this initiative is colossal, even though not all of the institutes are up and running and in some cases institutes that have been founded are moribund. Still, the CI headquarters has confirmed that their current projection for future growth is one thousand Confucius Institutes by the year 2020! Chen Jinyu, former vice chair of CI headquarters, accounted for the immense international popularity of CIs: "With regards to the operations of Confucian Institutes, brand name means quality; brand name means returns. Those who enjoy more brand names will enjoy higher popularity, reputation, more social influence, and will therefore be able to generate more support from local communities."[12]

Hanban and its comprehensive program of language education and selective cultural indoctrination might be best described as "systems engineering" (*xitong gongchen*).[13] Indeed, it is a well-engineered system, one that has added its own university. From a certain angle, it is a *system* that looks very much like a business—Hanban "owns proprietorship of the name, logo, and brand of the Confucius Institutes"—but is advertised as a "nongovernmental, non-profit organization."

Hanban is actually a division of the PRC's Ministry of Education, and its particular work is governed by the thirteenth responsibility identified in the ministry's mission statement:

> To organize and guide international educational exchanges and cooperation; to formulate policies of programmes for Chinese students studying abroad and foreign students studying in China. . . . To plan, coordinate and direct the work of promoting the Chinese language in the world.[14]

It is a broad agenda to be sure. Given the administrative composition of its recently established Confucius Institute Headquarters, Hanban's ambition is expectedly grand. Dr. Xu Lin serves as the director general and CEO of CI headquarters, and she is everywhere from Africa to Europe, Canada, the United States, and Australia, usually pictured with university officials, party members, and benefactors or addressing the thousands of Confucius Institute and Confucius Classroom representatives who attend Hanban's annual Confucius Institute Conference (in 2012 they will host the seventh such international conference in Beijing).

Xu Lin's work has been tireless as a representative and officiator of concluded agreements. One can explore the range of her industry by consulting the revamped online platform for Confucius Institutes at www.chinese.cn/. She is a very lively public speaker whose constant promotional pitch on behalf of the global spread of Confucius Institutes is that it engenders cultural understanding. In a recent address in Washington, DC, she offered a curious formulation of the advantages of intercultural communication brought by Hanban, saying, "I went to two hairdressers but both failed to do my hair the way I wanted it. That's why I am here because I strongly believe that in today's global village, we should learn more from each other and understand each other better."[15] Taking Xu's comment along with Chen Jiyu's previously cited assertion about the significance of the Confucius "brand," one recognizes that there are genuine limits to the understanding encouraged by the political export of an administered "culture."

Dr. Xu may be the face of the Institutes, but she answers to a group of very highly placed CCP officials: a representative of the State Council (the highest organ of the Chinese government), Liu Yandong, who chairs the headquarters; four vice chairs who represent the Ministry of Education, Overseas Chinese Affairs for the State Council, and the Ministry of Finance; and the deputy secretary general of the State Council. In addition, the headquarters has a China Executive Council composed of more ranking members of powerful ministries: Foreign Affairs; National Development and Reform; Education; Commerce; State Administration for Radio, Film, and Television; Information Office of the State Council; and the State Language Commission. The Confucius Institute Council is composed of one representative each from Canada, France, Germany, Hungary, Japan, Kenya, New Zealand, Thailand, the United Kingdom, and the United States, in addition to five different representatives from universities in Beijing, Shandong (the putative natal province of Kongzi), and Xiamen.

Coordination between the headquarters and the rapidly expanding Confucius Classrooms and Institutes is accomplished in accord with the CI constitution and the "Guide for Directors of Confucius Institutes." Each institute must prepare an annual report, with the original foundation agreements, minutes of the meetings of the institute's board of directors (which all institutes must have), correspondence, records of students and teachers in the program, enrollment figures, publicity material, photographs, video and print records of all media coverage, and a "registration record of fixed assets and bills." They are all subject to periodic assessment by the headquarters. As well, there is an annual Confucius Institute Conference where the year's achievements are chronicled and the finalists and winner of the "Best Confucius Institute" are announced and where thousands of representatives of institutes and classrooms worldwide can exchange best practices and immerse themselves in a several-day celebration of Chinese arts and culture. The scale of the enterprise is monumental and has the mass culture appeal of investment hysteria where attendees ring out applause and exclaim with joy at the mention of the addition of new members of an expanding financial pyramid.

Every Confucius Institute is a spectacular experiment in cultural outreach: (1) the cultural and financial outreach of a Chinese concern with a U.S. or foreign counterpart; (2) the defining conception of responsibility for expanding access to and fluency in standard Chinese; (3) the widening of opportunities for travel to and study in China; (4) the creation of a new network of academic partnership enabling exchange between universities and their faculties; (5) the establishment of mechanisms for training foreign teachers in the instruction of Chinese at the primary and secondary level; and (6) the forging or enhancement of ties between U.S. higher educational institutions and the surrounding communities in which they are located. Several of these aspects make it difficult to reduce this outreach entirely to propaganda and instead suggest a constructive role by the Chinese government in the complex and changing relations in U.S. patterns of learning. But, just as well, the placement of institutes within the centers, departments, and institutes of public and private universities is *without precedent* and threatens the independent pursuit of research that is the enabling premise of higher education.

CI SETUP, PRACTICE, AND OUTCOME

It is said that Confucius Institutes are modeled very loosely on the European cultural institutes: the Alliance Française, the British Council, Instituto Cervantes, and the Goethe Institute. There are a number of similarities in their design and objectives, but I believe when one attends to operational specifics, the comparison is imperfect, explicitly because these institutes are *not* located *within* higher educational institutions. The Confucius Institute system is largely underwritten by and must report to the Chinese government. This is undoubtedly why many commentators and a number of faculty at universities that have founded CI have charged that these institutes expect their staff to report on campus activities to Chinese consulates and embassies. Therefore, they are unlike the French and German entities, for example, which are legally independent cultural institutes. Another very prominent difference between them is that only the Confucius Institutes insist on institutional partnerships with host institutions such as cities, secondary schools, and in particular universities. This is not to say that there isn't a strategic impulse to promote cultural understanding behind the presence and programming of any of the famous European cultural exchange institutes; however, they do not serve as agents of their governments. In the case of the Confucius Institutes this simply cannot be said, and this fact is the cause of concern.

All but a very few of the CIs in the United States have been established at state universities, like the University of Maryland at College Park, where the first of these was founded at the close of 2004, or the University of Iowa in 2005 (see table 13.1). There is an explicit application procedure via review by Hanban, the website of which provides PDF versions of the application form. Potential foreign university partners and schools may apply for the funding, curricula, and teachers necessary to establish either a Confucius Classroom or an Institute.

A glance at this list of the Confucius Institutes and Confucius Classrooms opened since 2005 discloses the dominance of public institutions, often in states where funding for higher education is insufficient to sponsor new programs or to hire new faculty positions in foreign languages, even if that language is, like Chinese, in very high demand. Smaller universities in smaller communities, such as Kennesaw State, Middle Tennessee State, or Alfred, now have Confucius Institutes and basic Chinese language. Suddenly, with the help of Hanban you can add a teacher or teachers of Chinese, obtain textbooks and a model curriculum, and all you have to do as the host institution is provide modest support.

In some instances, especially in the case of the most distinguished U.S. private schools (Columbia, Stanford, Yale, University of Chicago, University of Pennsylvania), direct (and in a number of instances very persistent)

Table 13.1.   Confucius Institutes in the United States, 2004–2011

Location	Name	Date Opened
Akron, Ohio	Confucius Institute at the University of Akron	November 17, 2008
Alfred, New York	Confucius Institute at Alfred University	April 30, 2009
Anchorage, Alaska	Confucius Institute at the University of Alaska Anchorage	November 18, 2008
Ann Arbor, Michigan	Confucius Institute at the University of Michigan	November 5, 2009
Atlanta, Georgia	Confucius Institute at Georgia State University	October 15, 2010
Atlanta, Georgia	Confucius Institute in Atlanta	
Benton Harbor, Michigan	Confucius Institute at Western Michigan University	November 23, 2009
Binghamton, New York	Confucius Institute of Chinese Opera at the State University of New York at Binghamton	November 6, 2009
Boston, Massachusetts	University of Massachusetts Confucius Institute at Boston	November 2006
Bowling Green, Kentucky	Confucius Institute at West Kentucky University	May 20, 2011
Buffalo, New York	Confucius Institute at State University of New York at Buffalo	April 9, 2010
Charlotte, North Carolina	Confucius Institute at Pfeiffer University	December 2009
Chicago, Illinois	Confucius Institute in Chicago	May 10, 2006
Chicago, Illinois	Confucius Institute at the University of Chicago	June 1, 2010
Cleveland, Ohio	Confucius Institute at Cleveland State University	April 9, 2008
Clinton, South Carolina	Confucius Institute at Presbyterian University	November 6, 2009
College Park, Maryland	Confucius Institute at the University of Maryland	November 2005
College Station, Texas	Confucius Institute at Texas A&M University	April 28, 2008
Columbia, South Carolina	Confucius Institute at the University of South Carolina	November 17, 2008
Conway, Arkansas	Confucius Institute at the University of Central Arkansas	September 18, 2008
Dallas, Texas	Confucius Institute at the University of Texas at Dallas	October 2007
Denver, Colorado	Confucius Institute at the Community College of Denver	September 8, 2007

Location	Name	Date Opened
Detroit, Michigan	Confucius Institute at Wayne State University	January 31, 2008
Durham, New Hampshire	Confucius Institute at the University of New Hampshire	October 26, 2010
East Lansing, Michigan	Confucius Institute at Michigan State University	May 2006
Eugene, Oregon	Confucius Institute at the University of Oregon	October 1, 2010
Fairfax, Virginia	Confucius Institute at George Mason University	January 6, 2009
Memphis, Tennessee	Confucius Institute at the University of Memphis	August 2009
Honolulu, Hawaii	Confucius Institute at the University of Hawai'i at Manoa	November 6, 2006
Indianapolis, Indiana	Confucius Institute in Indianapolis	August 2007
Iowa City, Iowa	Confucius Institute at the University of Iowa	September 22, 2006
Kalamazoo, Michigan	Confucius Institue at Western Michigan University	August 2009
Kennesaw, Georgia	Confucius Institute at Kennesaw State University	August 17, 2009
Kingston, Rhode Island	Confucius Institute at the University of Rhode Island	September 16, 2007
Las Cruces, New Mexico	Confucius Institute at New Mexico State University	August 2007
Lawrence, Kansas	Confucius Institute at the University of Kansas	May 4, 2006
Lexington, Kentucky	Confucius Institute at Kentucky University	November 6, 2010
Lincoln, Nebraska	Confucius Institute at the University of Nebraska–Lincoln	October 29, 2007
Los Angeles, California	Confucius Institute at the University of California, Los Angeles	August 16, 2007
Menlo Park, California	Confucius Institute at Stanford University	December 15, 2009
Mesa, Arizona	Confucius Institute at Arizona State	October 2, 2007
Miami, Florida	Confucius Institute at Miami Dade College	April 29, 2010
Minneapolis, Minnesota	Confucius Institute at the University of Minnesota	September 19, 2008
Missoula, Montana	Confucius Institute at the University of Montana	January 25, 2010

(*continued*)

Table 13.1. *(continued)*

Location	Name	Date Opened
Murfreesboro, Tennessee	Confucius Institute at Middle Tennessee State University	April 21, 2010
New Brunswick, New Jersey	Confucius Institute at Rutgers	November 9, 2007
Newark, Delaware	Confucius Institute at the University of Delaware	October 29, 2010
New York, New York	Confucius Institute at the China Institute	August 2006
New York, New York	Confucius Institute at Columbia University	December 14, 2009
New York, New York	Confucius Institute at State College of Optometry	October 27, 2010
Norman, Oklahoma	Confucius Institute at the University of Oklahoma	August 2006
Oxford, Ohio	Confucius Institute at Miami University	August 2, 2007
Pittsburgh, Pennsylvania	Confucius Institute at the University of Pittsburgh	September 26, 2007
Platteville, Wisconsin	Confucius Institute at the University of Wisconsin–Platteville	April 12, 2008
Pleasantville, New York	Confucius Institute at Pace University	June 2, 2006
Portland, Oregon	Confucius Institute at Portland State University	May 16, 2007
Raleigh, North Carolina	Confucius Institute at North Carolina State University	April 23, 2007
Salt Lake City, Utah	Confucius Institute at the University of Utah	October 23, 2007
San Antonio, Texas	Confucius Institute at the University of Texas at San Antonio	February 10, 2010
San Diego, California	Confucius Institute at San Diego State University	March 26, 2009
San Francisco, California	Confucius Institute at San Francisco State University	April 15, 2005
Seattle, Washington	Confucius Institute of the State of Washington	April 26, 2010
St. Louis, Missouri	Confucius Institute at Webster University	March 5, 2008
Stony Brook, New York	Confucius Institute at Stony Brook University	October 16, 2008
Tampa, Florida	Confucius Institute at the University of South Florida	March 2, 2008
Tempe, Arizona	Confucius Institue of Arizona State University	October 22, 2007

Location	Name	Date Opened
Toledo, Ohio	Confucius Institute at the University of Toledo	December 2, 2009
Troy, Alabama	Confucius Institute at Troy University	September 3, 2008
Tucson, Arizona	Confucius Institute at the University of Arizona	May 16, 2008
University Park, Pennsylvania	Confucius Institute at Pennsylvania State University	September 26, 2007
Valparaiso, Indiana	Confucius Institute at Valparaiso University	February 14, 2008
West Lafayette, Indiana	Confucius Institute at Purdue University	

appeals were made by Hanban to establish an institutional partnership. Stanford, Chicago, and Columbia all decided to partner with a Chinese university under Hanban's aegis.

In 2010 Stanford and Chicago broke significant new ground for Hanban by announcing the establishment of Confucius Institutes. However, in each case the deliberations leading to this decision yielded counterproposals from the U.S. universities demonstrating an awareness of their distinguished status and a corresponding willingness to create new uses from the funding. Stanford, for example, which received in excess of $4 million, granted that the Confucius Institute would "support and promote teaching, research and scholarship relating to Chinese language, literature, and culture." Their Department of East Asian Languages and Cultures agreed to provide the space for the institute and to set up a Confucius Institute reading room, the volumes for which (as is always a contractually specified item in the Memorandum of Understanding) would be provided by Hanban. This is consistent with the global practice; however, Stanford added a new dimension: the first Confucius Institute endowed chair, the responsibilities of which include "teaching and advising in literary theory, classical poetry, classical Chinese and other genres, at both undergraduate and graduate levels."[16] The University of Chicago decided that it would accept the funding for the purposes of increasing the number of Chinese instructors and funding graduate fellowships and dissertation research and travel. The public announcement included another first: the use of Confucius Institute funding to underwrite "research." It was met with vigorous faculty opposition and a campuswide petition drive.[17] Yet it prevailed.

This was not so for the University of Pennsylvania (Penn) or the University of British Columbia (UBC). In the case of Penn the invitation from Hanban was a source of considerable provocation. The university's upper administration, in concert with Hanban, attempted to establish a Confucius Institute in the Graduate School of Education. The initiative was advanced without consultation with the Chinese studies faculty, who upon learning that the final agreement papers were being endorsed, exposed the proceedings, thus closing the door on the CI prospect. Although startled by the furtive manner in which the university and Hanban had conducted negotiations, the China faculty was strongly opposed to the very idea of the institute, saying, "we did not want a CI on our campus to compete with our own programs, to introduce inferior pedagogy, and to engage in various unwelcome 'soft power' initiatives . . . such as are going on everywhere else there are CIs."

UBC, one of Canada's flagship institutions with an eminent faculty and program in Chinese studies, was also approached but declined the offer. According to sources at UBC, there was persistent pressure from the university's higher administration as Hanban made three different appeals to establish an institute. A key difference in this case was the knowledge of the Chinese studies faculty, who admitted that the degree of closeness between Hanban and the Chinese government was a real concern, but just as important was a sense that the additional funding and staffing were of little value to UBC, where the Chinese language and literature programs were already fully developed. To this juncture (spring 2012) those universities that rejected Hanban's offers are the singular exceptions to the global rule of acceptance, with the most recent being Dickinson State University, whose faculty voted against the establishment of a Confucius Institute after it had been approved by the North Dakota Board of Education.[18]

In universities where there is an already well-established and professionally staffed East Asian studies program that confers doctoral degrees, for instance at UCLA, the approach by Hanban may not be rebuffed, as it was at Berkeley. Although in the case of the UCLA Confucius Institute, its establishment resembled the pattern followed at Penn and was not without controversy, as the faculty were on break and the initiative was foisted upon the university with the assistance of deans and administrators. This helps to explain why the CI there was set up in a wing of the university at some remove from the Asian Languages and Cultures Department. This is for a very good reason, and one that is broached in most every circumstance in which a CI initiative is proposed by Hanban with the assistance of a university administration: competition between a university's own program and that offered by Hanban is undesirable. The Confucius Institute at UCLA is housed in the School of Education, where a cooperative endeavor in the training of 122 newly certified teachers of Chinese for instruction in U.S. middle schools and high schools (also involving the College Board) has generated impressive results—now "school districts around the country [are able] to request a Mandarin teacher for a one- to three-year period."[19]

Usually, the initial investment from Hanban is for five years, after which the home institution may apply for renewal of the arrangement; extension of funding is not automatic. Customary financial arrangements for the establishment of an institute call for cost sharing, with Hanban expecting the amount they contribute to be matched by the home institution. However, there is some flexibility in these practices as demonstrated by the University of Chicago, which refused to accept a matching funds agreement and insisted instead on an initial direct outlay by Hanban of $2,000,000 over a five-year interval. Confucius Institutes are nonprofit enterprises, but there is an implied understanding that it is preferred that the foreign universities and communities find ways to offer programming that could offset the costs.

Standard initial investments, as mentioned previously, are between $50,000 to $100,000 per year over five years. Yet, as in the case of the University of Nebraska's Confucius Institute, the startup funds of $100,000 were complemented by an additional $270,000 in year three. Hanban selects the Chinese-language teachers, usually in concert with a partner institution in China. It also pays the salary and the travel expenses of the teachers, while the hosts arrange housing and cover the costs of infrastructure, which include the work visa, transportation, and food.[20] The establishment logistics vary little from setting to setting. Contracts are standardized and with the renewed vigor with which Hanban has seen to its professionalization following numerous complaints in the first several years, one can travel (as have I and my research assistants) to any number of Confucius Institute sites and find them to be virtually identical in curricula, events, instruction, and programming. An attentive browse through the homepages of any of the U.S. and European Confucius Institutes demonstrates this uniformity as well. Once agreements have been formalized for the venture, the host institution is presented with a brass plaque bearing its official title in the foreign language and the copyrighted "Confucius Institute" tile in Chinese: *Kongzi xueyuan* (see figure 13.2). The standard photograph of officials from Hanban, the Chinese partner university, and the host university at the ritual unveiling of the Confucius Institute plaque confirms official membership in the global network.

In the United States, upper-level university administrators—chancellors, presidents, provosts, vice presidents—can recognize the advantages offered by joint academic ventures with Hanban. If, like Kansas and Maryland, where there are well-established programs in East Asian studies and in Chinese language, but also a state or federal mandate to offer outreach education at urban and rural school districts or provide programs for teacher training and enrichment, a Confucius Institute is a perfect fit. From the vantage of a university leader the politics doesn't matter all that much. It is preferable to be meaningfully engaged in China than not. And one would

Figure 13.2. Formal Unveiling Ceremony, Confucius Institute, San Diego State University. Photograph courtesy of Confucius Institute at SDSU.

be very hard-pressed to find such leaders whose portfolio did not involve diversity, global initiatives, and internationalization. Establishing a prominent public mark of commitment to China and to the dissemination of Chinese-language learning is simply very canny academic business. As well, some university administrators believe that such agreements offer genuine prospects for productive research collaboration in which both the host and the partner university may benefit. This prospect has yet to bear fruit.

The pattern of developing these relationships with Hanban very often involves a top-down approach institutionally. Presidents or chancellors excited by the prospects of funds, new staff, and comparatively modest or negligible investment, not to mention the enhanced prestige of establishing a Chinese program and setting up faculty exchanges with China and scholarships for students to study abroad, will strongly encourage their deans to consider the prospects. This upper-level administrative initiative and pressure appears to be the norm in the founding of most Confucius Institutes. This fact may also help to explain the composition of so many of the CI advisory boards, in which there is a majority representation of high-level administrators and a comparative dearth of Sinologists or Chinese studies faculty.[21]

The benefits of establishing the institute are not limited to just the foreign university, its Chinese partner school, and the immediate community. Many CIs employ or arrange for the use of satellite technology to provide interactive video learning of Chinese to schools that cannot afford a teacher but where the demand for Chinese is marked. For example, the high schools of several communities in southwestern Pennsylvania (Blackhawk, Moon Area, Western Beaver, and Beaver Falls), along with two dozen others across the state, have benefited from this arrangement because of the Confucius Institute outreach program of the University of Pittsburgh. There are many such stories all over the United States, and they remind us of Hanban's chief objective to promote the development of Chinese-language learning.

There is usually a Chinese point person who can assist university administrators in seeing the advantages of such an arrangement; it is not unusual for this person to be named the director of the institute once it is founded. They may not be scholars of Chinese language or history or literature; indeed, they only need to have completed an undergraduate degree. They are very often ethnically Chinese or Chinese-American—a consequence of the eligibility criteria for directors, which states "foreign directors should ideally communicate in Chinese in their daily lives." All CI directors are vetted by Hanban and appointed by approval of its board. Once the individual institutes are established, some establish links on their homepage inviting contributions of any denomination to defray a portion of the operating costs.

Some of the programming, such as a calligraphy demonstration or a Chinese singing performance by young students or a New Year's celebration including a lion dance (de rigueur), is free, while others such as Chinese-language classes require a fee, the costs for which range from thirty to three hundred dollars for instruction plus materials. Most institutes provide a range of traditional programming such as acrobatics, Beijing opera, dance troupes, historical and family-friendly films, storytellers, and musical performances with traditional Chinese instruments such as *erhu* (two-string fiddle), *pipa* (four- or five-string lute), and *qin* (seven-string zither) along with Chinese vocalists. It is customary for a new Confucius Institute opening or convening conferences in Chinese studies or playing a part in invited lectures to host a special program of entertainment before the conference or lecture. In these cases a special program is designed to set the mood for the event such as the one hosted in February 2010 by the Confucius Institutes of Valparaiso University and the University of Memphis, at which the anthropologist of China Dr. Ohlier Povet was the honoree. The musical program for the event was appropriately titled "Harmony: A Concert Dedicated to the Confucius Institute at the University of Memphis Featuring Guest Soloists from China." The political theme is the musical theme, is the cultural theme, is the *political* theme.

CONFUCIUS INSTITUTES AND THE
MEANING OF GLOBAL OUTREACH

With so many institutes and classrooms popping up around the world and in the United States in particular, the Hanban initiative usually engenders commentary, more suspicious than appreciative. Certainly, in this moment of reactionary U.S. politics where the religion and cultural background of a sitting president are seriously questioned,[22] the expansion of a Chinese presence in secondary and undergraduate education is, for some, a cause for concern. This concern, in most cases, is based upon a Trojan Horse theory in which, as Peter Schmidt has observed, "China sees the promotion of its culture and its chief language, standard Mandarin, as a means of expanding its economic, cultural, and diplomatic reach."[23] Of course, this is *exactly* what the Chinese government is doing through Hanban's promotion of its language-learning services. Li Changchun, the propaganda chief of the CCP, has affirmed as much in stating that the Confucius Institutes are "an important part of China's overseas propaganda setup."[24]

Because the CIs are instruments of propaganda, they are necessarily controversial and should be anathema to colleges and universities. The CCP is indeed using these institutes as the thin edge of a wedge to argue its case for benefaction not confrontation as it persuades its foreign partners that it is serious about "cultural understanding." The controversy comes from particular consequences that are at odds with the untrammeled expression of ideas on a range of issues, some of which the Chinese government has never favored. The early versions of the Memorandum of Understanding— with reference to which all institutes are founded—states that the signatories accept the One-China Policy. Internal Hanban documents, secured by faculty in some institutions where applications were underway for the establishment of an institute, offer details of how CI representatives are to report to Chinese consulates and embassies. Such documents have also revealed a pattern of discriminatory hiring by Hanban of their teachers and staff. This is indeed disturbing. There is good reason to be cautious, but as yet there is no overwhelming evidence that politics has trumped the educational mission. There have been a few actual and near controversies that were the consequence of the political beliefs of the funding agency that ran afoul of the universities, the vitality of which depends upon an academic freedom unfamiliar in China.

To date there have been the incidents in the United States discussed above. But so far there have not been any events in which the academic freedom of the host university was *explicitly* threatened by authorities of Hanban. Most directors have gone on record in this regard to affirm the independence of their institutes.[25] This, though, does not mean that U.S. Confucius Institute directors do not take special care in arranging programming that is uncontroversial in the eyes of their benefactor. By this I mean that their mindfulness of the funding source has affected consideration of what is appropriate programming. At its worst, this amounts to a persistent self-censorship, a practice common to the political survival experience of Chinese citizens today.

There have been two very prominent events in Israel and Sweden that have cast an unflattering light on the overreach of the Confucius Institutes, Hanban, or Chinese embassy authorities. This kind of academic self-censorship, which is an issue for a good number of U.S. China scholars, seemed to be the case with Yoav Ariel in the spring of 2008. Ariel, in his capacity as dean of students (and a Sinologist), peremptorily closed a Falun Gong art exhibition at Tel Aviv University without having seen the exhibit. Students were appalled and filed suit against him for violation of academic freedom. In October 1, 2009, the presiding judge of the Tel Aviv District Court announced that the University "violated freedom of expression and succumbed to pressure from the Chinese embassy." *Ha'aretz*, a liberal daily, quoted the judge's finding that "the plaintiffs proved that the Chinese embassy finances various activities at the university including scholarships for students who study in China, a campus Confucius center where students can study Chinese, and conferences in Buddhism and Chinese philosophy. It seems that Professor Ariel feared endangering these activities, and therefore closed the exhibit."[26]

In a case involving the University of Stockholm, academic freedom was once again the concern when university staff made a formal complaint that the Confucius Institute was being used by the Chinese embassy to conduct surveillance, disseminate political propaganda, and "inhibit research on sensitive areas such as Falun gong"—essentially, a platform for spying.[27] They insisted that the university terminate its contract with Hanban and place the Nordic Confucius Institute outside of the university. While an independent review of the charges was inconclusive, the University of Stockholm did create a different format for the CI. Events of this kind offer confirmation of the criticisms of Hanban and the Confucius Institutes made by observers in Australia, Canada, India, and the United States: that China's investment in cultural understanding through language and culture studies will compromise the candid discussion, inquiry, and research that are essential to university life.

Nonetheless, concerns about academic freedom do not overwhelm the majority who find in CI an opportunity to enrich their personal experience and deepen their understanding of a place and a people they admire. And many parents of children learning Chinese in 42 schools of the Chicago Public Schools, are genuinely excited by the prospect of their kids learning Chinese, thus preparing them for the realities of the future. They probably know little about the background of what seems to be a sudden gift from above. The very idea that their children have the opportunity to learn a language critical to understanding a complex and rapidly changing world is reason in itself, regardless of the specific quality of the pedagogy, to appreciate Confucius Classrooms and Institutes. Moreover, as the College Board and the Asia Society engage Hanban in a targeted collaboration to accelerate the increase in the number of effective Chinese-language teachers in primary and secondary schools across the United States, it is very likely that the excitement of Chicago parents represents current popular sentiment.

With China's $6.9 billion "global media drive," the Confucius Institutes enterprise has broadened into international educational video. CI online instructional programming and SCOLA (Satellite Communications for Learning Associated) formed a partnership in January 2009, and SCOLA has been televising CI Chinese instructional videos on its Channel 3 at all participating colleges and universities. Thus, whenever foreign-language learning is underway and cultural competency is the emphasis, U.S. students have immediate access to the instructional media of Hanban, that is, in addition to the material in their own university or high school Chinese classes. CI headquarters has also launched a new universal online platform for aspiring Chinese-language learners at http://www.college.chinese.cn/college/en/, which claims "the best quality Chinese language resources in the world."

THE ROAD AHEAD

The oft-heard refrain *gaige kaifang* ("reform and openness") has guided the CCP in its fitful thirty-year struggle to define in accomplishment the meaning of this phrase. The Confucius Institutes may be recognized as the embodiment of the nation's urge to open itself to the world, to share its ample cultural resources, and to recover the international stature China once enjoyed. The ideological foundations of CI are not new, and the dramatic commitments the government has made in establishing them are consistent with the reform aspirations that brought Deng Xiaoping to prominence in 1979. What is different now is that the policy of "openness" has acquired scope and dimension greater than its inventor could have imagined, in fact great enough to put the experiment with reform in touch with peoples everywhere.

Persistent doubts about the real intentions of the Confucius Institutes and the suspicion that they will become a source for indoctrination rather than education remain. Concerns about public program content specifically, that lectures or films about "The Three Ts"—Tibet, Taiwan, and Tiananmen—will be forbidden, have not been confirmed; although I do know from private conversations with those involved in programming at some CIs that trepidation is engendered by the prospect of such events. There is also concern that support for graduate fellowships drawn from institute funds could influence the direction of research. But so far there have been no *documented* cases of this kind of conflict.

After-the-fact explanations of the contemporary moral relevance of Kongzi and Confucianism for alienated Chinese offer little reassurance to China's critics at home and abroad who warn of the perils of propaganda and mind control and inveigh against Hanban's systematic reduction of the diverse cultures of Chinese tradition to a uniform, quaint commodity. The actual content of the Chinese culture of Confucius Institutes will invariably be a concern because the impulse to export it on such a monumental scale even for noble educational purpose can only lead to a mass production inseparable from commerce and politics. The term most appropriate for CI programming is "culturetainment." The concept gets at the abridgment of Chinese civilization in the name of digestible forms of cultural appeal that can be readily shipped overseas. To that extent, it is possible the Chinese-language education provided by CI will fall short of standard proficiency.

In writing about the spectacle of Confucius Institutes, it is difficult to avoid skepticism or mistrust. The reasons for this suspicion are complicated, but I know that it has much to do with the singular inappropriateness of their institutional presence *within* schools, colleges, and universities and the fact that there is *no* separation between the political and the pedagogical. I do not mean to be harsh—people have to start somewhere in learning a language like Chinese, which, like English, is extremely difficult. The Confucius Institute culture industry does *produce* language learning, and it is in this particular respect that the true measurement of its future success will be obtained, particularly if its students can demonstrate high-level proficiency in Chinese as measured by a *genuinely* independent and *objectively* scored examination. Of course, without meaningful evidence of *real* student achievement, China, Confucius, and Confucianism will be forever understood as a conceptually flawed enterprise corrupted by cash.

One can only hope, that the more noble purposes of human contact through learning will become salient as the international programs of Confucius Institutes mature in the years ahead. Then, Five-Year Plans may well be overcome by a wider expanse of intercultural communication conducted in the democracy of a language containing the grand diversity of China's peoples and their many cultures, a diversity that defies mass production as it vexes authoritarian rule.

SUGGESTIONS FOR FURTHER READING

Books and Articles

Brady, Anne-Marie, ed. *China's Thought Management* (New York: Routledge, 2011).

Guo, Xiaolin. *Repackaging Confucius: PRC Public Diplomacy and the Rise of Soft Power*. Stockholm: Institute for Security and Development Policy, Asia Paper Series, 2008.

Paradise, James F. "China and International Harmony: The Role of Confucius Institutes in Bolstering Beijing's Soft Power." *Asian Survey* 49, no. 4 (July–August 2009): 647–69.

Redden, Elizabeth. "Confucius Says...Debate over Chinese-Funded Institutions at American Universities," *Inside Higher Ed*, January 4, 2012, http://www.inside highered.com/news/2012/01/04/debate-over-chinese-funded-institutes-american -universities.

Siow, Maria Wey-Shen. "China's Confucius Institutes: Crossing the River by Feeling the Stones." *Asia Pacific Bulletin*, no. 91, January 6, 2011, http://www.eastwestcenter .org/fileadmin/stored/pdfs/apb091_1.pdf.

Starr, Don. "Chinese Language Education in Europe: The Confucius Institutes." *European Journal of Education* 44, no. 1 (March 2009): part 1, 65–82.

Websites

China Daily, http://europe.chinadaily.com.cn/
China Media Project, http://cmp.hku.hk/
The Diplomat, http://the-diplomat.com/
Guardian, www.guardian.co.uk
Xinhua, http://www.xinhuanet.com/english2010/

NOTES

1. *Culture industry* here refers to the concept as advanced by Theodor Adorno and Max Horkheimer in "The Culture Industry: Enlightenment as Mass Deception," who

employed it to describe the ruthless reproduction of the uniformity of mass culture under monopoly capitalism. Theodor Adorno and Max Horkheimer, *Dialectic of Enlightenment* (New York: Continuum Books, 1972).

2. Hu Jintao, "Hold High the Great Banner of Socialism with Chinese Characteristics and Strive for New Victories in Building a Moderately Prosperous Society in All Respects," report delivered at the 17th National Congress of the Chinese Communist Party, October 15, 2007.

3. "Zhongyang waishi gongzuo huiyi zai jing juxing: Hu Jintao zuo zhongyao jianghua" (Hu Jintao Gives an Important Speech at the Communist Party's Central Work Foreign Affairs Conference, Beijing), *Xinhua*, August 23, 2006, http://news.xinhuanet.com/politics/2006-08/23/content_4999294.htm.

4. "DNA Test to Clear Up Confucius Confusion," *Reuters*, June 17, 2006, reprinted in *China Daily*, June 18, 2006, http://www.chinadaily.com.cn/china/2006-06/18/content_619560.htm. It must be pointed out in this instance that 1,000 yuan is a substantial sum of money for many Chinese.

5. "China Unveils Standard Portrait of Confucius," *Xinhua*, September 23, 2006, http://news.xinhuanet.com/english/2006-09/23/content_5129591.htm.

6. The official announcement was covered in *Xinhua*, which provided two images of the "standard portrait." See "China Unveils."

7. Quoted in Guo Xiaolin, "Repackaging Confucius: PRC Public Diplomacy and the Rise of Soft Power," Institute for Security and Development Policy, Stockholm, 2008, 35.

8. "What Is Confucius Institute?" Office of Chinese Language Council International (Hanban), July 2, 2010, http://english.hanban.org/article/2010-07/02/content_153912.htm.

9. It is not always easy to obtain detailed or reliable information about the operations of Confucius Institutes. The original funding outlays to partner institutions are not usually stated, and the promissory arrangements in subsequent years are ambiguous. From conversations with principals, some clerical staff, program participants, students, faculty, and others (who will remain anonymous), reading annual reports from a number of Confucius Institute sites, operations can be reconstructed. Hard evidence of financing and political ties is scarce, and it seems clear that it is not common practice to disclose funding details.

10. *The Daily Show with Jon Stewart*, June 7, 2010, http://www.thedailyshow.com/watch/mon-june-7-2010/socialism-studies.

11. Confucius Classrooms are the local hub for outreach education in Chinese at the primary and secondary levels of instruction. They are initiated via funding from Hanban and provide language and culture teaching materials, as well as a Chinese teacher for foreign classrooms. They are often developed out of university- or city-affiliated Confucius Institutes. The Asia Society, with Hanban, has set up its own set of Confucius Classrooms at sixty schools across the United States. They expect that these select schools will become "the model sites for the teaching and learning of Chinese."

12. Don Starr, "Chinese Language Education in Europe: The Confucius Institutes," *European Journal of Education* 44, no. 1 (March 2009): part 1, 65–82, esp. 78–79.

13. This was the description of the CCP's national program in patriotic education provided by the former, and now imprisoned, mayor of Beijing Chen Xitong.

14. "The Responsibilities of the Ministry of Education," Ministry of Education of the People's Republic of China, http://www.moe.edu.cn/publicfiles/business/htmlfiles/moe/moe_2797/200907/49988.html.

15. Tan Yingzi and Li Xiaokun, "Confucius Schools Bridge Cultural Divides," *China Daily*, April 28, 2010, http://www.chinadaily.com.cn/china/2010-04/28/content_9782204.htm.

16. "Confucius Institute Founded," *Horizons* newsletter, Center for East Asian Studies, Stanford University, 2010, 1. The dean who assumed the position of director of the Institute was pressured by the Hanban officials to avoid mentioning Tibet in regard to this new endowed chair. The dean declined to agree to this demand.

17. The faculty protest against the opening of a Confucius Institute was bound up with a number of other initiatives that signaled the sacrifice of intellectual integrity and academic freedom to the goals of an expanding corporatization at the University of Chicago. The relevant information on this debate may be accessed at http://uchicago-cores.org/debate/june14_response/.

18. "Dickinson State U. Reverses Decision on Confucius Institute," *Chronicle of Higher Education* February 9, 2012, http://chronicle.com/blogs/ticker/dickinson-state-u-reverses-decision-on-confucius-institute/40412.

19. Kylie Reynolds, "Mandarin Teachers Gain Training at UCLA," *Daily Bruin*, August 2, 2010.

20. Unfortunately, the official Hanban criteria for its Overseas Volunteer Chinese Teacher Program will appear discriminatory to its U.S. partner institutions, as its third qualification reads: "Aged between 22 to 60, physical and mental healthy, no record of participation in Falun Gong and other illegal organizations and no criminal record." For the official Hanban qualifications for volunteer instructors, see http://www.chinese.cn/hanban_en/node_9806.htm.

21. The director of the CI at Stanford is the dean of Humanities and Sciences, and at Middle Tennessee State the CI advisory board is headed by the university president, while at the Confucius Institute in Indianapolis, the chancellor of Indiana University–Purdue University at Indianapolis co-chairs the advisory board, whose members are deans, other university presidents, corporate CEOs, and vice presidents. Faculty, especially Chinese studies faculty, are noticeably less well represented in CI administrations.

22. In a Pew poll from August 2010, one that became (unaccountably) a focus of the "mainstream media," 18 percent of those polled believed that Barack Obama was not a Christian but a Muslim. An astonishing 35 percent of self-identified "Republican" voters in this poll asserted that he was a follower of Islam and, moreover, that he was not a native-born citizen of the United States.

23. Peter Schmidt, "At U.S. Colleges, Chinese-Financed Centers Prompt Worries about Academic Freedom," *Chronicle of Higher Education*, October 22, 2010, A8–A10.

24. This may explain why Li's prominent official presence at the ceremonies at University College Dublin in 2010 announcing the joint Chinese and Irish government cofinancing of the construction of a "flagship building" for a new Confucius Institute for Ireland provoked a very negative reaction in Ireland and beyond.

25. In both Europe and the United States my conversations with CI directors and personnel consistently yielded no evidence of interference in programming, even when it might be considered by Hanban authorities to be especially sensitive.

26. Ofra Edelman, "Court: TAU Bowed to Chinese Pressure over Falun Exhibition," *Ha'aretz*, October 1, 2009, http://www.haaretz.com/print-edition/news/court-tau-bowed-to-chinese-pressure-over-falun-exhibition-1.6933.

27. Starr, "Chinese Language Education," 79.

14

Tensions and Violence in China's Minority Regions

Katherine Palmer Kaup

On July 5, 2009, what began like any other Sunday in the capital of Xinjiang Uyghur Autonomous Region ended in terror and bloodshed, leaving over 150 dead and nearly a thousand injured in violent ethnic riots. In the afternoon, crowds gathered to demand government investigation of an ethnic brawl that occurred ten days earlier at a toy factory over two thousand miles away, in Guangdong Province. Two ethnic Uyghur men died in the Guangdong brawl, and over one hundred were injured, as hundreds of Uyghur workers and members of the majority Han ethnic group bludgeoned one another with fire extinguishers, chains, and makeshift weapons surrounding allegations that a Uyghur man had raped a Han girl. A witness to the Guangdong clash reported that "people were so vicious, they just kept beating the dead bodies."[1]

Accounts vary of exactly what happened the night of July 5 in Ürümqi. Around 7 p.m., police moved in to disperse the crowd. Protestors responded with violence, using clubs and rocks to push back the police. Eyewitnesses reported seeing a large crowd of Uyghur men then begin attacking Han passersby as the violence spread. Radio Free Asia video footage shows throngs of protestors sweeping down the streets, with several overturned and gutted vehicles burning in the background. By morning police had restored a precarious calm, and hundreds of riot police and People's Armed Police moved into the area, armed with machine guns and backed by armored vehicles. Pent-up ethnic tensions continued to flare that week, however, and on July 7 Han vigilante groups roamed the streets seeking revenge for the violence two days earlier. According to more than one report, groups of Han carrying chains, machetes, and clubs attacked Uyghurs across the city, at times unimpeded by onlooking police.

Western reports of the riots noted the underlying ethnic tensions result-ing from five decades of Communist Party policy in the region. Official Chinese sources instead blamed "hostile outside forces" for inciting the riots, particularly the "dissident" Rebiya Kadeer.[2] The Chinese government immediately shut down cell phone communication, Internet access, Twit-ter, and other forms of communication in Xinjiang as it struggled to spin the official story. Though domestic cell phone communication was largely restored by late July, Internet access was not reopened until several months later and only with a robust filtering system in place, allowing limited ac-cess to only officially approved sites. The government issued a series of special reports on Xinjiang throughout the fall, highlighting the region's achievements and economic progress. Any mention of tension in the re-gion was blamed on the "three evil forces" of ethnic separatism, religious extremism, and international terrorism, and on "hostile outside forces" in-cluding Rebiya Kadeer. Discussion of weaknesses in government policy was conspicuously absent. Government reports consistently emphasized that economic development was the cure for minority concerns and announced a host of new investments in the region to further speed economic growth.

WRESTLING WITH THE ECONOMIC AND POLITICAL COMPLEXITY OF MINORITIES

Less than two years earlier in March 2008, widespread ethnic protests erupted across Tibetan areas, leading to several deaths and thousands of arrests. What began in Lhasa as a peaceful commemoration of the 1959 Ti-betan Uprising ended as well in violence on that day. The sympathetic pro-tests that spread across the Tibetan plateau that spring lasted even longer and involved more ethnic minorities than those in Xinjiang, and like the events in the summer of 2009, they were followed by increased repression and a surge in government financial investment in the region as the party struggled to win the hearts of the minorities through economic develop-ment rather than redressing their more central demands for religious and cultural rights.

Why did protests in the capital of the Tibetan Autonomous Region lead thousands of Tibetans in over fifty counties to take to the streets in sympa-thetic demonstrations, at great personal risk? How do the Xinjiang events in 2009 relate to those just months earlier in Tibet? Why would a factory brawl two thousand miles away lead to such widespread violence in Xinjiang? Who are the Uyghurs and Tibetans, what do they want, and why is there so much resistance to Chinese government policy in the regions?

Before addressing these very important questions, it is necessary to look beyond just Xinjiang and Tibet to understand the importance of "the minority question" in China as a whole. Who are the minorities, and why are they so important to the Chinese government? Why can't the Chinese government meet their demands? Is there any way to ease tensions in these regions without leading to the demise of party rule or national unity?

Unfortunately, there are no easy fixes for ethnic tensions in China. The Chinese government is, and has been since 1949, quite concerned that many of the minority regions might break away from the People's Republic of China (PRC). In Xinjiang and Tibet, where ethnic identity is strongest and tensions with the state the highest, the government has used a heavy-handed policy to contain even the slightest hints of support for separatism, often conflating expressions of ethnic sentiment with calls for independence or the "three evils."

Human rights groups as well as U.S. government organizations provide an important service in monitoring and reporting on human rights violations occurring in Tibet and Xinjiang.[3] They often fail to acknowledge the complexities of ethnic relations in China, however, and attribute pernicious intentions to the Chinese government in its ethnic policies. Numerous human rights groups detail the Chinese government's encouragement of Han migration into Tibet and Xinjiang, for example, and condemn it as a mass campaign to dilute minority cultures and assimilate the minorities. They rarely discuss the discrepancies in educational levels between the Han and minorities and do not give enough weight to the possibility that the Chinese government feels there are too few skilled minority technocrats to push the central government's rapid economic-development strategy for the regions.

It would be much more constructive to question the wisdom of promoting such rapid economic development before minorities have enough trained personnel to participate in the development process than to accuse the Chinese government of purposefully destroying the interests of their minority citizens. The latter leads the Chinese government to take on an extremely defensive attitude and discount outside views of its minority policy as naive, impractical, or "veiled attempts to split the motherland."

Similarly, U.S. government reports regularly note that the Chinese government has used "terrorism" as a justification to crack down on religious practices and expressions of ethnic identity. Though the Chinese government does conflate expressions of ethnic identity with what it calls the "three evils," outsiders not understating the complexities of managing ethnic relations, including the fact that there have been isolated violent terrorist acts, provides the Chinese government an opportunity to reject outside suggestions for improving human rights as unsuitable for "China's domestic concerns." The tone of reporting on developments in Xinjiang and Tibet tends to be polemical, with both Chinese government sources and those criticizing the government failing to acknowledge the concerns of the other.

It is easy enough to list the human rights violations and numerous contradictions in government promises and policy implementation. Without acknowledging the complexities involved in managing ethnic relations in China, however, we are left with a one-sided interpretation of events and limited in our ability to influence change.[4] Unfortunately, because the Chinese government regularly denies reporters, scholars, and analysts access in minority regions, they are limited in their ability to assess the full complexity of the situation in these regions. The Chinese government would be better served to increase access rather than secretively guard the flow of information in minority regions, which increases suspicions both from outside analysts and among minorities themselves.

An overview of the key features of China's minority policy reveals that the fundamental approach to easing ethnic tensions is flawed; indeed, it works against the government's efforts to promote prosperity and equality in a unified, multinational state. By objectively acknowledging the difficulties facing government management of these regions and adjusting the tone of reporting on ethnic tensions, human rights groups and government organizations may have a better chance of engaging the Chinese government in substantive discussion on how to begin easing tensions without losing control.

WHO ARE THE MINORITIES
AND WHY ARE THEY SO IMPORTANT?

Though China's fifty-five officially recognized minorities make up barely 9 percent of the country's total population, in absolute terms this equals 120 million people, a population larger than all but ten of the world's nations. The minorities' political significance far exceeds their numbers. The minorities occupy over 60 percent of China's landmass; 90 percent of China's international borders fall in officially designated ethnic autonomous areas. Over half of the fifty-five ethnic minorities have significant counterparts across international borders and historically have been poorly integrated into the central Chinese state. In Xinjiang, for example, in addition to ethnic Uyghurs, there are large numbers of ethnic Kazakhs, Uzbeks, Kyrgyz, and Tajiks. These names should sound familiar, as Kazakhstan, Uzbekistan, Kyrgyzstan, and Tajikistan are independent countries neighboring Xinjiang (see figure 14.1). The Uyghurs are the only major ethnic group in Xinjiang without a state of their own, a fact not lost on either the Chinese government or the Uyghur population. Securing the loyalty of those living in minority border regions is of particular strategic concern to Beijing. Many of China's rich natural resources are concentrated in minority regions, including vast reserves of oil, gas, coal, hydroelectric resources, valuable minerals,

Figure 14.1. Xinjiang Province and Its Borders.

and natural forests. More than a third of China's oil and gas reserves are in Xinjiang. While minority territories are less developed than most Han territories, the minorities lack the technical skills and capital needed to develop on their own. Government efforts to develop the ethnic regions are often resented by minorities as signs of internal colonization, however.

China's ethnic groups are conceptualized much differently than those in the United States. Racial distinctions factor in very little. Rather, the Chinese government recognizes groups as official ethnic minorities using a four-part definition developed by Stalin in 1912.[5] According to this definition, a minority nationality must have its own unique language, territory, economic system, and culture. Significantly, the minorities have historical claim to their own territory, unlike most minorities in the United States save some Native American tribes. More than four hundred groups demanded recognition in the 1950s as the government promised minorities the right to become the "masters of their own homes" and establish regional ethnic autonomous governments with special economic and governing privileges.

Determining exactly which groups should be recognized as separate ethnic groups turned out to be extraordinarily complicated. What exactly is a "unique culture"? Should those who wear a certain type of ethnic clothing be classified as a unique group? What if they wear the same clothing but practice different religions? What if the style of clothing is the same, but the color different? To tackle these difficult issues, the government sent work teams to the countryside in the 1950s and divided the various ethnic groups into just over fifty officially recognized minority nationalities. In some areas, these ethnic boundaries continue to be disputed.

China's minorities vary widely, though almost all historically were pushed out of China's heartland into undesirable and generally infertile land in the border regions. Many of the minorities are separated from central China by rugged mountains or vast deserts, making those regions harder to integrate into the national and global economy. Though their economic circumstances have improved dramatically since 1949, minorities remain far below the Han average on all socioeconomic indicators, including education, health, and income.

Exactly which ethnic characteristics are most important to the different minorities varies greatly. For some minority groups, language, shared oral histories, artistic cultures, and purported common origin play a central role in ethnic identification and define them as ethnic groups. Religion is a defining characteristic for both the Uyghurs and the Tibetan populations, the former overwhelmingly Muslim and the latter Buddhist. Religions provide believers an alternative source of authority from the Chinese Communist Party (CCP), and consequently, the party views them with particular suspicion and controls them more rigidly than groups with less-unified religious identities.

The minority contexts in China's southwest and northwest are quite different. Western coverage of minority developments in China tends to focus on contentious policies in the northwest and not report on progress in the southwest. Politically, minorities in the southwest have been much easier to manage. Minorities in the southwest live in scattered communities, often divided by mountains and rivers, and interspersed with other ethnic communities. Though villages in the southwest tend to be inhabited by a single ethnic group, often neighboring villages are home to other single ethnic groups. Minorities in the northwest live in more cohesive communities, more clearly divided from other groups and divided from the central plains where Han predominate by vast desert or mountain ranges. The southwest minorities tend to have less-unified languages, often with no written script or with mutually unintelligible dialects. Their religions are also less unified than those in the northwest, many practicing animism and worshiping sacred objects specific to their village community, like a sacred tree. Few minorities in the south make historical claims to modern independent states, as the Tibetans and Uyghurs do in the north. Due to their scattered demographics, internal divisions, and lack of claims to independent nationhood, the southwest minorities have not demanded independence and instead advocate for greater privileges within the People's Republic of China. By contrast, many Tibetans and Uyghurs would prefer independence from the PRC. The government fears the "splittism" that comes from such aspirations and has cracked down forcefully on the slightest hint of calls for greater ethnic autonomy. Given the weaker cohesion of southwest groups and their fewer political demands on the state, government policy has been less imposing and restrictive than in the northwest.

Tensions between the Chinese government and the Tibetan and Uyghur populations have been particularly pronounced. As with all of China's minorities, the ethnic identity of both the Uyghurs and the Tibetans has evolved over time, and the boundaries of their identity cannot be rigidly objectified.[6] There are internal divisions in their languages and faith, though their sense of ethnic identity as Tibetans and Uyghurs and their historical claims to statehood are stronger than most other minority groups in China. The Uyghurs are a predominately Muslim population of Turkic descent. They migrated to the region from the West along the Silk Road beginning in the ninth century. The Tibetans define themselves largely by their unique form of Buddhism, their common origins and language, and their long history as a separate culture isolated from the outside by the formidable Tibetan topography. Though language policy in these regions is complex and the government has imposed a number of changes to the Uyghur written script since 1949, the Uyghur and Tibetan scripts are more unified and widely used than those of almost any of the southwestern groups.

REGIONAL ETHNIC AUTONOMY AND THE BUILDUP TO ETHNIC VIOLENCE

The ethnic riots in Xinjiang in the summer of 2009 cannot be viewed in isolation. To understand the clash and its full implications, we need to understand the promises made to minorities in the Regional Ethnic Autonomy Law and then more closely examine the law's application, particularly in Tibet and Xinjiang. The degree of violence can only be explained by the high levels of frustration and resentment accumulated over many years.

All government minority policy is premised on two key assumptions: economic development is the cure to resolving ethnic conflict, and Han Chinese are inherently more politically reliable than the minorities. These two key assumptions and the policies they inspire undermine the government's goal to create a "harmonious society" and preserve a multinational unitary state. The first assumption is heavily grounded in Marxist ideology, which contends that nationalities are mere reflections of class conflict. According to this theory, as class inequality fades with economic development, so too will ethnic consciousness and, eventually, nations. This underlying assumption informs *all* minority policy in the PRC and is as clearly evident today as it was during the early years of the Chinese communist revolution. High-level official statements, State Council regulations, national policies, party proclamations, and press reporting all confirm explicitly and through their policies that economic development is the primary tool in resolving ethnic conflict.

This emphasis can clearly be seen in the official press following the Xinjiang summer riots. In August, for example, the *Xinjiang Daily* reported that 5.4 billion yuan ($858 million U.S.) would be used to expedite highway construction in the region, explaining that "speeding up development is the best way to fight the 'three evil forces' of terrorism, separatism and extremism, which is blamed for the deadly July 5 riot in Ürümqi."[7] The 2009 State Council's White Paper on Ethnic Policy explicitly notes: "The state is convinced that quickening the economic and social development of minority communities and minority areas is the fundamental solution to China's ethnic issues. Overcoming the difficulties and solving the problems in the minority areas hinges on development."[8] The government's contention that Han Chinese are politically more reliable than minorities similarly peppers many of its policies and policy statements. One particularly clear example is the government's "Assist Tibet, Xinjiang, and Border Regions" policy that promotes the transfer of large numbers of Han Chinese government cadres explicitly to "combat domestic and foreign forces' vain attempts . . . to stir up ethnic separatism."[9] This policy, combined with the influx of Han technocrats to help speed economic development in Xinjiang, has fundamentally transformed the ethnic makeup in the region.

In 1949 only 6 percent of the Xinjiang population was Han, while today over 40 percent is. The Chinese government argues that these new Han immigrants are necessary to provide technical expertise for economic development in the region and to dampen local "splittist" tendencies. The influx of Han Chinese has increased ethnic tensions dramatically, however, and many both within and outside of Xinjiang view the policy as a concerted effort to dilute Uyghur cultural identity.[10] Many human rights groups accuse the Chinese government of "cultural genocide" in its treatment of Tibetans and encouragement of mass influxes of Han Chinese to the region.[11] Many Uyghurs report significant Han discrimination against Uygurs in and outside of the workplace, and Han dominate the best-paying jobs.[12]

The regional ethnic autonomy policy was developed before the Chinese Communist Party seized power in 1949 and codified into law in 1984 in the Regional Ethnic Autonomy Law (REAL). The law grants minorities a number of privileges and guarantees them a number of rights, though the implementation of these provisions has been problematic. The rights of minorities under the REAL can be roughly divided into three broad categories:

political, cultural, and economic. Additionally, the law bars discrimination on the basis of ethnicity. Closer examination of the tensions between the rights provided on paper and their enforcement will help us understand the brewing discontent that erupted in Tibet in 2008 and Xinjiang in 2009.

Political Rights

The REAL allows for the establishment of ethnic autonomous governments in all areas where there is a "concentrated ethnic community." Depending on the size of the population, these autonomous governments may be provincial-level autonomous regions or smaller prefectural or district-level governments. There are also over 1,100 autonomous townships scattered across the country. The head of state of the autonomous government must be drawn from the lead ethnic group. There are currently five autonomous regions, thirty autonomous prefectures, and 120 autonomous counties.[13]

The law calls for preferential hiring policies to ensure large minority representation in state offices and mandates proportional representation at the national level. Without a doubt, minority representation, within both the state and the party, has increased dramatically since 1949. The September 2009 government White Paper on Development and Progress in Xinjiang notes that the number of minority government and party officials in Xinjiang increased from 46,000 in 1955 to over 363,000 in 2009. Nonetheless, two crucial weaknesses in minority appointments limit real representation of minority concerns. First, though the REAL mandates that the head of the *state* in autonomous areas must be a member of the titular minority, no similar provisions are made for *party* offices, where real political power remains. Of the 125 administrative units in Xinjiang, not *one* has a first party secretary, the lead CCP office, who is a Uyghur.[14] Furthermore, only village-level heads are popularly elected; the rest are appointed by the party organization office. The heads of the autonomous regions, therefore, report to and represent the party, not the ethnic citizens of the territory. Until popular elections are put in place, something not at all likely in the near future, severe restrictions on ethnic representation will persist.

Cultural Rights

The law grants minorities the right to preserve and promote their unique cultures, practice "normal" religious activity, control their own educational curriculum and school policies, and use their own language. Protecting these given rights has been problematic, however.

The REAL provides minorities the right to "develop literature, art, the press, publishing, radio broadcasting, the film industry, television and other cultural undertakings in forms and with characteristics unique to the nationalities," though it provides them only the right to "*support* relevant departments and bureaus as they collect, organize, translate and publish historical and cultural books of the nationalities" (my emphasis). The Chinese government has been particularly careful that the official version of Han–minority relations is the only version publicly available and tolerates no independent discussion of historical tensions among the minorities. The Chinese government asserts that China is, and has been for nearly two thousand years, a multinational unitary state in which "political and cultural exchanges among different ethnic groups reinforced their allegiance to the central government and their identification with Chinese culture, and strengthened the cohesion force, vitality and creativity of the Chinese nation, giving rise to the unification and diversity of Chinese civilization."[15]

The state tolerates no deviation from this interpretation of history and quickly represses accounts of ethnic tension as facades for "inciting splittism." Uyghur doctoral student Tohti Tunyaz learned the hazards of contradicting official histories in 1999, when he was sentenced to ten years in prison for his doctoral research on 1930s Xinjiang politics. Though Tunyaz used materials gathered from the state-run Xinjiang University library and supplied by an employee of the state, he was sentenced for "stealing state secrets" and publishing materials "inciting splittism." Cultural works are also carefully censored to ensure that they reflect harmonious relations among minorities. Thirty-one-year-old Nurmemet Yasin was sentenced to ten years' imprisonment in 2005 for publishing a short story titled "Wild Pigeon" in a literary magazine, which the authorities claimed "incited racial hatred and discrimination." The moving story, available in translation on Radio Free Asia's website along with other of Yasin's writings, tells of a pigeon that opts to commit suicide rather than live a life without freedom. The story was apparently interpreted as an allegory for Han Chinese policy in Xinjiang.[16]

The government's promises to protect minorities' religious freedom have also not been honored. Though religion is not the sole marker of ethnic identity for any minority group, for several it is the most important and defining characteristic of their identity. The party thus interprets demands for religious freedom as demands for greater ethnic autonomy. When demands for religious freedom come from groups discontented with party policy in their regions, the party interprets religious gatherings as particularly menacing to its authority.

Religion has been an especially sensitive issue for the Communist Party, not just in ethnic regions, but across the country. Religion provides believers a source of authority separate from, and above, the Communist Party. Mao Zedong recognized that clamping down on religion too quickly can cause a backlash surge in religious activism and warned against heavy-handed policies to control religion. At the same time, the party is acutely aware of the power religious leaders have over their followers. The party has carefully controlled religious gatherings and censored religious sermons and publications. The Chinese constitution provides all citizens the right to practice "normal" religious activity. All religious clergy in China, however, must receive "patriotic education" and be licensed by the state. No place of worship can be built without a license by the state. It is illegal to worship in groups outside of officially licensed religious venues. Religious sermons must meet the approval of the state-run religious organizations that oversee each of the five officially recognized religions—in Tibet the Chinese Buddhist Association and in Xinjiang primarily the Islamic Association.

The Chinese government contends that minorities have the right to practice their religions freely. The government reports that all adult citizens are able to attend mosque and notes that there are currently 24,300 mosques in Xinjiang, up from just two thousand at the end of the Cultural Revolution. More than twenty thousand Islamic clergy have been trained in the state-run Xinjiang Islamic Institute. The state has invested funds to restore religious sites since 1978, and in 2008 it spent more than thirty-three million dollars restoring the Idkah Mosque and a nearby pilgrimage site. The government boasts that all Tibetans are free to practice their religion and that there are 1,700 places of worship and 46,000 monks in Tibet.[17]

Despite these figures, the government has clearly clamped down tightly on religious practice within the minority regions, particularly in Xinjiang and Tibet. A number of international human rights and U.S. government organizations report on these controls in detail.[18] Religious activity in Tibet and Xinjiang is controlled more tightly than in any other region in China. Following large-scale ethnic protests in Tibet in 1989 and the collapse of the Soviet Union in 1991, existing restrictions tightened dramatically. Though these policies and the discontent they incite have been well documented by international watch groups, the Chinese government emphatically contends that all citizens have religious freedom as long as they do not use it "to incite splittism." Additional restrictions were placed on religion in the months surrounding the 2008 Olympic Games out of government fear that the minorities would capitalize on the event to call international media attention to ethnic concerns. These new restrictions led to increased levels of tension that contributed to the protests and riots in minority regions between March 2008 and July 2009.

In the summer of 2007 the Chinese government issued a new "Regulation for the Management of Reincarnations."[19] Tibetans believe that some 1,600 religious leaders across Tibet are reincarnations and that their teachings have been consistently developed through reincarnated lineages. According to the new 2007 regulations, as these teachers pass away, the State Administration for Religious Affairs, rather than the monasteries, will now decide if their reincarnated lineages will be continued, and if they are, how the search for new leaders and their education will be conducted. It would be hard to interpret this maneuver by the self-professed atheistic Chinese Communist Party's state religious administration as anything but a strike at the heart of one of the key features of Tibetan Buddhism. The new regulation on managing reincarnations coincided with an increase of government propaganda against the Tibetans' beloved exiled religious leader, the Dalai Lama. The restrictive religious climate, combined with a new influx of Han Chinese through the recent completion of a much publicized rail line into Tibet from central China, created a tense climate on the eve of the March 2008 protests.

In response to the March protests, the Chinese government only tightened its controls over religion, further exacerbating tensions. Monasteries housing monks who participated in the protests were punished harshly. Though the government has consistently denied placing quotas on the number of monks allowed in monasteries, the "Measures for Dealing Strictly with Rebellious Monasteries and Individual Monks and Nuns" announced in summer 2008 that the number of monks allowed in "troublemaking monasteries" must be reduced in proportion to the number of monks from those monasteries who participated in the protests. The measure thus tacitly confirmed that quota restrictions exist for the number of monks allowed into monasteries. The government announced that it must "strike hard" against any attempt to use religion as a front for the "three evils." No country can tolerate religious organizations operating as fronts for illegal or violent activity, but the Chinese government's heavy-handed policies and the tone of their "life or death struggle against the three evils" has exacerbated tensions in the region rather than alleviated them.

A series of measures imposed in 2008 further increased the air of religious oppression in Xinjiang. In an effort to combat what it called "infiltration" in the schools, the Xinjiang government called for a mass campaign to promote the "Three Upholds, Two Opposes" (upholding the unification of the motherland, ethnic unity, and social stability, while opposing ethnic separatism and illegal religious activity). The campaign included a call to increase the promotion of several topics designed to strengthen ethnic unity, including instruction in atheism. Earlier, in 2005, the Communist Party secretary demanded that schools "make education in atheism part of the effort to transform social customs . . . and promote nationality development and progress."[20] In 2008 a wide-scale "two-point system" was implemented, requiring high-level officials to use both regular direct contacts and direct oversight of mosques and leaders in an effort to increase controls over religion.

The ability of minorities to use their own language as a medium of instruction in education has also been reduced in recent years.[21] In 2002 the government removed Uyghur as the language of instruction at Xinjiang University and increased its "bilingual education" campaign. The campaign promoted the use of Mandarin Chinese, which many contend has come at the cost of Uyghur language promotion. Though Mandarin is the primary language of business across the PRC and increased understanding of Chinese will increase integration of the minorities, the policy has been imposed forcefully by the government.

Economic Rights

The Regional Ethnic Autonomy Law guarantees minorities a greater degree of autonomy than nonminority areas in setting their local development strategies. These rights are vaguely defined, however, and have been difficult to implement in part because of the rapidly changing nature of the Chinese economy since the law was promulgated in 1984 and revised in 2001. The central government has awarded minority areas preferential subsidies and development packages and has invested heavily in them. The Chinese government's White Paper on Development and Progress in Xinjiang notes that Xinjiang's GDP increased by 86.4 times from 1952 to 2008 and industrial added value by 274 times. The government invested over 380 billion yuan in Xinjiang during this period and remitted 375 billion in subsidies to the Xinjiang government. Infrastructure in the region has improved dramatically, paving the way (literally, in the form of over 147,000 kilometers of new roads) for further economic growth. An extensive network of roads, railways, and air routes has enabled rapid economic development in the region. Similar economic development has occurred in Tibet.

Exactly who has benefited from this development is unclear, however. Human rights groups and many Western analysts argue that the central government has extracted vast resources from the region, particularly in oil and gas revenues, and that the overwhelming majority of high-paying jobs have been taken by Han Chinese shipped in by the central government to aid the region's economic development. The Chinese government carefully guards economic statistics that might shed light on this debate. Though the government regularly reports on economic growth in minority regions, it does not allow data that break down income and other economic indicators by ethnicity. Western contributors to a 2005 edited volume on Xinjiang development tried to explore these issues, and the Chinese government responded by denying them reentry visas into China. Several Uyghurs who have provided outside analysts with evidence of economic discrepancies between the Han and Uyghurs are now serving sentences in jail for "leaking state secrets."[22]

THE PATH AHEAD

Unfortunately, there is no easy fix to ease the tensions between the government and its minority peoples. The issues facing the Chinese regime are extraordinarily complex. Many of the minorities still do not speak Mandarin Chinese fluently, limiting their ability to engage in the national economy. The government recognizes that minorities are far below the Han majority in all socioeconomic indicators, including per capita income, educational levels, and access to health care. Given the low level of technically trained minorities and the need for such expertise to develop the minority regions economically, the Chinese government has resorted to moving huge numbers of Han Chinese into minority territories. A host of policies, including several supporting the Go West Campaign launched in 2000, encourage Han Chinese to spend time in minority regions in service resembling an internal Peace Corps effort. Given the tensions in the region, the low levels of economic development, and the often harsh geography of these minority regions, Han Chinese often do not want to serve in these areas. To encourage the Han participation needed to develop these regions rapidly, the Chinese government has offered incentive packages to those willing to serve in border regions. Han Chinese often, thus, not only take the best jobs in minority regions since they are better trained than the minorities, but also receive higher salaries for the same jobs performed by minorities.

The government's rush to develop the regions economically depends on massive Han Chinese participation, given the current educational levels among the minorities. In addition, the government has exacerbated the lack of trained minority personnel by encouraging minorities to seek employment in Han areas outside of the autonomous regions. The CCP argues that through working in central and coastal China, minorities develop important new skills and have higher earning potential, but the policy results in a severe drain of needed minority expertise within the autonomous areas. The government sponsors a number of exchange programs to bring personnel from minority regions to central regions and vice versa, and some technical schools seem to promote job placement in the interior. The government's continued encouragement of exchanges of workers between Han and minority areas is designed to increase minorities' links with central China and avoid minority leaders and professionals becoming exclusively attached to minority regions.

Although the issues are complex and none of the solutions to ethnic tensions easy, a shift in tone and policy from the Chinese government, human rights groups, and the Tibetans and Uyghurs living in exile could help. While economic development is certainly important to ease poverty and disparities in ethnic areas, in my opinion the Chinese government must develop an economic strategy that is not dependent on massive influxes of Han Chinese. Ethnic tensions will be alleviated more effectively through a slower development strategy led by, and benefiting, the minorities themselves. Increased investment in educational infrastructure within minority areas, together with incentive packages to encourage technically trained minorities to remain in minority regions, will serve national integration better in the long run than the current overly accelerated growth led by Han Chinese.

Human rights groups and U.S. policy makers should continue to report on Chinese government transgressions of its own rules and human rights policies. However, current reporting and policy proposals tend to oversimplify the challenges facing the Chinese government. Current religious controls in Xinjiang undoubtedly exacerbate Uyghur resentment of the government and provide fertile breeding ground for religious radicalism that might not exist in a less tense environment. The government is aware that tensions are high and recognizes that if one minority group launches a secession campaign, whether successful or not, others may follow. The Chinese government's refusal to discuss minority issues is exacerbated by outside analysts' relentless emphasis on human rights violations and minimal recognition of the legitimate challenges facing the Chinese leadership in minority regions. Only through going beyond the headlines and acknowledging the depth of the challenges—which do not easily fit into media sound bites—can we hope to find a path out of ethnic discord and violence.

SUGGESTIONS FOR FURTHER READING

Bovington, Gardner. *Uyghurs: Strangers in Their Own Land*. New York: Columbia University Press, 2010.

Goldstein, Melvyn. *The Snow Lion and the Dragon: China, Tibet, and the Dalai Lama*. Berkeley: University of California Press, 1999.

Harrell, Stevan. *Ways of Being Ethnic in Southwest China*. Seattle: University of Washington Press, 2002.

Kaup, Katherine. *Creating the Zhuang: Ethnic Politics in China*. Boulder: Lynne Reinner Press, 2000.

Mackerras, Colin. *China's Ethnic Minorities and Globalization*. London and New York: Routledge, 2003.

McCarthy, Susan. *Communist Multiculturalism: Ethnic Revival in Southwest China*. Seattle: University of Washington Press, 2009.

Rossabi, Morris. *Governing China's Multiethnic Frontiers*. Seattle: University of Washington Press, 2004.

Shakya, Tsering. *The Dragon in the Land of Snows: A History of Modern Tibet Since 1947*. New York: Columbia University Press, 1999.

Starr, Frederick. *Xinjiang: China's Muslim Borderland*. Armonk, NY: M. E. Sharpe, 2004.

NOTES

1. Andrew Jacobs, "At a Distant Toy Factory, the Spark for China's Ethnic Bloodshed," *New York Times*, July 16, 2009.

2. Yu Zheng, "Woman Behind Xinjiang Riot Caught Self-contradictory," *Xinhua*, July 11, 2009. Rebiya Kadeer is the president of the World Uyghur Congress and has since 2005 lived in the United States following her release from a Xinjiang prison where she was jailed for five years on the charge of "endangering state security."

3. See, for example, reports by Human Rights Watch, Human Rights in China, Amnesty International, the Congressional-Executive Commission on China, the United States Commission on International Religious Freedom, Tibet Information Network, Uyghur American Association, the National Endowment for Democracy, and others.

4. See "Human Rights in Xinjiang: Recent Developments," Congressional-Executive Commission on China Staff Roundtable, February 13, 2009.

5. See Joseph Stalin, *Marxism and the National Question* (New York: International Publishers, 1942). This work was first published as "The National Question and Social-Democracy" in 1913 in *Prosveshcheniye*, nos. 3, 4, and 5.

6. Dru Gladney, "The Ethnogensis of the Uyghur," *Central Asian Survey* 9, no. 1 (1990): 1–28.

7. "Xinjiang to Spend 5.4 Billion Yuan in Two Months to Hasten Highway Construction," *Xinhua*, August 4, 2009.

8. Information Office of the State Council of the People's Republic of China, White Paper, "China's Ethnic Policy and Common Prosperity and Development for All Ethnic Groups," September 9, 2009.

9. For a full English translation with the Chinese text, see "Government Policy Towards Minorities Depends on Sending Han Cadre to Minority Areas," Congressional-Executive Commission on China, Virtual Academy, May 23, 2005, http://www.cecc.gov/pages/virtualAcad/index.phpd?showsingle=13066.

10. See, for example, "Human Rights in China: Uygurs of East Turkestan," Unrepresented Nations and Peoples Organization, http://www.unpo.org/downloads/petition%20document%20english.pdf.

11. The Dalai Lama, for example, argues that "whether intentionally or unintentionally, some kind of cultural genocide is taking place [in Tibet]." "Dalai Lama Condemns China's 'Cultural Genocide' of Tibet," *Telegraph*, March 16, 2008.

12. Xiaowei Zang, "Uyghur-Han Earnings Differentials in Urumchi," *China Journal* 65 (January 2011): 141–55.

13. Information Office of the State Council of the People's Republic of China, White Paper, "Regional Autonomy for China's Ethnic Minorities," July 2005, http://www.china.org.cn/e-white/20050301/index.htm.

14. Nicholas Becquelin, "Staged Development in Xinjiang," *China Quarterly* 178 (2004): 358, 363.

15. Information Office of the State Council of the People's Republic of China, "China's Ethnic Policy and Common Prosperity and Development for All Ethnic Groups," September 27, 2009, http://www.chinadaily.com.cn/china/2009-09/27/content_8743072.htm.

16. See PEN America Center, "China/Uighur Autonomous Region: Nurmuhemmet Yasin," http://www.pen.org/viewmedia.php/prmMID/765/prmID/174.

17. Information Office, "China's Ethnic Policy and Common Prosperity."

18. See, for example, Human Rights Watch, "Devastating Blows: Religious Repression of Uyghurs in Xinjiang," April 11, 2005, http://www.hrw.org/en/node/11799/section/1; and the Congressional-Executive Commission on China 2009 and 2010 annual reports' special sections on Xinjiang and Tibet, available at http://www.cecc.gov/index.php.

19. Congressional-Executive Commission on China, *Annual Report 2007*, 196, http://www.cecc.gov/pages/annualRpt/annualRpt07/CECCannRpt2007.pdf.

20. Wang Lequan, "Maintain the Dominant Position of Marxism in Ideological Work and Adhere to the Four Cardinal Principals," *Seeking Truth* 2 (January 16, 2005).

21. Congressional-Executive Commission on China, *Annual Report 2009*, 258–59, http://www.cecc.gov/pages/annualRpt/annualRpt09/CECCannRpt2009.pdf.

22. For a detailed list of political prisoners in Xinjiang, see the Congressional-Executive Commission on China's political prisoner database, available at http://cecc.gov/pages/victims/index.php.

15

An Unharmonious Society: Foreign Reporting in China

Gady Epstein

There is much that the world's reading public knows, and wants to know, about China. A great deal of that knowledge and interest is in urban China, especially its monumental architectural modernism and its triumphal capitalism—money, markets, the manna of global commerce. However, it is rural China, where half of the population still lives, that the world's readers know precious little about, and it is here that an investigative reporter can escape the careful tailoring of news for public consumption and open a passage into the real-life experience of so many who live in China today. It was in the Chinese countryside where I began my very literal journey to understand China not long after I first arrived in 2002.

JOURNALIST AND POLITICS IN CHINA'S OUTBACK

At about noon on a Saturday in September of 2003, I was traveling the last mile of a twenty-hour journey to Yongquan Village (see figure 15.1) when I finally blew my cover. Like almost every foreign journalist doing stories in China, I had not sought permission for this trip as was technically required at the time. I had taken the usual precautions to avoid attracting official attention. I turned off my phone when I left Beijing for Chongqing, traveling light with my assistant and interpreter Wen Haijing (by this time, as opposed to years earlier, foreign correspondents could hire anyone we chose as assistants, with an open application process, and with Haijing, a native of Chongqing in southwest China, I was especially lucky; she was fiercely independent-minded, intellectually curious, and resourceful, in addition to

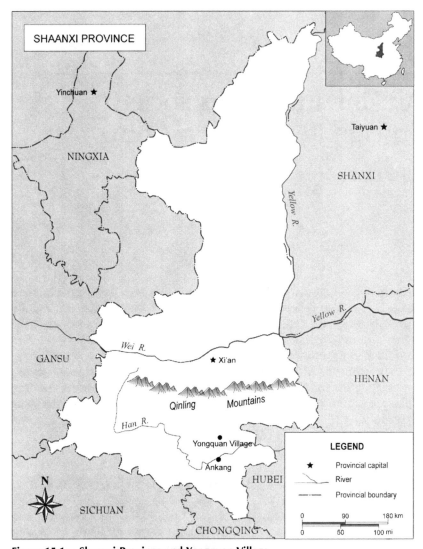

Figure 15.1. Shaanxi Province and Yongquan Village

being a gifted English speaker). We didn't check into a hotel, instead hopping onto an overnight train to Ankang in southern Shaanxi Province. After a quick breakfast of rice porridge and some awful Nescafé, we hired a cab for the fifty-mile drive to Yongquan Village, where three farmers had just attempted suicide in a five-day stretch. Something had gone very wrong with a government reforestation program, and I was on my way to find out why.

The problem was that, due to the very erosion problems that made reforestation an urgent necessity, the last two miles of dirt road to the village were impassable by car. Haijing and I had to get out and I hired two motorbikes to take us the rest of the way. Then we found out that there was about one more mile to our journey, a hike straight up the mountain. If I had done a good job until now of concealing that a foreign journalist was visiting a village that rarely if ever had seen foreigners before, it didn't matter now. I pulled my Red Sox hat on tight and low as I hiked up to Yongquan Village, but neither my hat nor my spectacles could do much to hide the literally big nose and white face announcing my foreign presence.

In the self-mocking, self-important parlance of foreign journalism in China, this was to have been a reporting "black op," a surgical strike. Get in, get your story without getting noticed, get out, and publish. Leave no marks, and definitely don't get your sources in trouble. This trip didn't work out that way, and I encountered one aspect of Chinese official attempts to control, interfere with, or influence the work of foreign journalists in China. But this is not the story you might think it is. What I encountered was not the sinister police state, not the terrifying shadowy security apparatus that I had read and heard so much about. Rather, what I encountered could be described as the little cogs of Chinese autocracy, the fearful, watch-for-your-own-back bureaucracy so often evident in China, from the ministries in Beijing to the provincial backwaters. That is not to say that this form of harassment cannot have its intimidating characteristics, but it is authoritarianism in the locally distributed, diluted form. Low-level officials would, by the end of this long day, take one of my notebooks (the wrong one) and delete photos from my camera (easily recovered), after having toasted their "American friend" in an entirely involuntary banquet. They followed their script, but they didn't stop Haijing and me from getting our story.

And as you will see, they didn't stop the poor farmers of this isolated village from telling their sad tale to a foreign interloper. In that way this story is instructive of how local officials and foreign journalists still interact now, some eight years later, even though the rules have changed to make it much easier for us to travel in China, and much harder for local officials to uproot us. The way foreign journalists are viewed by local officials when they come into town remains the same: we mean nothing but trouble.

After forty minutes of hiking up a steep mountain "path" of dirt, mud, and rocky stream with the guidance of the two motorbike riders, we reached the packed-mud hut of subsistence farmer Li Liwen. Li, fifty-six, began to explain to me why he had tried to kill himself by swallowing pesticide—because he had been fined for planting crops between trees on land he had given up for reforestation, even though the officials had allowed him to grow crops against the rules so he could have enough to eat. About ten minutes into our interview, two men walked in, wearing noticeably nicer clothes than anyone should be wearing here—long-sleeve dress shirts, slacks, and matching pairs of white sneakers with green star logos—the "bullet-proof polyester," to borrow a colleague's shorthand, of low-level government officials in China.

Their lack of authority was immediately clear in that they didn't try to stop my interview. They conferred in hushed tones with the guides who brought us here, but otherwise merely sat quietly on low peasant stools and observed my interview, accepting hot cups of tea from Li's wife. I continued asking questions, a bit delicately at first, as I was aware of my company, but getting blunt when I needed to. I wanted to keep asking questions of this man as long as possible, because I wasn't sure I'd get any more interviews on this day.

Eventually, though, the more senior of the men, thirty-six-year-old Wang Daxue, dressed in a purple shirt, started interrupting when Li would give an answer that didn't please him. He was visibly displeased when Li said he didn't have enough to eat, then started talking over him when he said the fine for growing crops between his trees was 560 yuan ($85 U.S. today)— "You have to tell the truth. That 560 is not the amount for just one *mu* (one-sixth of an acre)," he said, referring to the common measure of agricultural land in China. Wang interrupted again when the farmer was asked what he thought of the reforestation program and said he didn't know much about such things: "Did you attend the meetings?" And again he was perturbed when the villager was asked whether he thought the program was a good idea. "You have to tell the truth. If you lie, you'll be responsible." "I want to think about it," Li ultimately said. "Yeah, you think about it," the man in the purple shirt said with a tinge of menace in his voice. Li never did give a proper answer.

But oddly, the two men didn't stop my work. I asked my questions, took photos, then announced where I was going next, to the homes of the widows of the two other farmers, who had successfully committed suicide. They were probably not sure what to do with a foreign journalist in this village and may have been awaiting word on how to handle me. Whatever the reason, the cadres (I use "cadre" here as a catchall term for any functionary in the Communist Party bureaucracy) showed us the way to my next stop, about a twenty- or twenty-five-minute hard hike down, over, and then up another three-quarters of a mile of mountain. They stopped along the path to talk to another apparent cadre who was holding a baby outside his hut, and not long after we reached the next stop our escort had grown with the addition of the village's party secretary, a roly-poly man who hadn't missed too many meals.

Gradually I was getting enveloped into the very broad, thick, well-fed, *baijiu*-soaked lower midsection of the Chinese government (*baijiu* is grain alcohol, strong and acrid stuff, consumed like water by some cadres). This is not the China you read and hear about when you prepare to come here to work as a journalist, yet it is the part of the government you need to understand most to function well as a foreign journalist in China. Authorities and foreign journalists play many different versions of cat and mouse, and one should know the differences between each of these versions—from the ritual and mundane to the more serious and intrusive forms of surveillance and intimidation—to appreciate the real and imagined challenges of foreign reporting in China. How the Chinese government tries to keep tabs on us can vary, depending on who we are, what we're working on, and why. Also it matters, crucially so, *where* we're working, *when* we're working, and to *whom* we are speaking—sensitive places, sensitive anniversaries, sensitive dissidents.

Here, as I encountered the village party secretary, I once again was not prevented from doing my job. This local boss, a villager himself, had just seen two of his farmers, including a lower-level official under his command, commit suicide, and he must have had mixed feelings as two widows, their young children with them, told their stories to a foreign journalist. They implicated the government in their husbands' deaths, there was no doubt about that, and though the party secretary interrupted them and his cronies mildly intimidated them, the widows said what they wanted to say. One also provided my assistant with a handwritten account, which Haijing read and took notes from as several functionaries looked on, anxious to intervene but holding back.

Since there were no telephones here, this would be my only chance to interview the widows, and I did so for two hours. I also, here, later, and at the previous stop, interviewed our self-appointed escorts about the government reforestation program. We got their names and ages and more material, the rarely heard government's side of the story (rarely heard because officials like these often do not respond to foreign journalists' inquiries, out of either bureaucratic timidity, arrogance, or both). I developed a fuller appreciation for the distrust that can develop in any small Chinese town or village between the aggrieved and the party: "Tragedies like our family's have been caused by government officials," Chen's widow, Sun Zhufang, then just twenty-five years old, told me as she stood just a few feet away from three government officials. One of them, Chen Xiaokun, the Yongquan party secretary, said the episode was the fault not of the government but of circumstances: "The key is that the environment and the geographical conditions of our place are not very good," said Chen, then forty. "People are poor and the mountains are barren and the rivers are unforgiving, so that's the root cause for common people to do these kinds of things."

To back up his point, Chen and his fellow officials asked me if I wanted to see the site of a recent landslide in this very same village that had just killed seventeen people, including eight children, and which had made national news. I certainly did, especially since it was relevant to the story. They took me to the site: A flat block of concrete stood where a fifteen-room house had once been. A small, neatly stacked pile of bricks stood on the concrete, the beginnings of a monument to the dead, including the fourteen whose bodies had not been found.

Chen's explicit and implicit message here was, "These are the miserable conditions we face." Although self-serving, it is also true, and it puts the journalist-authority interaction in China in valuable context. Conditions are indeed harsh in many corners of China, especially the parts journalists want to see. Chinese people—not just officials—are well aware that when foreign journalists report on these backwaters, they will not paint a pretty picture of their country.

THE LESSON GOING FORWARD

To this day, this fundamental tension between the foreign reporter and the Chinese official provides an inherently adversarial backdrop anytime journalists parachute in to cover a story in China. But at the Chinese central government level, the official strategy for handling would-be parachutists is evolving into a more modern form of public relations management. Chinese leaders have long heard from their counterparts and from foreign PR firms that the most pragmatic way to handle the pesky media is with openness and transparency. Chinese authorities also have surely been told it is wiser to co-opt and steer foreign journalists, like embedded journalists in war, than to blockade them.

Since 2008, Chinese authorities have shown clear signs of adapting their approach. Partly this was a mechanical necessity, as Beijing had promised more freedom for journalists in winning the bid for the 2008 Olympics and needed to display a more open approach. Western nations had made Chinese restrictions on press freedom a point of contention in welcoming China more fully into the international community, and Beijing's willingness to soften its rules for the Olympics was viewed optimistically by some as an important inflection point. Beginning January 1, 2007, under a new provisionary rule, journalists no longer had to ask permission for reporting trips, doing away with a rule that was often a useful pretext for local officials to keep foreign journalists from reporting in any number of Yongquan Villages. But this rule change did not reflect an important ideological shift at the center. It may have removed some teeth from thousands of small-town officials, but it also merely acknowledged and codified the general practice of the day (aside from reporting trips to politically sensitive Tibet and areas of Xinjiang, which to this day are treated differently by authorities, regardless of what the rules say). By 2007 the Foreign Ministry had long tolerated foreign journalists' forays into the countryside, for reports on local problems were of little concern to Beijing. That was a significant lesson of my 2003 experience—even at the time, the stakes were high only for the few actors involved, not for Beijing. Central government officials may not love the stories that come out of these trips, but during the 2000s in particular, they came to understand that the individual impact of any such story was limited. That is, of course, both good news and bad news for the journalists going out on these adventures: for the most part, we can go where we like, but the fact that the government doesn't care that much may say something depressing about the social and political utility of the work—at least in the micro analysis of each individual story. I can hope only that I have given a voice to a story that otherwise would not have been told. In aggregate, though, the many stories told by foreign correspondents can provide the world with a rich, nuanced picture of what life in China can be like beyond the towers of glass and steel in Beijing and Shanghai.

It is instructive, then, to consider the sensitive areas where foreign journalists' interests and central government priorities collide: on the Tiananmen Square massacre, Tibet, Xinjiang, and Chinese dissidents. The government's approach to these issues is by no means uniform. The interests of security forces can trump all other considerations, and in 2011 those security interests were very much in the ascendant with the arrest of artist-dissident Ai Weiwei and hundreds of detentions, disappearances, and intimidating warnings to lawyers and activists. But in recent years Beijing had been developing a more sophisticated approach to handling foreign journalists in sensitive areas, spurred by a surprising catalyst, the Tibet riots of 2008—a spate of ethnically charged violence, directed largely by Tibetans at Han Chinese, that authorities responded to with an overwhelming and militarized crackdown. Surprising because of course no news event in the last few years brought China more negative publicity than the Chinese response to those riots; surprising because the most influential account that provided a positive spin for Beijing on the riots came from the one foreign journalist who happened to be in Lhasa when the riots broke out. The evenhanded accounts of the *Economist*'s James Miles, provided in print but also over broadcasts, gave a vivid portrayal of Tibetans' violence against innocent Han Chinese. He described how chaos reigned for as long as twenty-four hours before the Chinese government decided it was necessary to quell it. Miles's on-scene reporting ran counter to the conventional, expected narrative. And of course this was not a Chinese state media account—this was a respected Western journalist, and his version could not be dismissed as propaganda.

The problem, as Beijing surely saw, is that Miles's version of events, with no images and only words, did not win the day in the international imagination. Other images, of the crackdown in the aftermath, made it out of

Tibet over mobile phones and the Internet, published in newspapers and broadcast worldwide often without proper context. Young Chinese nationalists online—the so-called *fenqing* or "angry youth"—launched a campaign against the Western media, spearheaded by the website Anti-CNN.com. But sympathizers with the Tibetan protesters "won the news cycle," and the Chinese government would go on to take a brutal drubbing in the weeks ahead as the Olympic torch relay became a magnet for protests around the world. Only the devastating Sichuan earthquake, with its terrible death toll, was able to transform global scorn into global empathy for China that spring. Foreign journalists were generally allowed to cover that disaster without too much harassment, since clearly the story was initially nonpolitical. The Tibet issue receded into the background, and the Olympics turned out to be a PR success.

But it had been a close call for Beijing, and leaders must have been mulling this question: Would the Tibet issue have played out the same way if, say, foreign journalists were in Tibet in numbers to observe events unfold (under Chinese supervision, of course)? Just as important, was it futile to try to monopolize the story through Chinese state media in this era of instant and visceral transmission of events through alternate channels—mobile phones, the web, and of course the social networks of web 2.0? They must have concluded so, because sixteen months later, when riots broke out in Ürümqi in the remote and heavily Muslim northwestern region of Xinjiang, foreign journalists were not only welcome but were invited to get out there immediately to report.

The reason: the first day's rioters were Uyghurs, the victims were Han Chinese, and by all accounts, the security response was restrained. Foreign journalists, given essentially the red-carpet treatment in a region where their movements had often been restricted and scrutinized closely, covered the earnest Chinese attempts to control the situation. Online, with rumors spreading quickly over social networks, China took the step of using the so-called Great Firewall of Internet controls to block Twitter (which had been briefly blocked during the twentieth anniversary of Tiananmen a month earlier) as well as Facebook, and these blocks remain in place as of this writing. Authorities also shut down mobile communications in Xinjiang, and then the Internet as well for many months, a controversial step but, from the security forces' standpoint, effective. China decisively won this news cycle, and though that victory was tempered by ongoing criticism of Chinese policies toward ethnic minorities, it was a rare victory nonetheless. More important, it marked a shift in how foreign journalists and their attentive hosts would operate in China during high-profile crises (if the crises are relatively obscure to most of the world, authorities can and do impede individual foreign reporters without paying a PR penalty). The Communist Party showed it understands that although it can block Twitter and cut off mobile communications to a hot spot like Ürümqi after the riots, it can no longer prevent a big story from getting out to the rest of the country and the world. So in public relations speak, they set out to define the story before the story defined them. What was remarkable about this was that Party leaders were able to act so promptly and so decisively on multiple fronts. The government was *ready* to handle a PR crisis with a sophisticated authoritarian strategy, and clearly had been crafting this strategy since the disastrous handling of the Tibet unrest.

MANAGING DISSENT IN THE DIGITAL AGE

Now that Communist Party leaders have embraced the twenty-four-hour news cycle, will they come to regret it? I suspect not, because they can always change the rules of engagement to suit circumstances. Internationally, crisis PR works in your favor when you have a reasonable storyline to push and the situation on the ground is deemed under control. But the security apparatus always puts security first, above public relations. This much has been evident in the recent calls for a "Jasmine Revolution" in China modeled on the uprisings in the Middle East. The police systematically intimidated foreign journalists who attempted to cover the Sunday gatherings, or "strolls," that were supposed to take place all over China from mid-February into March—it is unclear how many participated or would have, in part because the government's response was so smothering, including detentions of activists and strict Internet controls. The intimidation took various forms, from calling journalists in for lectures not to go to certain sites without permission (which would not be granted if asked), to showing up at journalists' homes to remind them of the rules of reporting in China, to threatening to revoke journalists' visas. Some reporters thought the government was changing the rules of the game, but from my perspective, Chinese security authorities' governing logic concerning foreign reporters has never changed: we are allowed to do our jobs as we like most of the time, until we cross a sensitive line of their choosing.

Foreign journalists had grown accustomed to a sense of freedom and openness that existed in circumstance, not as much in fact, in part because the focus for many of us had changed. In 2009 China parried well with foreign journalists through a gantlet of sensitive anniversaries, including the fiftieth anniversary of the Dalai Lama's flight from Tibet, the twentieth anniversary of the Tiananmen Square massacre, and the tenth anniversary of the crackdown on Falun Gong followers—the last of which barely registered globally. Yet it was not public relations genius that helped China the most through this period; it was a more subtle, long-term shift in how foreign media covers China, partly in response to what readers and viewers of the world have the appetite to consume. Foreign journalists had become, on the whole, less adversarial on human rights, less inclined to upend the established order, and certainly more accepting of the status quo. At the same time, the news-digesting general public has had more than its fill of stories about injustices in China. Now, let me backpedal for a moment here: I am not saying there aren't a great number of foreign journalists who are passionate about human rights and injustice—perhaps even the majority are—and I am not saying that all readers don't want to read about human rights in China. The coverage of the Jasmine Revolution crackdown and of the Ai Weiwei arrest shows that when our perception of the China story is jarred, when Chinese authorities remind us forcefully of their priorities—security above all, at the tragic expense of human rights—foreign journalists can respond with a force and passion commensurate to the moment.

Here is what I am saying: There has been a dramatic shift in the "China story" as it is told by foreign journalists since I first arrived in 2002, and it correlates with China's rise as an economic and political superpower during that time. During that time it became clear that the notion that economic engagement with China would bring about political reform was, as former *Los Angeles Times* Beijing correspondent Jim Mann, who worked in China thirty years ago, wrote in his book *The China Fantasy*, a delusion. The world has made a choice to engage with China, to give into the reality of the status quo and essentially surrender on human rights. That process of realization may already have been underway in 2002, but it was certainly not yet fully and consciously realized. Many foreign journalists in 2002 still assessed China with a post-Tiananmen, post-Soviet-breakup mindset. It was the last year of Jiang Zemin's reign as general secretary of the CCP, a reign almost literally born from the bloodshed of Tiananmen, and there was a notion that Beijing's day of reckoning as an authoritarian state would yet come, maybe not in a few years but inevitably. There were earnest wagers about how long the communist regime would last. There were earnest questions about whether Jiang's successor, Hu Jintao, would champion political reform.

NEW LEADERSHIP, PERSISTENT PROBLEMS

In this context, human rights and injustice had a visceral, close feel for a foreign journalist. Stories of government abuses captivated readers, including one on the rampant spread of HIV through Henan Province via government-sanctioned blood-selling, and the fact that authorities tried to lock down the "AIDS villages" and keep foreign journalists out. These sordid details made reporting the story all the more honorable a pursuit. Overall, it felt like the winds of Tiananmen were still blowing in Beijing, that the economy might falter terribly, and that the regime was not on solid ground.

Then the government covered up the SARS epidemic of 2003, and the foreign media corps helped apply the necessary pressure to break the story to the world. All of the heroes of the SARS story were Chinese, like the journalist who helped me report on the real extent of SARS in Guangzhou in March 2003, when I was, to my knowledge, the first Western reporter to interview a recovered SARS patient in China. And like retired military doctor Jiang Yanyong, the whistleblower who leaked to *Time* magazine and others that SARS was a full-blown epidemic in Beijing. But though the heroes were Chinese, the foreign media perhaps could feel more righteous and confident of its power to help do good in China than at any time since 1989.

Much has changed since then. China recovered from SARS, its economy surged—and its new leaders consolidated power and tightened their grip over the political space: crusading journalists and rights defense lawyers began finding their jobs tougher and tougher year after year. I and other foreign journalists covered these travails, but for a number of reasons the attention span for human rights abuses in China had attenuated. The Iraq War and the international focus on terrorism certainly were factors, which also brought China and the United States closer together diplomatically. But by the end of the decade there was something else: that post-Tiananmen, post-Soviet-breakup mindset among foreign journalists had completely disappeared, replaced by an acceptance of the so-called China model, authoritarian state capitalism, and its central role in world affairs. The global financial crisis, and China's emergence from it apparently stronger than ever, cemented this mindset (I say only apparently stronger because history will have to wait some years to render a correct judgment on the China model, but for now appearances rule the day).

What does that mean for human rights coverage? Foreign journalists still provide it, but despite the brief and dramatic spikes in attention paid, the issue is almost completely drowned out by the political and economic news that are also of importance. The coverage, then, often has a defeatist ring to it, because it is clear that Chinese authoritarianism has essentially won, and knows it. This problem of human rights coverage is rooted deep in the human psyche, for there is only so much that many reporters and especially their editors can absorb before they tune out, and their readers may have tuned out before them. The human rights abuses are so numerous that we have become numb to the headlines, and there is virtually no room in people's minds to process them. Every individual tale must compete for attention with the unmediated geyser of global news and entertainment developments, not to mention the many distractions of everyday life. Beijing knows, to its great satisfaction, that this is no contest. Authorities can even get away with repeatedly kidnapping and severely torturing a Chinese "dissident" who was once named one of the best lawyers in China.

THE GAO ZHISHENG CASE: THE HARSH POLITICS OF LAW

That lawyer, Gao Zhisheng, was disappeared by authorities, in "black ops" fashion, from early 2009 to early 2010, and was again disappeared last year—and is still missing at the time of this writing. He had told me when I last met him in 2005, "The China you see and the China we feel are totally different. Maybe you see only the prosperity and development in China and also the many legal rights that the Chinese people should have on paper." He finished his point with a chilling truth: "Every day, I feel the truth of the development of the rule of law in China."

Once named one of the best lawyers in the country, Gao's crime was to advocate for those who have no rights, most notably the followers of the banned spiritual movement Falun Gong. For his crime, the secret police had already abducted Gao and tortured him for days on end. A kangaroo court had convicted and sentenced him for subverting state power. His wife and two children, relentlessly harassed by police, finally escaped while under surveillance in January 2009, fleeing for exile in the United States.

This is the other China Gao was talking about, "a state with the characteristics of the mafia," he told me, where no laws can protect lawyers like him. This China is a Stalinist anachronism: brutal and merciless when it encounters the most stubborn dissidents; thuggish when it thinks a good beating or detention on trumped-up charges will teach the appropriate lesson; merely intimidating when it believes that making some bluntly worded threats and scaring off a lawyer's paying clients will produce the desired results.

And this China gets results. There is a limit to how much intimidation and brutality most Chinese rights defenders can endure before deciding, finally, that it might be best for them and their families if they work within carefully defined boundaries. They remain under constant pressure even while operating in the mainstream, working in the China that is part of our more acceptable, comfortable discourse, the one where many earnest efforts are being made to improve rule of law, human rights, working conditions, and environmental protections.

I don't need to describe this China because it is the one with which the rest of the world engages every day and that the media generally has described (despite extensive coverage of crackdowns and many fine individual efforts to peer into and describe Gao's China). The Western democracies long ago concluded that engagement with the Chinese Communist Party is ultimately in the best interests of the Chinese people; Gao counters that engaging with the Chinese government is no different historically from "shaking hands with Stalin" at Yalta.

Obviously, engagement at this point is not a choice. It is reality. Many Chinese rights defenders work diligently within that reality, and some believe unrestrained activism like Gao's undermines their cause, weakening reform-minded bureaucrats within the government, strengthening the hard-line security factions. What Gao calls appeasement, they would call realism, and vice versa. It is a debate with no clear winner, only differing shades of struggle.

Gao, nominated for the Nobel Peace Prize like the more moderate 2010 laureate Liu Xiaobo, calls for more help from the West in that struggle. He blasts France and Germany for caring more about securing big Chinese purchase orders than about human rights. He affords praise for American values but says the United States, too, has a "bottom line" in dealing with China, and it is not human rights.

CHINA'S RISE AND STUMBLES

Whenever China journalists speak in public, we are almost invariably asked whether we are free to write what we want, or whether we feel we must watch what we say lest we offend our host government. In fact, foreign correspondents are generally entirely free to do our jobs in China. The roadblocks we face may be at times systemic ones—most people in government or in state-owned enterprises see little benefit in talking to a foreign reporter—but, outside of security crises, these barriers are generally not maliciously laid by officials seeking to thwart us. The Foreign Ministry, officially responsible for maintaining relations with foreign journalists in China, has sought to be more customer friendly over the years, offering occasionally valuable escorted trips that provide access to officials and sites journalists might not otherwise get. And no foreign correspondent has been thrown out of China since the 1990s. Authorities had been, until recently, more reticent to bully journalists than, say, China scholars, who definitely limit the scope of their research and writing to avoid getting barred from the country that is their life's work. Beijing has been more calculating in applying its leverage over journalists; ejecting a journalist is a risky and by definition headline-making step.

Recently, that calculation has been changing for the worse. In 2011 conditions for foreign reporters in China reached a low point not experienced in the long memory of veterans posted in Beijing. The aggressive security response to the so-called Jasmine Revolution has been accompanied by intimidation of a number of reporters, including explicit threats that their visas could be revoked. As China feels fully its growing influence in the world, and yet feels insecure at home, we can reasonably expect that authorities will continue to apply pressure to foreign correspondents, especially at sensitive moments or on the most sensitive subjects. They also will continue to target our Chinese assistants. Over the years many news researchers have been "invited to tea" by state security agents, who ask them to keep tabs on their bosses. As far as I know, these assistants choose to stand with their correspondents, and it is usually with an eye out for their welfare that we become more careful about running afoul of authorities.

And yet it remains true that for most of our everyday work, for 99 percent of what foreign correspondents do, the authorities seem not to care.

Why? That is partly a function of official confidence. China has arrived, and foreign journalists cannot do much to undermine the country's standing in the world. But a crucial factor is that authorities have a more pressing security priority: their own people, who can now, thanks to the Internet, instantly transform any incident of official abuse into a national scandal. The power of web 2.0, currently represented most ably by Sina's weibo (weibo is also the generic Chinese word for microblog), is more fearsome for authorities than any pen or camera of a foreign journalist ever was. This is the most recent and most important way in which the job of reporting has changed for foreigners in China: whereas once foreign journalists were a vital outlet for getting stories to the outside world, on the faint hope that officials would be embarrassed into reforming their behavior, now that outlet is the collective consciousness of the Chinese Internet, coiled and ready to vent fury and create the next explosive social meme (enter the phrase "My dad is Li Gang" into Google, and you'll see what I mean). One recent account in the Chinese press suggested that 70 percent of officials in China, mostly local, suffer from "Internet terror." That form of accountability can be nasty, brutish, and unwieldy, and foreign media has never offered anything approaching it.

So what is left for the foreign media, besides chronicling this rise of a great power? Quite a bit. The Chinese media is still straining at the shackles of the Propaganda Ministry. The Internet is still subject to aggressive self-monitoring and censorship that can smother important stories. The political system hasn't changed, corruption is rampant, and powerful state-owned enterprises tower over much of the economy. And, too, the common people in remote corners of China who are not as connected to the Internet—some of them want their voice to be heard. It is more imperative than ever that foreign journalists give them that voice, and provide candid, insightful reporting and analysis of the state of play in China today.

SUGGESTIONS FOR FURTHER READING

I recommend three books here, two by foreign correspondents who covered the China story as well as anyone and one about a much more noble profession, that of the Chinese journalist.

Bandurski, David, and Martin Hala, eds. *Investigative Journalism in China*. Seattle: University of Washington Press, 2010.

McGregor, Richard. *The Party: The Secret World of China's Communist Rulers*. New York: Harper, 2010.

Pan, Philip. *Out of Mao's Shadow: The Struggle for the Soul of New China*. New York: Simon & Schuster, 2009.

Afterword: What Future for Human Rights Dialogues?

John Kamm

China has registered prodigious economic growth since reforms were adopted thirty years ago, achieving double-digit annual gains even during the worst recession in the West since the Great Depression. Few have credited the human rights reforms that enabled growth to happen—the right to travel, to own property, to change jobs—all internationally recognized economic rights. Deng Xiaoping made "socialism with Chinese characteristics" acceptable by allegedly declaring that "to get rich is glorious," though it is by no means certain that he actually uttered those famous words.

What is, however, quite certain is that Deng never said that to speak freely is glorious, and during the period of economic reform, political reforms that might challenge the grip on power of the Communist Party have been resisted with the full power of the state, and the repression of free speech and free association has never slowed. Since 2008, the year of the Olympics, the Chinese government has launched wave after wave of political arrests and disappearances, to the extent that the population of political prisoners is at its highest point in many years.

Contrary to expectations in many capitals, China's increasing wealth and global reach have not translated into a lessening of political repression. On the contrary, the last few years have seen a great stepping up of imprisonments for political and religious activities and a concomitant reduction in acts of clemency for political prisoners.

When China was vulnerable in the immediate aftermath of Tiananmen, it adopted a policy of holding human rights dialogues with Western countries, with the United Nations, and in a few cases, with nongovernmental organizations to ward off sanctions and deflect criticism. No longer vulnerable—some might even say in the driver's seat—China is less interested in engaging the international community on issues related to human rights, and when it does so it is increasingly on its own terms. It is less and less willing to discuss the fate of its growing population of political prisoners.

This essay tells the story of the policy of human rights dialogues, their history and current state, and examines whether or not, and in what forms, discussing human rights with China can continue.

In March 1989 the Chinese People's Liberation Army (PLA) was used to quell protests in Tibet's capital of Lhasa. Martial law was declared by the party secretary and political commissar of the PLA in the Tibet Autonomous Region, Hu Jintao, current president of the People's Republic of China (PRC). The following month violent protests erupted in Xi'an. Peaceful protests, on a larger scale, began in Beijing after the popular reformist and ousted Party Central Committee secretary Hu Yaobang died on April 15. By late May the city was paralyzed, and students and workers in other cities all over the country began marching and taking other steps, including shutting down colleges and mounting strikes at key industrial enterprises. The response of the Chinese government was to send in the PLA and declare martial law in Beijing. Hundreds of civilians were killed and thousands were detained in Beijing and hundreds of other locations.

The response from the international community was swift and forceful. The United States adopted a number of sanctions, including a ban on high-level visits and an embargo on sales of military equipment to China. The European Union also adopted an arms embargo, one that stands to the present day despite efforts from time to time by member states to have it lifted. In August 1989 the United Nations Sub-commission on Prevention of Discrimination and Protection of Minorities passed a resolution criticizing the gross violations of human rights committed by the Chinese government in its suppression of peaceful protests by its citizens. It marked the first time in the history of the United Nations that a resolution censuring a permanent member of the Security Council had passed the most important body under the Human Rights Commission.

In the spring of 1990 an effort began in the U.S. Congress to strip China of its most favored nation (MFN) trading status. As a nonmarket economy defined by the Trade Act of 1974, China's trade status had to be renewed every year. An executive order had to be issued by the president extending the status, and Congress—which has constitutional authority over foreign trade—would consider whether to support or overturn the president's order. Congress decided to take a dual track, debating a resolution of outright disapproval at the same time as pursuing the idea of making future MFN renewals dependent on conditions tied to the country's human rights practices. In 1990 the House of Representatives adopted the latter approach, passing a bill that set a number of conditions on renewal of the status in

1991. The bill passed in the waning weeks of the congressional term, but it died before the Senate took action. In 1991 and 1992 the bill passed both houses of Congress, but it was vetoed by President George H. W. Bush. The vetoes were narrowly upheld in the Senate.

DIALOGUES TO COUNTER CENSURE AND SANCTIONS

Had China lost its access to the U.S. market in the early 1990s it is doubtful that the Chinese economic miracle that the world has watched unfold would have taken place. China's paramount leader at the time of the international response to Tiananmen was Deng Xiaoping, and he personally authorized human rights concessions to counter the threat of isolation. Among those concessions was the offer to Western countries to engage in "dialogues" on human rights. The first dialogues were held in 1991 with Switzerland (home of the Human Rights Commission that had censured China) and the United States (where the MFN debate had reached a critical stage).

The policy of holding human rights dialogues proved successful in countering the threat of Western sanctions and critical resolutions in the United Nations, though it was by no means the only policy that contributed to these ends (the decision to abstain instead of veto the Security Council's use-of-force resolution in the first Iraq War played a big role as well). The initiation of the dialogues with the United States and Switzerland in 1991 was followed by the start of dialogues with the European Union in 1995 and with Australia, Canada, Japan, Norway, and the United Kingdom in 1997. The initiation of the latter dialogues was decisive in convincing the United States and the European Union not to sponsor a China resolution at the 1998 session of the Human Rights Commission, effectively ending the threat of censure by the United Nations.

In 2003 China and Germany agreed to hold annual rights dialogues. In addition to bilateral dialogues with nine countries, China has held consultations on human rights with countries like Sweden and exchanges with developing countries like Brazil. Consultations are considered ad hoc affairs with no requirement of an annual or semiannual session. They are held with "developed" countries, and Beijing often insists that there be no discussions of its domestic human rights practices but that the focus should rather be on international human rights and humanitarian crises. After dialogues are suspended, Beijing sometimes resumes discussions in the form of consultations. This is apparently the case with Japan.

China began aggressively pursuing cooperation on human rights with the United Nations in the late 1990s, inviting special rapporteurs and concluding technical cooperation memoranda. To support this robust "human rights diplomacy," China stocked the Ministry of Foreign Affairs' International Department and its Geneva Mission with some of its top diplomats. It established a human rights division under the International Department and appointed a special representative for human rights dialogues. By the end of 2009 more than one hundred rounds of dialogues with the nine bilateral partners had taken place. "Unofficial" dialogues with the International Committee of the Red Cross (notably on issues relating to health in detention) and the Dui Hua Foundation, which has raised and received information on prisoner cases, are also overseen by the MFA's International Department. In 2008 Dui Hua initiated an exchange on juvenile justice with China's Supreme People's Court. Other dialogues that concern fundamental rights are those with the Tibetan community in exile handled by the United Front Department of the Chinese Communist Party, the Vatican over normalization of relations handled by the State Administration of Religious Affairs jointly with the Ministry of Foreign Affairs, and labor rights under ILO conventions handled by the Ministry of Labor.

"SAME BED, DIFFERENT DREAMS"

Beijing was careful never to publicly link its effort to avoid sanctions and censure with the holding of the human rights dialogues, instead stressing that dialogues were held in an atmosphere of "equality and mutual respect" with the goal of achieving "mutual understanding," by which was meant understanding on the part of its Western interlocutors that China was making impressive strides in the field of human rights. As China grew wealthier and more powerful, and as the United States' image as a human rights defender was tarnished by abuses committed in Iraq and elsewhere, China no longer feared sanctions and international censure. Their leaders and officials bristled at Western criticism and increasingly used forums like the rights dialogues to attack the human rights failings of its dialogue partners. (In one example, China criticized Norway for the government's control of the Evangelical Lutheran Church.) It began giving its Western partners prisoner lists of their own, but the practice appears to have been dropped after the partners expressed their willingness to address the Chinese side's concerns and provide detailed information on the cases.

Chinese leaders and their subordinates remembered how useful the policy of holding dialogues had been in the past. At the same time they apparently concluded that the practice of holding dialogues was proving useful to their foreign partners as well, deflecting criticism at home that the governments were doing nothing to address violations of human rights in China. Beijing eventually concluded that the Western governments needed the dialogues more than China needed them. The holding of dialogues came to be viewed as a favor to Western governments as well as a means to burnish China's international image. Withholding the favor of a dialogue became a favorite means of expressing disapproval with the foreign partner's policies and practices across a broad spectrum of issues.

DIALOGUE AS SHIELD BECOMES DIALOGUE AS WEAPON

In 1999 China suspended the human rights dialogue with the United States in the aftermath of the American bombing of its embassy in Belgrade (though it is likely it would have been suspended anyway as Washington had already announced its intention of sponsoring a China resolution at the annual meeting of the Human Rights Commission in Geneva). In August 2001 and during the spring of 2002, Japanese Prime Minister Junichiro Koizumi visited the Yasukuni Shrine honoring Japanese war dead, visits that touched off widespread protests in China. Part of China's response was to suspend the human rights dialogue with the country.

In subsequent years, rounds of the bilateral dialogues have been cancelled or postponed for a variety of reasons, including a foreign government's granting of permission to visits by the Dalai Lama or the Uyghur activist Rebiya Kadeer and other perceived slights, like Switzerland's staging of intergovernmental meetings to discuss China's human rights (known for a time as the Berne Process). After Switzerland stopped taking the lead in organizing such meetings, Beijing agreed to resume the dialogue, but it was derailed again when two Swiss cantons granted political asylum to three Guantanamo detainees, two Uyghurs, and one Kazak who were Chinese citizens. (A round was finally held in March 2011 in Switzerland.) In May 2007 the Chinese delegation to the EU-China human rights dialogue round held in Berlin walked out of the legal seminar held as an integral part of the dialogue. It was protesting the participation of two NGOs selected by the EU.

In December 2009 China executed a British citizen, Akmal Shaikh. The United Kingdom protested vigorously. The Chinese MFA postponed the round of the human rights dialogue that was to be held in January 2010 because British protests had "hurt the feelings of the Chinese people." When the UK and China initiated their dialogue in 1997, it was agreed that there should be two rounds a year. Though no understanding was ever reached, the Chinese side has, in recent years, only agreed to one round a year.

In late 2005 the UN special rapporteur on torture, Manfred Nowak, visited China. At the conclusion of his visit, Nowak issued a scathing report, and there wasn't another visit by a special rapporteur until late 2010, when the special rapporteur on the right to food made a visit (he too issued a critical report that singled out how Chinese food policies were affecting nomadic hunters and herders, much to the chagrin of his Chinese hosts). The Technical Memorandum of Cooperation between the Office of the High Commissioner for Human Rights and the Chinese government expired in August 2010, and it has not been renewed to date.

THE BURTON REPORT

Foreign governments, notably those of the United States and Canada, have also suspended dialogues with China, but only because of problems with the dialogues themselves. In 2003 then U.S. assistant secretary of state Lorne Craner decided that China had not lived up to commitments made in the 2002 round and that the United States would not hold a round in 2003. (Subsequently, Beijing showed little interest in resuming the dialogue and another session wasn't held until 2008.) Partly in response to a critical report authored by former Canadian diplomat Charles Burton, the newly elected Conservative government in Ottawa ordered a rethink of the Sino-Canadian human rights dialogue, effectively suspending it in 2006. As of this writing it has yet to resume. The European Parliament passed a resolution criticizing the EU-China dialogue in December 2009. Consideration was given to indefinitely suspending the EU-China dialogue after Wo Weihan, the father of two EU citizens, was executed on the last day of the dialogue held in Beijing in November 2008.

Although human rights groups have long been critical of the dialogues as lacking in transparency, measurable benchmarks, and accountability (an assessment of the UK-China dialogue issued in early 2011 by thirteen human rights groups dismissed the process as a "farce"), what was intriguing about the Burton report was that widespread dissatisfaction with the dialogue was expressed by both Canadian and Chinese officials. In criticisms heard of both the Canadian dialogue and the dialogues between China and other countries, many of the officials interviewed by Burton felt the dialogues were merely propaganda exercises. The rounds were often held on short notice and there was a lack of preparation. The Ministry of Foreign Affairs and their Western counterparts were seen as the wrong bodies to be organizing the dialogues as their jobs were to defend their respective countries' interests and not to push for real change in domestic human rights policies. There were frequent disagreements over the agenda and over whether or not site visits would be held. Participants were changed frequently, and the rank of leaders sponsoring the dialogue downgraded.

The Chinese side in particular objected to the presentation of lists of so-called cases of concern, holding that the mere handing over of a list represented an attempt to interfere in China's internal affairs and undermine the "independence of China's judiciary." Chinese resistance to accepting lists grew and became increasingly shrill. In early 2010 the author was advised by a senior Chinese diplomat that the days of China accepting prisoner lists were fast drawing to a close. Yet for many of the foreign countries that hold human rights dialogues the presentation of lists and the discussion of cases are the *raison d'être* of the dialogues. If lists can no longer be presented and cases discussed, it is unlikely that Western countries will agree to continue holding the human rights dialogues with China.

NOBEL PRIZE LEADS TO POLICY RETHINK

On October 8, 2010, the Norwegian Nobel Committee gave the 2010 Nobel Peace Prize to the Chinese dissident Liu Xiaobo. Beijing reacted furiously, calling Liu a common criminal and attacking both the committee ("a bunch of clowns") and the prize itself ("a blasphemy"). Spokesmen made clear that relations with Norway would be seriously affected, and in fact numerous meetings and visits were cancelled. A Chinese-Norway Free Trade Agreement, under negotiation for years and close to conclusion, became a dead letter. The future of Norway's human rights dialogue with China, considered one of the best of the dialogues, was put in jeopardy. Few observers believed a round would take place in 2011.

The Nobel decision contributed to what has been the most serious crackdown against protest and dissent in China in recent years. To make sure none of Liu's family members, friends, or associates could attend the award ceremony in Oslo, the Chinese government greatly stepped up detentions, house arrests, and disappearances of the country's small population of human rights defenders and activists. Soaring imprisonments and a sharp drop in sentence reductions and parole for prisoners serving sentences for endangering state security mean, that, by the end of 2010, there were more people in prison for political offenses than at any time since the Tiananmen protests of 1989.

Beijing was convinced that Western countries, particularly the United States, orchestrated the awarding of the prize to Liu Xiaobo. It launched an unprecedented effort to convince countries to boycott the December 10 ceremony in Oslo, threatening unspecified "serious consequences" for any country that sent its ambassador to the ceremony. The effort was a failure, as only nineteen countries invited to attend failed to do so. Among functioning democracies only the Philippines boycotted the ceremony, apparently as part of an effort to convince China not to execute three of its citizens. (The Chinese Supreme Court obliged by postponing the executions for roughly six weeks.) At one point it looked like Serbia would reject the invitation, but the European Union reportedly let Belgrade know that joining the boycott would affect Serbia's application to join the group.

Beijing canceled the second round of the 2010 dialogues that was supposed to have taken place in November or December 2010. This marked the first time since 1998 that a round of dialogues with the EU had been cancelled. The cancellation reflected Beijing's desire to reduce the number of rounds of the EU-China dialogue from two per year to one per year, as well as unhappiness over the strong support voiced by the EU for the decision to give the Nobel Peace Prize to Liu Xiaobo. There are other signs that the Liu Xiaobo decision has had an impact on China's thinking about holding human rights dialogues. As one Chinese diplomat told the author, "China no longer has an incentive to engage in human rights dialogues. The policy has failed to increase Western understanding of the real situation of human rights in China."

The first rights dialogue with a Western country after the Nobel decision was the one with Australia held in Beijing in December 2010. Instead of two days of discussion, the talks lasted one day. There were no visits outside of Beijing. The Chinese side refused to provide information on cases raised by the Australian side, which nevertheless presented a list. The Chinese side rejected Australian attempts to raise Liu Xiaobo's case, saying it wasn't a "human rights issue" but rather was an issue of respecting China's sovereignty and judicial integrity. A month later, a round of the dialogue with the UK was held in London. Details of what took place have not been

Figure A.1. Surveillance Camera Embedded in Exhibit, Pavilion of the Future, Shanghai World Expo. Photograph by Tong Lam.

released, but if what UK Foreign Minister Jeremy Brown had to say is any measure, the talks took place in a decidedly frosty atmosphere: "The UK and China are continuing to approach these discussions in a constructive spirit and covering the full range of issues in an open and frank manner."

After the round with the UK, diplomats attached to the MFA's International Department took advantage of the 2011 spring meeting of the Human Rights Council to have a two-day round of dialogue with Switzerland in Berne. Again, no written information on prisoners was handed over. From June 2010 to the round of the U.S.-China human rights dialogue held in Beijing in April 2010, the MFA refused to respond to any lists of prisoners presented in bilateral dialogues. The response to the U.S. representatives was reportedly short and lacking in details.

Although many Western critics of the dialogues claim that they have failed to exert a positive influence on human rights practices in China, this judgment is unduly harsh. Persistent European pressure on China's use of the death penalty, exercised through the dialogues and other means, played a role in Beijing's decision to carry out reforms of their capital punishment system, reforms that contributed to a sharp drop in the number of executions from more than ten thousand a year at the end of the 1990s to about five thousand a year in 2010. There is some evidence that the dialogues have contributed to other reforms of the criminal justice system, including perhaps a reduction in the use of reeducation through labor (though use of other forms of arbitrary detention have apparently increased.) Dui Hua's exchanges on juvenile justice with the Supreme People's Court have contributed to tangible improvements in the way China treats its juvenile offenders. The Legal Experts Dialogue held between the United States and China from 2003 to 2005 elicited an undertaking from China that prisoners serving sentences for endangering state security enjoyed the same access to sentence reduction and parole as other prisoners. Provincial regulations that have recently come to light suggest, however, that discrimination against political prisoners in the exercise of clemency remains a feature of the penal system.

There is little doubt though that the most tangible success of the rights dialogues has been the focus on cases of people who have been detained for the nonviolent expression of their political and religious beliefs. More than one thousand such cases have been raised in the course of twenty years of dialogue; the Chinese special representative for human rights dialogues told the author that, in the middle years of the last decade, he was fielding requests for information on more than three hundred prisoners each year. It has been well established that the presence on a list increases the prospects for a prisoner's early release and better treatment.

China's increasingly strident rejection of international criticism and its refusal to provide information or discuss the cases of prominent (and less prominent) detainees, coupled with a growing unwillingness among cost-conscious Western governments to hold dialogues simply for the sake of holding dialogues, could well spell an end to a useful but fatally flawed exercise of engaging Beijing on human rights through formal government-to-government dialogues. More and more Western officials worry that giving the impression of a dialogue that contributes to meaningful reforms in China only serves to provide cover for what has become a fierce campaign by the Chinese government to eliminate dissent, criminalize protest, and stall efforts at legal and democratic reform.

SUGGESTIONS FOR FURTHER READING

Burton, Charles. *Assessment of the Canada China Human Rights Dialogue.* Report by Charles Burton to Canada's Department of Foreign Affairs and International Trade, April 2006.

Dui Hua Foundation. "China's Global Presence Shifts Dialogue Away from Domestic Rights Abuses." *Dialogue,* no. 29 (Fall 2007): 1–3.

———. "Speaking of Human Rights: US Dialogue Policy for China Still Taking Shape." *Dialogue,* no. 35 (Spring 2009): 1–3.

———. "Legal Experts Dialogue: Promising, Complex Channel for US-China Talks." *Dialogue,* no. 37 (Fall 2009): 1–3.

Foot, Rosemary. *Rights Beyond Borders.* New York: Oxford University Press, 2000.

Human Rights in China. "From Principle to Pragmatism: Can "Dialogue" Improve China's Human Rights Situation?" June 1998.

Kent, Ann. *China, the United Nations, and Human Rights: The Limits of Compliance.* Philadelphia: University of Pennsylvania Press, 1999.

———. "States Monitoring States: The United States, Australia and China's Human Rights, 1990–2001." *Human Rights Quarterly* 23, no. 3 (August 2001): 583–624.

Kinzelbach, Katrin, and Hatla Telle. "Talking Human Rights to China: An Assessment of the EU's Approach," *China Quarterly* 205 (2011): 60–79.

Ming, Wan. *Human Rights in Chinese Foreign Relations: Defining and Defending National Interests.* Philadelphia: University of Pennsylvania Press, 2001.

Index

About the Contributors

David Bandurski is the editor of the *China Media Project* in the Journalism and Media Studies Center at the University of Hong Kong. He is the coeditor of *Investigative Journalism in China* (2010) and a frequent commentator on Chinese media whose writings have appeared in *Far Eastern Economic Review*, the *Wall Street Journal*, *Index on Censorship*, as well as the *South China Morning Post*. He was corecipient of the Merit Prize in Commentary in 2006 and in 2007 received a Human Rights Press Award.

Susan D. Blum is professor of anthropology at the University of Notre Dame. A fellow of the Helen Kellogg Institute for International Studies and former director of the Center for Asian Studies, Blum has written extensively on language, identity, and nationalism in China. She is the author of *My Word! Plagiarism and Chinese Culture* (2009), *Lies That Bind: Chinese Truth, Other Truths* (Rowman & Littlefield, 2007), and *Portraits of "Primitives": Ordering Human Kinds in the Chinese Nation* (Rowman & Littlefield, 2001), and editor of *Making Sense of Language: Readings in Culture and Communication* (2009).

Timothy Cheek is professor and the Louis Cha Chair in Chinese Research at the Institute of Asian Research at the University of British Columbia. His research, teaching, and translating focus on the recent history of China, especially the role of Chinese intellectuals in the twentieth century and the history of the Chinese Communist Party. His books include *The Cambridge Critical Introduction to Mao* (2010), *Living with Reform: China Since 1989* (2006), *Mao Zedong and China's Revolutions* (2002), and *Propaganda and Culture in Mao's China* (1997).

Gady Epstein, China correspondent for the *Economist*, has been covering China and Asia since 2002. From 2007 to 2011, he was Beijing bureau chief for *Forbes*. Previously, he was Beijing bureau chief and international projects reporter for the *Baltimore Sun*, where he won a Gerald Loeb Award for coauthoring a series on globalization.

Andrew S. Erickson is associate professor in the U.S. Naval War College's China Maritime Studies Institute and a fellow in the Princeton-Harvard China and the World Program at the Fairbank Center for Chinese Studies. His research, published in *Asian Security, Journal of Strategic Studies, The American Interest*, and *Joint Force Quarterly*, is available through his website, www.andrewerickson.com. Erickson is also co-founder of *China SignPost* (www.chinasignpost.com), a research newsletter and web portal covering key internal developments in China, its use of natural resources, its trade policies, and its military and security issues.

Lionel M. Jensen is associate professor of East Asian languages and cultures at the University of Notre Dame and visiting fellow in the Internationales Kolleg für Geisteswissenschaftliche Forschung at the University of Erlangen-Nürnberg. He is the author and editor of six books, including *Manufacturing Confucianism* and *China's Transformations*. He has just completed *Enchanted Texts: Kongzi, Zhu Xi and the Mythistory of Confucianism*.

John Kamm, a 2005 MacArthur Fellow, is the executive director of the Dui Hua Foundation, a human rights group based in San Francisco with an office in Hong Kong. Kamm was a business leader in Hong Kong when he first intervened on behalf of a political prisoner at a business dinner hosted by a senior Chinese official. In the ensuing twenty years he has worked on more than a thousand cases and has helped hundreds of political and religious prisoners. His work has been recognized by President Bill Clinton, who presented him with the first Best Global Practices Award in 1997, and by President George W. Bush, who gave him the Eleanor Roosevelt Award for Human Rights in 2001.

Wenqing Kang is assistant professor of history at Cleveland State University. He is the author of *Obsession: Male Same-Sex Relations in China, 1900–1950*, published by Hong Kong University Press in 2009.

Katherine Palmer Kaup, a National Committee on United States–China Relations Public Intellectuals Fellow, is James B. Duke Associate Professor of Asian Studies and Political Science as well as chair of the Asian Studies Department at Furman University, where she specializes in Chinese ethnic policy and the Regional Ethnic Autonomy Law. She is the author of *Creating* *the Zhuang: Ethnic Politics in China* (2000) and several articles on the impact that state policy and administrative divisions have had on ethnic identity and mobilization in China's southwest and in Xinjiang. In 2005 she was special advisor for minority nationalities affairs at the Congressional-Executive Commission on China.

Travis Klingberg is a PhD candidate in cultural geography at the University of Colorado at Boulder. His dissertation research (for which he received a Fulbright-Hays Doctoral Dissertation Award) focuses on the ways geographic narratives about China have been repeated and remade since the early 1990s as increasing numbers of domestic, independent tourists have traveled between China's cities and its rural western areas.

Orion A. Lewis is a research scholar at the Rohatyn Center for International Affairs at Middlebury College, as well as a postdoctoral research associate in the Program on Terrorism and Insurgency Research at Wesleyan University. His interests are at the intersection of comparative and international political economy, with an emphasis on China and East Asia. His work on China—explaining gradual press liberalization in a formally controlled system—has illuminated the role of political communication in authoritarian institutional change. Recent publications have appeared in *Harvard Asia Pacific Review*, *Theory in Biosciences*, and *Glasshouse Forum*.

Benjamin L. Liebman is the Robert L. Lieff Professor of Law and the director of the Center for Chinese Legal Studies at Columbia Law School. His current research focuses on the role of the media in the Chinese legal system, on Chinese tort law, and on the evolution of China's courts and legal profession. His recent scholarship includes "Toward Competitive Supervision? The Media and the Courts" in *China Quarterly* (2011) and "A Return to Populist Legality? Historical Legacies and Legal Reform" in *Mao's Invisible Hand*, edited by Elizabeth Perry and Sebastian Heilmann (2011).

Jonathan S. Noble, advisor of Asia initiatives in the Office of the Provost at the University of Notre Dame, specializes in Chinese contemporary culture, film, and performance. He has translated numerous essays and works on Chinese drama and popular culture. From 2005 to 2007, he was one of the inaugural fellows of the Public Intellectuals Program of the National Committee on United States–China Relations.

Tim Oakes teaches cultural geography at the University of Colorado at Boulder. He is the author of *Tourism and Modernity in China* (1998) and coeditor of numerous volumes on tourism, mobility, and culture in China, including *Translocal China* (2006) and *Faiths on Display* (2010). He is currently completing a monograph on heritage tourism in rural China.

Jessica C. Teets is an assistant professor in the Political Science Department at Middlebury College, Vermont. Her research focuses on the changing role of civil society, such as nonprofits, NGOs, and other associations, in authoritarian regimes. She is recently the author of "Post-Earthquake Relief and Reconstruction Efforts: The Emergence of Civil Society in China?" in *China Quarterly* (June 2009).

Alex L. Wang is senior attorney and director of the China Environmental Law Project, Beijing, of the National Resources Defense Council. He works with China's policy makers, fledgling environmental groups, and legal community to strengthen environmental protection. He blogs on China's environmental law, policy, and the power of the people at http://switchboard .nrdc.org/blogs/awang/ and www.greenlaw.org.cn.

Timothy B. Weston is associate professor of history and associate director of the Center for Asian Studies at the University of Colorado at Boulder. He is the author of *The Power of Position: Beijing University, Intellectuals and Chinese Political Culture, 1898–1929* (2004) and coeditor of *China beyond the Headlines* (2000) and *China's Transformations: The Stories beyond the Headlines* (2007). His research focuses on intellectuals, political culture, media, and public life in modern China. In 2009 he was named a National Committee on United States–China Relations Public Intellectuals Fellow.

CPSIA information can be obtained at www.ICGtesting.com
Printed in the USA
BVOW030838210612

293265BV00005B/5/P